This original study examines how Shakespeare and his contemporaries made the difficult transition from writing plays for the theatre to publishing them as literary works. Tracing the path from playhouse to printing house, Douglas Brooks analyzes how and why certain popular plays found their way into print while many others failed to do so and looks at the role played by the Renaissance book trade in shaping literary reputations. Incorporating many finely observed typographical illustrations, this book focuses on plays by Shakespeare, Jonson, Webster, and Beaumont and Fletcher as well as reviewing the complicated publication history of Thomas Heywood's work. Brooks stakes out new ground by uncovering the continually shifting relationship between theatre and publisher and defining the way in which the concept of authorship changed. His book represents an important contribution to the ongoing refiguration of two histories: English Renaissance drama and the early modern book.

Douglas A. Brooks is Assistant Professor of Early Modern Literature at Texas A&M University.

Cambridge Studies in Renaissance Literature and Culture 36

From Playhouse to Printing House

Cambridge Studies in Renaissance Literature and Culture

General editor
STEPHEN ORGEL
Jackson Eli Reynolds Professor of Humanities, Stanford University

Editorial board
Anne Barton, *University of Cambridge*
Jonathan Dollimore, *University of York*
Marjorie Garber, *Harvard University*
Jonathan Goldberg, *Johns Hopkins University*
Nancy Vickers, *Bryn Mawr College*

Since the 1970s there has been a broad and vital reinterpretation of the nature of literary texts, a move away from formalism to a sense of literature as an aspect of social, economic, political and cultural history. While the earliest New Historicist work was criticized for a narrow and anecdotal view of history, it also served as an important stimulus for post-structuralist, feminist, Marxist and psychoanalytical work, which in turn has increasingly informed and redirected it. Recent writing on the nature of representation, the historical construction of gender and of the concept of identity itself, on theatre as a political and economic phenomenon and on the ideologies of art generally, reveals the breadth of the field. Cambridge Studies in Renaissance Literature and Culture is designed to offer historically oriented studies of Renaissance literature and theatre which make use of the insights afforded by theoretical perspectives. The view of history envisioned is above all a view of our own history, a reading of the Renaissance for and from our own time.

Recent titles include

29. Dorothy Stephens, *The limits of eroticism in post-petrarchan narrative: conditional pleasure from Spenser to Marvell*

30. Celia R. Daileader, *Eroticism on the Renaissance stage: transcendence, desire, and the limits of the visible*

31. Theordore B. Leinwand, *Theatre, finance, and society in early modern England*

32. Heather Dubrow, *Shakespeare and domestic loss: forms of deprivation, mourning, and recuperation*

33. David M. Posner, *The performance of nobility in early modern European literature*

34. Michael C. Schoenfeldt, *Bodies and selves in early modern England: physiology and inwardness in Spenser, Shakespeare, Herbert, and Milton*

35. Lynn Enterline, *The rhetoric of the body from Ovid to Shakespeare*

A complete list of books in the series is given at the end of the volume.

From Playhouse to Printing House

*Drama and Authorship in
Early Modern England*

Douglas A. Brooks

CAMBRIDGE UNIVERSITY PRESS
Cambridge, New York, Melbourne, Madrid, Cape Town, Singapore, São Paulo

Cambridge University Press
The Edinburgh Building, Cambridge CB2 2RU, UK

Published in the United States of America by Cambridge University Press, New York

www.cambridge.org
Information on this title: www.cambridge.org/9780521771177

© Douglas A. Brooks 2000

This publication is in copyright. Subject to statutory exception
and to the provisions of relevant collective licensing agreements,
no reproduction of any part may take place without
the written permission of Cambridge University Press.

First published 2000
This digitally printed first paperback version 2006

A catalogue record for this publication is available from the British Library

Library of Congress Cataloguing in Publication data

Brooks, Douglas A.
From playhouse to printing house: drama and authorship in early modern
England / Douglas A. Brooks.
    p. cm. – (Cambridge studies in Renaissance literature and
culture; 36)
Includes bibliographical references and index.
ISBN 0 521 77117 X hardback
1. English drama – Early modern and Elizabethan, 1500–1600 – History and
criticism. 2. Authors and the theatre – England – History – 16th century.
3. Authors and the theatre – England – History – 17th Century. 4. Literature
publishing – England – History – 16th century. 5. Literature publishing –
England – History – 17th century. 6. English drama – 17th century – History
and criticism. 7. Drama – Publishing – History. 8. Renaissance – England.
9. Playwriting – History. 10. Authorship – History. I. Title. II. Series.
PR658.A9B76 2000
822'.309–dc21   99–16686   CIP

ISBN-13 978-0-521-77117-7 hardback
ISBN-10 0-521-77117-X hardback

ISBN-13 978-0-521-03486-9 paperback
ISBN-10 0-521-03486-8 paperback

In loving memory of Daniel Brooks, Mimi Brooks, and Adele Gittler

As it is written: "How abundant is Your goodness that You have concealed for Your reverent ones," and it is written: "He guards all of his bones, even one of them was not broken."
Yisgadal v'yiskadash sh'mei rabbav – Amein.

Wo es war, soll Ich werden   Sigmund Freud

Contents

List of illustrations *page* x
Preface xii
Acknowledgements xvii

    Prologue "Thou grewst to govern the whole Stage alone": dramas of authorship in early modern England   1

1 "A toy brought to the Presse": marketing printed drama in early modern London   14

2 "So disfigured with scrapings & blotting out": Sir John Oldcastle and the construction of Shakespeare's authorship   66

3 "If he be at his book, disturb him not": the two Jonson folios of 1616   104

4 "What strange Production is at last displaid": dramatic authorship and the dilemma of collaboration   140

5 "So wronged in beeing publisht": Thomas Heywood and the discourse of perilous publication   189

    Epilogue "Why not Malevole in folio with vs": the after-birth of the author   221

Notes 229
Bibliography 268
Index 284

Illustrations

1 Title page: *The Tragedie of Gorbodvc*, 1565. Reproduced by permission of the Huntington Library, San Marino, CA — page 25
2 Title page: *The Most Lamentable Romaine Tragedie of Titus Andronicus*, 1594. Reproduced by permission of The Folger Shakespeare Library, Washington DC. — 26
3 Title page: *The Tragidie of Ferrex and Porrex*, 1570. Reproduced by permission of the Folger Shakespeare Library. — 28
4 Title page: *All such treatises as haue been lately published by Thomas Norton*, 1570. Reproduced by permission of the Huntington Library. — 39
5 Page of text: *Volpone, or The Foxe*, 1607. Reproduced by permission of the Huntington Library. — 47
6 Title page: *The Second part of Henrie the fourth*, 1600. Reproduced by permission of The Huntington Library. — 72
7 Page of text: The Catalogue, *The Workes of Beniamin Jonson*, 1616. Reproduced by permission of the Folger Shakespeare Library. — 114
8 Title page: *Epigrammes, The Workes of Beniamin Jonson*, 1616. Reproduced by permission of the Folger Shakespeare Library. — 115
9 Title page: *The Forrest, The Workes of Beniamin Jonson*, 1616. Reproduced by permission of the Folger Shakespeare Library. — 117
10 Title page: *B. Jon: His Part of King James his Royall and Magnificent Entertainement*, 1604. Reproduced by permission of the Folger Shakespeare Library. — 123
11 Title page: *Part of the Kings Entertainment, The Workes of Beniamin Jonson*, 1616. Reproduced by permission of the Folger Shakespeare Library. — 125
12 Title page: *Mr. William Shakespeares Comedies, Histories, & Tragedies*, 1623. Reproduced by permission of the Folger Shakespeare Library. — 142
13 Title page: *Comedies and Tragedies*, 1647. Reproduced by permission of the Huntington Library. — 143

List of illustrations   xi

14 Fletcher portrait: *Comedies and Tragedies*, 1647. Reproduced by permission of the Huntington Library.   148
15 Title page: *The Travailes of The three English Brothers*, 1607. Reproduced by permission of The Huntington Library.   158
16 Title page: *A Faire Quarrell*, 1617. Reproduced by permission of the Huntington Library.   160
17 Title page: *The Virgin Martir*, 1622. Reproduced by permission of the Huntington Library.   162
18 Title page: *The Virgin Martir*, 1622. Reproduced by permission of the Huntington Library.   163
19 Title page: *Fifty Comedies and Tragedies*, 1679. Reproduced by permission of the Huntington Library.   169
20 Title page: *The Witch of Edmonton*, 1658. Reproduced by permission of the Huntington Library.   171
21 Title page: *The Workes of Beniamin Jonson*, 1616. Reproduced by permission of the Huntington Library.   184
22 Title page: *Pleasant Dialogves and Dramma's*, 1637. Reproduced by permission of the Huntington Library.   218

Preface

> The bud disappears when the blossom breaks through, and we might say that the former is refuted by the latter.
> G. W. F. Hegel, *The Phenomenology of Mind*

This book is a study of the profession of playwriting for the early modern London stage. My primary objectives are to reconsider the historical evidence about the authorial status of early modern plays and to show how the authorship of drama in the period was shaped by emergent modes of textual production.

D. F. McKenzie has observed that, "[e]very book tells a story quite apart from that recounted by its text . . . the product of social acts involving the complex interventions of human agency acting on material forms."[1] This book is largely about books or, more precisely, about the manifold materializing processes that constituted the passage from playhouse to printing house, that transformed acting scripts into published dramatic texts. Accordingly, I have tried to listen carefully to the stories that a half a dozen or so early modern English books tell and to make some sense of these stories by examining the complex interventions of human agency that acted upon them. What I heard, and have tried to pass on here, is a remarkably varied, sometimes contradictory group of tales that stubbornly refuse to be woven together into one coherent narrative. Indeed, what these books record, apart from the plays they were designed to preserve and promote, are dramas of authorship.

In Chapter 1, I focus on three books, the 1570 edition of *Ferrex and Porrex*, the 1612 edition of *The White Devil*, and the 1623 Shakespeare Folio, in order to treat generally some of the legal, material, and cultural issues linked to the authorship and publication of drama in early modern London. By juxtaposing drama-specific elements of the London book trade in the first decade of Elizabeth's reign with the publication activities of several playwrights in the early seventeenth century that nurtured a potential readership for the 1623 Folio, I show how the printing of plays facilitated the commodification of dramatic authorship and generated, consequently, an intensifying preoccupation with individualized authorial agency.

The subject of my second chapter is the pre-1623 Folio publication history of Shakespeare's plays, specifically the printed quarto editions of the two parts of *Henry IV*. Using these two books as a point of departure, I consider the role played by typography, royal authority, and the material status of books in chronicle and martyrological accounts of Sir John Oldcastle and editorial accounts of Shakespeare.

In Chapter 3 my primary concern is with the story told by Jonson's 1616 *Workes* folio. Noting how this collection binds together anomalously authorial play-texts with less authorial masque and entertainment texts, I argue that the hybrid structure of this book captures and preserves the complex struggle of authorship to reconcile the desire for individual autonomy with the need for external authoritative sanction. Because this struggle coheres with the two main performance venues (the theatre and the court) of Jonson's career as a dramatist, I contend that the printed page remains powerfully engaged with the stage.

The focus of the fourth chapter is the 1647 Beaumont and Fletcher folio and what it reports to us about the status of singular and collaborative authorship in the period. By considering the textual apparatus of the 1647 Beaumont and Fletcher folio in the context of evidence about multiple authorship in the period, I suggest that collaboration was incompatible with emergent notions of authorship as an individualized activity, and I argue that the 1647 folio documents its own failure to translate the collaborative writing conditions of the theatre into the single-author format of the printed drama collection.

In the final chapter, I examine a book that never came into being in order to consider what happens when the collaboration between playhouse and printing house falters. My subject is the complicated publication history of Thomas Heywood, whose career typified the profession of dramatist in early modern London. An extraordinarily prolific writer who contributed plays to several companies over a period of fifty years, Heywood's authorial canon remains dispersed and unauthoritative largely because he failed to play and be played by what Elizabeth Eisenstein aptly terms, "the game of books and authors."

The argument of this book frequently required me to reproduce various materializations of play-texts produced in early modern printing houses, and I have done what I can in the incunabula phase of the digital age to offer a conscientious simulacra of early modern orthographic and typographic "practices." Only long S "f" has been willfully modernized. Nevertheless, given that no two early modern books are exactly alike, all acts of reproduction – even photographic – are necessarily acts of interpretation and distortion. I can only hope that the facsimiles I have chosen to include will provide the reader with some sense of "being there."

Finally, although I hope this "little booke," to borrow from Spenser's first published work, will "thy selfe present," it is intended as the first installment of a three-part study of England's encounters with print. Part II, *All the Kings' Printers: The Imprint of Royal Authority in Early Modern England*, will examine the institution of the King's/Queen's Printer from 1504 to 1642 and the role played by print in the consolidation of the crown's authority. Part III, *In Such a Questionable Shape: The Imprint of Paternity in Early Modern England*, will argue that the awkward, incomplete transition from manuscript to print temporarily exposed and disturbed the epistemic foundations of patriarchal culture. Obviously – and how could it be otherwise – all three books are already bound between the covers of now and then.

Acknowledgements: "To the Iudiciall Reader"

A certain principle of thrift dictates that only one name mark off the edges of the text you have begun to read. In fact, like so many early modern dramatic texts, this book depended on the introduction and interference of several agents and intentions, and it is the product of a number of collaborations. At the playhouse I had the good fortune of working as an apprentice in a company whose sharers included David Scott Kastan, Anne Lake Prescott, James Shapiro, Jean Howard, Julie Stone Peters, and Peter Platt, all of whom read early versions of the manuscript. In the specific case of David, to borrow from Ben Jonson, "the invention was derived by me, and presented thus," but it was his "Mai(e)sties will." For that, and much more, I am very thankful. Anne was an early and ardent supporter, and Jim's inspired seminar in Tudor/Stuart drama set me on the path to the early modern. This book also benefited significantly from the input of my fellow apprentices, particularly Jim Cain, Bianca Calabresi, Thomas Festa, Moshe Gold, Juana Green, Jesse Lander, Zachary Lesser, Benedict Robinson, and Chloe Wheatley. In the specific case of Ben and Zach, both generously shared their research and pre-publication typescripts of articles with me. The book, as will be clear, has been greatly strengthened by their contributions.

Now as a junior sharer in a new playhouse, I am grateful to work in a company that includes Margaret Ezell, James Harner, and Paul Parrish, all of whom read a section of the manuscript. Finnie Coleman, Don Dickson, Anke Finger, Susanna Finnell, Maura Ives, and Craig Kallendorf, Jimmie Killingsworth, Howard Marchitello, and J. Lawrence Mitchell have also been very supportive. Three of my apprentices, John Gibbs, Christopher Morrow, and Pat Ocanas, have made many helpful suggestions.

Within the larger theatre of the profession, a number of players collaborated on this project. Cyndia Susan Clegg gave me copies of her publisher databases and pre-publication typescripts of articles, and helped me immensely during two visits to the Huntington Library. James

Riddell generously shared his considerable knowledge of Jonson's texts with me, and made work (and lunch) at the Huntington fun. Glyn Parry read a section of the manuscript, and frequently reminds me that the post-modern condition threatens to put the past "under erasure." David L. Gants was extraordinarily generous about sharing his work with me pre-publication, as were Gordon McMullan and David Norton. Thanks to the tremendous generosity of Julie Stone Peters, I was able to read a typescript of her forthcoming book, *Theatre of the Book: Print and the Stage 1480–1880* (Oxford: Clarendon Press, forthcoming 2000), a week before I reluctantly sent off the manuscript. While I greatly regret that time did not permit me to draw upon Julie Peters' astonishingly comprehensive research – her elegant and wide-ranging analysis in Chapter 1, "Experimenting on the Page 1480–1630," Chapter 6, "Accurate Texts, Authoritative Editions," Chapter 10, "Dramatists, Poets, and Other Scribblers," and Chapter 11, "Who Owns the Play? Pirate, Plagiarist, Imitator, Thief?" would have greatly informed and refined my argument – I am very happy in knowing that it will be available soon in published form. It is a stunning scholarly achievement. I am also grateful to Mark Bland for doing his best to set me straight on several points, and Peter Blayney showed me a lot of things that only he knows. Heidi Brayman Hackel has taught me a great deal about early modern readers. Paul Werstine and Laurie E. Maguire have inspired, encouraged, and supported my work in many ways.

Since I could not, as John Marston puts it, be "my owne setter out," I've been extremely fortunate at the printing house to work with Josie Dixon, Stephen Orgel and Sara Adhikari. They have been – in the words of Thomas Heywood's dedication to Nicholas Okes – "so carefull, and industrious, so serious and laborious to doe the Author all the rights of the presse." Professor Orgel and a reader whom Virginia Woolf might have called Anon made this a much better book than the one they first read. Sara Adhikari did a superb job of copy-editing the manuscript, and I am grateful for her patience, keen eye, and tenacity.

In light of all these collaborations, I take some comfort in Michel Foucault's notorious assertion that, "[t]exts, books, and discourses really began to have authors . . . to the extent that discourses could be transgressive," because it offers a somewhat narcissistic and masochistic guarantee that I alone will be punished for any of this book's transgressions.

An early version of a section of Chapter 3 appeared as "'If he be at his book, disturb him not': The Two Jonson Folios of 1616" in the *Ben Jonson Journal* 4 (1997): 81–103. I am grateful to Richard Harp and Stanley Stewart for kindly granting me permission to reprint that material here. An early version of a section of Chapter 2 appeared as "Sir John Oldcastle and the Construction of Shakespeare's Authorship" in *Studies in English Literature 1500–1900* 38:2 (Spring 1998). I am grateful to Robert Patten and the editorial board for kindly granting me permission to reprint that material here.

I also want to express my gratitude to those institutions that generously provided funds during the three years this book was researched and written. A George A. Schweppe Fellowship from Columbia University enabled me to spend a year free of teaching. A Faculty Mini Grant from Texas A&M University helped to pay for facsimiles and reproduction fees. A University Research Opportunity Program Grant from Texas A&M paid the salaries of two brilliant undergraduate research assistants, Kimberly Jones and Mathew Reynolds, who worked with me on this book and another project. Grants from the Huntington Library, the A. W. Mellon Foundation, and the South Central Modern Language Association financed two research trips to the Huntington Library. A grant from the Folger Institute enabled me to participate in Professor Blayney's seminar on the Stationers' Company and to do research at the Folger Shakespeare Library.

An anonymous musical group known only as the Residents first sparked my interest in authorship many years ago, and their work has continued to inspire me. Satesh Reddy made authoring this book much less dramatic than it would have been without him, and my good friend, Benedict Weisser, was a great source of support and inspiration. My family – Jeff, Ava, Harvey, Naomi, Marshall, Amy, Michael, Claire, Bill, Karen, David, and Eric – have encouraged my work in many ways. For eight years my greatest collaborator in all things day and night has been Victoria Rosner. John Web writes of Beaumont and Fletcher's collaboration that, "one Soule, informed . . . two wits." In our case, I pray that it be her Soule and wish I had her wit . . .

  Abke yanke buree he
  Abke rang safed he

Prologue: "Thou grewst to govern the whole Stage alone": dramas of authorship in early modern England

> Get thee to London, for if one man were dead, they will have much neede of such a one as thou art . . . and when thou feelest thy purse well lined, buy thee some place or Lordship in the Country, that growing weary of playing, thy mony may there bring thee to dignitie and reputation.
> Attributed to William Shakespeare

> The death of the author might be said to fulfill much the same function in our day as did the death of God for late nineteenth-century thought. Both deaths attest to a departure of belief in authority, presence, intention, omniscience and creativity.
> Sean Burke, *The Death and Return of the Author*

The title of my introduction comes from a commendatory poem written for the 1647 folio collection of John Fletcher and Francis Beaumont's plays. Fletcher collaborated with several playwrights during his career, and perhaps no more than six of the thirty-four plays in the volume were actually written in collaboration with Beaumont. Yet the writer of this verse presses on in his effort to transform the dozens of collaborations that produced the plays he celebrates – the collaborations between playwrights, between playwrights and playing companies, between playwrights and actors, between playing companies and scribes, between playing companies and censors, between playing companies and publishers, between publishers and printers, between printers and compositors – into one grand authorial voice. Lamenting earlier in the poem that "th' are imperfect births . . . Produc'd by causes not univocall," the writer's desire for univocality, for a choir of collaborators that sing in one voice, for a solitary governor/author who can serve as the plays' sole source of authority has been remarkably durable.

In this book I hope to frustrate the desire for univocality that continues to generate much of the scholarship on early modern English drama by examining aspects of play production and publication in the period that correspond poorly with critical and editorial efforts to idealize the authorship of texts written for the London stage. Alternatively, my analysis of dramatic authorship suggests that play-texts were increasingly shaped not by individual authors, but rather by various networks of engagement that both enabled and inhibited the materialization of plays as they passed from the stage to the page. Furthermore, I argue that the circulation and publication of dramatic texts contributed to emergent notions of literary ambition in the period and to the construction of proto-modern notions of authorship.

The most formidable obstacle to such a project is the looming figure of Shakespeare who, as Richard Dutton astutely notes, "remains the dominant voice in the English-speaking world's construction of its definitive author – a voice essentially of pre-print culture, of closet or privileged readership, of (to a degree) social snobbery."[1] Similarly, Jeffrey Masten observes that, "[s]ince the eighteenth century, Shakespeare has been viewed as *the* individual Author and the author of individuality – the very anti-type of collaboration. 'His' texts have been read as chronologies of personal/generic development, as material for authorial psychoanalysis, as the organic efflux of the singular mind of genius, as maps of a peculiarly individuated language and imagery."[2] Translated into nearly one hundred languages and sold in nearly every country on earth, Shakespeare's plays have come to represent the standard by which "great literature" is measured, and the name of Shakespeare has become a synonym for authorship itself. The image of the playwright armed with quill pen and parchment is practically an international symbol for authorship and literary production, readily comprehensible even to those who have never read a Shakespeare play. Indeed, as Michael D. Bristol observes, "[b]elieving in Shakespeare is not altogether different from believing in Santa Claus: such belief articulates a deep sense of affiliation with a tradition of expressive forms and institutional practices."[3] Inevitably, the iconic status of Shakespeare as author has emerged in spite of the fact that the term "playwright" itself, inasmuch as it semantically suggests other professions such as shipwrights, wheelwrights, and cartwrights, allies the early modern dramatist with other craftsmen rather than with contemporary writers such as Spenser or Sidney.[4] The fact that a film largely concerned with Shakespeare's authorship recently won the Academy Award for "Best Picture" of 1999 and turned the Bard into something of a movie star should only complicate matters.

This book struggles to emerge from the shadow of Shakespeare's iconic authorship by celebrating printed dramatic texts as "imperfect births," and by exposing the various collaborations that enabled the production of plays in early modern England – even the production of Shakespeare's plays. To use the phrase "various collaborations," in the same sentence (as I have done) with the proper name of the most individualized of author figures, Shakespeare, might seem paradoxical, though perhaps somewhat less so now that the movie *Shakespeare in Love* has portrayed our hero flagrantly collaborating with a woman on the text of at least one play; but in fact it is precisely this paradox which, in large part, constitutes the limits of this investigation. Put another way, this book as a whole argues that the construction of an "ordinary poet" working within the necessarily collaborative structures of the theatre into the icon of individualized authorial agency is, like all such paradoxes, the effect of a desire. In its workings, this desire collapses a complexly diachronic and contingent set of narratives into a synchronic truth that must, for the sake of maintaining its own viability, continue to place its past under erasure.

Given the critical developments of the past twenty-five years, this book, like the printed dramatic texts it examines, is the product of a particular set of collaborations in a specific professional context. Beginning with Roland Barthes's 1968 manifesto, "The Death of the Author," the concept of authorship, long associated with the unifying relationship between an author and a body of works, has suffered some fundamental setbacks and reversals. Advocating a modernist criticism based on semiotics, Barthes challenged contemporary modes of interpretation in which,

The *explanation* of a work is always sought in the man or woman who produced it, as if it were always in the end, through the more or less transparent allegory of the fiction, the voice of a single person, the Author "confiding" in us.[5]

Subsequently, Michel Foucault raised the critical stakes significantly when he declared that, "[t]he coming into being of the notion of 'author' constitutes the privileged moment of *individualization* in the history of ideas, knowledge, literature, philosophy, and the sciences."[6] Arguing that a text's mode of being was characterized by what he called an "author function," Foucault asserted that a discourse containing this "author function" had four main characteristics:

(1) the author function is linked to the juridical and institutional system that encompasses, determines, and articulates the universe of discourses; (2) it does not affect all discourses in the same way at all times and in all types of civilization; (3) it is not defined by the spontaneous attribution of a discourse to its producer, but rather by a series of specific and complex operations; (4) it does not refer purely and simply to a real individual, since it can give rise simultaneously to several selves, to several subjects – positions that can be occupied by different classes of individuals.[7]

It would be difficult to overestimate the impact that these essays by Barthes and Foucault, as well as the critical controversy they sparked, have had on a range of disciplines during the three decades since they were first published. In the case of early modern literature, Foucault's influence on the work of Stephen Greenblatt and the critical school that was briefly labeled "New Historicism" has been extensively chronicled.[8] In the essay that might be considered a manifesto for New Historicism, "Towards the Poetics of Culture," Greenblatt observes:

> the work of art is itself the product of a set of manipulations, some of them our own . . . many others undertaken in the construction of the original work. That is, the work of art is the product of a negotiation between a creator or class of creators, equipped with a complex, communally shared repertoire of conventions, and the institutions and practices of society.[9]

Although critics have tended to view the primary influence of Foucault on New Historicist critics as their concern with power relations,[10] Foucault's essay on authorship was central to the project of cultural poetics. Despite this centrality, as Masten rightly observes, "[t]he most rigorous New Historicist revaluations of Shakespeare – for example, Stephen Greenblatt's analysis of the 'collective production of literary pleasure and interest' – have largely adhered to an individuated, non-collaborative Shakespeare."[11] Foucault's influence is even more apparent in recent studies of early modern authorship,[12] especially studies of Shakespeare's authorship.[13]

Given the periodization that generally defines and confines academic fields of literary study, scholars of early modern literature were bound to see the emergence of the "author function" as taking place on their watch. In the specific context of Shakespeare criticism, the Foucauldian legacy of the void and/or dispersed character of authorship has allegedly brought about what Leah Marcus calls "the demise of the transcendent bard."[14] The result, according to Bristol, is that "the specific artifacts known as Shakespeare's works are described not as the creation of individual authors, but rather as a local manifestation of larger discursive formations."[15] In Ian Donaldson's elegant summation of recent scholarly developments, "Shakespeare is no longer viewed as a timeless and transhistorical genius, but as a textual phenomenon that is constantly reconstructed, constantly reinvented, constantly reinterpreted by every age according to its needs, priorities, and preconceptions."[16]

Despite this intensive critical effort to deconstruct the author, Shakespeare remains the privileged model of playwriting in the period, an inheritance that continues to haunt our understanding of dramatic authorship. Renewed interest in the material book and textuality – nostalgically motivated in part by the advent of cyber-cultures – should eventually contribute a great deal to Shakespeare's displacement. Nevertheless, this effort will certainly be complicated by the fact that, as David L. Gants laments, "[t]he study of William Shakespeare and the transmission of his texts has dominated the field of endeavor known as Anglo-American bibliography ever since it began to emerge as a distinct discipline during the latter half of the nineteenth century."[17] Consequently, much of what has been called the "New Textualism" has only reinforced Shakespeare's centrality.[18] Since the approach to dramatic authorship I take in this book has been informed by recent scholarship in textual studies, I want to survey briefly some of the important developments.

In 1981 Stephen Orgel published an essay, the title of which alluded to Foucault's essay on authorship by asking, "What is a Text?"[19] Orgel's reply, uttered in the New Textualism's infancy and sustained by a commitment to displacing the author, was rather succinct: "We know nothing about Shakespeare's original text."[20] Subsequently, Orgel would assert that, "every word we possess by Shakespeare has been through some editorial process."[21] Echoing Orgel's position in a more recent study, Marcus cautions that, "[n]o single version of a literary work, whether Renaissance or modern, can offer us the fond dream of unmediated access to an author."[22] Similarly, Randall McLeod laments that, "[t]he edited world is not going to disappear just because it is revealed to be wrong,"[23] and Paul Werstine reminds us that, "twentieth-century editing has proved resistant to the innovations of textual theory."[24] Not surprisingly, college bookstore shelves are crammed with new editions of Shakespeare's plays, including Arden (third series), Oxford, New Cambridge, Signet, Bantam, Folger, Norton, and Riverside.[25]

Simultaneously emboldened by the death of the author, and promoting itself as an "after-theory" phenomenon,[26] the New Textualism is in fact a reaction against a previous, though equally dispersed and amorphous, school of textual criticism generally identified as the New Bibliography. This reactionary aspect of the New Textualism is often touted as one of its strengths, if not its central mission.[27] Referring to the New Bibliography's origins, Werstine observes that, "[t]he early twentieth century had a taste for lurid romance,"[28] a taste that was initially exposed to the public in 1909 when one of its founding members, A. W. Pollard, published its first major work, *Shakespeare Folios and Quartos: A Study in the Bibliography of Shakespeare's Plays 1594–1685*.[29] The author was still alive, metaphysically at least, "logocentric" was not yet a derogatory term, the German word for "deconstruction" would be coined seventeen years later by Martin Heidegger in *Sein und Zeit*,[30] and a small group of bibliographers, casting about for a moral tale to explain away the confusing evidence they had collected, stumbled upon what Peter W. M. Blayney aptly depicts as "a stirring melodrama in which Good players, with occasional help from Good stationers, struggled against a few Bad stationers and usually won."[31] Pollard examined seventeen of the extant Shakespeare quartos and decided that some were "good" and some were "bad." Subsequently, he suggested that the "good" quartos were printed from Shakespeare's own manuscripts or "foul papers," as they came to be labeled, and he and a few earnest disciples – John Dover Wilson, W. W. Greg, and R. B. McKerrow – developed a range of narratives to account for the "bad" quartos.[32] Some were based on playhouse copies, some were based on copies that had been shortened and revised by playing companies for performance in the provinces, others were produced from texts that were memorially reconstructed by rogue actors who sold them for a little pocket money to printing houses.[33] Underwriting these narratives, according to Blayney, were the following "unfounded myths":

> that acting companies usually considered publication to be against their best interests; that some publishers were so desperate to satisfy their eager customers that they would acquire plays by any dishonest means; that if a stationer failed to register a play he was probably trying to conceal its origins; that if he registered it but failed to publish, he was probably acting on behalf of the players to forestall piracy by someone else.[34]

Nearly all of Pollard's terms and narratives were destined to be transformed from optimistic speculation about the texts of a single author into a general theory of dramatic texts and their authorship in the work of Greg.[35] In *The Editorial Problem in Shakespeare: A Survey of the Foundations of the Text* (1942) Greg was still willing to concede that an "inquiry into the nature of the manuscripts that were used as copy for the early editions of Shakespeare's plays" necessitated "entering upon a region of inference and conjecture" based on "a considerable body of evidence at our disposal" consisting of "possibly half a hundred playbooks from which we may hope, in one or another, to learn something to our purpose."[36] By the time "The Rationale of Copy-Text" (1949) appeared, the future of editing drama had brightened considerably. Recalling at the outset an earlier time when "the genealogical classification of manuscripts as a principle of textual criticism . . . appeared to provide at least some scientific basis for the conception of the most authoritative text,"[37] Greg concluded this seminal essay by arguing – in the specific case of *Richard III* and *King Lear* – that the folio texts of these plays be used as copy-text for scholarly editions because they "are in some parts connected by transcriptional continuity with the author's manuscript, whereas the quartos contain, as it is generally assumed, only reported texts, whose accidental characteristics can be of no authority whatever."[38] In less than a decade, "bad" had gotten worse, while "inference and conjecture" had been utterly displaced by editorial certitude about the "transcriptional continuity" between Shakespeare's manuscripts and the 1623 Folio. After more than "half a hundred" years of intensive bibliographical research, Greg was finally in a position to endorse the Folio's title page's claim that it fronted Shakespeare's plays "Published according to the True Originall Copies." Some twenty-five years later E. A. J. Honigmann would assert that, "[o]ne reason for the astonishing successes of the New Bibliography has been its emphasis on checking inferences about printed books by comparison with collateral manuscripts of the same period."[39]

Greg's "Rationale of Copy-Text," which Fredson Bowers subsequently called "the most influential textual document of this century,"[40] became something of a sacred text in the editorial community, primarily because it made the task of editing so much easier. After Greg's "Rationale," according to Werstine,

> it came to be assumed that editors already knew all they needed to about everything except the details ... In other words, editors thought that, for many of Shakespeare's plays, only the book's manufacture stood between the authorial manuscript and the present day editor and reader.[41]

The result of this editorial self-confidence was that Shakespeare's authorship became the body of evidence against which all dramatic texts were compared, and authorship became central to the interpretation of dramatic texts. As Werstine observes,

> And so, except for the printing house(s) that manufactured the particular book(s), the whole of early modern culture got consumed by an increasingly engorged author-function, which ate up the army of scribes, the theatrical industry (with its players, bookkeepers, costume-buyers, theatre owners, and thousands of patrons), and the government with its censors.[42]

Such was the New Bibliographic author-monster that had to be slain. With translated rumors of the death of the author drifting in from France, the time was certainly right.

The earliest blows were struck in the form of Michael Warren's "Quarto and Folio *King Lear* and the Interpretation of Albany and Edgar," Steven Urkowitz's *Shakespeare's Revision of King Lear*, and Warren and Taylor's collection of essays, *The Division of the Kingdoms*; but never were wounds more nurturing. Seeking to rehabilitate the 1608 text of *Lear* from eternal damnation in the New Bibliographic hell of "bad" quartodom, Warren, Urkowitz, Taylor *et al.* argued for its validity as one of two versions of the play that Shakespeare wrote.[43] Thus, except for a few dozen textual errors that couldn't possibly be purposeful, both *Lear*'s were happily restored to their author, and memorial reconstruction gave way to "versioning" as the critical explanation for their remarkable differences. Honigman had already proposed a similar interpretative solution when he argued that variants between multiple extant copies of a given play could be explained in terms of the "vagaries of authors in copying out their own work,"[44] but even Honigmann had to admit that applying his "argument about Shakespeare's 'second thoughts' to *King Lear* will seem foolhardy to anyone acquainted with the extraordinary complications of the two texts."[45]

Not long after these once-divided textual kingdoms were reunited under the peaceful reign of the author, the versioned *King Lear* became the centerpiece of Wells and Taylor's *William Shakespeare: The Complete Works*. With regard to this progression, de Grazia and Peter Stallybrass observe, "[f]or over two hundred years, *King Lear* was one text; in 1986, with the Oxford Shakespeare, it became two . . . As a result of this multiplication, Shakespeare studies will never be the same."[46] Ostensibly, the Oxford edition responded to the death of the author by attempting to restore Shakespeare's plays to the highly collaborative environment of the theatre in which they were initially written – a rather unlikely environment for staging Foucault's "privileged moment of *individualization*."[47] When Wells first introduced the Oxford edition to an audience at the Sheldonian Theatre on 28 October 1986, he declared that its editors had chosen "when possible, to print the more theatrical version of each play" because "[t]he theatre of Shakespeare's time was his most valuable collaborator."[48] Furthermore, he emphasized "our treatment of stage directions," arguing that "[e]ditorial theorists, preoccupied by the words to be spoken, have almost totally ignored the subject of stage directions, even though they are central to a presentation of Shakespeare's, or any dramatist's, art."[49] Similarly, Taylor asserted that the Oxford Shakespeare "attends, systematically and characteristically, to all the signals conveyed by spelling, punctuation, stage directions, lineation, typography, act and scene division, line numbering."[50]

But if Shakespeare had finally been subjected to the death sentence first handed down by Barthes and Foucault, then editorially executed by Wells and Taylor, some scholars have been less than convinced. Referring indirectly to some of the critical developments that generated the Oxford edition, Masten, for example, astutely notes that, "[e]ven the recent influential studies positing revision in certain Shakespearean texts are careful always to situate Shakespeare as the agency of revision, preempting the possibilities of diachronic collaboration."[51] For de Grazia and Stallybrass, who warn that "we are in danger of remaining hypnotically fascinated by the isolated author," the "notion of 'Shakespeare the reviser' . . . readily lends itself to a Man-and-Works criticism, for each multiple text constitutes a canon in miniature in which the author's personal and artistic development can be charted from revision to revision."[52] For Jonathan Goldberg, the versioned *Lear* means that "Shakespeare reigns supreme, author now of two sovereign texts."[53] Similarly, Werstine looks back at the *King Lear* controversy from which the Oxford edition was born and sees only a resurrection in the form of an "author function [that] swallowed up virtually all of the culture in which [the play] was inscribed/performed/printed" – an author function that was force-fed by editors who believe "that printed texts can be read virtually as if they were authorial manuscripts."[54] Corroborating Werstine's skepticism about the current status of authorship in textual studies, Dutton's recent analysis of the manuscript circulation of plays raises serious questions about what Dutton – referring to the *Complete Oxford Shakespeare* – characterizes as "the primacy increasingly often accorded performance as the only true, or at least most authentic, manifestation of the Shakespeare text."[55] Alternatively, Dutton's argument, which will be examined at some length in Chapter 1, suggests that there may have been readers of dramatic texts in early modern England who not only distinguished between plays as they were initially written by a given playwright and as they were subsequently adapted for performance but also valued more highly the former.

"Through a twisted dialectic," Barthes writes, "the Text, destroyer of all subject, contains a subject to love."[56] Rather than displacing Shakespeare as the model for the study of dramatic authorship, the New Textualism has more or less guaranteed that he will continue to govern the whole stage alone. This development is all the more regrettable because Shakespeare's status among contemporary playwrights was somewhat anomalous. First, as Peter Thomson notes, Shakespeare "was uniquely successful, but part of that success was the outcome of his ability to accommodate his creativity within the confines of London's emergent professional theatre."[57] Second, unlike Ben Jonson or John Webster – to name only two contemporary playwrights who, as we shall see, may have viewed the printing house as a positive alternative to the playhouse – Shakespeare seems to have been reluctant to see his plays published, and rather untypically indifferent about the quality of those plays that did find their way into print during his lifetime. As Samuel Johnson long ago noted, "[n]o other author gave up his works to fortune and time with so little care; no books could be left in hands as likely to injure them as plays frequently acted, yet continued in manuscript."[58] Dutton has recently shed much needed light on this puzzling, often misinterpreted aspect of Shakespeare's career,[59] and I will return to his important findings in Chapter 1. Third, the authority of those Shakespeare plays that did get published during his lifetime had little to do with his authorship in the first place. As Orgel importantly observes, "[t]he authority of the published text was, for the most part, that of the publisher: he owned it; the author's rights in the work ended with his sale of the manuscript. The publisher was fully entitled to alter the manuscript if he saw fit – the manuscript was his."[60] Shakespeare, of course, probably never sold any manuscripts of his plays, so his authority over his texts was limited to the collaborative environment of his playing company where, as Dutton rightly notes, "he was a company man, too identified with an ethos in which any removal of company property warranted expulsion from its ranks, too bound to a small group by ties that went beyond a mere contractual framework . . ."[61]

In early modern London, the death of the author was in some sense merely a workaday hazard of publication; the city's printing houses and bookstalls were crammed with orphaned texts. Jonson, as Scott McMillin notes, was the "dramatist who cared about literary status, and who made a campaign out of turning plays into respectable literature."[62] Accordingly, he did more than any of his contemporary playwrights to usurp the publisher's authority by involving himself in the publication process; and although recent commentators have tended to interpret this involvement as an early attempt to attain something akin to authorial property rights, Mark Rose correctly observes that, "[b]y no means can [Jonson] be mistaken for the modern figure of the author as a private individual whose worth is calculable in terms of the property he or she created."[63] Jonson himself makes a similar appraisal of his authorial predicament when he acknowledges to Alphonso Ferrabosco that, "When we doe give, ALPHONSO, to the light, / A Worke of ours, we part with our owne right."[64]

Appropriately, title pages of published texts, including plays, almost always included the names of a given text's publisher and/or printer,[65] and frequently indicated where the text had been printed and could be purchased. Moreover, because plays were generally the property of a given playing company prior to publication, title pages of plays frequently included some form of company attribution. During the roughly sixty-six-year period of the professional theatre (1576–1642), company attribution on extant printed title pages remained more or less constant at about sixty percent.[66] Author attribution, on the other hand, was hardly a priority on title pages, especially during the first few decades of the professional theatre when less than twenty percent of the extant published plays featured the name of an author.[67]

In the particular case of Shakespeare, the primacy of the publisher over the author is perhaps the only thing about his authorship that is typical. The specifics of Shakespeare's involvement with printers and publishers will be examined in Chapter 1, but it is worth noting here that his earliest plays were published anonymously, and that he did not emerge as the author of a coherent body of printed texts until seven years after his death, when the two main holders of authority over a play-text in his day, the publisher and the playing company, joined forces to bring out a folio collection of his plays. In its most literal or physical sense, then, the death of the author did play a fundamental role in the coming into being of the notion of Shakespeare as an author, though "the privileged moment of *individualization*" that is constituted by this notion had little to do with the "history of ideas, knowledge, literature, philosophy, and the sciences." Instead, as befits a materially large, involved, and expensive publication project, the 1623 Folio's address "To the great Variety of Readers" (A3r)[68] is primarily concerned with encouraging customers to buy the book. Ostensibly written by John Heminge and Henrie Condell, two shareholders in Shakespeare's playing company, the King's Men, the structure of the reader address makes it utterly clear at the outset that business comes first, and the individualization of Shakespeare as an author comes second. However, even the effort to individualize Shakespeare's authorship is largely motivated by the primary goal of representing the book as a valuable commodity.

Beginning in the second line of their address, Heminge and Condell concern themselves with ensuring that readers fully grasp the fact that reading and spending go hand in hand. The prospective buyer of Shakespeare's "collected and publish'd" (22) writings must, of course, be literate, though only minimally so, because even the reader "that can but spell" (1) is given the privilege of being counted as a potential customer.[69] After the basic characteristics of the Folio's market niche have been established, Shakespeare's future readers are instructed that "the fate of all Bookes depends vp- / on your capacities : and not of your heads alone, / but of your purses" (3–5). Then Heminge and Condell acknowledge their clientele's supposed yearnings: "Well ! It is now publique, & you / wil stand for your priuiledges wee know : to read, / and censure" (5–7). Next, it's the hard sell, complete with the testimony of an expert on the sale and purchase of books: "Do so, but buy it first. That doth best / commend a Booke, the Stationer saies" (7–8). Then, the semantic barrier between money and words is succinctly dismantled as readers are advised to "Iudge your sixe-pen'orth, your shillings worth, your five shil- / lings worth at a time, or higher, so you rise to the just rates, and wel- / come" (10–12).[70] Finally, the purveyors of Shakespeare's corpus revert one more time to the hard sell to make their last pitch: "But, what ever you do, Buy" (12).

Heminge and Condell's prologue to Shakespeare's posthumous career in print is an impressive performance worthy of two men who had spent their lives in the theatre, and it is clear that their loyalties are divided between their purse and their late colleague's person. Of the address's thirty-nine lines, the seventeen lines of the first paragraph are devoted to selling Shakespeare, while the twenty-two lines of the second take up his authorship. Two lines into the second paragraph, the word "Author" itself appears for the first and last time as the object of a desire "that / the Author himselfe had liv'd to have set forth, and overseen his owne / writings" (18–20). In his absence, self-serving grave robbers have sacked his literary sepulcher and flooded the market "with diverse / stolne, and surreptitious copies, maimed, and deformed by the frauds / and stealthes of iniurious impostors, that expos'd them" (23–25). Alternatively, Heminge and Condell counter with a kind of medieval resurrection narrative in which they assure their readers that they offer Shakespeare's remains "cur'd, and perfect of their limbes; and all / the rest, absolute in their numbers, as he conceived thẽ" (26–27). Then, once the contents of his authorial tomb have been restored and preserved, they present a cured and perfectly embalmed image of the author himself as "a happie imitator of Nature" and "a most gentle expresser of it. His mind / and hand," they inform us, "went together : And what he thought, he vttered with that / easinesse, that wee haue scarse receiued from him a blot in his papers" (27–30). No space has been left in this mythic account of the writer's craft for the kind of debates that have raged on for much of this century about the nature of the playwright's manuscripts or his involvement in the revision of his plays. Nothing – not the scribe, not the censor, not the actor, not the "valuable collaborator" that is the theatre, not the Stationers' Company, not even the printing house – except a quill pen and an inkwell mediate between what Shakespeare thought and what has become available for the first time to his prospective readers.

Now that authorship is viewed in the academy as a "discursive formation" or as a complicated negotiation between a creator and the society in which she or he creates, we can look at this effort to re-embody the author for a future readership and see it as the shrewd marketing ploy that it was. But to do so is to underestimate the influence this account has had on the study of dramatic authorship. In the formative years of the New Bibliography, for example, Pollard was convinced that Shakespeare and members of his company worried that play manuscripts existing in multiple scribal copies could be stolen and performed by other companies and/or printed.[71] Thus, as Werstine observes, Pollard argued

that Shakespeare would turn over to his company manuscripts of his plays in his own hand – not scribal transcripts of them. Pollard based this part of his argument on the words of Heminge and Condell in the front matter to the

Shakespeare First Folio ... Pollard construed the actors' reference to Shakespeare's papers as a statement of fact to the effect that Shakespeare handed over his plays to his company in his own handwriting.[72]

Marcus asserts that, "[t]he Bard generated by the First Folio is a figure for Art itself as Renaissance humanists like Ben Jonson wished to imagine it, existing in lofty separateness from the vicissitudes of life, yet capable, from its eminence, of shedding influence, 'cheere,' and admonition."[73] Certainly Jonson contributed to the materialization of Shakespeare's authorship accomplished by the 1623 Folio. The publication of Jonson's *Workes* in 1616 inaugurated the era of the printed drama collection, and he contributed two dedicatory poems to the Shakespeare Folio. Nevertheless, there is nothing lofty about Heminge and Condell's address. It was written to sell a book. Bristol observes that, "[w]hat the theatres were able to accomplish was the transformation of otherwise familiar performance practices into cultural merchandise."[74] For Douglas Bruster, the oft-noted tendency of Shakespeare's plays "to offer (even affirm) simultaneously, without contradiction, contradictory themes, messages, and ideological stances" is "a product of early modern market forces which shaped dramatic commodities to answer the various manifestations of social desire."[75] Although Heminge and Condell, fellow sharers in London's most financially successful playing company, were well acquainted with the theatrical market and the rich potential of transforming drama into a commodity, they were somewhat out of their milieu when it came to transforming Shakespeare's "papers" into a commodity that could be exchanged for fifteen shillings unbound (or one pound bound)[76] among strangers at the bookstalls at St. Paul's churchyard. Indeed, they acknowledge their lack of experience in this area when, upon instructing readers for the first time to "buy it first," they defer to the expertise of "the Stationer." Stationers, of course, knew all about buying it first, because, as John Feather notes, "[b]y the end of the sixteenth century literature, in the broadest sense, had become a commercial commodity. The rewards of that commerce, however, were for the printer, publisher and bookseller, rather than for the author."[77] In the particular case of the 1623 Folio, Heminge and Condell could hope that the publication of Shakespeare's plays in a collection might stimulate some modicum of renewed interest in the dead playwright's work, leading perhaps to revivals of some of his plays in the playhouse. But it was a printing house, owned by the Jaggards, that stood to gain a modest profit if approximately 800 readers heeded Heminge and Condell's exhortations to "buy it first" and took the rather large volume of plays home with them from St. Paul's. It took them nearly a decade to do so.

1 "A toy brought to the Presse": marketing printed drama in early modern London

> Some Play books since I first undertooke this subject, are growne from *Quarto* into *Folio*, which yet beare so good a price and sale, that I cannot with griefe relate it, they are now(e) new-printed in farre better paper than most Octavo or Quarto *Bibles*, which hardly finde vent as they.
> William Prynne, *Histrio-mastix*

> Books are objects. On a table, on shelves, in store windows, they wait for someone to come and deliver them from their materiality, from their immobility.
> Georges Poulet, *Criticism and the Experience of Interiority*

I begin at the end, or rather, as befits a study of authorship written in the post-modern era when new and often indistinguishable digital sources of authority are usurping the thrones once occupied by the book-bound, after the death of an author. Given Shakespeare's decision to leave the theatre and the world without first performing what Louis A. Montrose terms "an act of textual self-monumentalization,"[1] the 1623 Folio tells a story of its dependence on the introduction and interference of several agents and intentions. The Folio's principal publishers, Edward Blount and Isaac Jaggard, were responsible for unauthorial, but nonetheless complex, negotiations with other publishers to acquire the existing publication rights for several plays previously printed in quarto editions.[2] They also had the responsibility of finding and hiring a printer, though this task was simplified considerably by the fact that Isaac's father, William Jaggard, was available. Keeping the project in the family must have taken precedence over the fact that the elder Jaggard had been blind for some years by the time copy was being cast off for the First Folio in the early months of 1622. Heminge and Condell were crucial to the project because, presumably, they were the source of those unpublished and unblotted manuscripts of Shakespeare's plays that remained in the possession of the King's Men after his death. Additionally, as Blayney observes,

[Shakespeare's] surviving fellows would have welcomed the planned edition as a tribute and memorial to one of the company's most successful playwrights.

Furthermore, while relatively few of his plays may have remained in regular performance by the 1620s, the book would remind the public that many once-popular plays were still available to be revived on demand.[3]

In other words, not only had the First Folio made possible the typographic resurrection of Shakespeare's plays "cur'd, and perfect of their limbes; and all / the rest, absolute in their numbers," but it may have also set the stage for the resuscitation of the playwright's moribund career in the theatre as well. Although Heminge and Condell probably never set foot inside of a printing house before 1622, the publicity potential of publication was one aspect of Shakespeare's transformation into cultural merchandise, of his commodification, with which they would have had some familiarity.[4]

"We do not know," according to Blayney, "whether the idea of publishing the Folio was first conceived by the players or the publishers, but the two groups had to cooperate before the idea became a reality."[5] We do know, however, that the generic idea of publishing a folio collection of contemporary plays had initially emerged from a period of intense collaboration between Jonson and a printer named William Stansby, though Montrose has recently argued that Edmund Spenser's "publication process, unfolded over the last two decades of the sixteenth century ... provided Jonson's most immediate and most significant native precedent and model."[6] In the specific case of Heminge and Condell's contribution to the First Folio, especially their use of the reader address to link the value of Shakespeare's plays as purchasable commodities with the idealization of his authorship, neither Spenser's nor Jonson's "publication process" provides a clear precedent.

Spenser's "publication process" was at least partly inspired by Chaucer's career in print, as it began to be managed by William Caxton shortly after he ushered England into the age of mechanical reproduction.[7] Jonson would have seen how a folio could lend impressive shape and substance to a writer's life during his visits to William Stansby's printing house. As actors in a playing company, Heminge and Condell had at one time or another probably mouthed the words to a number of prologues that promoted a particular play and its author. Nevertheless, the text on which their 1623 performance is based is not unique to the theatre. Rather, it looks back to and derives many of its lines from a substantive tradition that originated not in the playhouse, but in the London book trade at a point when it began to play an active role in the commodification of drama and dramatic authorship. Examining an early phase of this tradition will provide us with some perspective on seventeenth-century efforts to materialize, embody, and commodify early modern drama – and its authorship – through publication.

If the playhouse and the printing house had to cooperate before the idea of the First Folio could become a reality, such cooperation is difficult to reconcile with Andrew Gurr's assertion that, "the companies that bought the plays were actively hostile to the idea of printing them . . . There was no reason to make the product durable or to record it for future generations. So the plays lived in a medium as ephemeral as the sounds through which they came to life."[8] Similarly D. F. McKenzie claims that in the early seventeenth century there was "a professional *dis*junction of play-wrights and printers . . . print was not the proper medium for plays." [9] McKenzie himself admits that, "the textual models we have adopted for the drama reflect only the commercial opportunism of printers in the early seventeenth century, a time when the theatre was alive and confident of its own distinctively oral and visual mode."[10] But the text of Jonson's folio, of Shakespeare's Folio, indeed, the texts of any number of quarto editions of plays tell very different stories in which printers and playwrights, and sometimes players, worked together to introduce plays to new and different markets. There may have been opportunism at the heart of such early seventeenth-century efforts to market drama, but it is hard to see such efforts as anything but joint business ventures in which the primary function of the author was his capacity to give a commodity a minimum of recognition and value. In this sense, Foucault's oft-quoted claim that, "[t]ext, books, and discourses really began to have authors . . . to the extent that authors became subject to punishment, that is, to the extent that discourses could be transgressive,"[11] can't quite be right either.

In the specific case of the 1623 Folio, the author that emerges is anything but transgressive, and Heminge and Condell make this clear, at least rhetorically, when they assure the reader that, "these Playes have had their triall alreadie, and stood out all Appeales; and do now come forth quitted rather by a Decree of Court" (15–16). This image of innocent plays sets the stage for the subsequent image of the author as "a happie imitator of Nature" and "a most gentle expresser" (28), but it does not cohere well with Foucault's notion of transgressive discourse. Bristol asserts that,

> it is clear that those who invented the theatre had specific interests of their own, most notably an interest in economic survival . . . all the principals in these enterprises were entirely indifferent to the possibility either of subversion of state power or of its affirmation. The political outlook of the shareholders was more likely to be linked to a preoccupation with their right to enjoy the profits of their own labor.[12]

No doubt it was precisely this right that shareholders had in mind when, as Orgel observes, they "commissioned the play, usually stipulated the subject, often provided the plot, often parceled it out, scene by scene, to several playwrights."[13] The diary kept by the theatrical entrepreneur, Philip Henslowe, in which he recorded his dealings with London companies, players, and playwrights from 1592 to 1604, provides ample evidence for Orgel's observation. Nevertheless, Henslowe's diary also suggests that the early modern London playhouse was a rather busy place that had no space for the "coming into being of the notion of 'author'" or time for "the privileged moment of *individualization* in the history of ideas, knowledge, literature, philosophy, and the sciences" that this authorial notion constituted.

Although we do not know whether it was the King's Men or a father–son printing business that commissioned the "Booke" that would broadcast the death of the author even as it materially gave birth to the author's individualization, it does seem clear that the "Booke" got the two companies together, and that their motive for cooperating to produce it was anything but metaphysical. In the particular case of the 1623 Folio, Roger Stoddard's assertion that, "[w]hatever authors do, they do not write books,"[14] is only half the story. The other half is that, whatever else the Folio did, it did write Shakespeare's authorship by giving shape to and rendering legible a set of discourses that required an author to make the "Booke" a marketable commodity. Indeed, as Feather observes more generally, "[t]he professional author, like the professional publisher, is a product of the age of the printed book."[15] Furthermore, if we move back in the history of printed drama in England from the Folio's appearance in the marketplace to the points at which Foucault's "punishment" or McKenzie's "*dis*junction" began to emerge, we find neither the "coming into being of the notion of 'author'" nor a conflict between printers and playwrights. Rather, in both cases we find the seeds being planted for a set of collaborations that would make published dramatic texts and, consequently, dramatic authorship possible.

With regard to the transgressive author, this historical retracing of steps begins with the Privy Council under Edward VI, a legislative body that seems to have been unaware of or indifferent to a rift between printers and playwrights. Indeed, as Greg Walker observes, "[a]lthough the introduction of printing may have had a considerable impact upon the availability of dramatic texts to both actors and readers, it is clear that its impact upon the perceptions of the political authorities was initially far less powerful . . . Their response to drama on the printed page was largely to ignore it, even in situations where one might expect them to have acted."[16] In April of 1551, a Royal Proclamation seeking to expand existing Acts against "Beggars and Vagabonds" took aim at "vagabondes, tellers of newes, sowers of sedicious rumours, players, and printers without license, and divers other disordered persons,"[17] forbidding them from engaging in their respective specialties and threatening them with fines and imprisonment. Clearly there was no feasible method for licensing "tellers of newes, sowers of sedicious rumours," or "divers other disordered persons," for that matter; but the syntactic ambiguity of the phrase "players, and printers without license" makes it unclear whether players could be licensed, or only printers. As if anticipating this minor interpretive crisis, the proclamation adds the following sentence:

> Nor that any common players, or other persons, upon like paines, do play thenglish tong, any manner Enterlude, Play or matter, without they have special licence to shew for the same, in writing under his majesties signe, or signed by vi. of his highness privie counsaill.[18]

Thus was born what Richard Dutton identifies as "the first definite attempt to institute a formal system of licensing of materials to be performed, which implicitly also meant censorship."[19] Print, according to McKenzie, may not have been "the proper medium for plays" in the early seventeenth century, but in the middle of the sixteenth century – one hundred years after its invention – both the printed page and the stage were considered improper enough to be grouped together in the same regulatory paradigm.[20]

Two years later, within months of Mary I's accession, an edict promising "Freedom of Conscience" again brought the press and the theatre together, and added "Religious Controversy" to the group.[21] Hoping perhaps to clarify the ambiguous phrasing of the earlier Act, the Proclamation of 18 August 1553 moved the position of the reference to licensing up to the front and shifted the objects of its concern from persons to things. The resulting Act, "Prohibiting Religious Controversy, Unlicensed Plays, and Printing," aspired to the "reformation of busy meddlers in matters of religion, and for redress of preachers, printers, and players," and claimed to be motivated by Mary's remembrance of "what great inconvenience and dangers have grown to this her highness' realm in time past through the diversity of opinions in questions of religion."[22] Declaring it "well-known" that there are

> evil-disposed persons which take upon them without sufficient authority to preach and to interpret the word of God after their own brain in churches and other places both public and private, and also by playing of interludes and printing of false fond books, ballads, rhymes, and other lewd treatises in the English tongue,[23]

the proclamation then announced its *raison d'être*:

> Her highness therefore straightly chargeth and commandeth all and every her said subjects of whatsoever state, condition, or degree they be, that none of them presume from henceforth to preach, or by way of reading in churches or other

public or private places (except in the schools of the universities) to interpret or teach any Scriptures or any manner points of doctrine concerning religion; neither also to print any books, matter, ballad, rhyme, interlude, process, or treatise, nor to play any interlude except they have her grace's special license in writing for the same.[24]

Dedicated to eliminating *in utero* the birth of what Jürgen Habermas would describe as the "domain of our social life in which such a thing as public opinion can be formed,"[25] the third Royal Proclamation of Mary's reign was powered by fear of the public sphere, and the locus of its anxiety in the first few months of England's compulsory return to Catholicism was the unholy trinity of preaching, printing, and playing. Moreover, the division glimpsed here between the propriety of the "schools of the universities" and the impropriety of "other public or private spaces" may have laid the foundation for subsequent attitudes toward playing and playwrights, exemplified most famously by Thomas Nashe's letter "To the Gentlemen Students of Both Universities." Nashe distinguishes between "how eloquent our gowned age is grown of late" and "the servile imitation of vain glorious tragedians,"[26] between the university stage and the public playhouse. The proclamation's distinction between what is allowed in universities but not elsewhere is further emphasized by its concern over what gets printed and subsequently read in the vernacular. Taking care, like the previous proclamation of 1551, to specify its anxiety over the "playing of interludes and printing of false fond books, ballads, rhymes, and other lewd treatises in the English tongue," the 1553 Act intimates that academic Latin plays as well as lewd treatises written in Latin do not pose a threat to the realm.

Recent studies by Frederick Kiefer and Bryan Crockett have explored in considerable depth the historical, metaphorical, thematic, rhetorical, and even gestural links between playing and printing, and playing and preaching, respectively. Within the limited context of mid-sixteenth-century regulatory concerns, however, initial governmental efforts to license plays and players simply failed to register the "professional *dis*junction of play-wrights and printers" that has been a premise of so many scholarly and editorial approaches to printed drama since the early New Bibliographical studies of Pollard and Greg. Rather, printing and playing pose equal threats within Edward's and Mary's successive legislative efforts to maintain order in their realms. Furthermore, the word "playwright" never appears in either of the proclamations examined above, nor does the word "author," for that matter. Instead, as the 1553 proclamation's consistent use of infinitive verbs such as "to preach," "to interpret," "to print," and "to play" suggests, it is the proscribed activities themselves – not their actors – that disturb the monarch's sleep.

Authorship enters into the regulatory picture two years later in a Royal Proclamation, "Enforcing Statute against Heresy; Prohibiting Seditious and Heretical Books," which promises "a great punishment" for "the authors, makers, and writers of books containing wicked doctrine and erroneous and heretical opinions contrary to the Catholic faith and determination of the holy church,"[27] but there is no reference to plays, interludes, or playing.

Playwrights do finally get some recognition in a Special Commission of 24 December 1581, which granted Edward Tilney enough power to take on the role of state censor of drama, but the reference is somewhat ambiguous. Providing Tilney with the authority to hire workers to perform his court duties, the Commission also authorized him

> to warne commaunde and appointe in all places within this our Realme of England, aswell within franchesses and liberties as without, all and every plaier or plaiers with their playmakers, either belonginge to any noble man or otherwise, bearinge the name or names of usinge the facultie of playmakers or plaiers of Comedies, Tragedies, Enterludes or whatever other showes soever, from tyme to tyme and at all tymes to appeare before him with all such plaies, Tragedies, Comedies or showes as they shall in readines or meane to sett forth.[28]

It can probably be assumed that the term "playmaker" here refers to what we would call "playwright." Nevertheless, the following table of title page and Stationers' Register attributions for first editions of plays written and published during the decade leading up to the Special Commission indicates that the use of the verb "to make" for authorship is rare, appearing only twice before the 1581 ruling, once after; and none of them made it into the Stationers' Register.

It is at least conceivable that "playmaker" refers to one who makes a play in the sense of one who produces or subsidizes a play. Henslowe, who mentions a number of playwrights by name, relies only on phrases such as "in earneste of a boocke" or "in pt of payment for a booke" to indicate that a given name or set of names has been paid for the writing of a play. Words like "author," "playwright," and "playmaker" never appear.

A subsequent 22 June 1600 Privy Council order seeking to redress "bothe the greatest abuses of the plaies and plaienge houses," reduced the licensed public theatres to "two houses and noe more allowed to serve for the use of the Common Stage Plaies," ordered that the "two severall Companies of Plaiers assigned vnto the two howses allowed maie play each of them in there severall howse twice a weeke and noe oftener," and threatened "[c]ommittinge to prison the owners of Plaiehouses and players as shall disobey & resist these orders."[29] Although Janet Clare asserts that censorship "is perhaps the most potent external force which

Date	Title	Title-Page Attribution	Stationers' Register
1569	Patient Grissil	Compiled by John Phillips	Compiled by John Phillips
	The Longer thou Livest the More Fool thou Art	Compiled by W. Wager	
	The Disobedient Child	Compiled by Thomas Ingelend	
	The Marriage of Wit and Science		
1571	Damon and Pithias	*Made* by Maister Edwards	
1573	Free-Will	Wrytten fyrst in Italian by FNB, and translated into Englishe by Henry Cheecke	
1575	Gammar Gorton's Needle	*Made* by Mr. S. Mr of Art	
	The Tide Tarrieth No Man	Compiled by George Wapull	
1577	All for Money	Compiled by T. Lupton	
	1&2 Promus and Cassandra	Compiled by George Whetstone	Compiled by George Whetstone
	The Most Virtuous and Godly Susanna	Devised by Thomas Churchyard	Gathered by Thomas Churchyard
1581	The Entertainment before the French Ambassadors	Collected, gathered, penned & published by Henry Goldweill	Collected, gathered, penned & published by Henry Goldweill
1594	Friar Bacon and Friar Bungay	*Made* by Robert Greene	

interacts with the creative consciousness,"[30] no reference is made in this order to writers, makers, gatherers, devisors, collectors, penners, or compilers.

During the second half of the sixteenth century, the period in which both the professional theatre and the printing of drama emerged, efforts were made to regulate both players and printers. In the 1590s, the Privy Council of London received a number of petitions from the Lord Mayor and/or aldermen calling for the total suppression of the playhouses.[31] And, of course, legislative attempts to control printers were frequently made by various individuals or groups, especially during periods of religious or political controversy, though ultimately – in the specific case of London – it was the Stationers' Company, according to Feather, that "could and did regulate the production and sale of books in the City."[32] Furthermore, although playwrights probably did write transgressive discourses (Jonson and Nashe's *Isle of Dogs* may have been one of them),[33] rarely do these authors seem to have been a major source of anxiety for the rulers and/or legislators who initiated these regulatory efforts. And finally, there may have been some hostility from time to time between playwrights and printers in the second half of the sixteenth century, but it was not serious enough to warrant the attention of those who sought to monitor and regulate either group. Given all of these qualifications, it is rather remarkable that the first transgressive discourse to benefit from the individualizing authorial potential of punishment was written by a playwright who did more than anyone in his age to make print "the proper medium for plays." According to Dutton,

> *Sejanus* would seem to be the first occasion on which any dramatist was made to answer *by the government* for his text – that is, treating a play-text as if it were a printed book and treating Jonson as if he were, for example, Dr. Hayward. Indeed, the possibility that the examination followed the *publication* of the play in 1605 rather than its 1603 *performance* should not lightly be discounted.[34]

The King's Men, the playing company that staged *Sejanus*, "seem not to have been involved in the inquiry," Dutton adds. If the Privy Council under Edward VI had been unwilling or unable to differentiate between players and printers in 1551, fifty years later the same legislative body was still refusing to cooperate with, to borrow McKenzie's phrase, "the textual models we have adopted for the drama." Even Dutton's use of italics in the passage quoted above typographically tell a tale not of "*dis*junction," but one of deliberate conflation in which *publication* and *performance* are fused together *by the government*. Appropriately, Jonson may have used the printed book to elude a regulatory system that was primarily structured to mediate between the playing company and the state, for as Dutton notes, "the pedantic apparatus of sources with which Jonson shrouded the quarto text, protesting (probably too much) the play's innocence as disinterested history, were an anticipation of trouble rather than a response to his arraignment."[35] In the printed text – the performance text is not extant – that individualized Jonson in the eyes of the Privy Council, a writer of history books named Cordus frets over the future of Pompey's theatre, is accused of treason, and his books are burnt.[36]

Jonson himself simultaneously acknowledged the individualizing potential of this transgressive moment and expressed its importance to his emergence as an individualized author in terms of the difference between the stage and the printed page by informing readers of the *Sejanus, His Fall* quarto that,

> this Booke, in all numbers, is not the same with that which was acted on the publike Stage, wherein a second Pen had good share: in place of which I have rather chosen, to put weaker (and no doubt lesse pleasing) of mine own, then to defraud so happy a Genius of his right, by my lothed usurpation (¶3).

In the specific context of dramatic authorship, this statement represents an important development, and its implications will be considered more fully in Chapter 3.

For Jonson, then, the distance between the playhouse and the printing house was the space of his authorial singularity, a singularity that could only be achieved and maintained in the printed text. If the members of the Privy Council chose to ignore this distance in their search for a transgressive singularity, certainly history was on their side. For it is one of the great, but rarely acknowledged, ironies of scholarship on early modern English drama that both the printing trade, organized and embodied as the Stationers' Company, and the English vernacular dramatic tradition, written and performed at the Inns of Court, came into their own at precisely the same historical moment during the early years of Elizabeth's reign. The Company was incorporated on 4 May 1557, the day its charter of incorporation was officially approved, and by the summer of 1562, "the shape of the Company was clear," according to Cyprian Blagden.[37] In that year, the Company fully settled into its new location at Peter's College, Elizabeth confirmed its charter, and city officials granted it the privilege of having its own livery.[38] Some five years after being incorporated, the Company had more or less fully emerged as England's primary institution for monitoring and regulating publication. At another guildhall known as the Inner Temple, Norton and Sackville's *Gorboduc* was being performed, and another institution was beginning to take shape.

Until Elizabeth's accession, the majority of the tragedies performed and/or published in London were translated from Greek to Latin by the likes of Roger Ascham (*Philoctetes*, 1543), and Thomas Caius (*The Tragedies of Euripides*, 1550). Beginning in 1558, however, with the performance of Seneca's *Thebais*,[39] translated into English by Thomas Browne, a number of "Englished" Senecan plays appeared one after the other in the first five years of Elizabeth's reign.[40] It is impossible to determine for certain what motivated this significant spate of interest in translating Seneca,[41] but it is not difficult to speculate how Browne's translation of *Thebais*, and its subsequent performance, might have encapsulated the Inns of Court's views on the Elizabethan succession. The play's treatment of the final dynastic crisis of the House of Cadmus would have resonated in the legalistic mind of England's juridical body with the Tudor dynasty, and even the specifics of the Tudor succession from one sister to another are mirrored in the play's depiction of a succession struggle between two brothers.

By 1562, however, the proliferation of "Englished" Senecas abated just long enough for Norton and Sackville's *Gorboduc* to be performed at the

Inner Temple. *Gorboduc*, like Seneca's *Thebais* four years earlier, also tells the story of a succession struggle between brothers. The importance of this performance cannot, perhaps, be overstated. As Walker observes, "Gorboduc is rightly considered a landmark in English literary history. As the earliest extant five-act verse tragedy in English, the earliest attempt to imitate Senecan tragic form in English, the earliest surviving English drama in blank verse, and the earliest English play to adopt the use of dumb-shows preceding each act, it offers itself as a point of departure for much of the Renaissance dramatic experimentation of the following decades."[42] Moreover, in the case of *Gorboduc* there is no longer any cause to speculate about how it was received because a recently discovered manuscript in the British Library's Yelverton collection preserves one audience member's impressions of the play's premiere performance in January of 1562.[43] Indicating that, "[t]here was a tragedie played in the Inner Temple of the two brethren Porrex and Ferrex K of Brytayne," the viewer/proto-New Historicist critic recalls "that many things were saied [in the play] for the Succesion to put things in certenty."[44] Commenting on this rare extant eyewitness account of a play in performance, Norman Jones and Paul Whitfield White assert that *Gorboduc* is "an object lesson in what happens if the problems of marriage and succession are not solved."[45] For Walker, *Gorboduc* is the first play "deliberately to intervene in [the] ongoing debate about the queen's marriage plans and the future of the realm."[46]

In the same year that the Stationers' Company emerged as the primary institution for monitoring and regulating the London book trade, the first home-grown English tragedy was sating London's still limited appetite for the genre by successfully adapting Senecan tragic conventions to English topical matters (specifically Elizabeth's marital and reproductive choices). If the first performance of *Gorboduc* and the ratification of the Company's charter by city and crown were, in fact, parallel moments of historical importance, the chronological convergence of page and stage that I have sketched in here would be nothing more than a coincidence. What does, however, seem significant is that the publication history of *Gorboduc* sets playhouse and printing house on a collision course which, though it remains largely misinterpreted in the textual scholarship on printed drama, will ultimately produce the 1623 Folio and, consequently, the notion we have of Shakespeare as an author.

Published initially on 22 September 1565, the title page of the first printed octavo edition (Fig. 1),[47] is slightly more crowded with print than, say, the title page of the quarto edition of *Titus Andronicus* (Fig. 2) published three decades later. Nevertheless, it is strikingly similar to

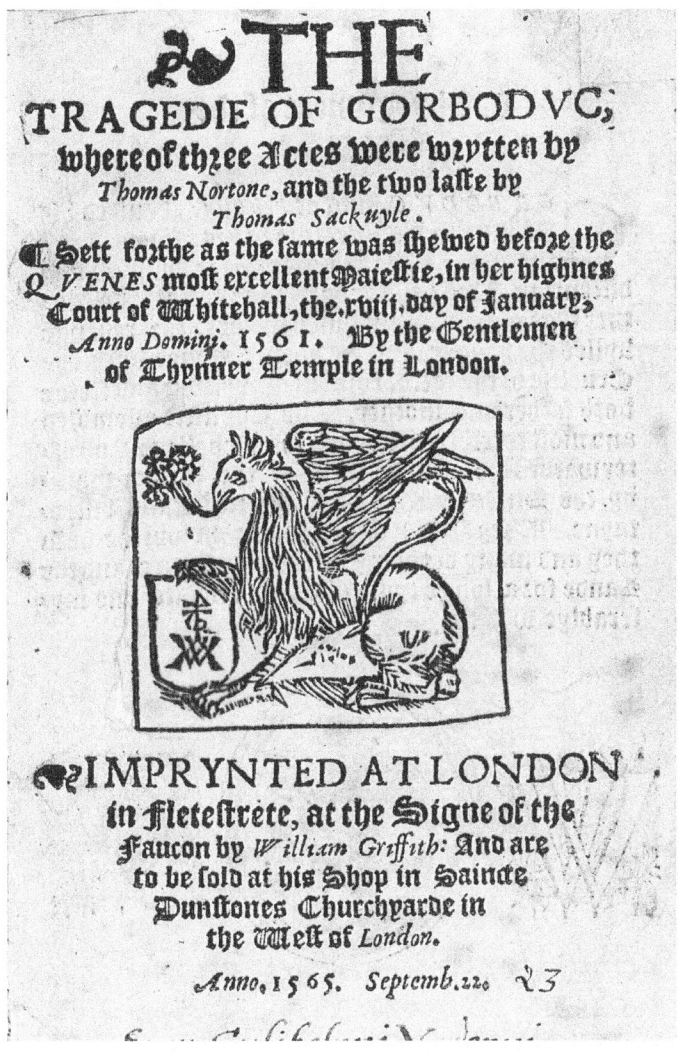

Figure 1 Title page: *The Tragedie of Gorbodvc*, 1565

hundreds of extant title pages of early modern dramatic texts that would be printed over the next seventy-five years. All the information that would become standard for title pages of printed plays can be found in the proper place. The title, "THE / TRAGEDIE OF GORBODVC," appears at the top of the page, facts of publication and sale appear at the bottom:

THE MOST LAmentable Romaine Tragedie of Titus Andronicus:

As it was Plaide by the Right Honourable the Earle of *Darbie*, Earle of *Pembrooke*, and Earle of *Sussex* their Seruants.

LONDON,
Printed by Iohn Danter, and are to be sold by *Edward White* & *Thomas Millington*, at the little North doore of Paules at the signe of the Gunne.
1594.

Figure 2 Title page: *The Most Lamentable Romaine Tragedie of Titus Andronicus*, 1594

Marketing Printed Drama 27

IMPRYNTED AT LONDON / in Fletestrete, at the Signe of the / Faucon by *William Griffith:* And are / to be sold at his Shop in Saincte / Dunstones Churchyarde in / the West of *London. / Anno,* 1565. *Septemb.* 22.

Above the emblem that dominates the center of the page, the particulars of the play's performance, as well as an indication of the printed text's fidelity to that performance, are provided :

Sett forthe as the same was shewed before the / QVENES most excellent Maiestie, in her highnes / Court of Whitehall, the xviij day of January, / *Anno Domini.* 1561. By the Gentlemen / of Thynner Temple in London.

Thus, the "*dis*junction" of printers and playwrights is represented here spatially as a kind of balance of power by the emblem that separates the two activities that have converged to make the printed dramatic text possible. Nearly all extant dramas printed subsequently would follow this format on their title pages. There is something truly extraordinary about this title page though, something that would not be replicated afterward. Just below the play's title appears an astonishingly precise statement about the play's authorship: "whereof three Actes were wrytten by / *Thomas Nortone,* and the two laste by / *Thomas Sackuyle.*" It would be difficult to exaggerate the singularity of such an attribution, and the mind boggles at how much scholarly labor might have been spared if all subsequent dramas had been so precisely attributed.[48]

When a second octavo edition (O2)[49] of the play is published five years later, the title page (Fig. 3) has undergone a radical transformation. The balance of power noted on the previous title page has been undone, and the locus of authority for the publication has been snatched away from the authors.[50] The careful ascription to Norton and Sackville has been removed, ostensibly compelling the play to join the ranks of the roughly 150 extant plays from the period that were published anonymously; in its place are proffered the two names of the play's new title: "The Tragidie of Ferrex / and Porrex." Where once prospective readers were informed that the play they were about to buy was "Sett forthe as the same was shewed," now they are assured that this new edition has been "set forth without addition or alte- / ration but altogether as the same was shewed / on stage before the Queenes Maiestie, / about nine yeares past." The increased promotion here of the printed play's fidelity to a single performance is oddly juxtaposed with the vagueness of the phrase "about nine yeares past." Where once an emblem ran interference between stage and page, now a single, ambiguous phrase, "Seen and allowed," indicates the presence of a new locus of authority, though it isn't exactly clear what it is that has been "Seen and allowed."[51] The performance? The text? The title page? Certainly, the emblem that was displaced has been

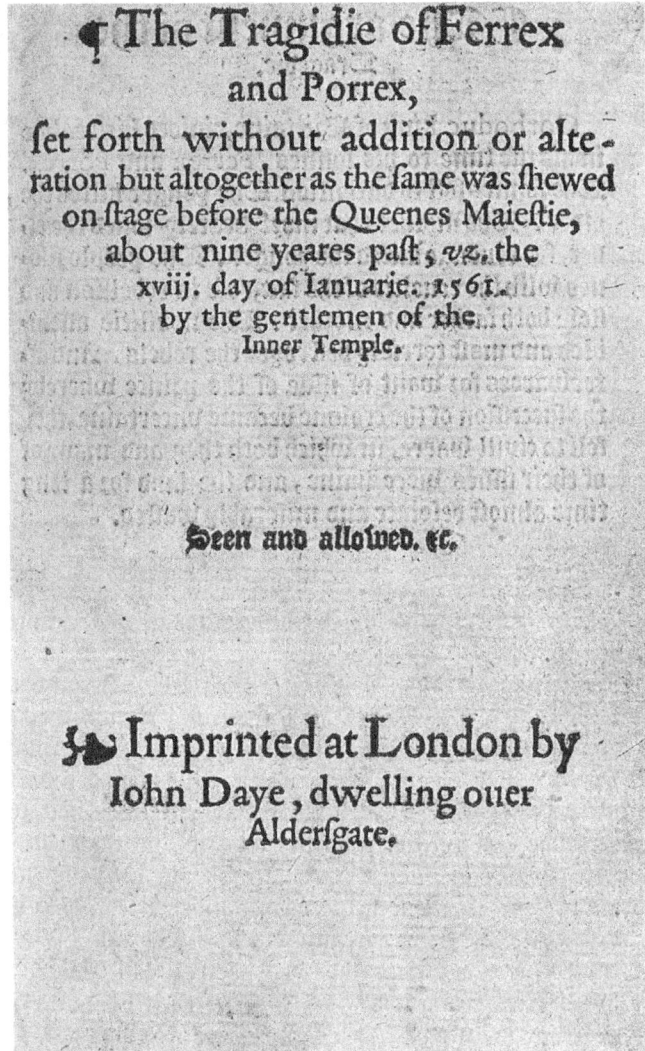

Figure 3 Title page: *The Tragidie of Ferrex and Porrex*, 1570

seen and not allowed. At the bottom of the page, publication information is provided, though in a greatly reduced form. The play, we are informed, has been "Imprinted at London by / Iohn Daye, dwelling over / Aldersgate." No "Signe" for identifying the printing house is offered, nor is there any information as to where the play may be purchased. We know merely that a printer named John Daye, the only proper name on

Marketing Printed Drama 29

the title page, dwells over Aldersgate. We also know, according to a 13 December 1572 letter written by Archbishop Parker, that Daye had previously complained,

> that dwellinge in a corner, and his brotherne [members of the Stationers' Company] envienge him, he cannot vtter his bookes which lie in his hande[s] ij or iij thousand powndes worthe, his frendes have procured of Powles a lease of a little shop to be sett vp in the [Paul's Cross] Church yearde, and it is conferred. And what by the instant request of sum enviouse booksellers, the maior and Aldermen will not suffer him to sett it vp in the Church yearde, wherein they have nothing to Doe but by power [i.e. force].[52]

In short, Daye, who had been involved in the printing and/or publishing of hundreds of books and pamphlets since 1546, was in a rather embattled position within the London community of printers and booksellers at about the time he printed the second octavo edition of Norton and Sackville's play.

Doing business in the marketplace of print changed dramatically with the incorporation of the Stationers' Company a decade after Daye began operating a press, and although he was the first printer to be issued a patent by Elizabeth shortly after her accession,[53] by the time his patron, the archbishop, was compelled to write on his behalf some thirteen years later, things were no longer going his way. Stranded in a "corner," and stuck with two or three thousand pounds' worth of unsold books – many of which he may have been given the privilege to compile at *his own expense* a decade earlier – Daye clearly had powerful friends and equally "force"ful enemies. Indeed, as Blayney observes with reference to Parker's letter, "It is worth wondering whether [the booksellers'] objections were indeed prompted by envy, or whether Daye's chosen site (probably in the Atrium) lay in front of existing sheds."[54] If, as Blayney intimates, Daye was planning to build his bookshop in front of existing shops, thereby preventing them from uttering their books, then it is quite likely that he was the subject of considerable resentment within at least a small group of his fellow stationers. Furthermore, as the following table indicates, of the forty-six items that Daye printed and/or published during the two-year period in which he would have been working on O2, eleven of those works were attributed to Norton, and *Ferrex and Porrex* was the penultimate.[55]

Having committed himself to printing or reprinting the bulk of Norton's oeuvre, Daye clearly had a lot at stake in deciding to produce a second edition of England's first tragedy. And it is at least probable that Norton's books were among those "which lie in his hande[s] ij or iij thousand powndes worthe" a year or so later.

Thus the birth, or perhaps the second coming, of English vernacular

Title	Author	Date	STC	Frmt.
1569 A discourse touching the pretended matche betwene the duke of Norfolke and the queene of Scottes.	[attrib. to T. Norton, T. Sampson, or Walsingham]	1569?	13869?	8¤
[anr. ed.]	ibid	1569?	13870	8¤
A warning agaynst the dangerous practises of papistes. [see 18686–1570]	Thomas Norton?	1569?	18685.3	8¤, 4s
[anr. issue] Sene and allowed.	Thomas Norton?	1569	18685.7	8¤, 4s
1570 All such treatises as haue been lately published by T. Norton. [6 pts.]	Thomas Norton	1570	18677	8¤
A bull [Noveritis quod anno] graunted by the pope to doctor Harding and other. [14 Aug. 1567]	Thomas Norton	1570	18677.5	2¤ (2)
[anr. ed.]	Thomas Norton	1570	18678	8¤, 4s
An addition declaratorie to the bulles. Scene [sic] and allowed. [2nd bull is Regnans in excelsis]	Thomas Norton	1570	18678a	8¤, 4s
[anr. ed.] Seen and allowed.	Thomas Norton	1570	18678a.5	8¤, 4s
A disclosing of the great bull ["An answer to the Bull" ent. 1569–70]	Thomas Norton	1570	18679	8¤, 4s
The Tragidie of Ferrex and Porrex, set forth without addition or alteration, but altogether as the same was shewed on stage before the Queenes Maiestie, about nine yeares past.	Thomas Norton	1570	18685	8¤, 4s
[A warning against the dangerous practises of papists; anr. ed. of 18685.3–1569; signed "T. Norton"] Newly perused and encreasced [sic].	Thomas Norton	1570?	18686	8¤, 4s

tragedy seems to have been tainted by the mundane, workaday, squabbles of the marketplace, and I think it is in this context that Daye's astonishing preface to O2, "The P.[rinter] to the Reader" (A2), should be read. Taking up an entire page and placed between two pages offering "The argument of the / Tragedie" and "The names of the Speakers," respectively, the rhetoric of the preface simultaneously recalls the "Church yearde" imbroglio – "his brotherne envienge him" – reported in the archbishop's letter and foreshadows the central conflict of the play itself, a succession feud between two "brotherne." Daye informs prospective customers that the printed play they hold in their hands was once part "of the grand Christmas in the Inner Temple," and he assures them that although it was "first written about nine years ago by the right honorable now Lord Buckhurst, and by T. Norton," it was "never intended by the authors thereof to be published." Next he warns the reader that a previous edition of the play was produced by a contemptible printer who "entised into his house a faire maide and done her villanie, and after all to-bescratched her face, torne her apparel, berayed and disfigured her, and then thrust her out of doors dishonested" (A2r). Thus does Daye's preface introduce an early generation of readers of printed English vernacular drama to the discourse of textual piracy, conceptually and thematically paving the way for the "*dis*junction" between playwrights and printers of which McKenzie finds evidence in the seventeenth century.[56] In the space of only a few lines, Daye essentially rehearses all of the main issues that would eventually constitute the foundation of twentieth-century bibliographic, editorial, and scholarly approaches to dramatic texts produced in early modern England. There is the privileging of a theatrical manuscript over a corrupt printed text and the assertion that the authors – to borrow from Gurr's observation quoted above – "were actively hostile to the idea of printing" their play. Then there is the allegation of textual piracy that will come to be one of the central tenets of the New Bibliography's project to produce moralizing narratives about the inauthorial status of dramatic texts.

Using Daye's preface to his edition of *Ferrex and Porrex* as one of her principal examples, Wendy Wall has recently argued that,

[i]n the early modern period, writers, printers, and compilers rethought manuscript authority and printed literary wares through a wealth of tropes, forms, and textual apparatuses; as a result they devised a language of justification and disavowal that activated various gendered dynamics and subsequently promoted gendered models of Renaissance authorship.[57]

Because this "language of justification and disavowal" and the "various gendered dynamics" it activated are the primary focus of Wall's study, she locates Daye's preface in a "rhetoric of disclosure that other writers use so easily," one in which "all hint at the titillating possibilities for figuring publication when they describe how their passions were so indecorously made public."[58] Daye is not, of course, the play's writer, but the distinction between printer and writer gets conflated in Wall's account, and she does not identify Daye as either the author of the prefatory text or the printer of the edition in the three pages she devotes to examining the rhetoric of the play's preface. Referring instead to Anthony Scoloker, who "mocks the publishing author who feigns postures of reluctance or fear," she begins her treatment of the 1570 text by asserting that "Scoloker could easily have been commenting on the introductory language used in Thomas Sackville and Thomas Norton's *Gorboduc* (1570)."[59]

What is perhaps most instructive about Wall's discussion of this complex foundational moment in the history of printed drama for my limited purposes in this chapter is her handling of the identities of the two men who printed the first and second editions of England's first vernacular tragedy. Indeed, early on she provides the proper names of the two authors who had little or nothing to do with the text's publication, but never names or identifies the two printers whose conflict has fueled much speculation about the alleged piracy of play-texts. In this inconsistency alone, her analysis illustrates how the relation between printing house and playhouse has often been obscured. For this reason it bears quoting at length:

> The *stationer* opens this work by comparing the text's previous corrupt printing to a ravished virgin. In his address, the scenes of writing and reading are fraught with images of sexual violation and wantonness. In particular he condemns the *irresponsible printer* who put the book forth . . . The *stationer* first uses the metaphor of the ravished maiden to describe the text's victimization: she has been ruined by the *vicious printer* who rakishly seduced and abandoned her. In the latter part of his preface, however, the *publisher* begins to attribute the text's "wantonness" to her inability to stay within chaste boundaries . . . As the *stationer* draws out this analogy, he shifts the blame from the *rapist printer* to the wanton text . . . The *publisher* concludes his preface by simultaneously declaring the woman/text "loosed" once again and by urging the reader to follow the authors' lead and reprivatize the book within the safety of the home . . . In this extraordinary preface, the *publisher* calls up the image of sexual violation to describe the text's emergence into the public eye . . . By boasting that the *author* has "re-dressed" and redeemed the text by re-establishing her "forme," the *publisher* titillates his audience with the image of the text in its previously disheveled state (emphasis added).[60]

Paraphrasing the text of Daye's preface, Wall labels Griffith, the printer of the 1565 octavo edition of *Gorboduc*, an "irresponsible printer," a "vicious printer," and a "rapist printer." Alternatively, Wall consistently refers to Daye as a "stationer" a "publisher," and even an "author," labels that would seem to be somewhat at odds with the title of the preface, "The P. to the Reader." The initial "P." is taken by most editors to be an abbreviation of publisher, though the distinction between printer and publisher had not yet stabilized. As Laurie E. Maguire notes, "sixteenth- and seventeenth-century epistles to printed texts, headed 'From the Printer to the Reader,' often mean from 'From the Publisher to the Reader,' 'printer' being used simply in the sense of 'the one who caused the text to be printed.'"[61]

In fact, Griffith was himself a stationer in quite good standing at the

Marketing Printed Drama 33

time, one of some forty printers who entered their texts "for his license for pryntinge" during the period – 22 July 1564 to 22 July 1566 – that *Gorboduc* was first being irresponsibly violated, victimized, and ravished. Furthermore, Griffith entered twenty-six different works for licensing by the Stationers' Company,[62] and yet his name never once appears among the list of ninety-two names of printers who, during the same period, were forced by the Company to pay "fynes for brakynge of good orders." Alternatively, Daye printed and/or published only twenty works during the same period, none of which is individually entered for license, and the Stationers' Register indicates that he was fined "for mysvsyng of master [the] warden."[63] And it is worth noting that Griffith's 1565 edition also seems to have been "seen and allowed" by the Stationers' Company because it received the following entry in the Company's register: "Receved of Wylliam greffeth for his lycense for pryntinge of a Trag[e]die of GORBODUC where[of] iij actes were Wretten by Thomas norton and the laste by Thomas Sackvyle."[64] Beneath this entry, however, Arber endorses Daye's version of events by adding the following note: "This is the surreptitious edition of *Ferrex and Porrex*, the first printed English Tragedy."[65] Arber's rhetoric here echoes Heminge and Condell's charge that readers of Shakespeare's previously printed plays "were abus'd with diverse stolne, and surreptitious copies" (A3r: 23–24). Thus, although Daye was not able to "utter" his books to the customers within Paul's Churchyard, subsequent readers have been only too willing to listen to him. To do so is to disregard the fact that, as Cauthen notes, "Q1 was not so corrupt that, if corrected, it could not be used for the copy-text for Q2" and that "Q2 omits an eight-line passage, perhaps for political reasons."[66] So much for Daye's claim on the title page that the text has been "set forth without addition or alte- / ration but altogether as the same was shewed / on stage."

The material details of the play's printing history necessarily complicate any effort to portray Daye as more upstanding than another allegedly irresponsible and abusive printer – as a stand-in for the absent and indifferent writers who fulfills the paternal responsibilities of the author function. Indeed, Wall's Daye becomes the Foucauldian "principle of thrift" for a work which, according to the inevitable fate of early modern books, has come to exist in variant forms.

Having acknowledged that the stationer/publisher is "urging the reader to follow the author's lead and reprivatize the book within the safety of the home," Wall does not see Daye's preface as the elaborate and masterful sales pitch that it is. Therefore, she takes him at his word when he asserts that if his edition of the play is not appreciated he "shall wishe that she had taried still at home with me." We know, of course, from the archbishop's letter that Daye is nearly drowning in "ij or iij thousand powndes worthe" of unsold books at this moment, but Wall's main concern is to situate the preface within what we might call, with a nod to Greenblatt, an early modern discourse of wander in which, as she puts it, "the text's 'wantonness'" is linked "to her inability to stay within chaste boundaries."[67]

It is certainly true that Daye is relying on a set of images or tropes culled from a heavily gendered discourse that his readers would have been quite familiar with. Twenty years later Spenser's Una informs the naive Redcrosse – in the thirteenth stanza of the *Faerie Queene*'s first canto – just as he is about to confront the poem's first monstrous mother, "This is the wandring wood, this Errours den / A monster vile, whom God and man does hate."[68] Una's expertise in things wandering would have come as no surprise to readers familiar with Richard Hyrde's 1529 English translation of Juan Luis Vives's well-respected handbook, *The Instruction of a Christian Woman*. According to Vives, "Womans thought is swyfte and for the most parte unstable walkyng and wandrynge out from home and soone wyl slyde by the reason of hit owne slyperness I wot nat howe far."[69] In the first letter of "William Baldwin to the Reader" of the 1559 edition of *A Mirror for Magistrates*, Baldwin asserts that the collection is to serve "as a myrrour for al men as well noble as others, to shewe the slippery deceytes of the waverying lady."[70] Moreover, in *Gorboduc*'s critical lines on royal succession, Mandud worries that, "we remain with out a certain prince / To wield the realm, or guide the wand'ring rule."[71] Given that Elizabeth was an unmarried virgin, the reference to a "wand'ring rule" reverberated with Plato's theories on the symptomology of hysteria, subsequently endorsed by Galen and later Edward Jorden, who, as Helen King observes, published "the key hysteria text of the early seventeenth century,"[72] *A Briefe Discourse of a Disease Called the Suffocation of the Mother*, shortly before Elizabeth's death in 1603. According to Plato, "[t]he animal within them is desirous of procreating children, and when remaining unfruitful long beyond its proper time, gets discontented and angry, and *wandering in every direction* through the body, closes up the passages of the breath."[73]

In Daye's proto-New Bibliographic version of the tradition, "the said Lord [Sackville] was out of England" and "T. Norton Farre out of London," while the text of their play, previously "berayed and disfigured" by Griffith, has now "after long wandring" come "at length home to the sight of her frendes who scant know her but by a few tokens and markes remayning." And yet, to move directly from Daye's gendered rhetoric of the printed page to the early modern discourse of gender is to pass over the rather significant fact that Daye is himself at this moment "Farre out of" Paul's Churchyard, and therefore a "wandring" bookseller looking to come "at length home" to a place where he can make a living off the books he has already printed at his own expense. To locate Daye's commonplace early modern tropes of violation and defilement in the discourse of gender relations is to miss the primary end to which he is employing them: the re-embodiment and commodification of a play-text that had already been printed and marketed by someone else. Consequently, in much the same way that he claims to have re-legitimated the woman/text "for her frendes sake and her owne," Daye's primary goal is to legitimate his edition to ensure his own financial sake. Accordingly, as we have seen above, he begins his preface by informing the reader that "this Tragedie was for furniture of the grand Christmas in the Inner Temple" and "after shewed before her Maiestie." With the latter claim he is following Griffith, who reports on the title page of his edition that "the same was shewed before the QVENES most excellent Maiestie," although, as Cauthen notes, "Queen Elizabeth was not present at the first performance, but there is no doubt that she soon heard of the play . . . it violated her edict (19 May 1559) forbidding plays which touched on religion or politics."[74] The queen did eventually get to see a royally commanded performance of the play at Whitehall, not the Inner Temple. While it is impossible to determine whether the text was altered for that performance, within Elizabeth's own legislative vision of what should and should not get staged, *Gorboduc* was already illegitimate well before Griffith got his "irresponsible" hands on it. Once the play wandered into the printing house, however, its fortunes continued to plummet because, according to Daye, it was "never intended by the authors thereof to be published."

Such disclaimers were, as Wall carefully documents,[75] quite popular among early modern authors, for whom they no doubt served as a convenient – if often ineffective – way of not being accountable for what they wrote. Indeed, it was just such accountability that prompted Jonson to be anomalously involved with the printing of the nine plays included in his 1616 *Workes* folio. Daye was not, however, the author of *Ferrex and Porrex*. Thus, the "professional *dis*junction" that emerges from the preface to the second octavo edition of England's first vernacular tragedy is between two printers, and Daye's next move – in accordance with the master narrative that would come to underwrite the New Bibliography – is to seek refuge in the discourse of piracy.[76] "Yet one W. G.," we are informed, "getting a copie therof at some yongmans hand that lacked a little money and much discretion in the last great plage. an. 1565. about V yeares past . . . put it forth exceedingly corrupted." All the elements are there: a greedy and immoral printer, a young man in need of a little pocket money, and even the plague makes an appearance as if to presage the production of a diseased or "exceedingly corrupted" text. When Marcus writes that "Shakespeare has to be kept free of any taint of commercialism, because that taint is reserved for the contaminators – to some extent the printers, who sold his precious creations in cheap popular editions, but more especially those pirates the memorial reconstructors, who perverted his language out of greed and ignorance,"[77] she could just as easily be recalling Daye's account of the previous edition's publication.

But what is even more remarkable about the rhetoric of Daye's preface is that it echoes the archbishop's depiction of the printer/bookseller's recent troubles in Paul's Churchyard. Where Parker writes of Daye's "brotherne [members of the Stationers' Company] envienge him," of "his bookes which lie in his hande," and a confrontation with "sum envious booksellers" who "have nothing to Doe but by power," Daye complains of Griffith "getting a copie therof at some yongmans hand," of a text that "shall be still reproched with her former missehap, or quarelled at by envious persons," and, finally, of a text that is "lesse ashamed of the dishonestie done to her because it was by fraude and force." I am not suggesting that Daye is relying on Parker's letter to write the preface to his edition, but rather that Daye's recent difficulties in the Elizabethan literary marketplace – as described by the archbishop – represent the primary subtext for his prefatorial effort to market his edition of Sackville and Norton's play. In other words, Daye sees himself as a victim of circumstances in Paul's Churchyard that are beyond his control, and therefore a readily accessible early modern gendered discourse of victimization informs and structures his attempt to discredit a fellow printer.

There are obvious differences between Daye's clumsy and maudlin attempt to transform an early English imitation of Senecan tragedy played before a small, educated audience at the Inner Temple and Whitehall into a marketable commodity, and Heminge and Condell's knowing and strategic effort to assist the 1623 Folio's publishers with the nearly unprecedented task of translating and compressing a very successful professional career on the London stage into a single elegant book. In the first place, there was no market for printed vernacular tragedy except, ironically, the one created by a previous edition of the play that Daye does his best to discredit, and a handful of printed translations of Seneca's plays. Indeed, the market for printed drama was so new that the conventions of title-page attribution in the highly collaborative writing environment of the professional playhouses had not yet emerged. Therefore, the play's first printer/publisher naively parceled out the text into two sections and attributed them to their respective authors. In the subsequent three decades, during which the first theatres would be built, plays would generally be published anonymously or occasionally attributed to a single author. The first extant printed drama after *Gorboduc* to be attributed to more than one author, *A Looking Glasse for London and England* (1594), merely indicates that it was "Made by Thomas Lodge Gentleman, and / Robert Greene / In Artibus Magister." Then, of course, there is the fact that Norton and Sackville are still very much alive when Daye gets the idea to publish a new edition of their play, though as was the case with the Folio, he does what he can to deny his edition's relation to its origin in social production. He accomplishes this denial by leaving the authors' names off the title page, claiming that the authors had never intended the play to be published in the first place, and asserting that both authors were far out of London when the play was initially printed. Like Heminge and Condell, Daye even does his best to efface the text's origin in mechanical production by slandering the play's previous printer.

The similarities between the two publishing ventures, however, are much more striking than the differences, and their respective reader addresses agree on a number of points about how plays that have ceased to be viable in performance can be transformed into valuable commodities in the marketplace of printed books. Helping to establish what would become an important convention of printed drama, Daye recalls an earlier phase of the book's commodification in which "the grand Christmas in the Inner Temple" was the marketplace. Where the Folio's plays had their first trial before audiences "at *Black-Friars*, or the *Cockpit*," *Gorboduc* was played before England's juridical body as well as its doubled embodiment, "her Majesty." Where Heminge and Condell acknowledge the self-regulating marketplace and claim that the plays have "now come forth quitted rather by a Decree of Court," Daye puts the phrase, "Seen and allowed," on the title page. Moreover, the two ventures attempt to enhance the legitimacy and value of their respective books by recounting two distinct phases of their embodiment and commodification. The first phase, conducted outside of a self-regulating market, has produced commodities that are, in Daye's case, "exceedingly corrupted," "berayed and disfigured," and "dishonested"; in Heminge and Condell's case, they are "maimed, and deformed by the frauds / and stealthes of iniurious impostors." Daye even goes so far as to identify the injurious impostor "that expos'd" it "by fraud and force." A second phase has produced a commodity which, owing to Daye's involvement, has come from its authors' "new appareled, trimmed, and attired . . . in such form as she was before." Owing to Blount and Jaggard's involvement, Shakespeare's plays "are now offer'd to your view cur'd, and perfect of their limbes . . . as he conceived thẽ."

If, however, we listen a little more closely to the book that Daye worked so hard to legitimate in 1570, we hear a story that is even more remarkably similar to the one told some half a century later by the 1623 Folio than that which can be gleaned from the respective books' reader prefaces. Though it has to my knowledge never been remarked upon in critical discussions of England's first vernacular tragedy, Daye's edition of *Ferrex and Porrex*, like the play-texts that Heminge and Condell strive to authorize and authenticate, was also printed as part of a collected works volume dedicated to a single author. Indeed, unlike the first edition of the play that was published five years earlier as an individual octavo text, Daye's subsequent edition of the play appeared as the sixth text of an octavo collection (A1r–H3v) dedicated, according to the volume's title page, to bringing together between the covers of a single book, "All such treatises as have / been lately published by / Thomas Norton : the ti- / tles whereof appeare in / the next side" (Fig. 4). The sixth of those titles, as I have already intimated, printed on "the next side" of the title page announcing a published collection of Norton's treatises, does not belong to a treatise at all but rather to a dramatic text written collaboratively by Norton and another author.

Despite recent critical efforts to confirm the play's status as a bold admonition to Elizabeth to rethink her stated position on marriage and reproduction, "The Tragidie of Ferrex and Porrex," as the play is renamed for this collection of Norton's writings, is not a treatise, nor for that matter was it written wholly by the author who, as advertised on the title page, stands as the volume's *raison d'être*. The grouping together of a play about the pending Tudor succession crisis with other works that feature titles like "To the Quenes Maiesties / poore deceiued Subiectes of the North / Countrey, drawn into rebellion / by the Earls of Northum- / berland and West- / merland" or "A warning agaynst the / dangerous practises of Papistes, / and specially the parteners of the late rebellion," to name the first two texts included in the volume (A1r–D4v and A1r–O4r, respectively), would probably not have troubled any early modern readers who figured out where Daye's shop was and paused long enough to peruse the volume's table of contents before deciding whether or not to purchase it. Indeed, if generic consistency had been a prerequisite for publishing a single-author collection, Jonson's 1616 *Workes* folio would have been a very different – and much smaller – book.

The authorial status of Daye's collection, however, is another matter. Both the internal title pages for the two works referred to above do, in

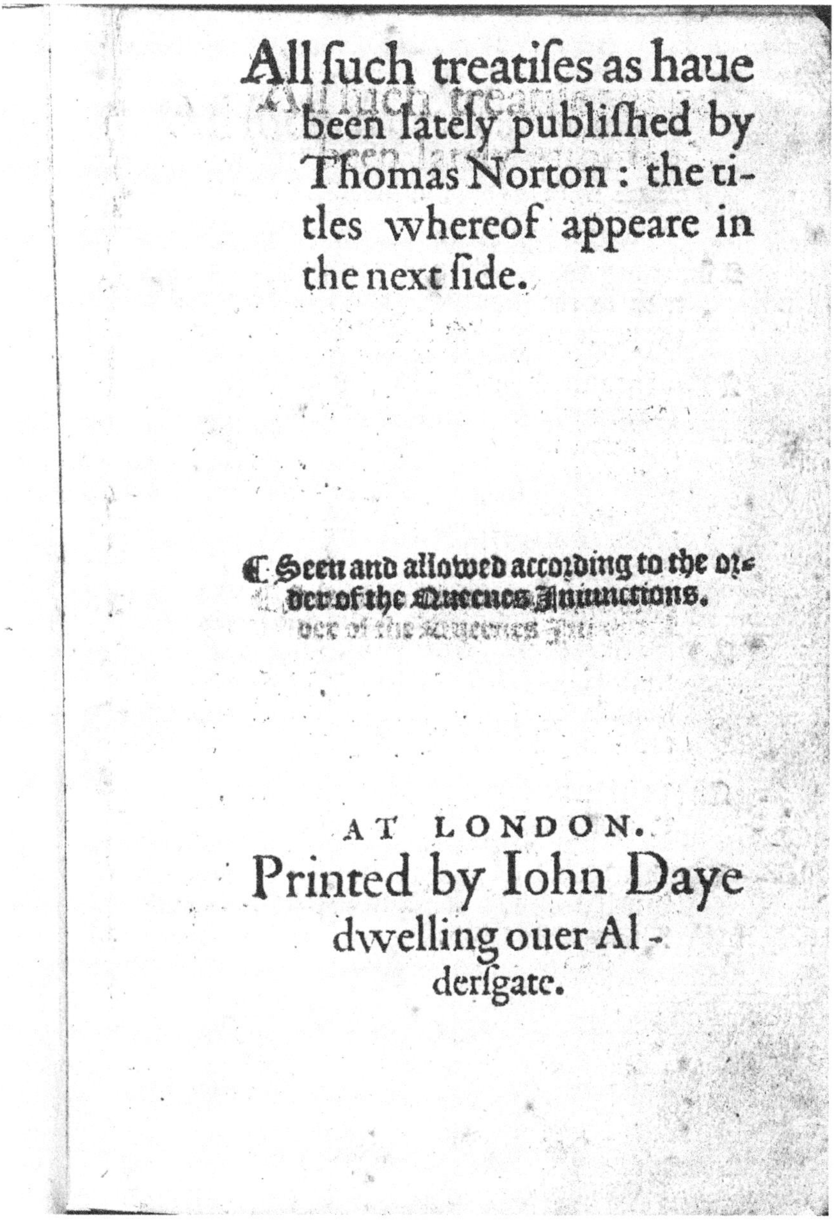

All such treatises as haue been lately published by Thomas Norton: the titles whereof appeare in the next side.

¶ Seen and allowed according to the order of the Queenes Iniunctions.

AT LONDON.
Printed by Iohn Daye dwelling ouer Aldersgate.

Figure 4 Title page: *All such treatises as haue been lately published by Thomas Norton*, 1570

fact, indicate that they were "Written by Thomas Norton. / And newly perused and en- / creased." Both texts identify Norton as the author and even assert that he had an opportunity to review and revise them before they went to press. Additionally, the second work, which takes a rather bold stand on issues of Catholic unrest in the first decade of Elizabeth's reign, is further author-ized by the following statement printed on the verso of the title page:

The Author protesteth that as he mea- / neth not herein to hurt the fame of any sin- / gular person unnamed whose doings im- / port no perill to her Maiestie, so can there / to no personage any worse abuise be gi- / uen, than to applie that to them selves / which thy neede not. If any be greeued / with cause, they must remember the fault / to be in their faultes, and not in him (A1v).

Given what we know about Daye's embattled position among some of his fellow stationers, it should come as no surprise that the Norton collection as a whole, like the play's reader preface discussed earlier, evokes something of a paranoid publishing enterprise. Indeed, each of the six "treatises" is accompanied by the phrase, "Seen and allowed according to the or- /der of the Queenes Iniunctions," a shorter version, "seen and allowed," or, as the title page of the work that immediately precedes the play puts it – orthographically anticipating the shift in genre just ahead – "scene and allowed." In this context, it is hard to know if Norton in fact wrote the disavowal quoted above, or if, alternatively, the same person who wrote the sordid tale of a play's textual violation, penned it on his behalf. Either way, the highly authorial status of the texts included at the beginning of the volume contrasts markedly with that of the volume as it progresses.

By the time the text of the second edition of *Gorboduc* appears, the internal title page printed for the edition has, as I noted earlier, given the play a new title and stripped it of its singularly precise author attribution. It is at least probable that half a century later Heminge and Condell chose to exclude *Pericles* and *Two Noble Kinsmen* from the 1623 Folio because, knowing the plays had been written in collaboration with other playwrights, they may have deemed them inappropriate for a collection devoted to a single author. Jonson did not include any of his early plays written in collaboration with other playwrights in his 1616 *Workes* folio collection, an act of selective self-canonization that may have influenced Heminge and Condell. Yet the concept of collaboration itself, even in its strictest authorial sense of two or more writers contributing to one text (a notion of collaborative authorship which I suggest in Chapter 4 emerged largely as a construction of the early modern publishing industry), is extremely difficult to distinguish from the concept of singular authorship in the specific case of a company playwright like Shakespeare. Indeed, if in fact the exclusion of collaboratively authored plays had been a primary factor in Heminge and Condell's thinking about what plays to include in the 1623 Folio, then arguably *Henry VIII*, *1 and 2 Henry VI*, and *Macbeth* would also have been excluded.

In the case of Daye's collection of Norton's writings, on the other hand, the dilemma of reconciling a collaboratively authored play with a single-author collection did not prevent the work from being included. Instead, a compromise formation, materialized on the title page as the absence of an attribution, was apparently enough at this early stage in the history of English printed drama to resolve the differences between an earlier creative venture, and a subsequent effort to make it into a marketable commodity. Thereafter, the authorial status of the volume plummets.

Being the sixth of the six treatises listed on "the next side" of the collection's title page, the final optimistic line of Norton and Sackville's tragedy, "But wrong can never take deepe roote to last," ought to have been the last line of the book. It is not, and it may never have been. What follows, instead, in the book as it is currently bound (Huntington 59846–59851), are another six treatises totaling some 216 octavo pages of text. None of these texts is announced on "the next side" of the volume's initial title page, and none of them was written by Norton. The following is some information about the texts that constitute the remaining half of the collection as it is currently preserved.

(1) (No title page): "A discourse touching the pretended match betwene the Duke of Norfolke and the Queene of Scottes." (Anonymous)
(2) (No title page): "Saluten in Christo" (STC 11505); End Page: "At London, xiij. of October 1571"; "your loving Brother in Latine. R. G" (Richard Grafton?)
(3) (Title page): "The effect of the declaration made in the Guildhall by M. Recorder of London, concerning the late attempts of the Quenes Maiesties evill, seditious, and disobedient subiectes." (STC 11036); "Imprinted at London by John Daye dwelling over Aldersgage." (Anonymous)
(4) (Title page): "Ane admoni- / tioun direct to the / trew Lordis mantenaris of / the Kingis graces Authoritie" (STC 3967); M. G. B (George Buchanan); "Imprinted at London by John Daye, accordyng to the Scotish copie Printed at Strivi-lyng by Robert Lekpreuik. Anno Do. M. D. LXXI.
(5) (Title page): "Ane detectioun of the duinges of Marie quene of Scottes, touchand the murder of hir husband, and hir conspiracie, adulterie, and pretended marriage with the Erle Bothwell." (STC 3981); "Tr. out of the Latine quihilke was written by G. B."

(6) (No title page): "The copie of a letter written by one in London concernyng the credit of the late published detection of the doynges of the ladie Marie of Scotland." (STC 17565) (Anonymous)

Of particular interest here is the fifth treatise which, in itself, constitutes something of a single-author collection inasmuch as it includes sections devoted to "The writynges and letters found in the sayd casket, which are auowit to be written with the Scottishe Quenis awne hand" and "Certain French Sonnettes writen by the quene of Scottes to Bothwell, before hir marriage with him . . ." Both of these sections link their legitimacy and interest value to their certitude about the queen's authorship.

My analysis of the paper and the printing of the second half of the book as it is currently bound suggests that the remaining works included in the collection, some of which don't even get their own title pages,[78] were printed in Daye's shop and subsequently gathered there – as much as two years later – with Norton's works for sale as a single, bindable book. Consistent with this analysis, the STC entries for five of the six works also attribute their printing to Daye. In this sense, Daye plays the role of the author function for the entire collection, being the only consistent singular identity connected with the volume. Moreover, in gathering a range of attributed and anonymous writings with six works by a "single" author, Daye may have seized upon what he thought to be a much needed opportunity to "vtter" some of those "bookes which lie in his hande[s] ij or iij thousand powndes worthe" at exactly the same time that the archbishop's letter was written. Similarly, half a century later, Heminge and Condell would clear out a little space in the playhouse chest where acting scripts were stored by attempting to market "old" Shakespeare to a new and very different kind of audience.

Doubly anomalous – as a dramatic text written in collaboration with another author – in the context of the volume in which it has been preserved, Daye's 1570 edition of Norton and Sackville's play materially occupies a liminal and transitional space between the single-authored and attributed "treatises" that precede it and the mostly anonymous hodge podge of texts that follow it. As we shall see in subsequent chapters, such a space came to be the ontological domain of much of the extant printed drama produced for the professional theatres in early modern London.

But perhaps the most significant parallel between the Norton collection of 1570 and the 1623 Folio is the high level of collaboration between printers and playwrights that the two books rely on and seem to promote. If we take them at their word – and twentieth-century editors of both works generally have – the printers/publishers of these two ventures begin from authorial manuscripts, profess a direct link to their respective authors (via the collegial mediation of Heminge and Condell in the latter case). Moreover, they claim they are striving to enhance their respective authors' reputations both by rekindling the public's interest in plays whose life on stage has ended and by supplying readers with well-printed, authoritative texts to replace ostensibly inferior ones they may have purchased previously. Nearly twenty years after Daye claims to have salvaged Norton and Sackville's literary standing, Richard Jones, the printer of a quarto edition of Marlowe's two *Tamburlaine the Great* plays, will take this effort one significant step further by editing – for the sake of improving – Marlowe's work before publishing it. In the reader address to his edition, Jones informs prospective customers that, "I haue (purposely) omitted and left out some fond and friuolous Iestures, digressing (and in my poore opinion) far vnmeet for the matter, which I thought, might seeme more tedious vnto the wise, than any way els to be regarded."[79] If we move forward from here to the first two decades of the seventeenth century, the period in which McKenzie locates a major rift between playhouse and printing house, we find playwrights and printers/publishers working together to forge a new market for published dramatic texts which, contrary to McKenzie's view that, "the theatre was alive and confident of its own distinctively oral and visual mode," had failed to find an audience when performed. In attempting to translate theatrical failures into successes at the book shop, printers/publishers and playwrights joined together to create a new and prestigious identity for printed drama that would culminate in Jonson's 1616 *Workes*, the 1623 Shakespeare Folio, and – most complexly – the Beaumont and Fletcher folio of 1647.

There are a number of extant contemporary commentaries on the early modern London stage and its luminaries, Francis Meres's *Palladis Tamia* (1598)[80] being perhaps the most frequently quoted. I want to focus, however, on the following lines from a note "To the Reader" included in the 1612 quarto edition of John Webster's play, *The White Devil*:

For my owne part I have ever truly cherisht my good opinion of other mens worthy Labours, especially of that full and haightned stile of Maister *Chapman*. The labor'd and vnderstanding workes of Maister *Johnson*: The no lesse worthy composures of the both worthily excellent Maister *Beamont* and Maister *Fletcher*: And lastly (without wrong last to be named) the right happy and copious industry of M. *Shake-speare*, M. *Dekker*, and M. *Heywood*, wishing what I write may be read by their light.[81]

Although Webster cautions his reader against equating the order in which he mentions these seven dramatists with some qualitative judgment of their merits as writers, I suspect that he has arranged his list of "cherisht" colleagues according to a hierarchy which, although indiscernible from the perspective of current critical practices, nevertheless holds a significant insight into the profession of playwriting in early seventeenth-century England. More precisely, I want to suggest that Webster's list of playwrights provides, in Barbara A. Mowat's phrase, "a point of entry into the very large and intricate topic of early English theatre and literature."[82] If, as Mowat astutely notes, "the printing and selling of plays for readers made the boundary between theatre and literary culture increasingly porous,"[83] I would add that some playwrights and publishers in the first decade of the seventeenth century also hoped to use the printing and selling of plays to erect a new and rather non-porous boundary between theatre audiences and well-educated readers. Indeed, as Heidi Brayman Hackel observes, "[t]he typography of playbooks suggests that publishers considered educated readers among the potential buyers of their books, and records of contemporary book ownership confirm that they succeeded in marketing playbooks to a broad range of readers."[84]

Whereas Meres organized his discussion of dramatists in terms of genre, taking care to specify which writers were best for tragedy or comedy, I suspect that Webster's assessment of the milieu in which he works is guided by an insider's knowledge of the profession, especially in terms of the relationship between playhouse and printing house. Chapman is praised for his "full and haightned stile," while Jonson is credited for producing "labor'd and vnderstanding workes." Four years later, Jonson would make good on the compliment by controversially publishing his folio collection of plays, masques, and epigrams under the title of *Workes* – a fairly involved printing project which, according to C. H. Herford and Percy and Evelyn Simpson, may have been in the planning stages when Webster's play went to the press.[85] Already inseparable some thirty-five years before the folio of 1647 would attempt simultaneously to monumentalize and domesticate their collaborative relationship, Beaumont and Fletcher are recognized for their "no lesse worthy composures." Lastly, Webster groups Dekker, Shakespeare, and Heywood together, praising them for their "right happy and copious industry."

Looking closely at the initial performance and publication history of *The Knight of the Burning Pestle*, staged in 1607 and printed six years later, Zachary Lesser argues that the play's publisher, Walter Burre, took a calculated risk in publishing a play that had been unpopular with theatre audiences because he believed that, "he could exploit a new and important cultural division in the theatrical market."[86] Hoping to generate a market for printed drama consisting of well-educated readers who would not be discouraged from buying a play because it failed to be popular on stage, Burre used the only tool available to him, the printing press. Among the specifically typographic features which, according to Lesser, characterize this nascent effort is the use of what Greg identified as "continuous printing" – a method of setting type in which verse lines broken between two speakers are set on one line to create a complete metrical unit.[87] In using the term generally to indicate any instance in which "each new speech, instead of (as is usual) beginning a fresh line of print, follows on from the last, with the speaker's name (or prefix) within the line,"[88] Greg included cases of space-saving due to problems with casting-off, of one- or two-word reactions from another speaker, and of prose uses. Alternatively, Lesser restricts his use of the term to cases in which the typographic strategy was clearly used to create a full verse line, and asserts that, "[c]ontinuous printing values the literary and poetic in the playwright's lines – their meter and form – over the theatrical necessity of clearly identifying the speaker of those lines, turning a stage play into a printed poem."[89] The practice of continuous printing, which began in the universities with translations from classical drama, certainly had a distinctly elitist heritage and, as drama began to become more acceptably literary matter, the number of continuously printed plays increased. For this reason, Lesser argues that,

> the technique came to seem "literary" and classical, serving to distance the play from its theatrical origins and from the "vulgar" plays which win the favor of audiences in the theatre. Of the first twenty plays printed continuously, dating from c. 1530 to 1604, all but four are either university drama, literary translations, or closet drama.[90]

Moreover, as Lesser observes about the more than seventy dramatic texts that appear to have been marketed to an upscale readership,

> [t]hese plays are twice as likely as the average printed play to contain Latin on their title pages, with those published after 1580 having an even higher likelihood. Over a third of them contain some indication of the author's social status on the title page, from university student, fellow, or Master of Arts, to "Gent." and "Servant to her Majesty," and including one countess (Pembroke); again, this is twice the percentage of overall plays. Fewer than a quarter of these plays were performed at outdoor theatres, far below the general rate, and they are overrepresented for "closet" drama, or drama intended purely for the study rather than the stage.[91]

Inevitably, the presence of such features as Latin epigrams and continuous printing conferred a certain literary status upon a given printed dramatic text, and it is probable that seventeenth-century publishers such as Burre trusted that a specific readership's familiarity with such features would enable it to readily distinguish their plays from less literary fare –

in much the same way that publishers of romantic novels today rely on cover art to make their books instantly recognizable to a specific audience (Fig. 5). In the case of continuous printing, Lesser argues:

> like the black-letter font frequently used for the speeches of Dutch characters in printed drama, continuous printing may have come to seem a "necessary" convention for this type of play. Such typographical "inevitability" highlights the fact that these plays came to be seen as clearly different from others, and, as part of the interwoven relationship between publishers and purchasers, it is both a response to the desires of select readers and a means of creating a group of select plays.[92]

If we apply these important insights of Lesser's analysis to Webster's assessment of his esteemed playwriting colleagues, we will see that the order in which he mentions them is particularly pregnant with meaning.

The 1612 quarto edition of *The White Devil*, printed by Nicholas Okes for Thomas Archer, includes all of the distinctly literary features discussed above. For Webster, whose only previous attributed publications consisted of a title-page credit for writing the additions to the 1604 quarto text of John Marston's *The Malcontent*, and collaborations with Thomas Dekker on *Northward Hoe* (1607) and *Westward Hoe* (1607), the printed text of *The White Devil* – replete with singular authorial attribution ("Written by Iohn Webster"), Latin epigram ("Non inferiora secutus"), and continuous printing – typographically constitutes something of a literary debut. Moreover, the self-consciously literary status of the play is reiterated thematically in the prefatory note "To the Reader," which not only appeals to an educated readership through its reliance on six lines of Latin – including a quote from Horace ("Haec hodie Porcis comedenda relinques") – but also rather explicitly attempts to designate its target readers. Like Jonson, who complained in the dedication to the 1605 quarto text of *Sejanus, His Fall* that the play in performance had "suffered no less violence from our people here than the subject of it did from the rage of the people of Rome,"[93] Webster begins this effort to legitimize the printed text of *The White Devil* by discounting the reception his play received in the theatre as the consequence of an inadequate performance venue and an inept audience:

> In publishing this Tragedy, I do but challenge to my selfe that liberty, which other men have tane before mee; not that I affect praise by it, for, *nos haec nouimus esse nihil*, onely since it was acted, in so dull a time of Winter, presented in so open and blacke a Theater, that it wanted (that which is the onely grace and setting out of a Tragedy) a full and vnderstanding Auditory: and that since that time I have noted, most of the people that come to that Play-house, resemble those ignorant asses (who visiting Stationers shoppes their vse is not to inquire for good bookes, but new bookes) I present it to the generall view with this confidence.[94]

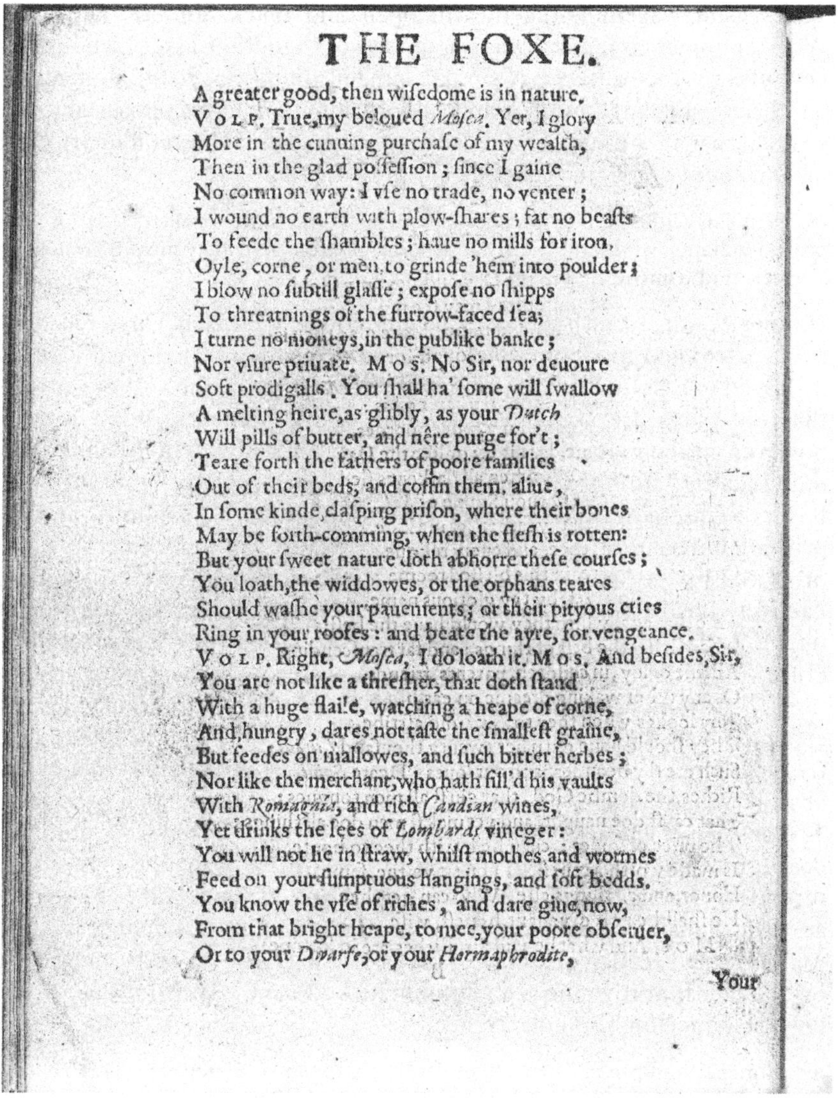

THE FOXE.

A greater good, then wisedome is in nature.
VOLP. True, my beloued *Mosca*. Yet, I glory
More in the cunning purchase of my wealth,
Then in the glad possession; since I gaine
No common way: I vse no trade, no venter;
I wound no earth with plow-shares; fat no beasts
To feede the shambles; haue no mills for iron,
Oyle, corne, or men, to grinde 'hem into poulder;
I blow no subtill glasse; expose no shipps
To threatnings of the furrow-faced sea;
I turne no moneys, in the publike banke;
Nor vsure priuate. M o s. No Sir, nor deuoure
Soft prodigalls. You shall ha' some will swallow
A melting heire, as glibly, as your *Dutch*
Will pills of butter, and nêre purge for't;
Teare forth the fathers of poore families
Out of their beds, and coffin them, aliue,
In some kinde clasping prison, where their bones
May be forth-comming, when the flesh is rotten:
But your sweet nature doth abhorre these courses;
You loath, the widdowes, or the orphans teares
Should washe your pauements; or their pityous cries
Ring in your roofes: and beate the ayre, for vengeance.
VOLP. Right, *Mosca*, I do loath it. M o s. And besides, Sir,
You are not like a thresher, that doth stand
With a huge flaile, watching a heape of corne,
And, hungry, dares not taste the smallest graine,
But feedes on mallowes, and such bitter herbes;
Nor like the merchant, who hath fill'd his vaults
With *Romagnia*, and rich *Candian* wines,
Yet drinks the lees of *Lombards* vineger:
You will not lie in straw, whilst mothes and wormes
Feed on your sumptuous hangings, and soft bedds.
You know the vse of riches, and dare giue, now,
From that bright heape, to mee, your poore obseruer,
Or to your *Dwarfe*, or your *Hermaphrodite*,

Your

Figure 5 Page of text: *Volpone, or The Foxe*, 1607

The season was dull, the theatre open and black, and the audience, Webster comes to realize, was comprised of "ignorant asses" who prefer new plays to good plays. A similar lament about playgoers' preferences had been articulated more graphically by an anonymous playwright four years earlier in a note "To the Reader" included in the 1608 quarto text of *The Familie of Love*. There the author complains:

> Plaies in this Citie are like wenches new falne to the trade, onelie desired of your neatest gallants, whiles the'are fresh: when they grow stale they must be vented by Termers and Cuntrie chapmen.[95]

Having wandered into the same gendered discourse that Daye relied on as he attempted to characterize a prior "exceedingly corrupted" edition he hoped to displace from the market with a new one, the author suggests that old plays are about as appealing as old wenches. What is new, however, in the preface to Webster's typographically literary debut as an individualized author is that he relies on the example of ignorant book buyers to discredit his theatre audience. Conflating the playhouse and the printing house in order to justify his play's failure in the former in a text produced by the latter, Webster is not at all – to recall Gurr's assertion – "actively hostile to the idea of printing" his play. Rather, he has sought refuge in the press because he has a very good reason – again recalling Gurr – "to make the product durable or to record it for future generations." Although plays, according to Gurr, "lived in a medium as ephemeral as the sounds through which they came to life," they also frequently died there well before they could fulfill their function as abstract commodities.

Webster provides several explanations for *The White Devil*'s untimely death, but, having absolved himself of responsibility for the play's poor reception on stage, he then anticipates and defends himself against another plausible explanation for the play's failure. Presumably because well-educated readers may try to blame the play's short performance life on the fact that it is "no true Drammaticke Poem," Webster once again lays the blame on his audience:

> for should a man present to such an Auditory, the most sententious Tragedy that ever was written, observing all the criticall lawes, as heighth of stile; and gravety of person; inrich it with the sententious Chorus, and as it were life'n Death, in the passionate and waighty *Nuntius*: yet after all this divine rapture, O dura messorum ilia, the breath that comes frõ the vncapable multitude, is able to poison it, and ere it be acted.[96]

Clearly, then, Webster wants to have it both ways. On the one hand, he faults his audience for not having the intellectual wherewithal to appreciate the serious literary merit of his work; on the other hand, he fends off potential critics who would fault his play for not being literary enough by asserting that he writes for an "vncapable multitude" whose bad breath would "poison" even "the most sententious Tragedy." Stranded as he is in this rather paradoxical authorial position, it's little wonder that Webster next confesses, "I was a long time in finishing this Tragedy," and then feels compelled to justify his belatedness by comparing himself to Euripides in the following apocryphal anecdote:

Alcestides objecting that *Eurypides* had onely in three daies composed three verses, whereas himselfe had written three hundreth: Thou telst truth, (quoth he) but heres the difference, thine shall onely bee read for three daies, whereas mine shall continue three ages.[97]

For Webster, the distinction between low art and high art, between short-lived popular fare and properly literary works destined for eternal fame – a distinction already deployed earlier when he faults readers who prefer new books over good books – is itself eternal and trans-historical. Clearly then, the theatre, which traffics in a medium as ephemeral as sounds, was not the best place for a play that had barely survived a single afternoon's performance, especially one written by an author who compares himself to a classical tragedian whose plays "shall continue three ages." And so, Webster deliberately sets out to make his "product durable" and "to record it for future generations" by handing it over to a printer. More importantly, though, he delivers it to a printer who is beginning to rely on a set of typographic conventions to create and foster a market of readers who may not only buy a play like *The White Devil*, but may also accord it the kind of respect and appreciation its writer thinks it deserves. Thus, in the case of one printed dramatic text, something like literature has been typographically born out of a theatrical failure. Viewed from this perspective, Webster's next and final move, listing the names of seven writers whose "worthy Labours" he admires, must be seen as a fantasy of inclusion, though, as I have begun to suggest, the elite club to which he hopes to gain access was by no means uniform.

George Chapman's literary reputation was already secure by the time *The White Devil* was printed, though it was not a reputation wholly earned on the floorboards of the London stage. In 1598, his completion of Marlowe's *Hero and Leander* as well as his translation of Homer, *Seven Books of the Iliads*, were published, and one year before the publication of Webster's play, his translation of the entire *Iliad*, *The Iliads of Homer Prince of Poets*, appeared. Three years later his translation of the *Odyssey* was published, and a year later *The Whole Works of Homer*. Indeed, Chapman's translations of Homer may have earned him a privileged position in Webster's prefatory effort at authorial self-construction for, as Mowat observes, "[t]he several editions of Homer published between 1561 and 1616 illustrate the gradual construction of a great Author in England's early modern period."[98] Because he contributed a significant final chapter to this lengthy, collaboratively produced narrative, Chapman was in a particularly excellent position to benefit from it.

Having studied at both Oxford and Cambridge, and having done more than any of his contemporaries to make the "Prince of Poets" available to English readers, Chapman alone gets praised for his "haightned stile," a compliment that Webster also applies to "the most sententious Tragedy" with its characteristic "heighth of stile." Beyond these significant literary credentials, Chapman had also produced a body of plays which, compared to Webster's output at this stage in his career, was considerable. Between 1598 and 1612, nine plays – *The Blind Beggar of Alexandria* (1598); *Humorous Day's Mirth* (1599); *All Fools* (1605); *Monsieur d'Olive* (1606); *The Gentleman Usher* (1606); *Bussy d'Ambois* (1607); *The Conspiracy and Tragedy of Charles Duke of Bighorn, 1&2* (1608); *May Day* (1611); and *Widow's Tears* (1612) – were published under his name, and one collaboratively written play – *Eastward Hoe* (1605) – was attributed to Chapman, Ben Jonson, and John Marston. Only one other extant play – *Sir Giles Goosecap* (1606) – from this fourteen-year period has been subsequently attributed to him, suggesting the extent to which his authorial status was consistently ratified through publication during his lifetime. Only one of Chapman's dramatic texts – *The Gentleman Usher* (1606) – was published in the self-consciously literary style of *The White Devil* before the latter play appeared. A second play, *The Revenge of Bussy d'Ambois* (1613) appeared a year after Webster placed Chapman at the top of his list of playwrights who had earned his "good opinion." Arguably, the recognition accorded to Chapman in the preface of *The White Devil* gave his publisher some ideas about how his next play should be printed and marketed. Moreover, a dedicatory epistle written by Chapman to Sir Thomas Howard establishes the play's literary credentials at the outset when it asserts,

Since workes of this kinde have beene lately esteemed worthy the Patronage of some of our worthiest Nobles, I have made no doubt to preferre this of mine to your vndoubted Vertue, and exceedingly true Noblesse : as contayning matter no lesse deserving your reading, and excitation to Heroycall life, then any such late Dedication (A3r).

Subsequently, Chapman, like Webster before him, refers to the play's theatrical phase, its "scenicall presentation," in which "it might meete with some maligners" (A3v).

Alternatively, Jonson, who left school to be apprenticed as a bricklayer and is mentioned professionally for the first time ten years later in a July 1597 entry in Henslowe's diary,[99] was known primarily at this stage in his career as a playwright who wrote plays for the theatre, and masques and entertainments for James I's court. Despite – or perhaps because of – his exclusive focus on writing for the public and private stage, Jonson did more in the period prior to the publication of Webster's play to bolster the literary reputation of and create a new reading market for printed drama than any of the six other playwrights Webster mentions.[100] Jonson's belief – so fully articulated in the preface "To the Readers" of the 1605 quarto of *Sejanus, His Fall* – that the publication process could deliver some modicum of success to a play that had failed miserably on the stage must have deeply influenced Webster's thinking about the literary status of his authorial debut – especially in terms of how he viewed the relation between the playhouse and the printing house. But Jonson went well beyond merely justifying his play's theatrical failure and defending its poetic integrity: within the same brief prefatory note, he also alerts his readers to the scope of his literary ambitions by explaining the method of quoting classical sources he relied on in preparing the text for publication, and he promises them that he will soon publish his own translation of Horace's *Ars Poetica*.

Subsequently, in the dedication included in the first quarto edition of *Catiline, his Conspiracy* (1611), Jonson takes another shot at literary self-fashioning by critiquing popular audiences in terms that would be appropriated a year or so later by Webster. Complaining of the "so thicke, and darke, an ignorance, as now almost couers the Age," Jonson nevertheless takes comfort in the knowledge that the play's dedicatee, William, Earl of Pembroke, will "in these Iig-giuen times . . . countenance a legitimate Poëme" (A2r–A2v). With the distinction between jigs and legitimate poems in place, Jonson then offers different addresses to their respective audiences: one is aimed at the "reader in ordinarie" who will "commend out of affection, selfe tickling, an easinesse, or imitation"; the other addresses the "Reader extraordinary" (A3r) who, like the Earl of Pembroke, not only knows a great piece of literature from popular trash, but also perhaps has the money to buy it. A year later, in the address to the reader of *The Alchemist* (1612) Jonson takes aim at playwrights who "are esteem'd the more learned, and sufficient for this, by the Multitude," and blames this unfortunate fate on "the disease of the unskilfull, to thinke rude things greater then polish'd: or scatter'd more numerous than compos'd" (A3r–A3v).

More significantly, Jonson takes greater advantage of the publication process to mark his plays typographically as literary than any of the other playwrights Webster mentions. Of the five Jonson plays published between 1605 and 1612 – *Sejanus, His Fall* (1605); *Volpone* (1607); *The Case is Altered* (1609); *Catiline, his Conspiracy* (1611); and *The Alchemist* (1612) – four of them feature Latin epigraphs on their title pages, and all of them make use of continuous printing.[101] Thus, although G. E. Bentley has written of Jonson's 1616 folio that "probably no other publication before the Restoration did so much to raise the contemporary existence of the generally belittled form of plays,"[102] it also seems clear that Jonson had already begun to take advantage of the printing house to further his literary ambitions as much as a decade earlier.

Only two authors into Webster's list, the nature of its hierarchy is already apparent. Chapman, the university man with an established literary reputation who also writes plays, comes first; Jonson, the professional playwright who has aggressively used publication to create for himself a literary reputation, comes second. The case of Beaumont and Fletcher who, compared with Chapman and Jonson, were relative newcomers to the profession of writing for the stage and come next on Webster's list, is a little more complicated. Together, they had received attribution on the title page of *The Woman Hater* (1607), with Fletcher's name appearing first. A quarto edition of Fletcher's play, *The Faithful Shepheardesse*, was subsequently published in 1610, and although no edition of a play individually attributed to Beaumont during this period has survived, both authors had had plays they wrote – collaboratively or individually – performed since 1606.[103] Though not quite as accomplished as Chapman or Jonson, Beaumont and Fletcher's presence in Webster's exclusive club nevertheless makes a great deal of sense.

Like *The White Devil*, Beaumont's play, *The Knight of the Burning Pestle*, also had a rather poor showing at the box office when it was first performed in 1607, as the play's publisher, Burre, makes clear in his dedication to Robert Keysar, the manager of the theatre in which the play was initially performed:

SIR, this vnfortunate child, who in eight daies (as lately I haue learned) was begot and borne, soone after, was by his parents (perhaps because hee was so vnlike his brethren) exposed to the wide world, who for want of iudgement, or not vnderstanding the priuy marke of Ironie about it (which shewed it was no ofspring of any vulgar braine) vtterly reiected it: so that for want of acceptance it was euen ready to giue up the Ghost, and was in danger to have bene smothered in perpetuall oblivion.[104]

Published a year after Webster's play, Burre's prefatory note – written by a publisher, not an author – blames *The Knight*'s theatrical failure on an audience who "vttterly reiected it" because they were in "want of iudgement" and lacked "vnderstanding." Beaumont's literary reputation

Marketing Printed Drama 53

was not publicly at stake because Burre published *The Knight* – printed continuously with Latin epigraph on its title page – anonymously.

Burre, however, stood to lose a substantial sum of money if the play did as badly in the bookshop as it had done in the theatre. His willingness to take such a risk is perhaps indicative of his conviction that, as Lesser notes, "the techniques which enabled him to attract his buyers could turn a failed stage play like *The Knight* into a successful publication."[105] Moreover, Burre, who had previously published four of Jonson's plays – *Every Man in his Humour*, *Cynthia's Revels*, *Catiline*, and *The Alchemist* – had considerable experience marketing unpopular dramatic texts. Although Beaumont and Fletcher may have had little involvement in Burre's effort to give *The Knight* a new lease on life, both had already made their sympathies quite clear in dedicatory poems they contributed to the 1612 quarto edition of *The Alchemist*. Beaumont worries that the wit of Jonson's play will be lost on the "common people . . . till thy Readers can grow vp to it" (A3v). Similarly, Fletcher blames the play's unpopularity in the theatre on playgoers who prefer vulgar forms of comedy such as "mad *Pasquill, / or Greene's* deare *Groatsworth*, or *Tom Coryate*" (A3v).

A comparable lack of confidence in audiences had already been rehearsed two years earlier when, in a note "To the Reader" of *The Faithful Shepheardesse*, Fletcher advises potential purchasers of the book that the play

is a pastorall Tragie-comedie, which the people seeing when it was plaid, having ever had a singular guift in defining, concluded to be a play of country hired Shepheards, in gray cloakes, with curtaild dogs in strings, sometimes laughing together, and sometimes killing one another: And missing whitsun ales, creame, wassel & morris-dances, began to be angry.[106]

Having anticipated some of the ways the play is likely to be misunderstood, Fletcher offers an elaborate definition of the hybrid genre he has chosen to work in, then concludes, "Thus much I hope will serve to iustifie my Poeme, and make you vnderstandit, to teach you more for nothing, I do not know that I am in conscience bound."[107] As was the case with Jonson and the quarto text of *Sejanus*, Fletcher looks to the printed book to provide him with an opportunity – unavailable to him when the drama was performed – to educate his audience so that his play may finally be appreciated. Jonson and Chapman sign on to assist him with this project by contributing commendatory poems to the quarto edition of the play, both of which strive to legitimize Fletcher's play by distinguishing between theatre audiences and readers. Disparaging audiences who "had, before / They saw it halfe, damnd thy whole play, and more, / Their motives were, since it had not to do / With vices, which they look'd for, and came to," Jonson goes on to assure Fletcher and the reader that the play will have a more deserving after-life by being immortalized in print:

> I, that am glad, thy Innocence was thy Guilt,
>   And with that all the *Muses* blood were spilt,
> In such a *Martyrdome*; To vexe their eyes,
>   Do crowne thy murdred *Poeme*: which shall rise
> A glorified worke to Time, when Fire,
>   or moathes shall eate, what all these Fooles admire. (A3v)

In the next chapter I will examine how the construction of Shakespeare's authorship borrowed from the discourse of "*Martyrdome*." However, it is worth noting how Jonson's attempt to distance the printed text of Fletcher's play from the theatre relies on a resurrection narrative that simultaneously echoes the complaints of contemporary anti-theatricalists – "it had not to do / With vices, which they look'd for, and came to" – and anticipates Heminge and Condell's effort some two decades later to market a collection of a dead playwright's plays. For Jonson, print enables such a resurrection by transfoming "thy whole play" into a "worke." Similarly, Chapman begins his commendatory verse by reminding Fletcher that, "There are no sureties (good friend) Will betaken / For workes that vulgar-good name hath forsaken," but ends by assuring him that, "like your Booke do you / Live in ould peace : and that for praise allow" (A3r).

Thus, Beaumont and Fletcher had recently begun to play the literary game that Webster was hoping to enter into with his first individually authored play. Not surprisingly, as Richard Dutton notes, "Jonson, Webster, and Beaumont and Fletcher – all wrote over-length plays, either with the expectation of a print readership, or knowing that they would be circulated in manuscript."[108] Oddly however, Webster then moves on to praise three playwrights who have each been professionally involved in the theatre for nearly two decades. Though he assures us they have been named "lastly (without wrong last to be named)," we would do well to follow Freud's advice on the derivative character of negation. When, as Jacques-Alain Miller observes,

> a patient, discussing a dream, claims "It was not my mother," the analyst is called upon to make the interpretation that it was indubitably her, for the word is present, and the negation beside it is the mark of repression.[109]

Indeed, despite Webster's attempt to neutralize the dubious impression that he fears will be created by mentioning Shakespeare, Dekker, and Heywood last, the hierarchical logic that structures his list dictates their placement. McLuskie reads this line of the preface and argues:

Marketing Printed Drama

In linking the names of Shakespeare, Dekker, and Heywood, Webster was referring to playwrights associated with the three most important companies then working in London: the King's Men in the Globe and Blackfriars, Prince Henry's Men at the Fortune theatre, and Queen Anne's Men at the Red Bull, the theatre in which Webster's play was first performed.[110]

There were, of course, only six companies performing plays in the year Webster's preface was published, and only three up until 1610, when James's son, the Duke of Albany and York, formed a company. A year later, his sister, the Lady Elizabeth, started a company and the former Blackfriars Boys re-emerged as the Children of the Queen's Revels.[111] For all practical purposes, then, there were only three companies of any major standing by 1612. To suggest, therefore, that Shakespeare's, Dekker's, and Heywood's association with these companies is what links them in Webster's assessment is to offer little more than a tautology. Given the context in which they appear, it seems more likely that Webster put them together because their strong associations with playing companies marked them as popular playwrights who had lower literary ambitions than the other writers who precede them in his list. In other words, those playwrights who aspire to the "heighth of stile" go at the top, while those who appeal to the groundlings go at the bottom.

Unlike Jonson, for whom the press came to represent the possibility of distancing himself and his career as an author from "the loathed stage," Shakespeare involved himself in the publication of only two works, *Venus and Adonis* and *The Rape of Lucrece*.[112] As Bentley observes with reference to these two poems, "[Shakespeare] not only provided dedications, but gave his readers excellent texts, far cleaner than those displayed in any of his play quartos." [113] Alternatively, Shakespeare seems to have been singularly indifferent about whether and how the plays he wrote made it into print, an indifference that has troubled critics from Samuel Johnson to the present. Noting this singularity, Bentley observes:

[Shakespeare] himself refrained from ushering [his plays] into print in the fashion of so many of his contemporaries in these years – Ben Jonson, John Marston, Samuel Daniel, Barnabe Barnes, John Day, Lewis Machin, Thomas Middleton, Nathan Field, Thomas Heywood, John Webster, John Stephens, Wentworth Smith, Thomas Dekker.[114]

Struggling to rationalize this exceptional lack of interest in publication, Michael J. B. Allen and Kenneth Muir fall back on intentionality when they assure us that Shakespeare's plays "were composed for performance only, not for reading, and belonged to the company in which he was a sharer, became indeed part of its stock."[115] This apparent selflessness with regard to the ownership of his texts is, perhaps, more easily comprehended when viewed in the context of Shakespeare's unparalleled professional involvement with the same company. According to Bentley:

> from the formation of the Lord Chamberlain's company in 1594 to Shakespeare's death in 1616 there is no evidence that he ever wrote any play for any other company – a longer period of fidelity than that known for any other dramatist, and one which was never interrupted.[116]

The consummate company man, rather than an individualist, Shakespeare's status as a sharer, as an "ordinary poet" for the King's Men, no doubt discouraged him from engaging in the kind of authorial self-promotion for which Jonson has often been celebrated. More precisely, this status may have *prevented* him from publishing his plays.

In a recent essay, Dutton has shed much new light on the ties that may have bound Shakespeare to the playhouse and kept him out of the printing house.[117] Looking at "the total picture of which plays got into print and when," Dutton observes that this evidence suggests that plays written by company playwrights such as Shakespeare "were the only ones to which the companies held a copyright respected by the Stationers' Company and the licensers for the press."[118] And while Dutton is not wholly convinced by this evidence, he tentatively concludes that "it does seem that the works of 'ordinary poets' were more rigorously denied the press than those of other authors."[119] In other words, even if Shakespeare had entertained fantasies of typographically fashioning himself in the manner Jonson pursued, he may not have been able to explore them.

Anomalously loyal – or obligated to – the company that translated his talent for writing popular plays into considerable financial and cultural success, such ties must have shaped Shakespeare's attitude toward the process of authorship itself. As Robert Clare observes,

> Theatre is a collaborative art. To be a "sharer" in a company, as Shakespeare was, was to be entitled to part of its profits; but the word has wider implications in any company where collective creativity is properly respected, to which he is unlikely to have been blind.[120]

Whereas Jonson was keenly aware that the "Stage" and the "Booke" afforded him distinct opportunities for authorship, and relied on the publication process to excise his early collaborative works from his authorial canon, Shakespeare seems to have been quite content – or compelled – to sidestep an emergent author function for the collaborative activities of the company. Faced with the necessity, according to Dutton, of straddling "the old world of courtly letters, largely wedded to manuscript culture and the new world of commercial print," Shakespeare committed his sonnets to print, but was probably not able to do so with his plays. This may not mean, however, that his plays were not written for the same educated audiences that bought the printed texts of his sonnets, but that, as Dutton argues, those audiences read and valued Shakespeare's plays in manuscript, and that "Heminge and Condell knew this in commending his plays to a wider readership."[121]

To Dutton's important argument I think we must add that the differences between the way Shakespeare and Jonson handled publication may also stem from a generational difference between the two dramatists. Shakespeare was older and already nearing the end of his theatrical career by the time playwrights like Jonson and publishers like Burre began to realize the potential of publication for creating a second market for plays. It is suggestive that Jonson's folio appeared in 1616, the year of Shakespeare's death, and that Shakespeare left the making of his literary reputation to two other sharers in the company, without whose effort to publish his plays in folio seven years after his death, only twenty would have survived in various quarto editions. Appropriately enough, it was a prefatory poem written by Jonson, "To the memory of my beloved, / The AUTHOR / Mr. William Shakespeare: / And / what he hath left us," which was chosen to follow the "CATALOGVE" page that sets out in three generic groupings what Shakespeare had left us. Referring to the first half of this poem, James Shapiro asserts that,

> before Jonson can write of "my gentle Shakespeare" Shakespeare must become in some sense Jonson's Shakespeare . . . It is precisely because Shakespeare is reimagined in Jonsonian terms that Jonson is able to call him, imperiously, "our Shakespeare" . . . Jonson reconstructs Shakespeare in the image Jonson has carefully created for himself: one who is to be compared with classical antecedents, whose ends are admonitory, a guiding light to the stage, a reviser, and a born and made poet.[122]

I would add that because Shakespeare is no longer a man in flesh, he is finally in a position to become a "man in print." Jonson's poem celebrates this transformation because, according to David Riggs, it substantiates his "lifelong contention that plays are (or should be) a serious form of literature."[123] More generally, the preliminaries of the 1623 Folio seek to remake Shakespeare in Jonson's image, for, as Riggs notes,

Heminge's and Condell's prefatory letter, "To the Great Variety of Readers," echoes Jonson's induction to *Bartholomew Fair*, his preface to *The Alchemist*, his epigram "to My Bookseller," and his *Discoveries*. The prefatory poems by Jonson, Hugh Holland, James Mabbe, and Leonard Digges transform Shakespeare into a specifically literary figure whose works have achieved the status of modern classics; the closest analogue to these tributes are the poems prefixed to Jonson's 1616 folio.[124]

Jonson himself seems to subtly allude to this effort to refashion Shakespeare in his own image when he writes in his prefatory poem that "a good Poet's made, as well as borne, / And such wert thou. Looke how the fathers face / Lives in his issue . . ." (B1v: 26–28). In the strictly material context of the early modern printing house and the London book trade, Jonson did in some real sense father Shakespeare by providing a model for the subsequent material embodiment of his career as a playwright.

Despite Heminge and Condell's efforts on the dead dramatist's behalf, Shakespeare's reluctance to publish his plays has been a bit embarrassing, given his singular position in the West, and commentators have frequently apologized for it or erroneously attributed it to paranoia about piracy. Christopher More, for example, attempts to justify Shakespeare's lack of interest in publication by arguing that he was willing to see his poems in print, but was compelled to protect his plays from other acting companies who would want them published so they could steal them for future performances. As More puts it, "[a]lthough most plays in Shakespeare's day were written in verse, they were meant to be performed and not read, since publication would have given rival theatre companies access to them."[125] More's view of the perilous circulation of plays between rival companies was initally proffered by A. W. Pollard and subsequently championed by E. K. Chambers. There is, however, no evidence that, for example, early published plays by Jonson such as the two *Every Man* plays or *Sejanus* were ever performed by any other company except the one for which they were originally written, the King's Men.[126] Nor is there any evidence, as Dutton notes, that Shakespeare's plays were performed in London by any other company after they were published in the 1623 Folio.[127] But perhaps the strongest argument against the playwright's fear of piracy has resulted from Dutton's careful scrutiny of the regulatory systems that monitored the activities of the playing companies during Shakespeare's day. At least one significant reason why publication probably did not enable rival companies to augment their repertoires of performance texts is that, according to Dutton, "[w]hen the Master of the Revels granted a licence to perform a play it was specific to the companies which acquired it and could only be passed on to others with their consent."[128] In other words, once a play had been – to borrow from a title page in Daye's Norton collection – "scene and allowed," it could legally be performed solely by the company who had submitted it to the Master of the Revels for inspection. Only if we view the London stage from the distorted perspective of Shakespeare's current cultural status is it possible to believe that an early seventeenth-century playing company would run the

Marketing Printed Drama 59

risk of being reprimanded – or even closed down – in order to perform a Shakespeare play that was already licensed to the playwright's company.

More's view of the division between dramatic and non-dramatic poetry does, however, have some historical legitimacy. Such a division was indeed rehearsed in Webster's day, most notably by Sir Thomas Bodley, who instructed his head librarian, Thomas James, to exclude "almanacs, plays, and proclamations"[129] from his collection of printed books in the same year that *The White Devil* was published. But it is also clear that Webster and some of the playwrights he admired had a much higher opinion of their own work. Jonson, Beaumont, Fletcher, and Webster repeatedly made it known in print that certain plays were deserving of the posterity that publication and Bodley's library promised. They were not much concerned whether such plays would, when published, become available to rival companies. Furthermore, since Jonson, Webster, and a publisher like Burre readily admitted that their respective plays were "vtterly reiected" by theatre audiences, rival playing companies would have been foolish to try to stage them.

On the other hand, in 1612 Shakespeare was nearing the end of a twenty-year playwriting career during which his attention to the "vulgar" tastes of theatre audiences and his indifference to publication were rewarded handsomely. It should come as no surprise, therefore, that although many of Shakespeare's plays found their way into print with the help of some twenty different publishers, only one of them, the 1608 quarto text of *King Lear* published by Nathaniel Butter, may have been marked typographically for the kind of select, literary readership to which "failed" playwrights like Jonson sought to market themselves. Indeed, the *Lear* quarto, the first play Nicholas Okes printed, was also the only play to prominently feature Shakespeare's name at the top of the title page, a strategy of authorial self-presentation used by Jonson and his printers on a number of quarto title pages published before 1608. Yet, even this sudden and anomalous typographic over-determination of the playwright's authorship probably had little to do with literary ambition or authorial self-promotion, nor does Butter and Okes's title-page reflect any particular reverence on their part for the playwright destined to become our greatest author. Rather, the material reality of *Lear*'s initial publication is somewhat inglorious. The edition probably ran to no more than seven hundred copies, and it seems unlikely that it sold very quickly, because no further edition of the play appeared until Thomas Pavier attempted to publish a collection of Shakespeare's plays eleven years later. If Butter and Okes expected their first Shakespeare play to turn a quick profit, that expectation did not keep Okes from taking approximately one hundred other printing jobs during the period that he printed *Lear*. Nor was literature a great priority at Okes's recently acquired printing house. During the period 1607–1611, Okes churned out texts in these general categories: Religion: 48; Education: 18; Literature: 16; History: 9; Almanacs: 8; Speeches: 4. Of the sixteen texts we might consider literary, nine were plays, and Shakespeare wrote only one of them.[130] In short, Okes and Butter's quarto edition of *Lear* represented only another job to them, one which they hoped would eventually return some kind of profit. They certainly did not trust their financial well-being to its success in Butter's bookshop.

A year after *Lear* appeared, *The famous Historie of Troylus and Cresseid* was published. It was the first Shakespeare quarto to include an address to the reader. Written by Henry Walley, who would publish Fletcher's *Shepheardesse* a year later, the preface is an attempt to distance the play from uneducated theatre audiences. Walley assures the "Eternall reader," an eternity secured through publication, that "you have heere a new play, neuer stal'd with the Stage, neuer clapper-clawd with the palmes of the vulger, and yet passing full of the palme comical."[131] After comparing Shakespeare's dramas with "the best Commedy in *Terence* or *Plautus*" and prophesying that "when [Shakespeare] is gone, and Commedies out of sale, you will scramble for them, and set vp a new English Inquisition,"[132] Walley returns to the subject of the play's theatrical innocence:

Take this for a warning, and at the perrill of your pleasures losse, and Iudgements, refuse not, nor like the lese, for not being sulllied with the smoky breath of the multitude; but thanke fortune for the scape it hath made amongst you.[133]

Whereas other publishers/playwrights encouraged prospective readers to ignore a play's reception in the theatre, Walley tries to convince readers to buy a play which, according to him, was never staged. Ironically, the anomalously anti-theatrical status of Walley's edition would be re-inscribed as an absence within the publication project that founded materially Shakespeare's literary reputation. Apparently, readers did not scramble for the 1609 quarto, so that when the 1623 Folio publishers were acquiring the texts or manuscripts of the plays they wanted to include in their collection, Walley was unwilling to allow *Troylus and Cresseid* to be reprinted because a folio edition of the play would have cut into the already poor sales of his edition. Ultimately, Walley capitulated, and Blount and Jaggard included a text of *Troylus* after the first few copies of the Folio had been printed and sold; but the lateness of this inclusion precluded the play's title from being listed on the "Catalogue" page.[134] The only other reader address to preface a Shakespeare quarto is a note from "The Stationer to the Reader" that was written by Thomas Walkley and included in the 1622 edition of *Othello* printed for him by Nicholas Okes. In the thirteen years that separate the two addresses, the theatre has all but disappeared as a defining oppositional context for promoting the publication process. Instead, one year before the appearance of the Folio, Shakespeare has already emerged as a Jonsonian author figure with his name and his "worke' at the center of Walkley's commodification strategy: "To commend it, I will not, for that which is good I hope every man will commend, without intreaty: and I am the bolder, because the Authors name is sufficient to vent his worke" (A2r).[135] Six years after the death of the author, a proper name has come to guarantee a proper work.

Although two of Shakespeare's publishers (Walley and Walkley) briefly tried to capitalize on his popularity by isolating the dramatist from the theatre audiences that had made him popular, Shakespeare did not constitute a role model for a playwright like Webster whose unpopularity with those same audiences helped to nurture his literary aspirations. Accordingly, Shakespeare's status in Webster's list is anomalous – except in the context of the two other playwrights who are also praised for their "right happy and copious industry."

Thomas Dekker was also a company man, not as a sharer, but rather as a piece worker or freelancer who, McLuskie notes, never had more than a "precarious hold on a theatrical career."[136] In the 1590s he worked for Henslowe, and was the first playwright listed in the latter's diary to receive a payment for his work. In this case, however, the work consisted of adding to others' plays:

pd vnto Thomas dickers the 20 of desembr 1597 for adycyons to fostus twentie shellinges and fyve shellinges more for a prolog to Marloes tambelan so in all J saye payde twentye five shellinges . . .[137]

During the first decade of the seventeenth century he wrote *The Honest Whore* (1604), *The Whore of Babylon* (1606–1607), and – with Thomas Middleton – *The Roaring Girl* (1611) for the Prince's Men at the Fortune Theatre, though he was not mentioned in the patent issued for Henry's company in 1606.[138] While Dekker's contributions to the Prince's Men were consistent with what Gurr identifies as the "company's continuing allegiance to the city,"[139] in the same year that Webster published *The White Devil*, the Middlesex General Session singled the company out for "certaine lewde Jigges songes and daunces used and accustomed at the playhouse called the Fortune in Guilding lane."[140] Such an accusation would have injured Dekker's standing amongst playwrights like Jonson who complained that their plays were poorly appreciated in "these Iig-giuen times." But by 1612 Dekker had used the dedication to *If This Be Not a Good Play the Devil is in It* to distance his work from his former employers and declare his preference for the Queen's Men, though he was not mentioned in the patent issued for Henry's company in 1606. Referring to the new company that performed his latest play, Dekker writes:

Acknowledgment is part of payment sometimes, but it neither is, nor shall be (betweene you and me) a *Canceling*. I have cast mine eye vpon many, but find none more fit, none more worthy, to *Patronize this*, than *you*, who have *Protected it*. Your *Cost, Counsell*, and *Labour*, had bin ill spent, if a *Second* should by my hand snatch from you *This Glory*.[141]

Knowing that a playwright was judged by the company that kept him, Dekker had switched his loyalties as the Fortune's fortunes began to plummet. Nevertheless, Dekker probably made the move a little too late, because a decade earlier he and Jonson had already publicly debated over the considerable disparity between the working conditions of the professional theatre and the fantasies of more literary-minded playwrights. In *Poetaster* (1602), Jonson satirized Dekker as a character named Demetrius Fannius, whom he forced to admit near the play's conclusion that Jonson

kept better company (for the most part) than I: and that better men lov'd him, than lov'd me: and that his writings thriv'd better than mine and were better lik't and grac't: nothing else (5.3. 450–453).

In the same year Dekker responded in *Satiromastix, or the Untrussing of the Humorous Poet* by having a character based on Jonson's promise that he will not

sit in a gallery, when your Comedies and Enterludes have entred their Actions, and there make vile and bad faces at everie lyne, to make Gentlemen have an eye to you, and to make players afraide to take your part (5.2. 298–301).

A similar dig at Jonson, aimed specifically at the recently published quarto of *Sejanus, His Fall*, was subsequently made by John Marston in a note "To the generall Reader" of the 1606 quarto text of *The Wonder of Women or the Tragedie of Sophonisba*. There Marston warns readers "that I have not labored in this poeme, to tie my selfe to relate any thing as an historian but to inlarge every thing as a Poet, To transcribe Authors, quote authorities, & translate Latin prose orations into English bla[n]k verse, hath in this subject beene the least aime of my studies."[142] Jonson, of course, had done all three of these things a year earlier in *Sejanus;* and, as if to drive home his anti-Jonsonian point, Marston next refers to his addressee as his "equall Reader." Three years later, Dekker indirectly criticized the elitist attitudes of playwrights like Jonson by depicting the commercial realities of writing for the theatre in *The Gull's Hornbook* (1609):

> The theatre is your poets Royal Exchange upon which their Muses – that are now turned to merchants – meeting barter away that light commodity of words for a lighter ware than words – plaudits . . . Players are their factors who put away the stuff and make the best of it they possibly can . . . Your gallant, your captain had wont to be the soundest paymasters . . . when your groundling and gallery commoner buys his sport by the penny and like a haggler is glad to utter again by retailing.[143]

Playing companies were often structured like corporations with shareholders, but for Dekker the theatre embodies the transitional configurations of nascent capitalism with playwrights as the primary investors.[144] Working in what Paul Yachnin suggestively terms, "The Knowledge Marketplace," muses-turned-merchants trade words for plaudits in an effort to convert a "socially degraded and morally suspect" product into "culturally legitimate currencies."[145] Players, according to the early modern sense of "factor,"[146] serve as proto-stockbrokers entrusted with a given playwright's investment of time, effort, and talent. Moreover, the clientele courted by Jonson and others in their prefaces pay top dollar, while the vulgar audiences disparaged by so many playwrights and publishers both reject works they can't appreciate, and scalp tickets.

The theatre was by no means a risk-free venture; if Shakespeare made a killing, Dekker – who got paid outright for whatever he could sell – was never far from the debtor's prison. Although he might have benefited from the literary self-fashioning that playwrights such as Jonson and Webster strove for, neither he nor his publishers pursued it extensively. Prior to *The White Devil*, only *The Whore of Babylon* was marketed to customers at Paul's Churchyard who were being trained gradually to distinguish at a glance between what Bodley termed "idle books, and riff-rafs"[147] and what Jonson called "a legitimate Poëme" – between, as Webster succinctly put it, "new bookes" and "good bookes." Nathaniel Butter published the text with a Latin epigraph on its title page and continuous printing a year before he may have encouraged Okes to gentrify Shakespeare's *King Lear*. In the same year, three of Dekker's collaborations with Webster – *Northward Hoe*, *Westward Hoe*, and *Sir Thomas Wyat* – were published. Three decades after the publication of *The Whore of Babylon*, a second play by Dekker, *The Wonder of a Kingdome* (1636), was dressed up typographically by its printer (Robert Raworth) and publisher (Nicholas Vavasour) for a select, literary readership.

As the last of the "lastly" named playwrights commended for their "right happy and copious industry," Heywood's literary status is particularly suspect. Although Chapman, the university man and translator of Homer, had the strongest literary credentials of the playwrights mentioned by Webster, it is not altogether clear that Heywood had the weakest. A number of his contemporaries praised him for his learning, especially his knowledge of languages.[148] We can also identify him with the "Thomas Heywood" who entered Emmanuel College, Cambridge, as a pensioner in 1591, though a subsequent tradition, begun by William Cartwright in his 1658 edition of *An Apology for Actors* indicates that "the gentleman was a Fellow of Peter-house in Cambridge."[149] Despite this considerable academic pedigree, Heywood was the most enthusiastic apologist for the theatre and therefore the group's most vocal and articulate spokesman about the perils of print publication.[150] Additionally, if we take him at his word in the note "To the Reader" of *The English Traveller* (1633), then he was also by far the most prolific for there he writes that, "[t]his *Tragi-Comedy* [is] one reserued amongst two hundred and twenty, in which I haue had either an entire hand, or at the least a maine finger."[151]

Heywood's relationship with the printing house is the most complicated of all the playwrights examined so far, and it will be the focus of Chapter 5. However, what distinguishes him in the present context is the legitimacy or privilege he accords to theatre audiences. Webster and some of the other playwrights he mentions, primarily sought to justify publication in their preliminaries by differentiating between theatre audiences unable to appreciate the literary value of their plays in performance and readers of the printed text constituting a much more suitable audience. Playwrights like Jonson and Webster considered publication deliberate and purposeful. Heywood, in contrast, informs his readers that *The English Traveller* came "accidentally to the Presse," and that he was forced to legitimize it after the fact: "I having Intelligence thereof, thought it not fit that it should passe as *filius populi*, a Bastard without a Father to acknowledge it."[152] Heminge and Condell had made similar claims two decades earlier about the "stolne, and surreptitious copies" constituting Shakespeare's career in print prior to their efforts to restore it to its paternal legitimacy with the help of Blount and Jaggard. Compelled by the vicissitudes of the London stage to work as a freelancer for the last twenty years of his life, Heywood died one year before the closing of the theatres with little assurance that any of his former colleagues would step in after his death to resuscitate his corpus as Heminge and Condell had done for Shakespeare's. None did.

If, as Elizabeth Eisenstein has observed, "the modern game of books and authors" could be played only after printing technology was invented,[153] scholars of early modern English drama have worked under the assumption that Shakespeare was the only game in town. Alternatively, this brief analysis of *The White Devil*'s reader address suggests that authors not only played a number of games, but also that they played them and were played by them, in very different ways. In the chapters that follow, I attempt to reconstruct what happened during four of those games.

2   "So disfigured with scrapings & blotting out": Sir John Oldcastle and the construction of Shakespeare's authorship

> Let vs returne vnto the Bench againe,
> And there examine further of this fray.   *Sir John Oldcastle* I.i.124–5

> We always seem to be dealing with ghosts when troubling over an author's identity.
>   Scott McMillin, *The Elizabethan Theatre & The Booke of Sir Thomas More*

A decade ago the editors of the *Oxford William Shakespeare: The Complete Works* replaced the name of the character called Falstaff in *1 Henry IV* with a hypothetically earlier version of the character's name, Sir John Oldcastle. The restoration of Oldcastle to the Oxford edition makes it the first authoritative text to undo an alteration which, as scholars have long suspected, Shakespeare himself must have made sometime between a non-extant 1596 performance text and the 1598 quarto of the play. The resulting scholarly debate over this editorial decision has touched on a number of significant issues linked to the authority and authenticity of "Shakespearean" texts, and it has raised important questions about how these texts were shaped by the material, religious, and political conditions in which they were produced.[1] In the case of *1 Henry IV*, critics have struggled to reconstruct how an early version of the text with Oldcastle as the protagonist of the unworthy knight plot might have placed the play and its author in a complicated position between an individual's reputation and a nation's. Indeed, it is likely that a play featuring a fat rogue named Oldcastle would have insulted William Brooke, a titular descendant of the knight's Cobham Lordship who served briefly as Lord Chamberlain at about the time *1 Henry IV* was first performed. Moreover, such a play certainly would have slurred the character's namesake, the Lord Cobham, a Lollard who was executed for treason and subsequently transformed by William Tyndale, John Bale, and John Foxe into one of England's greatest Protestant martyrs. Consequently, scholars have used the publication of the Oxford edition to speculate on Shakespeare's authorial intentions.

In this chapter, I want to shift the discussion away from what

Sir John Oldcastle 67

Shakespeare might have intended by focusing instead on a significant aspect of the dramatist's authorship that has been under-examined in the recent debate over the Oxford *1 Henry IV*. I argue that the initial deletion of Oldcastle from an early text of *1 Henry IV* and its subsequent restoration to the Oxford edition constitute two important textual points in the history of Shakespeare's authorship; and I attempt to trace this history from the authorial attribution on the quarto title page of *2 Henry IV* (1600), to the present moment in literary studies when Shakespeare's position as a canonical author faces re-evaluation. Concomitantly, I try to account for the importance of Oldcastle's name to Shakespeare's authorial status by suggesting that the posthumous construction of Oldcastle's martyrdom has certain elements in common with the posthumous construction of Shakespeare's authorship.

In 1619, three years after Ben Jonson published a folio collection of his plays, Thomas Pavier hit on the idea of publishing a collection of Shakespeare's plays.[2] At first the venture must have seemed a sure bet, though probably not an exceedingly profitable one.[3] Pavier already owned the rights to what he deemed were four of Shakespeare's dramas, and apparently he had access to at least six other "Shakespearean" quartos. Ten plays would have constituted a substantial volume, and Pavier merely hired an elderly, nearly blind printer named William Jaggard and had him reprint earlier editions of plays with consecutive pagination as a newly set quarto collection.[4] Having died some three years earlier, Shakespeare had no objections to this effort to capitalize on his name; but even if he had, there would have been precious little to be done about it. John Feather oberves that, "the idea of rights in copies, that is, the unique right to print a particular text, was well-established before the end of the 1580s, and probably earlier."[5] Such rights, however, belonged only to Freemen of the Stationers' Company, not to authors. A law that could provide Shakespeare – rather than the King's Men – with something like copyright protection was nearly a century down the time line.[6]

Things did not go well for Pavier. The following order from the Court of Assistants foiled the publisher's ur-scheme to make Shakespeare's ascending star pay: "vppon a ler from the right ho^{ble} the lo. Chamberlleyne It is thought fitt & so ordered That no playes that his ma^{tyes} do play shalbe printed wthout consent of some of them."[7] Undaunted by the Lord Chamberlain's intervention, Pavier and company proceeded to publish seven of the ten plays as separate editions. Having back-dated the title pages of the six plays he did not own so as to produce simulacra of their original printings, Pavier thought he could pass them off as remainders of first editions. His scam might have gone undetected to this day had practitioners of the New Bibliography not determined that the title pages of the plays had been printed from the same type and on the same stocks of paper.[8]

Whatever its contemporary or subsequent success as an effort to make the Bard "a man in print," Pavier and Jaggard's undertaking remains notable not only for its willingness to reprint what have come to be known as bad quartos, but also for its eagerness to attribute plays to Shakespeare's pen.[9] In a very real sense, 1619 can be said to have commenced the era of Shakespeare apocrypha. Of the three Pavier/Jaggard reprints that were not selected by John Heminge and Henrie Condell for the "authorized" Folio of 1623, only *Pericles* – one of the seven plays added in the 1664 reprint of the 1663 third folio – has been granted the sacred authorial status of a Shakespeare play. The play's close call with non-canonization is succinctly characterized by David Bevington who observes that perhaps the First Folio's editors "experienced copyright difficulties or could not lay their hands on the prompt book, but it is also possible they either suspected or knew that Shakespeare was not sole author."[10]

Another 1619 reprint, *A Yorkshire Tragedy*, subsequently lapsed into authorial anonymity, and the last of the rogue reprints, *1 Sir John Oldcastle*, has endured what the editor of a recent critical edition of the play calls "a varied and tempestuous printing history,"[11] a fate not uncommon to those plays which at one point or another are branded "Shakespeare apocrypha." The title page of the 1600 edition of *Oldcastle* indicates that the play was "Printed by V. S. for Thomas Pavier."[12] V. S. is one Valentine Simmes, a printer of some reputation who printed several Shakespeare quartos as well as some plays staged by the Admiral's Men.[13] As with many such quarto editions of plays, no author is mentioned. By the time of the 1619 reprint, however, "William Shakespeare" appears on the title page, and it is Pavier's turn to be reduced to "for T. P." The newfound importance bestowed on Shakespeare's authorial status is certainly consistent with an effort to publish a collection of plays three years after Jonson's *Workes* and four years before the First Folio; but in the case of the *Oldcastle* reprint the author's name appears, oddly enough, on a title page that is falsely dated "1600" so Pavier can sidestep Stationers' restrictions by passing it off as the remnant of an earlier edition. Like the striking of the clock in *Julius Caesar*, the Shakespearean author function is textually compelled to make an appearance before its time, though, as Scott McMillin observes, "[b]y 1600 [Shakespeare's] name obviously sold books – it appeared on four of his five plays first published in that year."[14]

Oldcastle presents scholars with a range of complications linked to the authorship of early modern drama. On 16 October 1599 Henslowe noted in his diary that Thomas Downton had received ten pounds "to pay m^r monday m^r drayton & m^r wilsson & haythway for the first pte of the lyfe of Sr Jhon Ouldcastell . . ."[15] The play is the product of at least four minds and pens, and a subsequent diary entry complicates the issue of its parentage by acknowledging payment to "Mr Mundaye & the Reste of the poets at the playinge of Sr John oldcastel."[16] In short, *Oldcastle* is a truly collaborative work, an attribute that does not bode well for a play compelled to compete in the marketplace of literary history with the canonical authorship of Shakespeare's works.[17]

We can only expect that a collaborative work like the *Oldcastle* play by Munday and the rest of the poets would be consigned to the margins in the age of the emergent individual author. That the play was temporarily allotted a slightly elevated status owes something to its brief stint as Shakespearean apocrypha, no matter how dubious its link to Shakespeare was even at the moment it was first printed. If anyone knew that *Oldcastle* did not flow from Shakespeare's pen, it was precisely Pavier who, nineteen years before he tried to publish a collection of Shakespeare's plays, was as close to the play's point of origin as anyone could be without having written it or acted in it. We know, for example, that some ten months after Henslowe paid Downton £10 for the play, Pavier shows up in the Stationers' Register on "11 Augusti / 1600" as having

> Entred for his copies under the
> handes of master VICARS and the / wardens.
> These iij copies
>   viz
> The first parte of the history of the life of
> Sir John / OLDCASTELL Lord COBHAM[18]

Moreover, the initial printing history of the play is fairly well documented and straightforward. Peter Corbin and Douglas Sedge, for example, observe with some confidence that an

> examination of Q1 suggests that the copy for it was authorial rather than a prompt copy. Inconsistencies in characters' names in speech prefixes and stage directions are considerable . . . It is unlikely that such inconsistency, coupled with indefinite or permissible stage directions . . . could have been tolerated by the prompter.[19]

Here, oddly enough, the theatre – metonymically embodied in the person of the prompter – intervenes as a force of textual consistency and stability. The prompter is given the pre-print responsibility of generating a coherent work, perhaps because in this particular case the prompter comes numerically closer to the individualized status of a Shakespeare or a Jonson than the four or more collaborators who patched *Oldcastle* together.[20] Equally odd is the fact that the process of collaborative authorship, rather than the oft-villainized print shop, seems to get blamed in Corbin and Sedge's analysis for those "inconsistencies [that] may, to some extent indicate the individual habits of the four different collaborators."[21] In short, nearly everything about the "authorial copy" of *Oldcastle* is straightforward except its authorship, and this paradox may begin to explain why critics in the past have been reluctant to ask the most obvious question about the 1619 reprint. Knowing full well in 1600 that the play he published in quarto was the collaborative product of four authors as well as the property of Henslowe, how could Pavier republish it nineteen years later as a Shakespeare play? Was there no one alive who would know or care?

The range of possible answers is fairly limited, and none of them can be reconciled easily with the looming figure of the great author. One probable scenario is that the authorial status of a given early modern play was so inconsequential that Pavier felt free to manipulate the identity of its author/s as the particular publishing circumstances required.[22] In Shakespeare's case, there is ample textual evidence of such inconsequence if we consider the fact that the title pages of the following quartos were printed without any indication of authorship: *Titus Andronicus, The First Part of the Contention Betwixt the Two Famous Houses of York and Lancaster, The True Tragedy of Richard Duke of York, Romeo and Juliet* (Q1 and Q2), *Richard III, 1 Henry IV,* and *Henry V.* Nearly half of the plays that appeared in print before the 1623 Folio laid no claims to Shakespeare's paternity. Furthermore, only Nathaniel Butter's 1608 quarto edition of *King Lear* – printed for him by Nicholas Okes – accords top-of-the-title-page billing to

"M. William Shak-speare:"

Set in larger type than it had ever appeared before, the author's name is linked to the title of the play, "True Chronicle Historie of the life and / death of King LEAR and his three / daughters" with the possessive pronoun "*H I S*" set in italicized and widely spaced capital pica letters.[23] The only other place in which Shakespeare could have seen his name set in comparably large type was blazoned across the title page of the 1609 Sonnets, in capital letters.[24] In strictly typographic terms, Shakespeare the poet fared better as a published author during his lifetime than Shakespeare the playwright.

Okes and Butter's title page announces rather loudly that here is an author and here is a play, and the correspondence between them is a typographically emphatic genitive. No doubt one probable motive for typographically emphasizing the possessive pronoun on *Lear*'s 1608 title page is to differentiate Shakespeare's "True Chronicle Historie of the life and death of King LEAR and his three daughters" from a non-Shakespearean "True Chronicle History of King LEIR and his three daughters" published in 1603.[25] In this sense, the typographic emergence of Shakespeare's authorial self-hood is fashioned for him courtesy of Okes and Butter, according to an epistemological schema that has been influentially characterized by Stephen Greenblatt as "resolutely dialectical."[26] Indeed, so powerful is this publishing venture's urge to drag Shakespeare into authorhood that, strangely enough, the author's name is printed a second time in the same large type as a head-title on the first page of play-text (B1r), this time beneath a border ornament ($9\frac{1}{2}$ by $1\frac{1}{4}$ cm.);[27] and once again a genitive relation between author and play is emphasized: "M. William Shak-speare / *H I S* / Historie, of King Lear."

Certainly Nathaniel Butter wanted this play – or any other manuscript he brought to Okes's print shop – to sell quickly, and it is tempting, therefore, as Blayney aptly puts it, to "imagine the delighted book-buying public flocking eagerly to the shops to buy the latest master work from the pen of their favorite playwright."[28] The reality is much less exciting. The first print run of Shakespeare's *Lear* was probably no larger than seven hundred copies, and some quantity of that first print run must have remained unsold more than a decade later because no other edition was published between 1608 and 1619 when Pavier attempted to publish a quarto collection of Shakespeare's plays and included a text of the play.[29]

Typographically speaking, however, things were not usually so dramatic for Shakespeare's status as an author in print. The chronological first quarto of a Shakespeare play to mention the playwright, *Love's Labour's Lost* (1598), merely indicates in small type near the middle of the title page that it has been "Newly corrected and augmented / *By W. Shakespeare*"(A1r). The logical assumption is that Shakespeare was newly correcting and augmenting what he himself had written, but the title page itself stubbornly refuses to assert the play's authorship. Two years later, the title page of *2 Henry IV* forecloses on the need to assume authorship by including, for the first time, the phrase, "*Written by William Shakespeare*" (A1r) (Fig. 6).

It bears repeating that this "*Written by William Shakespeare*," which appears near the bottom in the smallest type on the page, is the first instance of an unambiguously authorial attribution to Shakespeare on the title page of an early modern play. Authors correct, sometimes they augment, and frequently enough in the past they have endeavored to correct and augment other authors' work: the early history of editing

THE
Second part of Henrie
the fourth, continuing to his death,
and coronation of *Henrie*
the fift.

With the humours of *sir* Iohn Falstaffe, and swaggering
Pistoll.

As it hath been sundrie times publikely
acted by the right honourable, the Lord
Chamberlaine his seruants.

Written by William Shakespeare.

LONDON
Printed by V.S. for Andrew Wise, and
William Aspley.
1600.

Figure 6 Title page: *The Second part of Henrie the fourth*, 1600

Shakespeare is resplendent with such authorial correction and augmentation. Moreover, plays such as Thomas Kyd's *The Spanish Tragedy* bear witness to the extent to which a play could be augmented by another playwright – in this particular case, Jonson. Arguably, however, authors primarily write, and it is therefore extraordinarily significant that the first title page to attribute the writing of a play to Shakespeare belongs to a play which appears after its prequel, *1 Henry IV*, had recently embroiled our playwright in something of a political – and perhaps religious – scandal. In some limited sense, then, this title page provides evidence for Foucault's claim that, "[t]exts, books, and discourses really began to have authors (other than mythical, 'sacralized' and 'sacralizing' figures) to the extent that authors became subject to punishment, that is, to the extent that discourses could be transgressive."[30] Having presumably selected Sir John Oldcastle as the signifier for a fat rogue knight in an earlier (non-extant performance text) version of *Henry IV*, Shakespeare was compelled to give the character an alternative name in a subsequent printed version of the play. The alteration seems to have been chiefly motivated by the fact that Sir John Oldcastle was the name of a proto-Protestant martyr and an ancestor, by marriage to Elizabeth Brooke, of William Brooke, the seventh Baron Cobham and Lord Chamberlain from August of 1596 until his death in March of 1597.[31] Two years later, the title page of the collaborative *Oldcastle* play would do its best to set the public record straight on the knight's pedigree by announcing that it housed "The first part / Of the true and hono- / rable historie, of the life of Sir / *John Old-castle, the good* / Lord Cobham" (A1r). By then, however, it was too late for Shakespeare who, in the formative years of his development as a playwright, had put his writing hand into the stove of religio-political engagement and got it burnt.

Whether Shakespeare intended to travesty the house of Cobham or indifferently went with the name of the Lollard thorn in Henry V's side because it was already in his major source text, *The Famous Victories of Henry V*, has been the subject of much critical debate, especially since the recent critical controversy over restoring Oldcastle to the text of *1 Henry IV*.[32] For now, however, I think it is important to try to see the restoration debate in the strictly material terms of Shakespeare's career in print. Viewed from this perspective, it seems extremely significant that the Oldcastle/Falstaff problem, which has generated a number of critical questions that go to the heart of authorial intention, is so closely linked to Shakespeare's typographic emergence as an author. If the issue of intentionality has always been foundational to the entire range of questions that can be asked of authorship and individuality, and if the Oldcastle/Falstaff crisis represents the first instance in Shakespeare's career as a published playwright that something he wrote raised serious questions – then and now – about his intentions, then the printing history of Shakespeare's texts provides us with a remarkable convergence of the material evidence of his status as an author with the metaphysical grounds of authorship itself. And yet this convergence has gone unremarked in the recent critical debate over the authorial/textual fate of the name Oldcastle in *1 Henry IV*, perhaps because, as D. F. McKenzie observes, "[d]ialects of written language – graphic, algebraic, hieroglyphic and, most significantly for our purposes, typographic – have suffered an exclusion from critical debate about the interpretation of texts because they are not speech-related."[33]

As was the case with the spectacular typographic appearance of the playwright's name on the title page that seeks to differentiate "*H I S*" "True Chronicle Historie of the life and / death of King LEAR and his three / daughters" from an earlier play by another dramatist, *1 Henry IV* is also "resolutely dialectical" in its relation to an earlier, anonymously authored *The Famous Victories of Henry V*. Sometime between 1596, when Shakespeare began his remake of the first part of *The Famous Victories of Henry V* for performance as *The History of Henry IV,* and 1598, when a quarto of *Henry IV* was first printed, the character of Sir John Oldcastle became Sir John Falstaff.[34] The 1598 quarto of *Famous Victories*, printed by Thomas Creede, lists "Sir John Oldcastle, alias Jockey" in the Dramatis Personae;[35] the 1598 quarto of *Henry IV* does not. In other words, the textual locus of *1 Henry IV*'s oppositionally constructed identity is precisely the oppositional matter of Oldcastle vs Falstaff, and Shakespeare must have removed the name Oldcastle from a performance text of *1 Henry IV* and put Falstaff in its place in time for the change to be preserved in print.

Just when Shakespeare performed this bit of surgery on a performance text, however, has been the subject of considerable scholarly debate. Based on a number of factors ranging from the spring 1597 composition date of *Merry Wives* to the monopoly Shakespeare's company held on the Christmas performance season at court, Gary Taylor argues that Oldcastle "apparently became 'Falstaff' before *Part One* was performed at Court at some time between 26 December 1596 and 8 February 1596/7."[36] Working from a chronological reconstruction of when Lord Cobham (William Brooke) could have seen – and thus ordered a change in – the "Oldcastle" version of the play before his death on March 5/6, Robert J. Fehrenbach concludes that Brooke must have protested the slur on his family's name "between the Christmas Revels and 24 January, and the performance Cobham saw of *1 Henry IV* had to have been on one of the four days of Christmas."[37] Janet Clare, who recalls A. R.

Humphreys' argument that the name-change was forced upon Shakespeare after both parts of *Henry IV* had been written,[38] logically concludes that the epilogue, which "is indeed over-long and cumbersome," would have been a revision of the original Oldcastle version of *2 Henry IV*'s epilogue.[39]

Although the actual moment when matters of the world forced themselves on the materiality of Shakespeare's text can probably never be recovered, this much seems certain: by the time *2 Henry IV* is published, the question of a character's name has given way to the initial attribution of Shakespeare's named authorship on the play's title page; and the play's epilogue specifically calls attention to the very oppositional construct that pre-empted the newly typographic status of the author's name: "for Olde-castle died Martyre, and this is not the / man" (L1v: 27–28). In other words, Shakespeare's *1 Henry IV* is not an earlier errant version of itself; the earlier version is not *Famous Victories*; and Falstaff is not Oldcastle. Finally, even the "Newly corrected and augmented / By W. Shakespeare" that constitutes the first appearance of the author's name in print underwrites this scene because presumably *1 Henry IV* was newly corrected (and perhaps augmented) to excommunicate Oldcastle from a version of the play before it was printed. In this sense, the publication of the authorially unattributed *Henry IV* quarto, cleansed of all but a punning reference to Oldcastle (2. 2. 40–41) and a metrical irregularity haunted by the three syllables of his name (2. 2. 102), anonymously constitutes Shakespeare's transition from the corrector/augmentor of *Love's Labour's Lost* to the writer of *2 Henry IV*.

More than anything else, this brief two-year segment from the complicated printing history of Shakespeare's texts suggests that the playwright's newly typographic status as an author got forged in the smithy of adversity. Materially, this predicament receives vivid representation in the printed quarto text of *2 Henry IV* which couples the title page's originary attribution of *written* authorship with the final page's notorious epilogue and "our humble Author['s]" (23) attempt to clear up any misunderstandings that may have resulted from an early version of the first installment of *Henry IV*. Within a year or so of having written *Romeo and Juliet*, Shakespeare had learned first-hand what could be in a name. Remarkably, the playwright may have used the term "author" in a self-referential fashion only twice in the entirety of his extant dramatic texts, and both times in a seemingly self-effacing way: first as "our humble Author" in the epilogue to *2 Henry IV*, then as "Our bending Author" who writes "[t]hus farre with rough and all-unable pen" in the epilogue to *Henry V* (F. TLN 3368–3369).[40]

The extant material evidence from the printers of Shakespeare's texts suggests that the dramatist's career in print was more erratic than we might expect of our greatest author. It is possible, therefore, that Pavier's willingness to attribute *Oldcastle* to Shakespeare in 1619 – when an authorized version of Shakespeare's plays was still a twinkling £ sign in the eyes of Heminge and Condell – merely symptomized an emergent authorship that was still *in utero*. On the other hand, given the latent ontological density of authorship that typographically manifests itself in the scene of naming bounded by the publication of *Henry IV*'s two parts, it is equally conceivable that Pavier was counting on the Oldcastle/Falstaff controversy to lend his Shakespearean attribution some weight. Indeed, he may have thought he could get away with passing off a collaboratively authored play as the work of an individual playwright from a rival acting company because he was banking on a potential readership's capacity to relate, conflate, or confuse a play's title with a playwright's scandal over a lord's title. Moreover, the circumstances that rescued the *Oldcastle* play from certain ignominy within the greater body of early modern collaborative playwriting frequently disparaged by critics as "hackwork"[41] have continued sporadically to provide the play with a certain notoriety at a few key junctures in literary history. In keeping with its titular character's destiny as a Protestant martyr, *Oldcastle* has occasionally been resurrected – its most recent major sighting taking place in the past ten years or so.[42]

Compelled to straddle the nominative and the titular, the signifier "Oldcastle" apparently had enough resonance to endure the two decades that separated the initial controversy from a subsequent publishing venture that may have sought to capitalize on it. Assuming that Shakespeare was as important to the Jacobeans as he has become to us, this scenario is perfectly reasonable. Yet, although such an assumption contradicts what we know about Shakespeare's status amongst his contemporaries, there is scattered evidence to suggest that in the world of the theatre, at least, some slippage between the banished name of the Shakespeare character and the title of the Munday–Drayton–Hathway–Wilson collaboration was known to occur. Arguably, the first such mix-up – long noted by scholars – transpired some three years after Lord Chamberlain Brooke's death in the context of what seems to have been a performance of *1 Henry IV* that was staged in London for the visiting Flemish ambassador. In a letter written 8 March 1599/1600 by Rowland Whyte to Sir Robert Sidney, the governor of Flushing, Whyte informs his boss that "[a]ll this weeke the Lords have bene in London, and past away the tyme in feasting and plaies . . . on Thursday afternoon the Lord Chamberlain's players acted before Vereken *Sir John Oldcastle*, to his great contentment."[43] While it is certainly possible that Ambassador

Vereken was being treated to a performance of the Munday–Drayton–Hathway–Wilson collaboration, the following entry in *Henslowe's Diary* complicates the matter considerably:

> Lente vnto John thare the 7 of septemb3 1602
> to geve vnto Thomas dickers for his adicions X^s
> in owld castell the some of . . . .[44]

What this entry makes clear is that as late as 1602, two years after Pavier first published a quarto edition of the play, it was still popular enough for Henslowe to pay yet another collaborator (corrector/augmentor) to make "adicions." Such durability suggests that although *Oldcastle* had enough of an audience to sustain itself on stage three years after it was first performed, Vereken and his party were never part of that audience because the play remained the property of Henslowe's company, the Admiral's Men – not the Lord Chamberlain's players who entertained the ambassador. Since Shakespeare began writing plays for the Chamberlain's players in 1594, most scholars – with the notable exception of Eric Sams who argues that a pirated text of the Munday–Drayton–Hathway–Wilson collaboration could have been performed[45] – believe that Whyte was referring to *1 Henry IV* as *Sir John Oldcastle*.[46] Thus in the mind of at least one of Pavier's contemporaries the name of the Lollard martyr was returned from Shakespearean textual exile long enough to greet a visiting dignitary. Two years later, *The Merry Wives of Windsor* would restore the originary opposition of *2 Henry IV*'s epilogue by rendering the name *Sir John Falstaff* titular.

If, however ambiguously, *1 Henry IV* could be referred to as *Oldcastle*, the reference was also known to move in the other direction. In Nathan Field's 1618 comedy, *Amends for Ladies*, Seldon tells Lord Proudly,

> Good morrow to your Honor, I doe heare
> Your Lordship this faire morning is to fight,
> And for your honour. Did you never see
> The Play, where the fat Knight hight Old-Castle
> Did tell you truly what honor was?[47]

Scholars have never disputed that Seldon is referring to Falstaff's catechizing of honor in Act Five of *1 Henry IV*, perhaps because the reference to the "fat Knight" and the absence of a recognizable referent scene in the Munday–Drayton–Hathway–Wilson collaboration leaves little room for debate. Fifteen years later, a similar conflation of Falstaff's catechism of honor with the name of the fourth Lord Cobham appears in Jane Owen's *An Antidote Against Purgatory*. Recalling "Sir John Oldcastle, being exprobated of his Cowardlynes," Owen goes on to ask "*If through my persuyte of Honour, I shall fortune to loose an Arme,*

78   From Playhouse to Printing House

or a Leg in the wars, can Honour restore to me my lost Arme, or Legge?"⁴⁸ The signifier is the Lollard martyr, the signified is Falstaff's soliliquized response to Prince Hal:

> Well, 'tis no matter; honor pricks
> me on. Yea, but how if honor prick me off when I
> come on? How then? Can honor set to a leg? No. Or
> an arm? No. Or take away the grief of a wound? No.   (V. i. 129–132)

Beyond a kind of shared archetypal memory of an Oldcastle ur-text of *1 Henry IV*, this random group of allusions – and there are a few others⁴⁹–is united in its apparent indifference to the fact that the knight's name had been changed and that there were persons who brought that name-change about. As has often been the case in the theatre, a dramatic character – in this case, one who behaves like Falstaff and goes by Oldcastle – has taken on an extra-performance career and achieved a cultural credit balance that others could draw on.⁵⁰ One aspect of this cultural moment, however, is certain, and no scholar has entered into the Oldcastle/Falstaff debate without first mentioning it: sometime between 1625 and 1636 a Dr. Richard James, the scholarly librarian for Sir Robert Cotton, wrote a dedicatory epistle to Sr. Henry Bourchier which was prefixed to James's own manuscript edition of Thomas Hoccleve's "The legend of and defence of yᵉ Noble knight and Martyr Sir Jhon Oldcastel."⁵¹ Responding to a "young Gentle Ladie['s]" inquiry as to "[h]ow Sir John Falstaffe . . . could be dead in yᵉ Harrie yᵉ fifts time and againe live in yᵉ time of Harrie yᵉ sixt to be banisht for cowardize," James provides her with the following explanation:

That in Shakespeare's first shewe of Harrie yᵉ fift, yᵉ person with which he vndertook to playe a buffone was not Falstaffe, but Sr Jhon Oldcastle, and that offence beinge worthily taken by personages descended from his [title,] as peradventure by manie others allso whoe ought to haue him in honourable memorie, the poet was putt to make an ignorant shifte of abjusing Sr Jhon ~~Falstaffe or~~ Fastolphe, a man not inferior [of] Vertue though not so famous in pietie as the other, whoe gaue witnesse vnto the truth of our reformation with a constant and resolute martyrdom, vnto which he was pursued by the Priests, Bishops, Moncks, and Friers of those dayes.⁵²

All other things being equal – goes the logic of James's sage and avuncular counsel – piety coupled with family in high places win the race. Simply too well connected and pious to spend all of literary eternity as a fat, perspiring "buffone," Oldcastle was rescued by Shakespeare who was compelled to intervene and safeguard's the knight's "resolute martyrdom" by granting Falstaff an anachronistic textual resurrection.

Inadvertently, James managed to stake out an important patch of critical terrain for the future of Shakespeare studies. More significantly,

James's reading is the first extant acknowledgment that the name Oldcastle garnered the status of Shakespeare apocrypha before the play *Oldcastle* did. A quarter of a century before Heminge and Condell removed *1 Sir John Oldcastle* from the authorized published canon of Shakespeare's works by not including it in the 1623 Folio, the name Sir John Oldcastle had already been banished from the printed text of a Shakespeare play. This much, at least, "[w]e all know," according to Taylor, who has undertaken "the recovery and restoration of the original authoritative *logos*"[53] by reinstating the name Sir John Oldcastle to its "original" *performance* text prominence in the *printed* Oxford edition of *1 Henry IV*.[54]

Approximately two years after Oldcastle was hypothetically removed from a performance text of *1 Henry IV*, both names appeared for the first time as the titles of plays: the martyr lent his name to the Munday–Drayton–Hathway–Wilson collaboration; the knight of the garter donated his to the principal part of the title – "A Most pleasant and / excellent conceited Co- / medie, of Syr *Iohn Falstaffe*, and the / merrie Wiues of *Winsor*." (A1r) – that appeared on the title page of the 1602 quarto. According to an oft-repeated anecdote that surfaced for the first time exactly one hundred years later in John Dennis's *The Comical Gallant: or The Amours of Sir John Falstaffe*,[55] the Falstaff play satisfied a command from Elizabeth I for another play about the "base Knight" (*1 H.VI*: IV. 1. 14).[56] Indeed, anecdotal evidence suggests that Falstaff occupied a substantial amount of the queen's attention, for we learn from Nicholas Rowe, the first to produce a critical edition of Shakespeare's plays (1709), that Elizabeth was behind the "ignorant shifte" from Oldcastle to Falstaff as well. After repeating Dennis's theory that Shakespeare wrote another play for Falstaff because Elizabeth wanted the playwright "to shew him in Love," Rowe delivers a theory of his own:

Upon this Occasion it may not be improper to observe, that this Part of Falstaff is said to have been written originally under the Name of Oldcastle; some of that Family being then remaining, the Queen was pleas'd to command him to alter it; upon which he made use of Falstaff.[57]

By dint of his status as Shakespeare's first editor, Rowe's account consigned the scandal of the Oldcastle/Falstaff name-change to the playwright's editorial legacy. Less obvious, however, is this account's contribution to the mythic development of Shakespeare's status as an author.

If we recall the significance of the Oldcastle/Falstaff controversy to the typographic coming-into-being of Shakespeare's authorhood on the title page of *2 Henry IV*, then it almost makes an odd kind of sense that Rowe would attempt to stage a meeting between the bard and the queen on this issue. Writing in the same year that the Statute of Anne, the world's first copyright Act, had placed authorial rights on the juridical map by strictly limiting the term of copyright protection to fourteen years,[58] Rowe would have been hard-pressed to find much legal, political, or institutional support for his project to bolster and enhance the status of Shakespeare's authorship.[59] Yet, he seems to have sidestepped these inadequacies by linking Shakespeare to Elizabeth, by placing the still tremulous figure of the author in a direct encounter with a representative of institutionalized individuality, the monarch.[60] Perhaps Rowe even suspected that the institution of monarchy, having suffered a number of setbacks of late, was poised to be eclipsed by strategies of subjectivity that lie dormant within the paradigm of the author function. Such suspicions would not have been groundless.

Examining the links between "authorship and political systems in Anglo-American culture since the seventeenth century," Jeffrey Masten asserts that, "authorship (that is author/ity at a local, textual level) *does* substitute for absolutist on the larger historical scale . . . textual production seems to move from collective making to individual authorship, while modes of government begin, however, slowly to move from singular authority to more collective action." [61] There is, in fact, some evidence to suggest that authorship and kingship were set to cross ascending and descending paths, respectively, at precisely the moment in which Rowe was preparing Shakespeare for his annotated authorial star turn. In 1694, the Licensing Act of 1637 that had augmented the English government's control over censorship was allowed to lapse, largely because it had become a restraint on trade.[62] Whatever legal foundation stationers had formerly relied upon to protect their interests lapsed with it. No longer required to register their publications, printers seem to have come into their own as unrestricted venture capitalists in the same year that the Bank of England was founded.[63] By 1694, kings and printers had been working at an uneasy co-existence for nearly 200 years, so it stands to reason that the year's print-related developments – and their subsequent effect on the legal status of authorship some fifteen years later – were somehow associated with contemporary fluctuations in the institution of monarchy.[64]

Within close proximity of Rowe – in the case of Dennis (1702) – and subsequently with Rowe himself, Falstaff's fate – first as a lover, then as a stand-in for Oldcastle – is anecdotally decided between Queen Elizabeth and Shakespeare. No such direct encounter between monarch and author is envisioned by the publishers/compilers of the 1623 Folio who

Sir John Oldcastle 81

only deferentially and humbly presume to remind William, the Earl of Pembroke, and Phillip, the Earl of Montgomery, that once upon a time they had "*beene pleas'd to thinke these trifles some-thing*" and had "*prosequuted both them, and their Authour liuing, with so much fauour*" (A2r: 10–12). Working as they are in the evening of absolutist rule under James I, it doesn't even occur to Heminge and Condell to refer to the monarch at all except in the course of delineating Pembroke's title as "Lord Chamberlaine to the / *Kings most Excellent Maiesty*." Nor for that matter does Richard James, the learned correspondent whom Taylor characterizes as "our key witness for the intervention of the Cobhams,"[65] seem inclined to link Shakespeare to the monarchy. If we accept Taylor's carefully argued conclusion that "MS James 35 probably dates from late 1634 or early 1635,"[66] then some twelve years after the First Folio authorized Shakespeare and two years before the Star Chamber decree of 1637 sought to re-authorize Charles I, James opts for a passive construction: "the poet was putt to make an ignorant shifte of abjusing Sr Jhon." Only "the poet" and "Sr Jhon" get singled out in James's account where, in place of William Brooke as the offended party, we find a collective consisting of "personages descended from his [title]" and "manie others allso whoe ought to haue him in honourable memorie." Presumably, the "manie others" are right-minded Protestants who have remained mindful of the earlier Lord Cobham's "constant and resolute martyrdom."

Although James begins with a reference to "Shakespeare's first shewe of Harrie ye fift," the reality principle has already been introduced by way of the "young Gentle Ladie" who seeks his assistance. Puzzled that Falstaffe "could be dead in ye Harrie ye fifts time and againe live in ye time of Harrie ye sixt," she locates the enigma of the fat knight's textual existence in the historical context of two kings' successive reigns.[67] The missing piece of the puzzle is certainly her ignorance of a shift in the name of a character, but it is her unwillingness to suspend her belief in the order of things for the sake of the poet's artful construction that enables history to invade a history play. Having stumbled upon a tear in Shakespeare's text, the Gentle Ladie refuses to patch it up. In the resulting gap, a space is opened up for an author to trade places with a martyr in being admonished by a monarch.

Whether James's reluctance to make Elizabeth the agent of Oldcastle's displacement from *1 Henry IV* indicates that no such royal directive was ever issued will probably always remain a matter of speculation. There is, however, no precedent for his reluctance in the published accounts of Oldcastle's martyrdom that circulated in post-Reformation England. On the contrary, treatments of royal agency in the life and death of the Lollard martyr are perhaps best characterized in the *Oldcastle* play by a judge who remarks of the knight's adherence to Wycliffe's doctrine, "This case concernes the Kings prerogative / And's dangerous to the state and common wealth" (A4v). It must have been just this prerogative that motivated a newly crowned Henry V to summon Oldcastle to Kensington in the summer of 1413. Upon his arrival, the king read to him aloud "the more appalling passages"[68] from a few unbound quires of heretical writings that had been confiscated from a limner's shop in Paternoster Row and were said to be the Lord Cobham's property.[69] The basic plot elements for the subsequent drama of Shakespeare's authorship are already in place: an unpublished manuscript and a summons to its alleged proprietor from an annoyed monarch.

Among those chroniclers who were contemporaries of Oldcastle,[70] the knight was commonly viewed as "[a] strong man in bataile . . . but a grete heretik, and a gret enemye to the Cherch," as Capgrave puts it.[71] A century later, writers began to raise the specter of Oldcastle's execution to exploit what G. R. Elton characterizes as "at least a superficial resemblance"[72] between the remnants of Lollardy and the initial efforts by England to part ways with the Roman Catholic church. The first to recognize Oldcastle's potential for a history of English Protestantism was William Tyndale, who re-interpreted the Lollard's excommunication for heresy as an act of unjust persecution and published this reading as a brief appendix to the *Book of Thorpe*, an account of another fifteenth-century Lollard first printed in 1530. Responding quickly in his *Dialogue Concerning Tyndale*, Sir Thomas More made himself perfectly clear that when "the Lorde Cobham [was] taken in Wales and burned in London"[73] it was fire well utilized. Yet it was precisely "thys terrible kynde of death with galowes, chaines, and fyre,"[74] in John Bale's phrase, that made the greatest impression on the architects of English Protestantism who were searching for the basement and first few stories of an edifice begun in mid-air.[75] Writing in 1544, Bale gathered together and reshaped much of the chronicle material on the Oldcastle controversy into a form that later would be incorporated directly into John Foxe's *Acts and Monuments*. Nevertheless, the initial result of Bale's efforts was a substantive achievement in its own right, numbering some 112 pages and tracing its lineage directly to "a certen brefe examinacyon of the sayd Lorde Cobham" which "the true servaunt of God Willyam Tyndale put into the prent" (4r). While the main elements of Bale's account concern the church's persecution, its subsequent effort to minimize sympathy for Oldcastle's death, the betrayal of Lord Powis, and finally the knight's martyrdom, he also attends to oft-chronicled events such as the potential confrontation in St. Giles's field between the king and several of Oldcastle's fellow heretics who are rumored to be gathered there for the sake of subverting the commonwealth. But it is on the subject of a meeting between a lord and his king that Bale's Oldcastle begins to stray from the well-beaten path of the chroniclers.

Whereas previous accounts only mention the initial session in Kensington, Bale provides Henry V with two opportunities to set the errant knight straight on matters of church and state. Being "a manne of great byrthe and in faver at that tyme with the kynge" (13r), Lord Cobham is summoned to Kensington after the king has "gentyliye harde those bloud thurstye" (13r) complaints against him by "these hygh Prelates with theyr pharysees and Scrybes" (12v). No mention is made of the "certain erroneous bills" that earned the knight a hearing in the chronicles. When Oldcastle arrives, the king "call[s] him secretlye, admonyshyng him betwixt him and him / to submyt himselfe to his mother the holye churche / and, as an obedyent chyld, to acknowledge himselfe culpable" (14v). Up to this point, Bale has followed the basic outline of his chronicle sources. Then he quickly veers off the well-chronicled path. Gone are the confiscated unbound quires of heretical writings read aloud by Henry, and in their place Bale gives Oldcastle the chance to voice his dangerous religious leanings directly to the king. "Unto you next my eternall lyuyinge God," he assures Henry, "owe I my whole obedience / and submyt me thereunto . . . But as touchynng the Pope and his spiritualite /trulye I owe thē neyther sute nor servyce / for so moche as I knowe him by the scriptures to be the great Antichrist / the sonne of perdiciyon / the open adversarye of God and the abhominacyon standynge in the holye place" (14v). Having shifted the material grounds of Oldcastle's Lollardy from writings alleged to be his property to a transcription of the beliefs he himself voices, from *graphie* to *logos*, Bale has rather shrewdly upgraded a fifteenth-century heresy to the core doctrine of post-Reformation religious/nationalist propaganda under Henry VIII and later Elizabeth – a doctrine which he himself had helped to shape in plays like *King Johan*.[76]

Nevertheless, as often happens with such repressions, the *graphie* stages a return. By the second meeting with Henry V, Oldcastle has become something of an author, having written down in the interim an extended version of what he told the king during their first session. Bale gives it a centered title at the top of 16r, "**The Christen Beleue of** / the lorde Cobham," and even narrates the conditions of its authorship. With the "furye of Antichrist thus kyndled agaynst him" and other "deadlye danngers" facing him "on everye syde," Bale tells us that Oldcastle "toke paper and penne in hande and so wrote a Christen confessyen or reckenyng of his fayth (which foloweth here after) and both signed and sealed it with his owne han-de" (16v).[77] Hoping to bring together writing hand and royal hand, Oldcastle "toke the copye with him / and went therwith to the kynge trusting to fynde mercye and faver at his hande" (16v). Consistent with the early stages of authorhood, initially "the kynge wolde in no case receyue yt." Subsequently, however, Henry summons the writer into his privy chamber, and this time he reads:

And hauyng his appele the-re at hande redye written / he shewed yt with all reverence to the kynge. Where-with the kynge was than moche more dyspleased than afore / and sayd angrily unto him / that he shuld not pursue his appele. But rather he shuld tarrye in holde, tyll soche tyme as yt were of the Pope allowed. (20v)

Ultimately then, the monarch is always compelled to peruse a set of heretical writings linked somehow to Oldcastle. However, in the gap that separates the historical Lord Cobham of the chronicles from the proto-Protestant figure of Bale's *Brefe Chronycle,* those writings have undergone a significant alteration in their authorial status from confiscated property attributed to an alleged Lollard to the self-authored, self-presented work of a proto-Protestant martyr. Whereas the former gets the knight an audience with the king, the latter lands him "in holde" at the Tower of London; and this significant departure from the chronicle story-line is consistent with Bale's larger concern to make sure over the course of two meetings with Henry that proper name is linked to intellectual property, that Oldcastle own his heresies in the presence of the monarch. As a narrative trope, the king's direct admonishment and censure of Oldcastle plays a profoundly important role in Bale's effort to fashion a posthumous career for the knight as a martyr for the Protestant cause so as to give England, as Kastan observes about Foxe's Oldcastle, "the saving remnant on which the godly nation is built."[78] In other words, as one of God's elect, Oldcastle is being prepared by Bale to stand "foremost on the list of English reformers and Protestant martyrs"[79] for the elect nation.

First published in English two decades after Bale's account, the version of events included in Foxe's *Acts and Monuments*[80] puts Oldcastle and his religious beliefs at center stage and casts the monarch as a supporting character in the plot trajectory that leads to the knight's denouement in St. Giles's field.[81] If, as Collinson asserts, "John Foxe believed Elizabeth to be a second Constantine, the inaugurator of the last, peaceful age of the Church,"[82] Foxe seems to have been less impressed with Henry V. The role he crafts for the king – hard upon the demise of the Marian government – is that of an ineffectual ruler manipulated by the clergy and dogma of the Catholic Church into going against "the moste noble knyght sir John Oldcastell the Lord Cobham" for being "a mighty maintey-ner of suspected preachers in the dioceses of

Lo~-don, Rochester, and Derforde" (261). It is not a flattering part for a king to play, but it may have enabled Foxe to begin to address the well-chronicled fact that Oldcastle had a problem with royal authority. As such, the dilemma for Foxe must have been all too clear: having opted to follow in Bale's footsteps and retain Oldcastle as the type of the Protestant martyr, he also had to face the fact that the knight's involvement in treasonous activities against Henry V made him, in Kastan's apt phrase, "an uncomfortable hero of the Protestant nation."[83]

Foxe's solution is two-fold. First he undermines the notion of treason itself by suggesting that the king's position in the realm had essentially been usurped by a corrupt church. Referring to the clergy's efforts to turn the king against Lord Cobham, Foxe observes that "this was [the church's] policye to couple the kinges authoritye with that they had done in their former councel of craft, and so to make it therby the stronger" (275). Then, over the course of two decades and four editions of the *Acts*, Foxe essentially places Oldcastle's participation in the St. Giles's field rebellion under erasure by attacking the credibility of the chroniclers who reported it. The first rehearsal for this disappearing act is staged in the 1563 edition, which subtly makes the church the target of the rebellion:

syr Roger Acton Knight, master John Browne esquire, syr John Beverlay a learned preacher, and divers other more [were] atta-ched for quarrelling with certain priests, and so imprisoned . . . The complaint was made unto the king of them that they had made a great assemblie in S. Giles field at London (275).

Having reported these events as they appear in the chronicles, Foxe then goes after the chroniclers:

All this hath Thomas Walden in divers of his workes, whiche was at the same tyme a whight or Carmelite frier, and the kynges confessor, and partly it is toucheth both by Robert Fabian, and by Polidorius Virgilius in theyr English chronicles, but not in all poyn-tes rightli as is to be sene in our stories afore toucheth (275).

By the 1583 edition,[84] however, this gentle critique has grown into a whole new segment devoted to "A defence of the Lord Cobham against Nich. Harpfield, set out under the name of Alanus Copus" (568). Where Copus reports – in Foxe's paraphrase – that "after (saith he) the Lord Cobham was escaped out of the Tower, his fellowes and confederates convented themselves together, seditiousli against the King and against their countrye," Foxe sneeringly responds, "[a] marvelous matter that such a great multitude of 20,000 specified in storie, should rise against the King, and yet but three persons onlie known and named" (569). In fact, so convinced is Foxe that he has found the thread which, if yanked hard enough, can unravel the fabric of lies that constitute Oldcastle's involvement in treason, that he gives it another tug a page later when he marvels how "of all this twentye thousand aforesaid, never a mans name known, but onlie three, to wit, syr Roger Acton, syr John Browne, and Joh[n] Beverlay, a preacher" (570).

In this vision of the past, the king's problems with Oldcastle are really his problems with the papist church. For this reason, perhaps, Foxe gets the knight and the king together for their first meeting early on in the twenty-page section he devotes to Oldcastle's story; and his account of both meetings (261–262 and 264) is taken verbatim from Bale. Indeed, the only change Foxe makes in Bale's version is to typographically enhance the status of Oldcastle's authorial debut. We recall that Bale's printer breaks up the typographic flow of the narrative momentarily at the beginning of Oldcastle's written confession to give it a centered title of its own. At its conclusion, however, the text of the confession flows directly into the account of the second meeting with Henry. The only indication that the narrative has shifted from Oldcastle's written text back to the text that enframes it comes in a single sentence that reminds the reader of the confession's author and indicates its intended audience: "This brefe confessyon of his fayth / the Lorde Cobham wrote (as is mency-ned afore) and so toke yt with him to the court / offerynge yt with all mekensse unto the kynge to reade yt over" (19v–19r). Alternatively, Foxe's printer sets off the title and text of Oldcastle's confession at its beginning (263) and at its end (264), and he sets the body of the text in a smaller italic font. As a text within a text within yet another text, the excess of typographic distinction accorded Oldcastle's writing not only accentuates his status as an author, but also inadvertently calls attention to the fact that the authorship of the frame text written by Bale has been silently incorporated into Foxe's. Furthermore, it is extremely significant that the only other segment of Foxe's account which gets set in the same italic font is another text within a text, this time an equally set-off subsection attributed to Archbishop Arundel and entitled, "**The Diffinitiue sentence of /** his condemnation."

The identical typographic distinction accorded Oldcastle's confession and condemnation strongly suggests that Foxe and his printer have relied on the press to enhance Bale's earlier effort to dislodge Oldcastle's martyrdom from the realm of the *logos* and relocate it under the sign of *graphie*. Bale's account revises the story of Oldcastle's death from chronicle versions in which confiscated heretical writings lead to a confession, and that confession leads ultimately to the gallows, to a version in which a confession leads to a self-authored text, and that text leads ultimately to the gallows. Foxe takes the next logical step by

Sir John Oldcastle   87

marshaling the materiality of the printed text to establish a direct typographic link between Oldcastle's authorship and his martyrdom.[85] As a kind of proto-grammatologist, Foxe relies on the printing press to enable what Foucault terms "an insurrection of subjugated knowledge."[86] Indeed, Foxe himself seems to be quite conscious of this insurrection when he writes, "[h]ereby tongues are known, knowledge groweth, judgement increaseth, books are dispersed, the Scripture is read, stories be opened, times compared, truth discerned, falsehood corrected . . . all (as I said) through the benefit of printing."[87]

By the time Raphael Holinshed turns his attention to Oldcastle, it is nearly half a century after the Act against Appeals to Rome (1533), and the primary concern of his brief and fragmented account – spread out over some twenty-five pages devoted to the reign of Henry V – is to situate the Lord Cobham and "all his deuises"[88] within the complex dealings that are needed to maintain a delicate balance between the crown's authority and the church's. Nevertheless, Bale and Foxe seem to have been so successful at instantiating their version of the wayward knight that when Holinshed addresses the topic of the meeting between lord and king, only the grammatological trajectory of their narrative reconstruction remains:

> And after this, [Henry] himselfe sent for hym, and right earnestly exhorted him, and louingly admonished him to reconcile himselfe to God, and to his lawes. The lord Cobham not onely thanked him of his most fauuorable clemencie, but also declared first to him by mouth, and afterwards by writing, the foundation of his faith, and the grounde of his beliefe, affirming his grace to be his supreme head, and competent iudge . . . The King understanding and persuaded by his Counsell, that by order of the lawes of his Realme, such accusations touchyng matters of faith, ought to be tried by the spirituall Prelates, sent him to the Tower of London, there to abide the determination of the Cleargie.   (1166: 1–10, 13–18)[89]

No doubt the reference to Henry V as "supreme head" must have reminded at least a few readers of the fact that Elizabeth had been compelled to make do two decades earlier with the title of "Supreme Governor."[90] But if Holinshed is willing to toe the Bale/Foxe story-line that runs from speech to writing to Tower, he is also unwilling to completely abandon the frequently chronicled element of confiscated heretical materials. Faced with the task of reconciling two disparate traditions, he merely shifts the confiscation scene – from its original place as the impetus for summoning Oldcastle to Kensington – to a later point in the narrative after the knight has already escaped the Tower:

> In the same place were found bookes written in english; & some of those bokes in times past had bin trim- ly gilte, & limned, beautified with Images, the heads wherof had bin scraped off, & in ye Litany, they had blotted forthe the name of our Lady, & of other saints, til they came to ye verse *payce no- bis Domine*. Diuers writings were founde there also, in derogation of suche honour as then was thought due to our Lady. (1189: 8–17).[91]

No longer unbound quires, Holinshed renders the evidence with the eye of a bibliophile. And while the heretical books "so disfigured with scrapings & / blotting out" (18–19) are still sent to the king, this time they are passed along directly to the Archbishop Arundel "to shewe the same in his ser- / mons at Paules crosse in Londo~" (21–22). No appalling passages are read nor confessions heard because Oldcastle – already a fugitive from the law – is unable to make an appearance in the king's privy chambers.

Despite a number of important variables, what remains constant in all of these accounts of the meeting between Henry V and Lord Cobham is that as individuals, each figure is compelled at some point to speak for and represent a larger collective body. For the pre-Reformation version of the king, that body is the realm and the Roman Catholic church to which it has pledged its allegiance. For the post-Reformation Henry, it is an evil and corrupt papist clergy that has turned him into a kind of ventriloquist's dummy whose authority over the realm is essentially limited to mouthing church policy. Alternatively, Oldcastle begins his career in the chronicles as the most notorious member of a shadowy assemblage of heretics who mutilate books and read in English; but with the guidance and encouragement of the post-Reformation writers, he comes to find his own, individualized authorial voice, and in doing so speaks and writes for the elect Protestant nation heralding the renais- sance of the primitive church. The key determinant in all of these transformations seems to be the particular collective or community with which a given writer identifies.

It is likely that a comparable sense of community motivated Richard James to attribute the agency behind the Oldcastle/Falstaff name change to sanguinal descendants of the house of Cobham and spiritual descen- dants of a prominent Protestant martyr. Yet James's reluctance to single out, for example, Lord Chamberlain William Brooke or Queen Elizabeth as the agent of this emendation is already a nostalgic gesture, because once Shakespeare has written a version of *Henry IV* with Sir John Oldcastle in the Dramatis Personae, the legendary figure is essentially compelled to go it alone.

As the next substantive treatment of Oldcastle's life and death after Foxe's,[92] the Munday–Drayton–Hathway–Wilson collaboration takes most of its cues not from an identification with a given community, but from an individual playwright named Shakespeare. In the same way that Shakespeare's *King Lear* is resolutely dialectical with an earlier anonymous version, Munday, Drayton, Hathway, and Wilson's play constructs its identity and the identity of its eponymous hero throughout as a dialectic of genitives: our *Oldcastle*/Oldcastle vs Shakespeare's. Indeed, this oppositional construction is already under way in the prologue when the reader is informed:

> It is no pampered glutton we present,
> Nor aged Councellor to youthfull sinne.
> But one, whose vertue shone above the rest,
> A valiant Martyr, and a vertuous peere.   (A2r)

Here, it seems that prologue has followed hard upon epilogue, because the diction and sequence of these lines mirror and invert the disclaimer at the end of *2 Henry IV*. Whereas Shakespeare maintains that "Oldcastle died a martyr, and this is not [Tyndale, Bale, and Foxe's] man," Munday *et al.* respond by insisting that this is not Shakespeare's man because Oldcastle was a martyr. Moreover, in a profoundly proto-Hegelian sense, this non-Shakespearean "one, whose vertue shone above the rest," is already rehearsing the singularity that will come to characterize Shakespeare's status as an author.

Singling out the Munday–Drayton–Hathway–Wilson collaboration as "a key document in any effort to see how the history play in this period changed and yet stayed the same," G. K. Hunter observes that "of the several (two-part) history plays that Henslowe's team produced in 1598–99 . . . [*Oldcastle*] is the one that seems to bear the most direct and specific relationship to its Shakespearean predecessor."[93] In Hunter's view, this close relationship is significant because it "show[s] us how far Shakespeare provided a starting point for the new-style history plays of the seventeenth century."[94] Accordingly, the two parts of *Henry IV* represent a "turning point in the history of a genre,"[95] and Hunter not only locates a major shift in the generic history of the history play precisely "in the contrast between two transitional plays, *Henry IV* and *Oldcastle*,"[96] but also attributes the agency behind that shift to Shakespeare. Certainly Hunter gives Shakespeare more credit than an individual author working in the highly collaborative environment of the early modern stage probably deserves, but it is nonetheless significant that he finds the playwright innovating precisely at the point that his authorship is established typographically. Half a century after Bale's Oldcastle is given the opportunity to express his proto-Protestant beliefs, the historical figure finds himself mixed up in the emergence of Shakespeare's dramatic authorship in print. The transition glimpsed here from one author's confession to another's apology, from one innovator's controversial beliefs to another's controversy, corresponds closely to the parallel between Foxe's reliance on typography to link Oldcastle's written confession to his martyrdom and the typographic debut of Shakespeare as a writer on the title page of *2 Henry IV*.

Given the extraordinary ontological density of authorship generated from within the oppositional identity of *1 Henry IV* and *1 Sir John Oldcastle*, it is perhaps not surprising that the latter is more directly and specifically preoccupied with Shakespeare than any other history play by Henslowe's team of collaborators. Hunter inevitably stumbles on to this scene of individuation when he attempts to describe the main generic difference which for him so powerfully constitutes the contrasting relationship between Shakespeare's *Henry IV* plays and the Munday–Drayton–Hathway–Wilson collaboration. While Shakespeare's two plays are representative of historical drama which, according to Hunter, "defines the nation (implicitly) as a politico-military entity centered on the court," the collaboratively authored *Sir John Oldcastle* exemplifies "a historical drama that presents national consciousness as much more a matter of individual self awareness."[97] In other words, an individual author produces a drama of collective national consciousness, but a collective of authors responding to that author produce a drama of individual national self-consciousness. Furthermore, having located the beginnings of the new history play in precisely the same oppositional interstice where Shakespeare's authorship typographically appears, Hunter also retraces the complexly dialectical circumstances that seem to have prompted that appearance in the first place by selecting *Oldcastle* as the more individuated of the two dramas. What Hunter's analysis does not register, however, is the extent to which the character of Oldcastle in the Henslowe collaboration embodies this "individual self-awareness," especially in the play's version of the two meetings between the king and Lord Cobham.

A stage direction preceding the first meeting has "Old-castle kneeling to the king" (D2v) as Henry, the Earl of Suffolk, and a butler enter the king's chambers. Here the potential of the theatre to bring to life details

Sir John Oldcastle 91

that remain latent in the martyrological accounts seems to be realized; yet the moment Lord Cobham opens his mouth those accounts begin to speak to many in the audience who could not have read them. Informed by the king that, "[t]he Bishops find themselves much iniured" by his "grosse opinion" (D2v), Oldcastle's response comes from Bale via Foxe. Henry is assured that next to God, the knight owes his life to him. The "Pope of Rome" and his "shaveling priests," on the other hand, deserve nothing, and Oldcastle will not be convinced otherwise unless scripture can supply proof. Thus Munday and collaborators faithfully reproduce – in miniature – the spoken confession of a proto-Protestant's belief, a confession that seems to have been the *raison d'être* of the first meeting with the king for post-Reformation writers. But then something odd happens. Having briefly made his religious position clear and assured Henry of his loyalty, Oldcastle jumps the gun and introduces a written document one meeting ahead of the schedule initially determined by Bale. Asked what he is holding in his hand, the resulting conversation between king and lord provides the next phase of the grammatological trajectory that first becomes traceable in Bale's pioneering account:

> *Cob.* A deed of clemencie,
> Your Highnesse pardon for Lord Powesse life,
> Which I did beg, and you my noble Lord,
> Of gracious favour did vouchsafe to grant.
>   *Har.* But yet it is not signed with our hand.
>   *Cob.* Not yet my Liege   *one ready with pen*
>   *Har.* The fact, you say, was done   *and incke.*
> Not of prepensed malice,but by chance.
>   *Cob.* Vpon mine honor so, no otherwise.
>   *Har.* There is his pardon, bid him make amends,   *writes.*
> And cleanse his soule to god for his offence
> What we remit, is but the bodies scourge,   *Enter Bishop.*
> How now Lord Bishop.   (D3r)

Petitioning Henry on behalf of Lord Powis not only rehearses the act of clemency that Oldcastle himself will ultimately require of the king, but also enables Henslowe's team to foreshadow the fact, made much of by Bale and Foxe, that Lord Powis was the figure in the chronicles who assisted church authorities in capturing Oldcastle after he had escaped from the Tower and bringing him to his execution. No honor among Lollard lords, the trade-off being set up here is a pardon for a betrayal. Nevertheless, the stage business carried out in the margins of this exchange tells another tale – first glimpsed in Bale, then typographically enhanced by Foxe – in which authorship is linked to martyrdom.[98] A lot of ground has been covered since Capgrave's Henry read aloud appalling passages from confiscated unbound quires of anonymously authored heretical writings. Now Henry "*writes*" his own name on an official document just as "*one ready with pen and incke*" gives way to the entrance of a Bishop who accuses Oldcastle of being "this heretike, / This Jew, this Traitor to your maiestie" who has "our decrees most shamefully prophande" (D3v).[99] At the very moment Henry's signature gets one wayward soul off the hook, the Bishop of Rochester arrives carrying the seeds of another's undoing in his mouth. Here the monarch writes, while Oldcastle stands by and watches as Henry dismantles the Bishop's story of a messenger forced by the knight's supporters to "eate / The written processe, parchment, seale and all" because he lacks material proof that the episode took place. Indeed, the story is itself precisely one of absent material evidence. Confiscation has given way to consumption, but Oldcastle has learned an important lesson.

By the second meeting, the Bishop of Rochester is back with an unconsumed "precept" (G2v) for Oldcastle's arrest, and the knight stands before the king accused of treason. The issue that so vexed Foxe's desire to reconcile Oldcastle's Henrician past with his own Elizabethan present is now at center stage, but conspicuously absent is the matter – first introduced by Bale – of the "brefe confessyon of his fayth / [that] the Lorde Cobham wrote . . . and so toke yt with him to the court / offerynge yt with all mekensse unto the kynge to reade yt over." In its place is a document, "severally subscribed" (G3v) by the hands of three conspirators (the Earl of Cambridge, Lord Scroop, and Sir Thomas Gray), that Oldcastle has obtained for the purpose of turning it over to Henry. Consisting of an appalling "platforme" which, in the king's own incredulous reading, entails "bribes from Charles of France, either to winne / My Crowne from me, or secretly contriue / My death by treason?" (G3v), this single document does for Oldcastle in the world of theatre what Foxe could not do for him in the twenty folio pages of the 1583 edition devoted to "A defence of the Lord Cobham, agaynst Nich Harpsfield" – it exonerates him from a long and well-chronicled historical legacy of treason.

If, as recently as Holinshed, the main subject of the two meetings with Henry – the first "by mouth, and afterwards by writing" – had been "the foun- / dation of [Oldcastle's] faith, and the grounde of his beliefe," then the agenda for England's great martyr in the final years of Elizabethan rule has undergone a substantial transformation. The itinerary proposed by the Munday–Drayton–Hathway–Wilson collaboration progresses from a written and signed pardon for one disloyal subject to a written and self-signed blueprint for sedition from three others. In the process, the principal tenets of Oldcastle's proto-Protestant faith get marginalized in order to make more room for recovering his status as a subject who is loyal to his king. Whereas Foxe lets Oldcastle speak for the Protestant nation first, and then figures out a way to resolve the knight's king problem two decades later, Henslowe's team appears much more eager to subordinate his role as religious spokesman to his individual status as Henry's subject. Matters of faith have given way to matters of state. Both of the meetings in the *Oldcastle* play, as well as the documents which are so prominently submitted during them, not only shift the focus of attention from Cobham's alleged heretical beliefs to his relationship with Henry but also show the king in a position of strength rarely seen in post-Reformation accounts of Oldcastle's martyrdom. Consequently, the task of remembering Oldcastle's problems with orthodox church doctrine ultimately falls upon the hagiographic figure of John Weever's poem.[100] On his way to the second meeting with Henry, Weever's Oldcastle recalls how

> At last (thus tossed) I writ my faith's confession
> Unto the four chief articles answered;
> Of penance, shrift, saints, transubstantiation,
> Which 'gainst me all by *Arundel* were laid.   (992–995)

Some forty years after the Elizabethan settlement, Munday and collaborators are more than willing to grant the monarch an agency that Foxe's post-Marian account could not accommodate – especially if Oldcastle's vehement anti-papist beliefs were to give him spiritual superiority over a king who had not parted ways with the Catholic church. *Oldcastle*'s Henry is still manipulated, in this case by the Bishop of Rochester whose grudge against the Lollard troublemaker seems to be more personal than religious, but the king often gets the last word. Thus when Henry gives the Bishop a commission "To search, attach, imprison, and condemne, / This most notorious traitor as you please," Rochester first bows to the king's power, "It shall be done, my Lord, without delay," then confides in the audience, "So now I hold Lord Cobham in my hand, / That which shall finish thy disdained life" (G3r). The "That which," of course, refers to the king's writ, not the archbishop's or the pope's; the mentality at work here, however, seems to be inspired less by a church official – no matter how evil and papist – concerned with tracking down a heretic than by the motiveless malignancy of a Vice figure or a proto-Iago. Moreover, the encounter occurs before Oldcastle's first meeting with Henry, reflecting the playwrights' efforts to keep the king from turning the knight's fate over to the church once they've met. In Foxe's second meeting, on the other hand, Henry knows he's over his head on religious issues, so Oldcastle is handed over to the proper authorities. In the Henslowe team's version, however, the knight departs being assured by the king that the rebels he has exposed shall "have martial law : but as for thee, / Friend to thy king and country, still be free" (G3v).

With the monarch of the *Oldcastle* play on the mend, it stands to reason that the titular martyr would have suffered some setbacks. On the surface, at least, nothing could be further from the truth. While Foxe and other theologians saw Oldcastle as both saint and martyr, the figure offered by Henslowe's team emphasizes the saint, presumably because Part 2 – of which no extant copies remain[101] – would have focused on his martyrdom. As a result, the knight who provided Bale and Foxe with a conduit for espousing the key doctrines of the newly reformed faith is limited here to embodying the Protestant ideal of the good Christian man. Kind, generous, loyal, and forgiving, the dramatic figure who remains on stage under his own name is nevertheless obviously hobbled by the fact that his once-heretical beliefs have become the state religion, and that the most dramatic part of his religious life – his death – has been postponed by the generic exigencies of the two-part history play. Resembling a stiff imitation of his Savior more than his own historical self,[102] the Oldcastle of the Munday–Drayton–Hathway–Wilson collaboration is also seriously constrained by his humble origins as the negation of *1 Henry IV*'s version. Compelled to be as good as Falstaff is bad, the last dramatic incarnation of England's great martyr doesn't really escape Shakespeare's travesty as much as he exists for it. Perhaps Part 2 of *Oldcastle* managed to rekindle the fires of the nation's religious imagination by gruesomely staging the knight's double execution as graphically depicted in Foxe's woodcut; but the play has no known performance history and probably had already disappeared by 1619. Otherwise, Pavier no doubt would have tried to include it with Part 1 in his collection of Shakespeare quartos.

In short, the English theatre could be rather unkind to one of its own. Despite some well-placed act of intervention that may have got his name removed from *1 Henry IV* as well as the subsequent effort by Henslowe's crew to contain and neutralize an infection that continued to spread under the name of Falstaff, Sir John Oldcastle, Lollard, knight, martyr, and hero to the Protestant nation, never seems to have recovered from the blow dealt to his legacy by Shakespeare. Indeed, Weever's 1601 account, which is the next and last substantive treatment of the fourth Lord Cobham's life and death, begins after Oldcastle is dead and drags the martyr's ghost back from Elysium to be the narrator. One model for Weever's lengthy narrative poem was certainly *The Mirror for Magistrates*, which had gone through a number of editions between its initial printing in 1559 and subsequent additions of 1587.[103] Yet, according to

Honigman, Weever was "a very early admirer of Shakespeare,"[104] and his *Mirror* contains what may have been the first extant allusion to the playwright's *Julius Caesar*.[105] Another of Weever's poems, *The Whipping of the Satyre*, refers to Shakespeare's Falstaff as if the character has already acquired a cultural currency that required no introduction.[106]

Not long after Oldcastle makes it on to the English stage, his legacy winds up impossibly stranded between one of his greatest detractors and one of that detractor's first admirers. Haunted by Shakespeare through most of his brief career in drama, Oldcastle never recovers.[107] Two decades later, even the one extant play that sought to rescue his reputation from the abuse it suffered in an early version of *1 Henry IV* gets reprinted by its original publisher as a play written by Shakespeare. Remarkably, then, not only does the typographic emergence of Shakespeare's authorship on the title page of *2 Henry IV* follow hard upon the controversy that resulted from his alleged use of Oldcastle's name in an unpublished performance text of Part 1, but the decline of Oldcastle's fortunes as a founding father of the godly English nation also seems to coincide precisely with the debut of the author who, by the first half of the eighteenth century, will come to be promoted – according to Michael Dobson's apt characterization – as "both symbol and exemplar of British national identity."[108] It is tempting, therefore, to see the two *Henry IV* plays and *1 Sir John Oldcastle* as comprising an important transitional space in which Shakespeare's authorship replaces Oldcastle's martyrdom, in which the author-function comes to lodge itself where previously the martyr-function served to individualize and embody England's national consciousness. The representational trajectory of this displacement – ranging from the first post-Reformation accounts that transform Oldcastle into the Protestant nation's great martyr to those editorial and anecdotal accounts of the eighteenth century that transform Shakespeare into a national poet whose authority "exceed[s] the texts from which it supposedly derived"[109] – seems to register and be closely linked to fluctuations in that other individualized embodiment of the nation, the monarch.

I have suggested that the proto-form of Shakespeare's authorship can be glimpsed in Bale's and Foxe's representations of Lord Cobham's meeting with Henry V, and the initial construction of Shakespeare's authorial identity appears to be grounded in the dialectic that characterizes the relation between his version of Oldcastle and the official proto-Protestant-martyr version represented by Bale, Foxe, and the Henslowe collaboration. It follows then that representations of Shakespeare would ultimately incorporate elements from the construction of Oldcastle's martyrological identity. One such element that becomes discernible – just as Shakespeare begins to achieve a level of national importance comparable with Oldcastle's post-Reformation career – is his relationship with the monarch. John Dennis, as noted earlier, is the first to suggest that such a relationship existed, and he indicates that the subject of their brief interaction was the fate of the character who replaced Oldcastle in *1 Henry IV*.[110] In the dedicatory epistle for his 1702 revision of *The Merry Wives of Windsor*, Dennis informs George Grenville,

> I knew very well that [*Merry Wives*] had pleas'd one of the greatest Queens that ever was in the world . . . This comedy was written at her Command, and by her direction, and she was so eager to see it Acted, that she commanded it to be finished in fourteen days; and was afterwards, as Tradition tells us, very well pleas'd at the Representation.[111]

One century after *Merry Wives* is first published in quarto, the conception and production of at least one Shakespeare play has already become the subject of a tradition in which Elizabeth's status as "one of the greatest Queens that ever was in the world" not only recalls Oldcastle's standing as "one, whose vertue shone above the rest," but also anticipates Shakespeare's promotion to the position of national poet and "patron of bourgeois morality" from the 1730s onward.[112]

Inadvertently cast as a place-holder at the changing of the guard from a faded martyr to a shining author, the selection of Elizabeth as executor of Falstaff's destiny must be seen as a nostalgic response to a moment, late in the seventeenth century, when the monarchy as an institution was being dismantled by "ideologues of compromise"[113] in search of a pragmatic middle ground between royalists and parliamentarians. No doubt Portia's assertion that "A substitute shines brightly as a King / Until a king be by"[114] was always something of a fantasy, but by the end of the seventeenth century the fantasy – dislodged from the remaining elements of its official reality – had given way to an illusion. Nearly ready to emerge as England's master of illusion, Shakespeare is finally in the perfect position to take instructions from a monarch. Mere chronology, of course, dictates that Elizabeth be the monarch who intervenes on behalf of Falstaff; but it is significant nonetheless that Dennis arranges for a meeting between a figure who is on the verge of becoming "one of the greatest [authors] that ever was in the world" and a queen who, a century after her death, must have represented for him a privileged moment in the life cycle of the monarchy when it could still claim to be grounded in the reality of heredity and dynasty. Indeed, such a meeting underscores the extent to which authorship was poised, in the final years of the seventeenth century, to replace kingship as the paradigm for the individualized embodiment of the national consciousness. How could things have turned out otherwise? The earliest form of copyright, we recall, had been "rights in copies" granted to Freemen of the Stationers' Company by "the Royal Prerogative."[115] It follows, therefore, that when the individualizing potential of copyright protection began to shift from printers to authors, the position of the monarch also began to shift. If, as Hamlet asserts, "the king is a thing," then certainly the king can be some*thing* else.

As the "place-holder of the void," according to the terms of Slavoj Žižek's astute analysis of royal authority, the monarch is compelled to represent the "Master's sublime body" as "a pure 'reflective determination'" which "guarantees and personifies the identity of the State qua rational totality . . ."[116] A sizable crack had already appeared in the mirror of this reflective determination by 1649, and the sudden escalation of editorial and scholarly scrutiny trained on Shakespeare's texts in the first decades of the eighteenth century suggests that as the author was being prepared for the role of national poet, his sublime corpus was being prepared to displace the monarch's sublime body. Thus, Dennis's anecdotal account of Shakespeare and Elizabeth conferring on Falstaff's future marks an important spot in the trajectory of this displacement in much the same way that Bale's version of meetings between Oldcastle and Henry V captures and preserves an early moment in post-Reformation England when a martyr temporarily displaced a monarch as the figure who guarantees and personifies the identity of the Protestant state. Once Oldcastle himself is displaced by Falstaff in Shakespeare's *Henry IV*, only the "qua rational totality" element of Žižek's Hegelian formulation remains, literally embodied in the character's obesity.

If the author's corpus is going to fill in for the monarch's body, that corpus must, of course, be authentic and authoritative. As the first person to produce a scholarly edition of Shakespeare's plays, it is extraordinarily significant that Nicholas Rowe worked back from Falstaff to Oldcastle seven years after the publication of Dennis's dedicatory anecdote. Reiterating his predecessor's "Occasion of [Shakespeare's] Writing *The Merry Wives of Windsor*," Rowe moves directly on to another "Occasion [upon which] it may not be improper to observe, that this Part of Falstaff is said to have been written originally under the name of Oldcastle."[117] Thus Rowe sets himself up to do for Falstaff's textual past what Dennis had already done for the character's textual future: put the strings pulling Shakespeare's writing hand firmly in Elizabeth's hands. But there is more to it than just proffering – for the first time – the specific identity of the figure who stood behind the "ignorant shifte."

In their accounts of Oldcastle, Bale and Foxe had carefully subordinated royal authority to religious authority by placing the martyr in a position – with reference to the Catholic church – that was morally and spiritually superior to the monarch's. Following the lead of *Famous Victories*' anonymous author, Shakespeare essentially restored Henry V to his pre-Reformation position of superiority by reducing Oldcastle to the status of a reprobate, subsequently renamed Falstaff. A rigorous logic seems to be at work, therefore, when Rowe makes the first scholarly move toward preparing Shakespeare to replace the monarch as the nation's individualized embodiment of bourgeois morality: now that Shakespeare is being prepared to be morally superior to the monarch, his characterization of Oldcastle gets called upon to link Shakespeare and Elizabeth. Having set out to do for Shakespeare what Bale and Foxe had done for Oldcastle in their accounts of two meetings between the knight and his king, Rowe introduces a second meeting between the author and his queen in which Oldcastle's martyrdom is salvaged and secured. And while the distance between authorship and martyrdom might seem formidable, Rowe himself narrows the gap shortly after completing his edition of the *Complete Works* when he writes in the prologue to his play, *The Tragedy of Jane Shore* (1714),

> In such an age immortal Shakespeare wrote,
> By no quaint rules nor hampering critics taught
> With rough, majestic force he moved the heart,
> And strength and nature made amends for art.[118]

Although the copyright Act of 1709 had limited the authorial life of a given text to fourteen years, Rowe seems unwilling to let Shakespeare die.

As Shakespeare's first scholarly editor, Rowe must have given himself at least some of the credit for the author's immortality, but it is also true that the Restoration more generally initiated a period in the history of the English stage that was extraordinarily kind to Shakespeare's authorship. Dobson, for example, asserts that "something happened during the century between the 1660's and the 1760's . . . something which indeed had the effect of 'authorizing' Shakespeare . . . of canonizing Shakespeare himself as the paradigmatic figure of literary authority . . ."[119] Whether or not this transformation of Shakespeare's authorial status is linked – as I have suggested – to fluctuations in the status of the monarch, what seems indisputable is that the Restoration did for Shakespeare what the Reformation had done for Oldcastle. Promising from the scaffold that, like Christ, he would rise again on the third day, Oldcastle was compelled to wait more than a hundred years for Tyndale, Bale, and Foxe to resurrect him. Similarly, when Colonel Joseph Hart looks back at what a few key Restoration figures contributed to Shakespeare's career, he also looks to Christ – this time with considerable irony – for a model:

> Then comes the 'resurrection' – on speculation. Betterton the player, and Rowe the writer, make a selection from a promiscuous heap of plays found in a garret, nameless as to authorship . . . 'I want an author for this selection of plays!' said Rowe. 'I have it!' said Betterton; 'call them Shakespeare's!' And Rowe, the 'commentator,' commenced to puff them as 'the bard's,' and to write a history of his hero in which there was scarcely a word that had the foundation of truth to rest upon. [T]is is about the sum and substance of the manner of setting up Shakespeare.[120]

Hart attempts to deflate the puffed authorship that the Restoration bequeathed to Shakespeare, just as Shakespeare stuck a needle in the puffed martyrdom that the Reformation had bestowed upon Oldcastle, by reducing the Lollard to a cartoonish, overweight scoundrel. But what is truly remarkable about the Colonel's effort to expose the "setting up" of the posthumous Shakespeare is the way in which it inadvertently aligns itself with the initial setting up of the posthumous Oldcastle. For the latter figure, it was a pile of unbound quires of heretical writings subsequently attributed to him that had put Lord Cobham on the chronicled path to becoming first a Lollard nuisance, then post-Reformation England's greatest martyr. For Shakespeare, it turns out to be "a promiscuous heap of plays found in a garret, nameless as to authorship" which, subsequently attributed to him by his editors, enables "the bard" to become post-Restoration England's greatest author.

Having shadowed the trajectory of Shakespeare's authorship from its typographic inception on the title page of *2 Henry IV* to its scholarly reconstruction in Rowe's *Complete Works*, and beyond, it should come as no surprise that the 1986 restoration of Oldcastle's name to the text of *1 Henry IV* in the Oxford edition of *The Complete Works* comes hard upon the post-structuralist displacement of the author from its long-secure position as the guarantor and personification of humanist subjectivity.[121] Previously, the construction of Oldcastle as a martyr (the figure who usurped the king's authority to become the exemplar of the Protestant state), had anticipated the construction of Shakespeare as an author (the figure who usurped the king's authority to become the exemplar of the modern bourgeois state); now Oldcastle's return coincides with the dismantling of Shakespeare's literary authority. Kastan has observed that "[t]he restoration of 'Oldcastle' enacts a fantasy of unmediated authorship paradoxically mediated by the Oxford edition itself,"[122] but such mediation, along with its concomitant paradoxical fantasy of unmediation, has always been an essential component of Oldcastle's and Shakespeare's parallel posthumous careers. The former had Bale and Foxe, the latter, Dennis and Rowe; and it remains to be seen in the final pages of this chapter how a recent act of mediation, this time by Wells and Taylor, further enhances the link between martyr and author.[123]

Taylor has argued that when Sir John Oldcastle/Falstaff's final speech (V. 4. 162–166) is "put in the mouth of a fictional character called Falstaff, the words lose their historicity and ambiguity";[124] but his more radical position is that Shakespeare's portrayal of the Protestant martyr as a lying, cheating, thieving, promiscuous scoundrel indicates that the language's greatest author "may have been popishly inclined."[125] If Rowe's pioneering effort to transform Shakespeare into the individualized embodiment of the national consciousness included turning over the responsibility for Oldcastle's removal to "one of the greatest Queens that ever was in the world," Taylor's acceptance of responsibility for Oldcastle's restoration appears at a moment in literary history when, following what Roland Barthes famously referred to as "the Death of the Author," Shakespeare's status as one of the world's greatest authors is being profoundly re-evaluated. Oddly, his Oxford editors seem primarily interested in damage control, and indeed it is a rather nostalgic project that finally announces itself when Taylor concludes his defense of restoring Oldcastle to the text of *1 Henry IV*.[126] "I do not know," writes Taylor, "whether Shakespeare was ever a 'papist,' though I rather suspect it. But I do know that Oldcastle is what Shakespeare wrote; that Oldcastle is what Shakespeare meant; and that Oldcastle is what his contemporaries understood."[127] Being the subject of knowledge about Shakespeare and his audience leads Taylor to believe that he has achieved what he terms "the recovery and restoration of the original authoritative *logos*,"[128] a dubious achievement, perhaps, in the current critical climate. Jonathan Goldberg jumped at the chance to interrogate Taylor's logocentrism;[129] but what seems far more interesting about Taylor's position than his longing for *logos* is the way in which his knowledge of Shakespeare's authorial intentions is linked to his suspicion that Shakespeare was Roman Catholic.

As Taylor himself readily admits, he is not the first person to suspect that Shakespeare was a "papist." That honor probably goes to John Speed. In *The Theatre of the Empire of Great Britaine* (1611), Speed took umbrage with a Jesuit's Falstaffian portrayal of Oldcastle on the grounds that it was Falstaffian, that is taken from "Stage-plaiers" who were connected somehow to "this Papist and his Poet, of like conscience for lies, the one ever faining, and the other ever falsifying the truth."[130] What the Papist and Poet have in common is falsehood, not necessarily religious affiliation; and yet, Catholic writers in Shakespeare's day did ridicule Protestants for celebrating Oldcastle's martyrdom.[131] It is not difficult, therefore, to see why first Speed and then Taylor might try to link Shakespeare's capable trashing of the martyrological figure with, as Taylor puts it, "his willingness to exploit a point of view which many of his contemporaries would have regarded as 'papist.'"[132] Furthermore, as Taylor also notes, there is some documentary evidence that members of Shakespeare's family may have been Catholic. Sams, for example, who maintains that "[t]he young Shakespeare's earliest emotions and experiences were enshrined in the language and teaching of the old Catholic faith,"[133] characterizes John Shakespeare's Spiritual Will and Last Testament as "explicitly Roman Catholic . . . an elaborate profession of faith, not a legal testamentary disposition at all."[134] Similarly, Honigman, who advises us to "brace ourselves, then, for howls of anguish about a Catholic Shakespeare," believes that the playwright "started life as a Catholic and served for a while in the Catholic households of Alexander Hoghton and Sir Thomas Hesketh,"[135] and he quotes from John Shakespeare's Testament in support of his belief.

Taylor credits Honigmann's study – *Shakespeare: The Lost Years* – with providing "new evidence of Shakespeare's early links with recusants in Lancashire."[136] Had Sams's book – *The Real Shakespeare: Retrieving the Early Years, 1564–1594* – been available, Taylor might have referred to it as well. Obviously, neither of these books can provide an air-tight case that Shakespeare practiced the "old faith": Honigmann is compelled to explain away "Shakespeare's anti-papal rhetoric" by advising us that "we must never lose sight of the fact that the poet who described himself in the sonnets was a most unusual man";[137] Sams ultimately falls back on a strained reading of *Hamlet* to endorse his position on John Shakespeare's religion.[138] And yet, both studies indirectly point to a serious difficulty in Taylor's effort to link his restoration of "Oldcastle" to Shakespeare's supposed Catholicism. On the one hand, Taylor "rather suspect[s]" that Shakespeare was a "papist"; on the same hand, Taylor contends that the playwright was willing "to exploit a point of view which many of his contemporaries would have regarded as 'papist.'" But being a "papist" is not, of course, the same thing as exploiting a papist point of view, especially in the world of the theatre. Then there is also the problem of knowing what Shakespeare's contemporaries would have regarded as a papist point of view.[139] In fact, Taylor never does provide any substantive evidence of what Shakespeare's contemporaries would have regarded as papist. Instead, he does what both Sams and Honigmann are ultimately compelled to do – search through the plays for the playwright's religion: "In *Hamlet* Shakespeare exploited the Catholic belief in Purgatory; in *Richard III* he exploited Catholic beliefs about All

Souls' Eve; in both *Twelfth Night* and *Measure for Measure* he mocked the hypocrisy of Puritans."[140] Surely, one didn't have to be "popish" in 1596 to exploit Catholic beliefs or mock Puritans.

In the end, all roads lead back to the author. Being a papist and exploiting a papist point of view must ultimately be the same thing for Taylor because, although he claims that knowledge of Falstaff's origins will reintroduce "historical resonances" to Shakespeare's play, what in fact he has done is place the complex historical conditions of religious conflict in Shakespeare's England under erasure so that he can proffer a radical view of the author's origins. Thus, Taylor begins his search through Shakespeare's plays for a Catholic worldview exactly where Sams and Honigmann begin – at the beginning: "There is documentary evidence," Taylor asserts, "that both Shakespeare's father and one of his daughters may have been popishly inclined."[141] In short, all Taylor can really do to rehistoricize *1 Henry IV* is either go back to the "lost years" of Shakespeare's youth and speculate on his religious beliefs, or go on to other plays. Stranded between the author's life and his life's work, it is hard to see how Taylor has reinserted history into the text. Indeed, the one hole in the play which the "young Gentle Ladie" of James's account first noticed has finally been patched.

More than anything else, Taylor's defense of the Oxford *Complete Works* edition of *1 Henry IV* makes it clear that if Oldcastle is going to be resurrected again, this time on Catholic grounds, then Shakespeare must be exhumed first. Presiding over the author's latest resurrection, Taylor and Wells inadvertently introduce a rather different historical resonance, one that was initially sounded in the collaborative effort of Rowe and Betterton to produce the first biographical preface to the *Complete Plays* of 1709.[142] Even the Rowe of Hart's scathing, fictionalized account can be heard whispering in the editorial voice of Taylor and Wells, "[We] want an author for this selection of plays!" From a historical restoration to a textual one, Oldcastle has remained a constant; and yet, some things have changed. Whereas Rowe and Betterton's *Complete Plays* proclaimed, The King is dead! Long live Shakespeare!, Taylor and Wells's *Complete Works* defiantly argues, The Author is dead. Long live Shakespeare.

And yet, if to restore Oldcastle is to reconstruct Shakespeare as a recusant – that is, if banishing Falstaff from the authoritative texts of *1 Henry IV* rehistoricizes the author as the most famous member of a marginalized and persecuted religious sect – then not only has Falstaff been turned back into Oldcastle, but so has Shakespeare. In short, Taylor can be confident that Oldcastle is what Shakespeare wrote and meant, because Taylor has reconstructed Shakespeare as Oldcastle – or to be more precise, as the notorious pre-martyrological Lord Cobham who lived in the shadowy margins of England's national religion. Thus the figure who was for a time the godly nation's greatest martyr, has also played a fundamental role in the construction of that nation's greatest author, from the religio-political controversy that preceded his debut as a writer on the title page of *2 Henry IV*, to the controversy over the debut of Oldcastle as a character in an authoritative edition of *1 Henry IV*. But didn't we always already know all of this? Didn't we already know that banishing Falstaff meant dragging out the author to speak about Oldcastle? Isn't that exactly what happens at the end of *2 Henry IV* when the clown who played the fat knight reappears on stage speaking for the author about his Oldcastle problem?

3 "If he be at his book, disturb him not": the two Jonson folios of 1616

> Now that the Printer, by a doubled charge, thinkes it worthy a longer life, then commonly the ayre of such things doth promise . . .
> Ben Jonson, *Every Man out of His Humor*

> What happened to that text that used to lie before the scholar in a comforting materiality?
> Hayden White, *The Content of the Form*

In her study of early modern print culture, Elizabeth Eisenstein observes that "one must wait until a full century after Gutenberg before the outlines of a new world picture begin to emerge into view."[1] If we adjust this view to the specific history of printing in England, then one of the most striking elements of this new world picture must certainly be the emergence of the professional theatre. Indeed, the stage was set for a merger between printing house and playhouse when, a full century after William Caxton set up England's first printing press in 1476, James Burbage was granted the first royal patent for a company of adult players. By 1577, Burbage's playhouse, The Theatre, was in regular use, and a precedent had been set for London's leading companies to construct commercial theatres just outside the city's jurisdiction. We have this fortunate convergence of print and drama to thank for the survival of more than 400 total plays in 961 total editions written for the London stage between 1576 and 1642.[2] Yet the importance of the printing press is often belittled in the large body of scholarship devoted to the theatre. One probable explanation for the subordination of printing house to playhouse in discussions of early modern drama can be located in a long-cherished, almost mythic, narrative according to which playwrights and the companies they represented were reluctant to print their plays. This narrative owes much to playwrights like John Marston, who cautions in a note to the "Equall Reader" of *Parasitaster, or, The Fawne* (1633),[3] "If any shall wonder why I print a Comedy, whose life rests much in the Actors voice. Let such know, that it cannot avoyd publishing: let it therefore stand with good excuse, that I have beene my owne setter out" (R7). As with all such binaries, the one proffered by

104

Marston accords a primacy and superiority to the voice, relegating print to a secondary and improper position that must be monitored and somehow appropriated through personal vigilance. Such a view of the relation between drama and print has become a kind of received wisdom, in part because Shakespeare has long been the privileged model of dramatic authorship, and Shakespeare, as we have seen, had little or no involvement with publishing his plays.

In the past two decades, textual scholars of early modern drama have begun systematically to dismantle the once sturdy New Bibliographic edifice that for nearly seventy-five years housed the study of dramatic authorship and helped to keep Shakespeare at the center of critical attention. Although I suggested in my introduction that the new textual scholarship has not been without its conflicts and difficulties, it is also true that the loosening of the New Bibliography's interpretive stranglehold on early modern dramatic texts has given Ben Jonson the opportunity to compete with his more famous rival. While the status of printed drama will no doubt continue to be the subject of considerable scholarly controversy, one thing currently seems beyond debate: the publication of Jonson's *Workes* folio in 1616 represented a profound shift in the complex relation between playhouse and printing house in early modern England. Of course, neither Jonson nor his fellow dramatists were strangers to the press, and I suggested in Chapter 1 that Jonson and some of his contemporaries were turning to publication in the first decade of the seventeenth century to create a new market of readers for plays that had failed in the theatre. Nevertheless, the publication of Jonson's plays, entertainments, and masques in a folio collection that sandwiched seventy-five pages of epigrams and poems between 940 pages of dramatic text helped to transform the market for printed drama.

G. E. Bentley best captures the import of this watershed event when he remarks of Jonson's *Workes*, "probably no other publication before the Restoration did so much to raise the contemporary existence of the generally belittled form of plays."[4] In the past two decades, the 1616 folio has figured prominently in studies of early modern authorship and print culture. For many scholars, Jonson's folio stands as a singular achievement of emergent authorial awareness – especially with regard to the meaning of print. Joseph Loewenstein asserts that "the 1616 *Workes* marks a major event in the history of what one might call the bibliographic ego."[5] Richard C. Newton singles out Jonson as the poet/author who "in an important sense 'invents' (discovers) the printed book by using the book to distinguish what is his."[6] For Harold Love, "in the 1616 folio [Jonson] produced one of the great typographical monuments of his age."[7] Summing up the recent trajectory of Jonson studies, Elizabeth Hanson astutely observes:

> It is by now a critical commonplace that when Jonson left the loathed stage, one place he went was the printed book. The 1616 folio, *The Workes of Benjamin Jonson*, and its arrangement of texts to evoke a career, constitutes a sustained representation of Jonson's authorial labor. In many recent accounts of his career, Jonson's location of his authorship in the printed book heralds the proprietary author, who is linked through implication and theoretical filiation, to possessive individualism, modern subjectivity, and bourgeois culture.[8]

All of these accounts, published within the past fifteen years, would seem to run counter to the post-structuralist critical wisdom that the fundamental inter-referentiality of language as a system of signifiers precludes the words in a given text from referring to anything – including an author – behind or beyond that text. Jonson scholarship in the age of Roland Barthes's "The Death of the Author" generally embraces a notion of the dramatist that is precisely the one Barthes eulogized in his well-known essay. "The Author," according to Barthes, "when believed in, is always conceived of as the past of his own book: book and author stand automatically on a single line divided into a before and an after."[9] Jonson scholars have translated this belief into a truth to the extent that they frequently conjure images of the dramatist peering over the printer's shoulder to supervise the presswork on his book.[10] Other recent commentators, influenced by Foucault's notion of the transgressive author, have focused on the suffering imposed on Jonson by the harsh realities of Elizabethan and Jacobean censorship, a critical preoccupation captured best in the title of Evelyn Tribble's essay, "Genius on the Rack: Authorities and the Margins in Ben Jonson's Glossed Works." In short, the threatened displacement of Shakespeare from the center of scholarship on dramatic authorship has facilitated Jonson's idealization. This significant shift from a playwright who – for a number of possible reasons reviewed in Chapter 1 – refrained from publishing his plays to a playwright who relied extensively on the printing press to establish himself as an author is taking place at a moment in history when many people have begun to worry about the consequences of the digital age for the era of the printed book.

In a recent collection of essays devoted to Jonson's folio, Kevin J. Donovan observes:

> while recent scholarship enhances our sense of the folio's historical, literary, and cultural significance, reevaluation of Jonson's texts in the folio tends to diminish the preeminent authority accorded to the folio in the received text of Jonson as established in the monumental Oxford edition.[11]

Donovan's observation contains an important insight, one which I think suggests how the critical desire to idealize Jonson's involvement with the publication process might be frustrated. In this chapter I follow Donovan's lead by focusing on the 1616 folio in order to advance two closely related claims, one about the material book itself, and the other about its critical reception. First, I want to suggest that textual analysis of the 1616 *Workes* reveals a significant fissure in the monument to Jonsonian authorship that the folio has come to represent; and I want to account for this fissure by reconsidering the concept of authorship itself. Second, I want to suggest that the critical reluctance to acknowledge the inconsistent and unstable authorial status of Jonson's folio is rooted in – to borrow from the title of Jonas Barish's study – a certain anti-theatrical prejudice.[12] In other words, Jonson's book gets validated at the expense of the theatre because recent critical responses to the folio that privilege it as a material book pass over what it reports to us about the complex and changing status of playwriting in the period. The Jonson that emerges from this chapter is not the embodiment of the modern notion of the author, but rather a transitional figure. His main contribution to the history of dramatic authorship, the 1616 *Workes* folio, I argue, constitutes a permanent record of that transition.

Perhaps the greatest obstacle to assessing the nature of Jonson's achievement in 1616 has been Jonson himself. For the most part, our view of the folio comes to us through the distorting lens of Jonson's own deep commitment to classical and neo-classical strategies of authorial self-representation and promotion.[13] The task has been further complicated by the fact, noted almost forty years ago by Johan Gerritsen, that "[a]n authoritative account of the printing of the first collected edition of an English playwright, the Jonson folio of 1616, does not exist, and in fact cannot yet be given."[14] Writing more than thirty years after Gerritsen, Donovan can still lament that "little is known about the printing of Jonson's 1616 *Workes*," an ignorance he attributes to "the unfortunate rift in modern scholarship between literary interpretation and textual criticism."[15] Fortunately, such ignorance has been significantly reduced by the recent work of David L. Gants, whose dissertation[16] represents a major advance in our knowledge of the 1616 folio as a material book. Indeed, Gants's contribution to the bibliographic scholarship on Jonson's folio is such that it can only be paralleled with that of Charlton Hinman's to the study of the 1623 Folio. Furthermore, Mark Bland's current research has substantially increased our knowledge of Jonson as an author[17] and of the production of his *Workes*.[18]

The fissure or gap in the text of the folio that will initially concern me here, however, was first brought to light by C. H. Herford and Percy and

Evelyn Simpson as they prepared their edition of Jonson's work for Oxford. Acknowledging that Jonson's involvement with the publication of the folio was inconsistent, especially with regard to the printing of that volume's masques and entertainments, the editors reluctantly admitted:

> The Masques . . . show no sign of the author's correction except on the last two pages, where he transposed effectively the final speeches, making Astraea decide that she would return to earth in order to bask in the sunshine of King James's court. The text of the entertainments and the masques is often carelessly printed, and the Latin and Greek quotations in the notes are especially bad. Jonson cannot have read the proofs.[19]

The transposition here refers to the final speeches of Astraea and Pallas in *The Golden Age Restored* (4Q1v–4Q4), the work that concludes the volume. In the folio's hypothetically revised version of this work, Astraea gets the last word; in the hypothetically original version, Pallas speaks last.

Herford and Simpson speculated in Volume VII of their edition that "the original ending was used at the court performance and that the revision was an afterthought designed to give a more significant ending to the folio."[20] The editors provided a precise explanation of how this transposition was accomplished, noting that, "the printer unlocked the forme and transposed the stanza without disturbing the type."[21] In the wake of the Oxford edition, the final two pages of the folio have become the subject of considerable interest and debate. Jonathan Goldberg, for example, has pointed to the revision as one among many of Jonson's failed attempts to get what he wanted from James I.[22] More recently, however, James A. Riddell has convincingly argued, on both literary and bibliographic grounds, that the Pallas/Astraea version represents the original court performance and that since the transposition was a stop-press correction, Jonson may have had little to do with it.[23]

I am inclined to agree with Riddell's assessment, especially in light of Gants's recent work on the folio. Noting that throughout the book's 1,028 folio pages there are more than 2500 textual variants resulting from stop-press corrections and resetting,[24] Gants concludes from his analysis of these variants that Jonson "involved himself at some level in the proofing and correcting of the volume."[25] Nevertheless, Gants's study of the folio also suggests that Jonson's involvement was not at all consistent. Based on a gathering-by-gathering examination of textual variants, Gants has determined that substantive authorial revisions "occur with regularity throughout the early plays, less so in the later ones, and rarely in the poems, masques and entertainments."[26] Subsequently, Gants emphasizes the importance of this evidence, noting that "the overwhelming majority of the later press changes appear to come from the printing-house corrector and not from Jonson."[27] In short, what Gants's detailed bibliographical investigation makes abundantly clear is that although Jonson did oversee the printing of his *Workes*, he seems to have been much more interested in the textual fate of most of the volume's play-texts.

Thus, although Herford and Simpsons' basic assessment of Jonson's involvement in the printing of the *Workes* has been supported – and greatly refined – by new evidence, what interests me most about their editorial position is the rather remarkable fact that, as Donovan notes, they "chose the folio as copytext for all but one of the previously printed masques."[28] Given what we now know about the printing of the folio, this choice would seem to be particularly vulnerable to criticism. However, I think it is important to consider the Oxford editors' decision in context. Contrary to their own best efforts to establish authoritative texts, A. W. Pollard and his followers ultimately exposed the extent to which early modern authors, especially playwrights, had little if any involvement in preparing their texts for publication. To presume authorial involvement was not tenable because, as D. C. Greetham notes with reference to the work of the New Bibliographers, "[i]t was clear that in the Renaissance this was rarely so (particularly for drama) and that when an author did assume any prerogative (as in the famous case of Ben Jonson's *Works* of 1616) this was regarded as an aberration (again particularly for drama)."[29] Comparatively speaking, Jonson's folio is in fact anomalously authoritative, and Herford and Simpsons' near total reliance on it for their edition must be attributed not so much to the folio's status as a text, but rather to the authorial status of other dramatic texts produced in the same period. In this sense, the aberration that is Jonson's achievement – regardless of its actual, material singularity – was fashioned for him by his Oxford editors according to an epistemological schema that is no less resolutely dialectical than the schema discussed in the context of Shakespeare's authorship in the previous chapter.

In other words, although the folio in its entirety was not uniformly anomalous, certainly the decision to use all but one of its normative masque texts as copy-text suggests an underlying fantasy that it be so.[30] And yet, as is frequently the case with repression, inevitably the repressed staged its return, and it did so most noisily, perhaps, in W. W. Greg's "The Rationale of Copy-Text" (1949). In this seminal essay, which, according to T. H. Howard Hill, Greg began writing while working on a review of the Oxford edition of the *Masques*,[31] Greg questioned the bibliographic practice of relying solely on the earliest edition of a given work as the most authoritative copy-text for a scholarly edition, inasmuch as that practice precluded later – often, posthumously published – editions from being consulted.[32]

In the particular case of Renaissance drama, at least, Greg inadvertently laid the foundation for the death of the author some two decades before Barthes – and he did so, oddly enough, while examining the section of Jonson's folio which, as Gants's analysis makes clear, evidences almost no authorial involvement with the printed text. The implications of Greg's essay should be clear. Shakespeare's untimely death no longer precluded the First Folio from being considered as copy-text,[33] but Jonson's intervention in the printing of the 1616 folio rendered it anomalously authoritative within a larger body of printed texts for which authorial involvement was no longer a prerequisite to being considered authoritative. To normalize Shakespeare, Jonson had to be excluded from the norm.

In this exiled position, Jonson has been revived even as Shakespeare scholars have, for the most part, accepted the death of their author and gotten on with the business of adjectival post-mortems such as Greenblatt's *Shakespearean Negotiations* or Richard Wilson's *Will Power: Essays on Shakespearean Authority*. Jonson scholars, on the other hand, have more or less tacitly agreed to offer up accounts of modern authorship's infancy and to celebrate its conception in the publication of their author's folio. In this sense, Shakespeare's death gives way to Jonson's birth, and the year 1616 plays host to a kind of generational relay that is also figured spatially as a shift from the playhouse to the printing house. For example, as the only major dramatist examined in Tribble's book, *Margins and Marginality: The Printed Page in Early Modern England*,[34] Jonson is designated as the lone figure responsible for the translation of drama in early modern England from its lowly, marginalized beginnings to its central position in the literary canon, from the stage to the page – the latter being "a place where," as Tribble quotes Michel de Certeau, "the ambiguities of the world have been exorcised."[35] What gets lost in the translation has rarely been addressed; but what is gained, the Jonsonian author function preserved intact after its more famous contemporary has been deconstructed, is oddly consistent with a widely-held view of the printing press's capacity, as Eisenstein puts it, "to preserve and pass on what was known."[36] In much the same way that a tanner's skin becomes leathery, Jonson seems to have spent too many years inhaling the fumes in William Stansby's print shop.

Given Jonson's marginal status as an author involved in the publication of his plays, it is perhaps not surprising that a certain hesitancy or reluctance characterizes Greg's approach to his texts. As Bowers notes, "[Greg] is curiously uncertain when he treats Jonson, who of all

Elizabethan authors has the best claim to the supervision of most parts of a revised edition, as in his folio *Works* in 1616."[37] Greg's curious uncertainty stems perhaps from his desire to reconcile Jonson's texts with the model he had constructed for Shakespeare's texts. Nevertheless, it is important to emphasize that this appraisal of the folio as a revised edition with most of its parts supervised by the author belongs to Bowers, despite the attribution to Greg. Greg's assessment of the folio, based at the time he was writing "Rationale" on his analysis of the Oxford edition, was somewhat more skeptical.[38]

As I have already noted, Herford and Simpson found that only the final two pages of the folio's masques and entertainments showed any authorial involvement, and even here Jonson – or his printer – may have been taking his cues from the king's reaction to the initial performance. Similarly, Sara van den Berg gives the king agency by arguing that "the publication of Jonson's works in a folio edition was occasioned, in part, by James I's decision to collect and publish his works in a folio."[39] I will return to this argument later, but even if the king did encourage the transposition of speeches at the end of the folio, the resulting text itself, which bears little or no evidence of Jonson's supervision, hardly constitutes an authorial triumph in print. As an unedited and unsupervised printed text based, hypothetically, on an unprinted performance text that looks to have been altered immediately before publication of the folio to please the monarch,[40] *The Golden Age Restored* made its way from the stage to the page along the same path that any number of plays written for the public theatres must have traveled.[41] The remaining 173 pages of masques and entertainments – nearly twenty percent of the folio – perhaps did not benefit from even this minimal amount of authorial intervention. Although Timothy Murray contends that the *Workes* title page can be "read allegorically in the exaggerated spirit of the antitheatrical treatises,"[42] it seems clear that the authorial status of the folio's final section is all too familiarly theatrical. Indeed, as Thomas L. Berger observes, "[t]he textual problems in the masques and entertainments of Ben Jonson are at once typical of the larger problems of the period and of specific problems faced by editors."[43]

As an artifact of early modern publication, the 1616 folio captures and preserves a certain discontinuity or struggle that can be provisionally identified as a kind of caesura in Jonson's authorship between theatre and court. If, as James K. Bracken asserts, "Jonson himself went to considerable lengths to give his previously published plays the kinds of details which were appropriate to learned and serious works,"[44] the author seems to have expended much less effort on his masques and entertainments. And it is worth noting, that a comparable division splits the body of Greg's essay on copy-text. In the main text he writes of the Oxford Jonson, "Simpson's consequent decision to take the folio for his copy-text for the plays it contains will doubtless be approved by most critics. I at least have no wish to dispute his choice."[45] In a footnote appended to this observation, however, he writes, "Simpson's procedure in taking the 1616 folio as copy-text in the case of most of the masques included, although he admits that in their case Jonson cannot be supposed to have supervised the printing, is much more questionable."[46] Here the textual apparatus of the scholarly page reproduces the relationship between the folio's two types of dramatic texts in terms of their authorial status: the masques are subordinated to the plays.

Less the aberration that Greetham labels it than a hybrid, Jonson's folio is something of a textual hermaphrodite wherein the epigrams and poems mark the spot at which untypically authorial play-texts have been grafted on to typically inauthorial masque texts and other similarly inauthorial pieces. Indeed Gants's analysis of textual variants in the folio's eighty-five gatherings lends some credence to this observation, insofar as the epigrams' four gatherings show only a minimum of intervention by Stansby's corrector, while the four gatherings devoted to the poems show no correction whatsoever, either by Jonson or someone in Stansby's shop.[47] In other words, if, as van den Berg urges, Jonson's decision to publish his folio can be attributed to shifting strategies of royal self-representation, the self in question would have to be that most theatrical of English monarchs, Elizabeth, on whose behalf crown lawyers at Sarjeants Inn argued,

A king has a Body natural, and a Body politic. His body natural (if it be considered in itself) is a Body mortal . . . But his Body politic is a Body that cannot be seen or handled, consisting of Policy and Government . . . this body is utterly void of . . . natural defectors and Imbecilities, which the Body natural is subject to.[48]

A version of this often rehearsed notion of the king's two bodies can be glimpsed linking print to royal self-representation in published versions of *Hymenaei, or the Solemnities of Masque, and Barriers at a Marriage*, where Jonson, as Loewenstein notes, "speaks of the printed text itself as the ideal form of the masque."[49] In its initial published form, the *speech*, which appears as a preface to the 1606 edition of the masque[50] does indeed extol the preservative powers of print:

It is noble and iust advantage, that the things subjected to *Vunderstanding* have of those which are objected to *Sense*, that the one sorte are but momentaire, and merely taking; the other impressing, and lasting: Else the Glory of all these *Solemnities* had perish'd like a Blaze, and gone out, in the *Beholders* eyes. So short-liv'd are the *Bodies* of all thinges, in comparison of their *soules*. And though

Bodies oft-times have the ill lucke to be sensually preferr'd, they find afterwards, the good fortune (when soules live) to be vtterly forgotten. This it is hath made the most royall *Princes*, and greatest *Persons*, (who are commonly the *Personaters* of these *Actions*) not onely studious of Riches and Magnificence in the outward Celebration, (which rightly becomes them) but curious after the most high, and hearty *Inventions* to furnish the inward parts. (A3)

Like the Body politic, the "soule" remains long after the Bodies of all things (including the masque and their royal "Personaters") have perished; and in this case, it is the "impressing," rather than the versifying of Shakespeare's sonnets, for example, that facilitates immortality. But the situation becomes a little more complicated once this preface is preserved in the new body of the folio (4G6), that is, once Jonson gets involved in the embalming process. Loewenstein correctly observes that "[t]he interested publication of the masques, which simultaneously abstracted the literary work and embedded it in the intimate transactions between poet and stationer, seems, then, to have been an important determinant in Jonson's subsequent interest in his plays."[51] Nevertheless, the author's involvement with the "impressing" of the folio's play-texts dialectically renders the printed texts of the masques in that same volume less than ideal.

The printing of the masques and entertainments section of the folio, with its defects and imbecilities, did not, as Herford and Simpson first realized, benefit from the immortalizing touch of its author's supervision. Remarkably, "The Catalogue" (Fig. 7) attests to the point at which the book's two bodies are sutured together by dividing the seventy-five pages of non-dramatic text between two levels of authorial involvement: *Epigrammes* concludes the list of dramatic texts written for the theatre, and *The Forrest* heads the list of largely unrevised and uncorrected dramatic texts initially produced for king and court. Furthermore, inasmuch as the *Epigrammes* section has a separate title page (Fig. 8), an attribution – "The Author B. I." – and a two-page dedication to William, Earl of Pembroke, it looks back to the plays for its authorial status.[52] The folio materially reproduces this authorial link by juxtaposing the title page of the *Epigrammes* with the end page of *Catiline* which, in recalling that "[t]his Tragoedie was first / Acted in the year / 1611," signals the cut-off point for the folio's preoccupation with the professional theatre. The link between the plays and the *Epigrammes* is further substantiated by analysis of the folio's presswork, inasmuch as the text of *Epigrammes* was printed at some point between the printing of *Catiline* and *Every Man in his Humor*.[53] Finally, like a number of the plays in the folio, the *Epigrammes*, "[t]he ripest of my studies," according to Jonson, were, as Herford and Simpson put it, "carefully revised before

Figure 7 Page of text: The Catalogue, *The Workes of Beniamin Jonson*, 1616

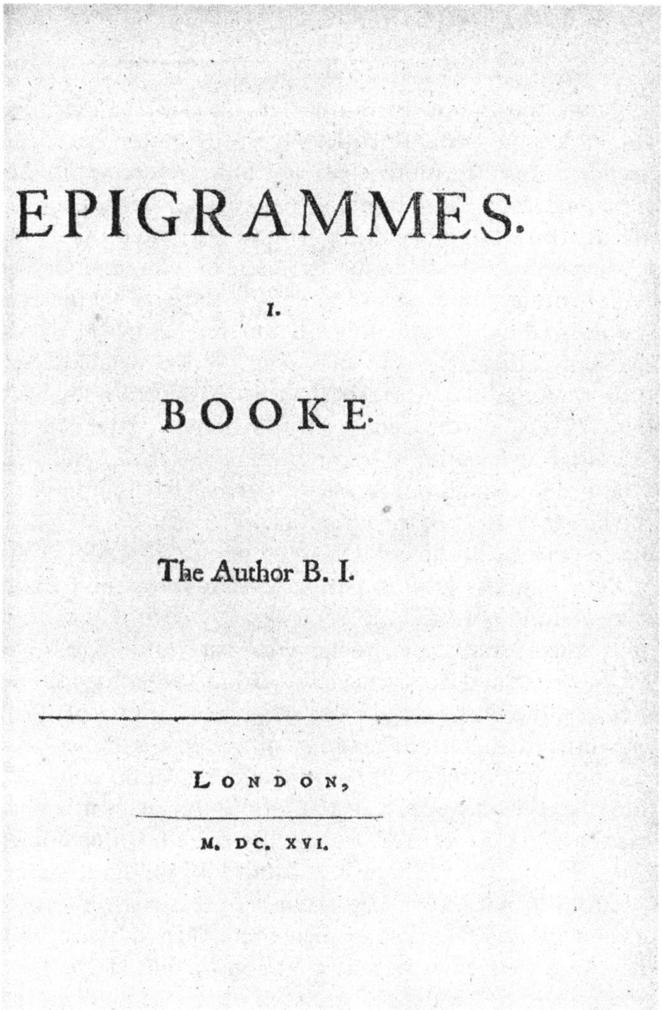

EPIGRAMMES.

I.

BOOKE.

The Author B. I.

LONDON,

M. DC. XVI.

Figure 8 Title page: *Epigrammes, The Workes of Beniamin Jonson*, 1616

they were sent to press."⁵⁴ As for *The Forrest*, Herford and Simpson merely remark that it "is also well-printed."⁵⁵

If the *Epigrammes* are inextricably linked to the plays, *The Forrest*, on the other hand, anticipates the authorial status of the masques because, like them, it has no separate title page, attribution, or dedications.⁵⁶ Authorized by nothing more than a titular reference to an abstract location beyond even the margins of the early Elizabethan playhouses, the poems are forced to make do with an unattributed title (Fig. 9) that is not much larger than the running title used in the remainder of the text, and they constitute – at least in the limited sense of textual apparatus – the least authorial work in the folio. Belonging neither to the theatre nor the court, and dedicated to no one, *The Forrest* would seem to be an entity unto itself, and it constitutes the least corrected body of text within the volume. Thus, at the center of the book – intended to enhance Jonson's status as an author by upgrading the lowly status of printed drama – appears a small collection of poems that is utterly anomalous within the larger context of the volume itself.

Placing the poems in the context of contemporary poetic miscellanies, van den Berg remarks their superior textual status and observes that, "*The Forrest* stands out among such books because Jonson rigorously edited it to demonstrate his poetic virtuosity and to establish a new paradigm of order and coherence."⁵⁷ Within the limited context of the folio, however, the claim for Jonson's rigorous editing of *The Forrest* is somewhat difficult to sustain because, although a number of the poems exist in manuscript form, there is no extant non-folio copy of the entire text of the poems as it appears in the folio.⁵⁸ As such, it is impossible to determine that *The Forrest* was as heavily revised, for example, as *Every Man in his Humor*,⁵⁹ and there is substantial bibliographic evidence to suggest that it did not receive the extensive press corrections from which *Every Man Out of His Humour* benefited.⁶⁰ In a strict bibliographic sense, therefore, we cannot be sure that Jonson edited *The Forrest*, if the term "editing" is to be used – as it has been generally – to describe Jonson's involvement in revising and correcting his text, as well as his supervision of the folio's printing.

Presuming that Jonson intended the entire volume to be as anomalously authoritative as the texts of the nine plays he included, Herford and Simpson speculated that the non-theatrical dramatic texts suffered from Jonson's lack of attention because he didn't have time to revise them or to keep a vigilant eye on the presswork for this section of the folio. The evidence for this speculation, a 20 January 1615 entry in the *Registers of the Company of Stationers of London* by William Stansby for Jonson's *Certayne Masques at the Court never yet printed*, enabled

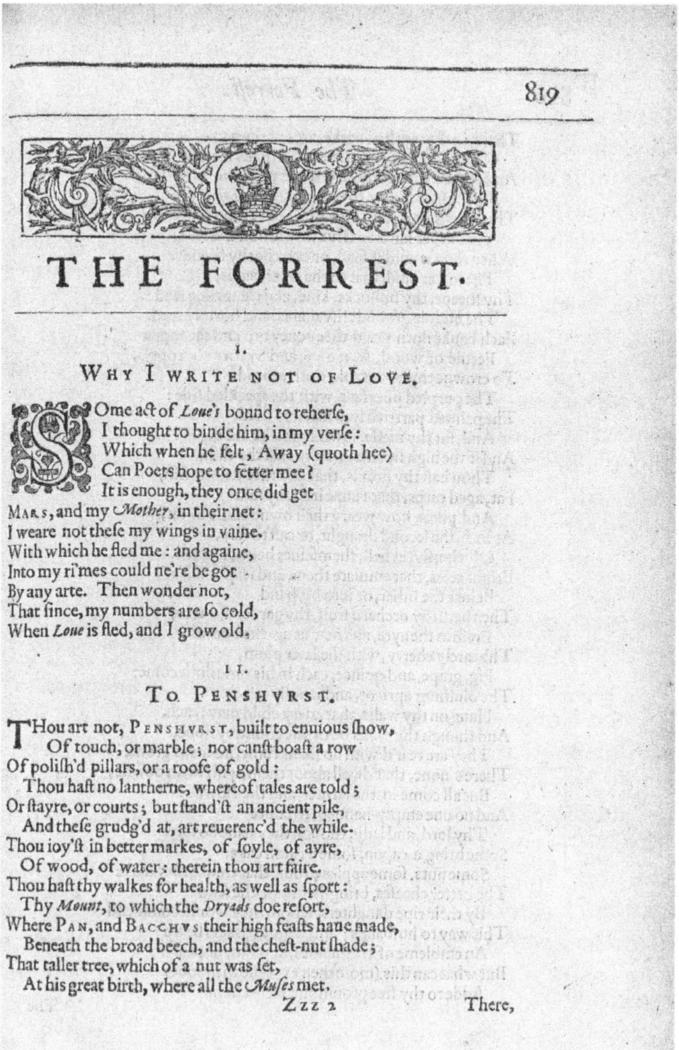

819

THE FORREST.

I.
WHY I WRITE NOT OF LOVE.

SOme act of *Loue's* bound to reherse,
 I thought to binde him, in my verse:
Which when he felt, Away (quoth hee)
Can Poets hope to fetter mee?
 It is enough, they once did get
MARS, and my *Mother*, in their net:
I weare not these my wings in vaine.
With which he fled me: and againe,
Into my ri'mes could ne're be got
 By any arte. Then wonder not,
That since, my numbers are so cold,
When *Loue* is fled, and I grow old.

II.
TO PENSHVRST.

THou art not, PENSHVRST, built to enuious show,
 Of touch, or marble; nor canst boast a row
Of polish'd pillars, or a roofe of gold:
 Thou hast no lantherne, whereof tales are told;
Or stayre, or courts; but stand'st an ancient pile,
 And these grudg'd at, art reuerenc'd the while.
Thou ioy'st in better markes, of soyle, of ayre,
 Of wood, of water: therein thou art faire.
Thou hast thy walkes for health, as well as sport:
 Thy *Mount*, to which the *Dryads* doe resort,
Where PAN, and BACCHVS their high feasts haue made,
 Beneath the broad beech, and the chest-nut shade;
That taller tree, which of a nut was set,
 At his great birth, where all the *Muses* met.
 Zzz 2 There,

Figure 9 Title page: *The Forrest, The Workes of Beniamin Jonson*, 1616

Herford and Simpson to vindicate Jonson by blaming Stansby for the inferior quality of the masques and entertainments. "It is probable," they contend, "that the printer, registering this section of the work in 1615 and producing it in 1616, hurried the printing."[61] Deceptively logical and credible, this attempt to uphold the author's unwavering commitment to the folio in its entirety nevertheless comes at a high price. Not only must Jonson be stripped of the agency that has traditionally constituted his achievement, but also the 1616 folio must itself be bifurcated. Claiming that copy for the *Workes* could not have gone to the printer much later than 1613,[62] Herford and Simpson find themselves compelled to provide an alternative account of the masques and entertainments fifty-eight pages later. The simultaneous presence of both positions within what the Oxford editors refer to as "An Historical Survey of the Text" essentially necessitates the theoretical production of two very different folios.[63] The one, begun in "1612 or at latest 1613," belongs to Jonson; the other, begun in 1616, belongs to Stansby.

Herford and Simpsons' argument for a start-date of 1613 has frequently been refuted since it first appeared in 1950.[64] Based on his analysis of type and paper used in Stansby's shop, Gerritsen argued nine years later that "the printing of the folio must have taken place in the course of 1615–16, and had reached mid-way by the spring of 1616."[65] Noting that a copy of the folio "was recorded in the inventory of stock held by the York bookseller John Foster made on 25 November 1616," Bland suggests that "the *Workes* was at press from January 1615 to the middle of November 1616."[66] Subsequently, Bland reasons that, "[i]f a rate of output of one forme a day was true of Jonson's *Workes*, then it would have been at the press for at least 86 weeks," implying that "production might have begun by April 1615."[67] What has not been sufficiently challenged, however, is the Oxford editors' contention that Stansby was responsible for the inauthorial status of the non-theatrical dramatic texts. In this context, it seems crucial to point out that the following entertainments and masques all predate the first performance of *Catiline* in 1611, the last play-text included in the folio: *B. Jon: his part of King James his royall entertainement . . . 15. of March 1603* (4B–4C5v); *A Panegyre on the Happie Entrance of James Our Soveraigne . . . 19, of March 1603* (4C6–4D2v); *A Particular Entertainment of The Qveene and Prince their Highnesse . . . 25, of June 1603* (4D3–4E1v); *A Private Entertainement of the King and Queene on Mayday . . . 1604* (4E2–4E5; *The entertainment of the Kings of Great Britaine and Denmarke . . . July 24, 1606* (4E5–4E6); *An Entertainment of King James and Queene Anne, at Theobalds . . . 22. of May, 1607* (4E6–4Fv); *The Qveenes Masques The First, of Blacknesse . . . 1605* (4F2–4G); *The Second*

Masqve. Which was of Beavtie . . . 1608 (4G–4G5v); *Hymenaei, or the Solemnities of Masque, and Barriers at a Marriage* (4G6–4I5v) (dated 1606 in STC 14774); *The Description of the Masqve, with the Nuptial Songs . . . 1608* (4I6–4K4v); and *The Masqve of Qveenes, Celebrated From the house of Fame . . . Febr.2 1609* (4K5–4M2v).

Furthermore, because most scholars of the folio maintain that Jonson marked up quartos as copy for the printers when they set up the folio's eight previously published plays,[68] it should be noted that of the entertainments and masques listed above, the following were also published previously and were, therefore, available to be marked up by the author as much as a decade before Stansby went to the Company of Stationers to register *Certayne Masques at the Court: B. Jon: His Part of King James his Royall Entertainement* (STC 14756); *Hymenaei, or the Solemnities of Masque, and Barriers at a Marriage* (STC 14774); *The Qveenes Masques The First, of Blacknesse* and *The Second Masqve. Which was of Beavtie* published together in 1608 as *The Characters of Two Royall Masques. The one of Blacknesse, the other of Beautie* (STC 14761); *The Description of the Masqve, with the Nuptial Songs* (STC 14770); and *The Masqve of Qveenes, Celebrated From the House of Fame* (STC 14778). While none of these texts was revised for the folio, *The Golden Age Restored*, a previously unpublished masque performed, according to the date on the folio text, practically on the way to the print shop, looks to have been subjected to at least one substantive – though not necessarily authorial – revision.

Upon closer inspection, the performance/publication history of the folio's entertainments and masques suggests that, like Prufrock, Jonson did indeed have time for revision, and that some of the earlier texts were first performed and published while he was most heavily revising the quarto texts of the plays. It now also seems likely that Jonson had a rather limited window of opportunity – between January 1615 and November 1616 – to supervise the printing of the folio in its entirety. Whatever time Jonson did have to get involved with the work at Stansby's shop, it would appear that he used it almost exclusively to monitor the preparation of his plays – although time itself, contrary to his Oxford editors' assertion, may not have been the basis for making them a priority. Indeed, Gants's analysis of the folio's printing sequence suggests that Jonson was "scrambling to finish the promised revisions" of *Every Man In* as the Masques were being printed.[69]

Certainly the exigencies of the early modern print shop imposed themselves on Jonson. But if we want to retain some of Jonson's agency and not hold Stansby totally accountable for the disparity in authorial involvement that differentiates the folio's two sections of dramatic texts, then we need an alternative theoretical approach to the folio's authorial status that forecloses on the temptation merely to praise Jonson for his accomplishment and blame him for his failure. Such an approach requires us to shift the critical spotlight away from the author and train it on two important issues that have been under-examined in discussions of the 1616 folio: the venues in which the folio's dramatic texts were produced and the concept of authorship itself.[70] The former enables us to begin to see the folio as what Jerome McGann calls a "language event,"[71] while the latter puts us at the heart of Jonson's achievement.

In his analysis of Jonson's collaboration with Inigo Jones, Loewenstein points the way to a reconsideration of the folio in terms of venue when he suggestively remarks, "[t]he court stage was not the democratic place of the public stage, not a homogeneous space in which the pretensions of an Amorphous might flourish."[72] For Loewenstein, this distinction between the two types of performance spaces to which Jonson contributed his texts has significant implications for Jonson's authorship, particularly in the case of *The Masque of Blacknesse*. Because this masque provided the queen with the opportunity to make what Loewenstein aptly terms a "royal intrusion," it endowed the court stage with "greater ideological power" even as it "deprived Jonson of that ultimate authority he had hoped to gain over the courtly stage."[73]

Promising Jonson what it could not possibly deliver, *The Masque of Blacknesse* nevertheless affords us a glimpse of the frustrating ambivalence which, Jacqueline T. Miller suggests, is characteristic of authorship in general. Noting that "authority and authorship are sometimes complementary, sometimes conflicting concepts," Miller asserts that the complex relation between these two terms "mirrors the difficult relation that exists between a writer's desire for, on the one hand, individual authority or creative autonomy and, on the other hand, the authoritative sanction that external sources provide."[74] Given the preoccupation of the entertainments and masques with theatricalized strategies of royal self-representation, it seems plausible that when the texts of these court dramas were included in the folio, they were left to rely on the more typical authority of the court, rather than on Jonson's anomalous textual authority. I want to suggest that the irreconcilable conflict Miller locates in the author's desire for both individual autonomy and externalized authority is preserved in Jonson's folio as the difference in the authorial status of that volume's two sections of dramatic texts.[75] And this conflict, I would add, could not be accommodated easily within the New Bibliography's project to establish authoritative texts, inasmuch as that effort necessarily limited the sources of a given work's authority to its author and/or its extant texts.

It would appear then that for those texts in the folio that were written for the public stage – where authorship was predominantly collaborative – Jonson seems to have marshaled the printing press to assert his individuality. In this sense, the folio enlarges upon and refines Jonson's previous attempts to use publication as a strategy of individualization, a strategy that Jonson himself had concisely depicted eleven years earlier when he informed readers of the *Sejanus, His Fall* quarto that, "this Booke, in all numbers, is not the same with that which was acted on the publike Stage, wherein a second Pen had good share: in place of which I have rather chosen, to put weaker (and no doubt lesse pleasing) of mine own, then to defraud so happy a Genius of his right, by my lothed usurpation" (¶3).[76] Intimating that the "Stage" and the "Booke" afford distinct opportunities for authorship, Jonson makes it clear that the publication process has given him the power to transform the authorial status of the work from a collaborative performance text to an individualized printed quarto text. Subsequently, he takes even greater advantage of this power by using the folio to excise collaborative works such as *Hot Anger Soon Cold*, *Page of Plymouth*, *The Scot's Tragedy*, *Eastward Hoe*, and the *Isle of Dogs* from his authorial canon.[77]

On the other hand, for those texts in the folio that were written for the court – where individuation is chiefly vested in the figure of the monarch – Jonson seems to have taken very little interest in exploiting the individualizing potential of the press. Having essentially abandoned the texts of the folio's masques and entertainments, when Jonson does mention their publication in the preface to *The Masque of Blacknesse*, he refers to them as "*carkasses*" from which "the *spirits* had also perished" and asserts that he is bringing them to press "In dutie, therefore, to that Majestie, who gave them their authoritie, and grace" (4F3). Here, in the published version of the first masque written in collaboration with Inigo Jones, Jonson concedes the queen's authority, but neither mentions Jones nor refers to the collaboration that produced the court performance except – as we shall see – to acknowledge the queen herself as a royal collaborator.

Tribble has taken Stephen Orgel to task for referring to the marginal glosses in his edition of the masques as "footnotes," because "the modern footnote is an eighteenth-century invention reflecting a firm subordination of subtext to text."[78] Regardless of the terminological anachronism, Orgel's instinct seems correct. In much the same way that a footnote grounds the discussion of a topic by referring to an established authority in the field, the heavy reliance on marginal glosses for the printed versions of the masques (and the entertainments) is symptomatic of the author's desire to get his footing by grounding his authorship in an authority other than his own. But this desire, I would add, also gets inscribed as an absence in Jonson's failure to make the masques and entertainments as anomalously authoritative as the plays. In this sense, James I does not, as van den Berg claims, "occasion the folio" so much as he occasions its least characteristically Jonsonian section. Furthermore, I would suggest that Jonson's deference to an alternative source of authority also gets inscribed as the presence of an absence, and it does so precisely in the form of a revision on the title page of the folio's first entertainment – the first work Jonson wrote for the king.

In its initial published form, the title page of Jonson's contribution to James's procession into London reads "B. Jon: / HIS PART OF / *King James* his Royall and Magnifi- / *cent Entertainement through his* / Honorable Cittie of London, / Thurseday the 15. of / March. 1603" (Fig. 10).[79] Recalling that James I and Jonson published their folios in the same year, it bears noting that the spelling of Jonson's name – or appropriately enough, a part of his name – appears changed for the first time in print on the title page of this entertainment, his first for the king. Shortened to "Jon," the abbreviation anticipates the notorious missing "h" that will come to characterize the author's idiosyncratic spelling of his name. Alternatively, the title page for *Poetaster or The Arraignment* (STC 14781), printed in 1602, attributes the play to "Ben Johnson."[80] Published some twelve years before the folio, the top billing accorded a *part* of the author's name is further emphasized typographically by the use of capital letters to combine attribution with possession in the phrase "HIS PART OF" – an emphasis that is itself emphasized a page later when the reader is informed that, "Vpon the Battlements / in a great capitall Letter was inscribed, / LONDINIVM:" (A2). Serving to link a classical author – "According to Tacitus" – with the name of the city that metonymically marks the beginning of James I's English reign as an entry into the Capitol, the capital letters also simultaneously recall the beginning of Jonson's work as an author for the king on the previous page, as well as the double appearance of the city's name in the title of the work – "Honorable Cittie of London" – and in that work's publishing history: "Printed at London by V. S. for / Edward Blount, 1604." Typographically, at least, authorship, royal performance, location, and publication are complexly entangled at the founding moment of Jonson's professional relationship with James I.

Contrasting Jonson's entertainment for the king's entry with Elizabeth's entertainment, *The Queenes Maiesties Passage*, a coronation progress which was carefully documented for immediate publication by Richard Mulcaster, Tribble rightly notes that the latter was published anonymously as a "pamphlet"[81] – a status that she guards carefully since

> **B. JON:**
> # HIS PART OF
> *King James* his Royall and Magnifi-
> cent *Entertainement through his*
> Honorable Cittie of London,
> Thurseday the 15. of
> *March. 1603.*
>
> So much as was presented in the first and last of
> their Triumphall Arch's.
>
> With his speach made to the last Presentation, in the
> *Strand, erected by the inhabitants of the Dutchy,*
> and *Westminster.*
>
> Also, a briefe *Panegyre* of his Maiesties first and well
> *auspicated entrance to his high Court of Parliament,*
> on Monday, the 19. of the same
> Moneth.
>
> With other Additions.
>
> Mart. *Quando magis dignos licuit spectare triumphos.*

> Printed at London by V.S. for
> Edward Blount, 1604.

Figure 10 Title page: *B. Jon: His Part of King James his Royall and Magnificent Entertainement*, 1604

she never acknowledges the subsequent attribution to Spenser's teacher.[82] Compelled to locate the shift in the authorial status of these two royal entertainments, she contrasts Jonson's entertainment with "Thomas Dekker's rival account," subsequently published as *The Whole Magnificent Entertainment*, so that she can distance herself from the theatre and conclude,

> Dekker presents "the whole" while Jonson presents "his part," an expression of possession that informs the entire treatise and, arguably, all of Jonson's work. This distinction between the whole and the part ultimately gets played out upon the text page itself, as Jonson glosses his own words, breaking up the text so that the reader's attention is constantly directed toward the margins, where Jonson's learning – the source of his "authority," as he says – is displayed (132).

Mulcaster's anonymous entertainment is a "pamphlet," while Jonson's is a "treatise," a word which, according to the *OED*, refers to "a book or writing which treats of some particular subject; commonly (in mod. use always), one containing a formal or methodical discussion or exposition of the principles of the subject." Clearly Tribble's interest in Jonson's use of scholarly apparatus to display his learning informs her choice of words here because, marginal glosses notwithstanding, the text of the entertainment does not pretend to present a methodical exposition of any subject's principles. Rather, as is the case with the pamphlet produced by Mulcaster – who did in fact produce a learned treatise on "the hole matter, which children ar to learn" (A3)[83] – it is primarily descriptive. But perhaps a more serious difficulty with Tribble's position is her contention that the "expression of possession" implicit in the phrase, "his part," "informs the entire treatise and, arguably, all of Jonson's work." This is not the *whole* story, because, in fact, once the whole of Jonson's part subsequently becomes a part of Jonson's whole, the title page for the folio edition of the entertainment for the king's entry provides a strikingly different account.

On the title page that is prepared for the folio text (4B) (Fig. 11), several parts of the earlier quarto title page have been removed, including the part that proclaims Jonson's possession of the text. Abstracted from the rivalry with Dekker and the actual event, both now long past, the new title page no longer accords top billing to "B. Jon," and it reduces the remainder of the title from "HIS PART OF / *King James* his Royal and Magnifi- / cent *Entertainement through his* / Honorable Cittie of London, / Thurseday the 15. of / *March. 1603*" to merely "PART OF THE / KINGS / ENTERTAINMENT / IN PASSING TO / his / Coronation." Because the "PART" no longer belongs to Jonson, possession is solely accorded to James: the text authorized by the folio title page is the *king*'s entertainment, and it represents what has been

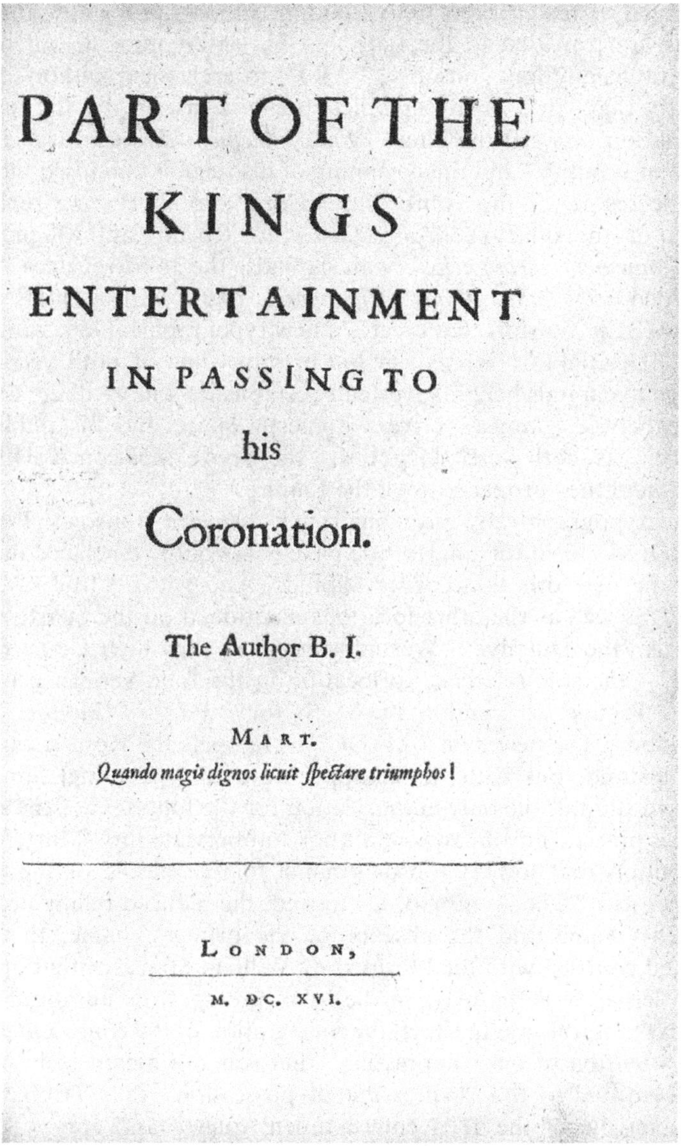

PART OF THE KINGS ENTERTAINMENT

IN PASSING TO

his

Coronation.

The Author B. I.

MART.
Quando magis dignos licuit spectare triumphos!

LONDON,
M. DC. XVI.

Figure 11 Title page: *Part of the Kings Entertainment, The Workes of Beniamin Jonson*, 1616

preserved of *his* entrance into London. Furthermore, now that capital letters are provided to the king and his entertainment, but no longer typographically link Jonson's "PART" to a classical author's name for the city that "in a great capitall Letter was inscribed," the metonymic association between the king's *"Entertainement through his* / Honorable Cittie of London" and the beginning of his reign is collapsed into a more specific record of the event: "his / Coronation." Having replaced the italics of the quarto's *"King James* his Royall and Magnifi- / *cent Entertainement through his"* with capitals, the folio replaces the italics accorded to *"the Kings Chamber"* (A3) with "THE KINGS CHAMBER," a shift that creates a new typographical link with "MONARCHIA BRITANNICA" in the previous line of both versions. The change to capitals here inadvertently establishes a more direct correspondence between James's private domestic space and his public realm, between, as both versions put it, "the above mentioned Title of the City" and the "proper seate of the Empire."

The typographically prominent link between Jonson's PART and LONDINIVM in the quarto title page gets doubly displaced in the folio once the new title is accorded capitals. And with "Cittie of London" gone – as well as the other locations mentioned on the quarto title page such as "the Dutchy," "Westminster," and "his high Court of Parliament" – the sole reference to location in the folio version gets reduced from "Printed at London by V. S. for / Edward Blount, 1604" to "London." The new date, "M. DC. XVI.," gets the Roman capitals this time around, but with the disappearance of V[alentine] S[imms] and Edward Blount, the only authorization for the folio text of the entertainment is provided by an ancient author – abbreviated to "Mart." – and an attribution that lowers Jonson's name to the middle of the page and reduces it to "The Author B. I." Indeed, the reduced billing accorded to Jonson's name and the absence of the printer's name, the latter in marked contrast with the "Printed by William Stansby" that appears on the title pages of the plays in the folio, presages the authorial status of the text that follows. In short, the folio edition of the *Kings Entertainment* calls attention to one "impressing" that was not meant to be "lasting"; and contrary to the "expression of possession" that Tribble finds so characteristic of the 1604 entertainment quarto and Jonson's work in general, the title page of the folio version offers up a text that is considerably less proprietary – especially in terms of its printing and authorship. Moreover, placed side by side, the title pages for the quarto and folio versions of the *Kings Entertainment* reproduce, respectively, the essential ambivalence of authorship as conflicting desires for individual autonomy and externalized authority. Considered diachronically, however, the two title pages suggest that Jonson's career as an author was moving from the former desire to the latter – a trajectory that not only gets preserved materially in the folio's arrangement of its two sections of dramatic texts but also runs contrary to the singular authorial achievement the folio itself has come to represent.

Obviously, the title page for a quarto edition of a work meant to be sold individually on the merits of its author and of the events to which that author contributed would require one kind of title page, while that same text, inserted twelve years later into a large folio volume of works by the same author, would require something quite different. And yet, if, as Loewenstein asserts, Jonson's inclusion of a masque in *Cynthia's Revels* reflects his desire "to extricate himself from the confused literary market of the public theatres and to insert himself into what might be called a neoconservative patronage market,"[84] then the first page of the folio's body of entertainments and masques seems to suggest that such patronage comes with its own share of difficulties.[85] At the most superficial level, the difference between the folio's two sections of dramatic texts, as well as the two forms of printed authorship (anomalous and typical) they represent, can be attributed to differences in venue. This point would seem to be so self-evident that it hardly requires further comment. But, in fact, the situation is considerably more complicated. Although scholars almost unanimously agree that the fundamental distinguishing characteristic of Jonson's authorship is his involvement with the printing of the 1616 folio, at least one significant determinant of that distinction appears to be neither the author nor the press. Instead, the performance site of a given dramatic work seems to have initially played a role in determining the authorial status of printed texts that get included in the folio.[86] Concomitantly, as Bland astutely observes, "Jonson and Stansby altered the spatial relationship of the text to the page" in the hopes of giving material form to "the idea of the book as its own theatre."[87] In either scenario, the page remains at least partially engaged with the stage, an engagement that is hard to miss in a work like *The Masque of Blacknesse*, the first selection in the folio devoted, according to the section's title page, to "MASQVES AT COVRT" (4F2).

Orgel has written that English theatre "was real in the way that 'real estate' is real; it was a location, a building."[88] Precisely this kind of locational and architectural realness initially authorizes the text of *The Masque of Blacknesse*, which begins with a recollection of its performance: *"Personated at the Court, at* WHITE-HALL, *on / the Twelv'th night, /* 1605" (4F3).[89] The double locative – at the court and at Whitehall – is further reinforced by the use of capital letters to typographically emphasize the real, material nature of the specific performance site as an authorization for this particular text. Murray argues that there is a strong correlation "between the authority of a medieval manuscript attributable to a certain archive and the originality of a prompt-book held in the vaults of an acting company" because "[t]heir place or location of holding – their physical presence – determines authenticity."[90] While a striking representation of such locational authority operates semiotically on the folio's title page to hold or house its title, here at the beginning of the folio's first masque, only the capitalized name of a location remains to authenticate the text that follows. Having traveled the long and perilous road from a bricklayer's apprentice to the king's dramatist, Jonson makes the next logical career move by replacing himself with a building at court. No authorial attribution appears. In fact, although each of the nine plays in the folio has a separate title page which features an identical attribution – "The Author B. I." – none of the masques included in the folio has a separate title page nor any indication of authorship, an absence that becomes even more conspicuous in the Oxford edition, which reproduces the initial title page, and then supplies each masque with an individual title page of its own.[91] Indeed, the desire to make these texts authorial is so great that the Oxford editors also provide facsimiles of title pages for all masques and entertainments previously published in quarto – despite the fact, as was noted above, that they chose the folio as copy-text for all of these works. The reality preserved by the folio, however, is far less ideal because all of the masques must look back to and rely on the section's title page for an author, which is also the only page that provides the minimal detail of that section's printing as "London / M. DC. XVI." So, although Loewenstein may be correct in asserting that "the publication of the masques is to a large extent a necessary step toward the printing of the 1616 folio,"[92] once the folio gets printed, it places the publication history of the masques under erasure.

On the other hand, if, as was noted earlier, the title pages of the nine plays in the folio reminds the reader that the texts were published in "London" and "Printed by William Stansby," it is also true that not one of these plays gives any indication of where – as the end-page for each play reads – "This Comoedie" or "This Tragoedie vvas first acted." Alternatively, a text like *The Masque of Blacknesse*, which is very site-specific, was not "first acted"; rather, as was the case with *Hymenaei, or the Solemnities of Masque*, it was "personated," an odd usage for the folio which, coupled with the typographic over-determination of its site of personation, recalls Jonson's effort some sixty folio pages earlier to link the royal body with Penshurst.[93] Moreover, although Murray has called Jonson "an architect of print,"[94] here only the banqueting hall at

James's court links the king with the author.[95] In this sense, the *Masque of Blacknesse* looks back to and revives a classical architectural notion in which, "the (idealized) body," according to Anthony Vidler, "was, so to speak, directly projected onto the building ... [which] derived its authority, proportional and compositional, from this body, and, in a complementary way, the building then acted to confirm and establish the body – social and individual – in the world."[96] Vidler is quick to point out that Renaissance architects "from Alberti to Francesco di Giorgio, Filarete, and Leonardo subscribed to this analogy."[97]

Perhaps the link between the masque's reliance on "WHITE-HALL" for its authority and the absence of the Foucauldian author-function can be best understood in the context of recent work by architectural theorist Mark Wigley. According to Wigley's analysis of Renaissance architecture, "it is not that the building is being thought of as a body with the classical analogy. Rather, the body is thought of as a building."[98] This reversal enables Wigley to argue that the oft-remarked emergence of Renaissance individuality is an architectural consequence. "The idea of the individual," Wigley asserts, "can only emerge within the institutions of domesticity established by the construction of the textured surface that is the house."[99] Clearly this is the case for Jonson and James in the poem that begins on the first page of the "The Forrest"; but on the first page of the folio's first masque – and, indeed, at the beginning of the remaining six masques – the court itself is architecturally compelled to shoulder the individualizing burden of the author.

When authorship does eventually enter on to the scene to authorize the proceedings, it is not Jonson's. Instead, Jonson begins his explanation of *The Masque of Blacknesse* by calling on four authors – "[a]PLINY, [b]SOLINVS, [c]PTOLOMEY, and of late [d]LEO the *African*" (4F3) – and giving them *side*notes. Nevertheless, it quickly becomes clear that the authority for this text lies closer to home. Having credited these authors with "remember[ing] vnto vs a riuer in *Aethiopia*, famous by the name of Niger," he abruptly shifts the authorial responsibility for his masque to someone else: "Hence (because it was her Maisties will, to have them Black mores at first) the invention was derived by me, and presented thus" (4F3). While Jonson's use of the word "invention" here recalls the attribution that appears on the title page of the 1608 quarto edition of the masque – "Invented by Ben: Jonson" (A2) – the absence of this attribution in the folio serves to enhance the queen's contribution. Orgel rightly underscores the importance of this contribution when he observes that Queen Anne's request that the ladies perform in blackface becomes "the conceit of the masque, and the necessity of fulfilling such requests defines one very important aspect of these productions."[100] Moreover, by acknowledging the role Anne played in the masque's initial conception, Jonson, as Orgel argues in a subsequent essay, is "distinguishing the *invention* of the text from its *authority*."[101] Such a distinction is remarkably similar to Miller's generalized conception of authorship as a struggle between the need for individual autonomy and the need for externalized authority. Nonetheless, it bears little resemblance to the authorship of the folio's play-texts, which not only make little room for the kind of collaboration typical of the early modern London stage, but also rely on Jonson's anomalous involvement with the publication process for their authority.

Traditionally, critical appraisals of the 1616 folio have tended to ignore this disparity, choosing instead to evaluate the authorship of the entire volume on the basis of the authorial status of its plays. Donovan, as I noted at the outset, attributes such negligence to "the unfortunate rift in modern scholarship between literary interpretation and textual criticism." I want to go further here and suggest that this "unfortunate rift" can itself be located within a certain ideological economy, one in which the chief investment is the singularity of the author and the singularity of the authorial text. If "the modern game of books and authors" could only be played after printing technology was invented, I would add that critics of early modern printed drama have been inclined to attend this game only when it is played by individuals. Foucault influentially exposed the limits of this lonely playing field some three decades ago. Subsequently, we have come to be increasingly aware of how modern notions of authorship elide a much more fraught and complicated process of subjectification which, according to Louis Montrose, both "shapes individuals as loci of consciousness and imitators of actions," and positions them "within networks of power beyond their comprehension or control."[102] The 1616 folio not only materially captures and preserves this fundamental process of subjectification but also reproduces and aligns its subject's constitutive elements with the theatre and the court, the two performance centers of Jonson's career as a dramatist.

To offer such theoretical observations does not go far enough. Despite the fact that authorship is increasingly viewed as a "discursive formation," the Shakespearean model of the lone author as "a happie imitator of Nature" and "a most gentle expresser" continues to influence how scholars read and write about printed drama. In the case of Jonson, this Shakespearean model underwrites the idealization of his involvement with the publication process. Whereas Shakespeare's "mind / and hand went together: And what he thought, he vttered with that / easinesse, that wee haue scarse receiued from him a blot in his papers," Jonson's mind has been compelled to merge with the printing press to produce a singularly authorial printed book that isolates his authorship from the inhospitable collaborative environment of the theatre and the court. I have begun to suggest that such an approach is not appropriate for a significant number of the dramatic texts collected in the *Workes*. In the remaining pages of this chapter, I want to reconsider the whole of the folio's authorship in the context of what we have noticed about the authorial status of its masques and entertainments.

One of the remarkable "coincidences" in the history of Jonson's authorship is that his *Workes* appeared in the same year as a folio collection of James I's writings.[103] I will have more to say about this historical coincidence shortly, but in some obvious sense the appearance of two folio collections so close in time suggests that the compositor's table made possible a meeting between the king and the dramatist in much the same way that the banquet table in "To Penshurst" brought them together.[104] Although these two texts represent very different publication ventures, taken together they seem to reproduce the defining ambivalence of authorship itself: one collects writings by an author seeking authority; the other collects writings by authority seeking to be an author.

Other monarchs before James had tried their hand at authorship,[105] but James's decision to publish a folio collection of his works in the same moment that Jonson and other playwrights were beginning to rely on publication to elevate their standing as authors is suggestive. James had already acknowledged the importance of the press in the first year of his English reign by authorizing the patent to the Stationers Company to form what became known as the English Stock.[106] In doing so, the king introduced the next phase of an uneasy alliance between royal authority and printers that was inititiated in 1504 with the appointment of William Faques as the king's printer,[107] and subsequently formalized in 1511, when Richard Pynson was commissioned to print statutes legitimating Henry VIII's succession.[108]

Because James I and Jonson achieved comparably singular deployments of the printing press in the same year, this bit of synchronicity has made it tempting to link their respective achievements. As Jeffrey Masten notes, scholars have recently begun to investigate "the relations between modes of textual production, systems of government, and modes of subjectivity."[109] For Masten, the emergence of dramatic authorship is complexly linked to emergent notions of patriarchal absolutism in the early seventeenth century – notions that are encoded in James's *Workes* – and he sees "the king's book as a marker for a conjunction of discourses we would now separate into the fields of sexuality, textuality, and political authority."[110] Focusing primarily on the etymological "conjunction" of author and authority, a relation he repeatedly represents with "the slash in the term *authorlity*," Masten argues that this philological contingency shapes and is shaped by the textual apparatus of James's 1616 folio.[111] Masten's concern with such etymological relations and their early modern materialization in textual production is an important first step toward understanding how systems of authority are transformed by emergent technologies. What is needed, however, is a systematic historical study of interactions between monarchs and printers in the period, one that goes beyond etymologies (or issues of censorship, for that matter) and examines, in particular, the activities of kings' printers between the turn of the sixteenth century and the Restoration.

In the specific context of Jonson studies, Hanson observes that the playwright has served "as exemplar in recent accounts of author formation in the Renaissance – accounts which usually situate [Jonson] in a discursive field defined by poles of 'authority' (embodied variously in the King, Classicism, the law, and his own ethical claims) and 'subversion' or 'transgression' . . . and describe his authorship as the effect of a complex interplay between them."[112] Van den Berg's essay, "Ben Jonson and the Ideology of Authorship," is in many ways representative of these critical trends, especially the effort to link author and authority. Concisely expressing what underwrites much of the recent non-bibliographic scholarship on Jonson and the 1616 folio, she asserts that "[t]he ideology of authorship rests on two major humanist assumptions: the autonomy of the individual and the primacy of texts as vehicles of human community."[113] For van den Berg, the exemplary autonomous individual is Jonson, the exemplary text is his *Workes*, and she contends that "[p]ersonal and cultural circumstances combined to occasion the 1616 folio."[114] In the first case, van den Berg offers the following overview of Jonson's personal circumstances: "By 1616 Ben Jonson had survived the failures of *Catiline* and *Sejanus* and was at the height of his public career. He had a substantial body of works, dramatic and poetic, that met his criteria in contemporary terms."[115] *Personally*, of course, Jonson also had a substantial body,[116] and in "Ben: Jonson's Execration against Vulcan"[117] Jonson himself linked his body with his books in the sense that both were objects that could be destroyed.[118]

The only mention of the dramatist in Francis Meres's *Palladis Tamia* (1598) puts "Beniamin Iohnson" at the end of a list of fourteen "Poets" who are "our best for Tragedie,"[119] and so it is probable that Jonson took the professional failures of *Catiline* and *Sejanus* personally. When van den Berg turns her attention to those "cultural circumstances" which combined with the dramatist's "personal" circumstances "to occasion the 1616 folio," she doesn't offer a cultural circumstance so much as another individual who happens to be an author. "Jonson could become the first poet to capitalize on the new medium of print," she contends, "partly because James, who published his works in folio in 1616, replaced the performative, theatrical mode of royal self-representation with the new literary mode of print."[120] What is most striking about this assertion is the way culture gets individualized in the figure of the king-as-author, as if van den Berg is advancing the very ideology of authorship she seeks to expose. Accordingly, this ideology enables her to reduce enormous and complex transitions to a kind of meeting-of-the-minds between two men, a meeting in which, as Wendy Wall puts it, "the distinct realms of textual authority and cultural authority can shade into one another."[121]

In 1616, Jonson overcomes the stigma of print because his king has overcome it. In 1616, Jonson replaces the playhouse with the printing house as the chief mode of his authorial self-expression because his king has replaced performance with print as the chief mode of royal self-representation. The powerful connection between king and poet that grounds this view of Jonson's *Workes* was rehearsed some twenty years before the publication of the two folios when Francis Meres surveyed the contemporary English literary scene and remarked:

As Emperors, kings and princes have in their handes authority to dignifie or disgrace their nobles, attendants, subjects and vassals: so Poets have the whole power in their handes to make men either immortally famous for their valiant exploites and virtuous exercises, or perpetually infamous for their vicious lives.[122]

The two folios of 1616 add historical specificity to Meres's analogy by singling out a king's and a poet's relation to print. Further, Jonson himself essentially collapses the analogy into the figure of James in the fourth epigram ("To King James") where he writes, "How, best of Kings, do'st thou a scepter beare! / How, best of *Poets*, do'st thou laurell weare" (3Tv).[123]

Obviously there are precedents for van den Berg's claim, but the one that interests me most was examined in the previous chapter. In locating the agency for Jonson's folio in James's hands, van den Berg is following a pattern that underwrites the posthumous construction of Shakespeare as an author. In much the same way that the establishment of Shakespeare's authorship in print on the title page of *2 Henry IV* gets linked subsequently to anecdotal accounts of the playwright receiving instructions about the fate of Falstaff from Queen Elizabeth, Jonson's emergence in print is said to be made possible by King James. If a "privileged moment of *individualization*" is at stake in such an emergence, then this reconstruction of Jonson's cultural circumstances would seem to be based on an anachronistic conflation of two meanings of the word "subject": the first, according to the *OED*, is an early fourteenth-century reference to "[o]ne who is under the dominion of a monarch or reigning prince"; the second is a late seventeenth-century development in which the word comes to refer to "the thinking or cognizing agent; the self or ego." Royal subject, meet bibliographic ego.

The appearance of the two folios in the same year makes such a conflation tempting, but a closer look at the publication history of Jonson's folio suggests that, in the matter of trading in the stage for the page, the king could well have been the poet's subject. Stansby, Jonson's printer, was a well-known producer of play-quartos[124] who had also printed and/or published several fine scholarly books including folios by many of the dramatist's friends and acquaintances.[125] In registering *Certayne Masques* in January 1615, Stansby had legally prepared himself to publish precisely that section of the folio that comes closest to what van den Berg might identify as James's "theatrical mode of royal self-representation"; and the volume in its entirety was printed relatively quickly, in less than two years. James I's folio is half as long as Jonson's, and the second of its two pages devoted to listing "THE / SEVERALL TREATISES / ACCORDING TO THE TIME / WHEREIN THEY WERE WRITTEN, / And Their Place In This / Collection, &c." (E4–E5) indicates that the last of its "Five Spea- / ches" – and the final item of the volume – preserves an exercise in royal performance given before "the Starre- / Chamber" in "1616." Alternatively, the folio's final piece, "THE GOLDEN AGE RESTORED," reproduces a "Maske at Court, 1615" (4Q1v).[126] Thus, while Stansby's 20 January 1615 registration of *Certayne Masques* seems to point to a kind of closure to the project of compiling the texts that were to comprise Jonson's *Workes*, James's *Workes* remained open into 1616.

In the end, it is probably impossible to determine which of our two authors got the idea to publish a collection of their writings in folio first. Indeed, Bland has even speculated that the idea of publishing Jonson's *Workes* – "perhaps gathered together as a quarto collection with a general title-page" – may have initially come from Walter Burre, who not only owned or had a controlling interest in all of Jonson's most important plays but also held unsold stocks of the dramatist's quartos prior to the printing of the folio.[127] The frequent appearance of plays in print by Jonson's contemporaries without their involvement in publication, as well as Thomas Pavier's effort to publish a quarto collection of Shakespeare's plays lends some credence to Bland's speculation. If, on the other hand, the impetus for the *Workes* did come from Jonson, there is certainly ample evidence – examined in Chapter 1 – that the playwright had begun to view publication as a viable alternative to the stage at an early moment in James's reign when the king may have been too busy getting used to his new throne to think about publishing a folio collection of his writings.

Ultimately, both men could have defended their decision to come out with a collection of their works by identifying themselves with a respective group of authors. In James's case, this identification is enunciated for him by James Winton early in the folio's "THE PREFACE / TO THE READER" wherein he poses himself the question, "How are we bound to those, who have laboured in setting out the Councells, and, Works of the Fathers together?" (B2r) Here, for a moment, a book metaphor collapses community and collection together as Winton answers himself by suggesting that the act of binding the king's writings together binds the king to other writers whose works have been bound together. Alternatively, Jonson could point to folio collections in Stansby's print shop by friends and acquaintances such as John Florio, Thomas Coryate, Walter Raleigh, John Selden, and William Camden with some admixture of inspiration and envy.[128] He also could have leafed through a folio of Seneca's *Workes* printed at Stansby's shop in 1614 and been impressed.[129]

There is, however, a more serious difficulty with positing a causal link between the two folios of 1616: it participates in and furthers the project of translating a drama of the margins into the literary center by excluding the theatre. In other words, if James becomes "a man in print" in order to replace the performative mode of royal self-representation with the printed mode, then to give James the credit for Jonson's folio is to remain the king's subject (in the earlier sense), inasmuch as this accreditation can only be made if the theatre itself is displaced. Murray has argued that, "[t]he transfer of a text from playhouse to printed book displaces almost completely the textual invisibility prescribed by the stage."[130] Indisputable as this deceptively complicated formulation is, it nevertheless fails to tell an important part of the story in which Jonson scholars have been a little too eager to aid the playwright with the transfer of his text from the playhouse to the printing house by prescribing the invisibility of the stage.

Surely it would be difficult to undertake a serious study of James's folio and its implications for royal self-representation without giving some attention to the ways in which previous English monarchs utilized authorship and print to represent themselves. And it is no less problematic to consider Jonson's folio and its impact on authorship without locating it in the greater historical context of authoring drama for the early modern English stage. That such an approach has been largely absent from discussions of the *Workes* points to a kind of antitheatricality in Jonson scholarship.[131] One probable source of this anti-theatricality can be traced back to Jonson's contemporaries, for whom the anomalously authorial status of the 1616 folio was expressed as the opposition between the terms "play" and "work," a semantic quibble succinctly captured in Epigram 269 Of *Wits Recreations*:

> *To Mr. Ben Johnson demanding the reason*
>   *Why he call'd his playes works.*
> Pray tell me Ben, where doth the mystery lurke,
> What others call a play you call a worke.[132]

Noting that "the idea of the work" has been fundamental to maintaining "the privileged position of the author," Foucault asserts that, "[a] theory of the work does not exist, and the empirical task of those who naively undertake the editing of works often suffers in the absence of such a theory."[133] In the passage quoted above, the writer points to the originary moment of privilege in the dramatist's career and enunciates for Foucault the process of individuation that is the foundation of modern authorship by reducing the difference between "play" and "work" to the difference between "others" and "you." Even the economic resonances of the two terms simultaneously individuate Jonson and isolate him from the theatre. If, as Steven Mullaney asserts, "Drama earned its living by a theatrical sleight of hand, translating work into play,"[134] then Jonson seems to have headed off in the opposite direction. In doing so, however, he moved toward anti-theatricalists like John Northbrooke, for whom the theatre, according to Jean Howard, "stands for idleness."[135] Indeed, the title of Northbrooke's 1579 tract, *A Treatise wherein Dicing, Daunsing, Vaine Plaies or Enterludes with other idle passtimes . . . are reprooved*, groups "Plaies" together with forms of play. After Jonson's folio, the opposition of work and play became something of a theme in printed collections of dramas. For example, William Sheares, the publisher of Marston's *Workes*, refers to the "approbies and aspersions" that have been "cast upon plays," and writes in his "Epistle dedicatorie" to Lady Elizabeth Cary,

is it because they are Playes? The name it seems somewhat offends them, where as if they were styled Workes, they might have their approbation also? I hope that I have now somewhat pacified that precise Sect, by reducing all our Authors Severall Playes into one Volume, and so stiled them the Works of Mr. John Marston. (A3–A3v)

The publication of Jonson's plays in a volume of the author's *Workes* offered other playwrights the means of protecting their plays from the "approbies and aspersions" that were the inevitable consequence of a culture that remained largely anti-theatrical, despite the popularity and success of the London stage. But to give Jonson sole credit for this innovation is to fall back into an ideology of authorship that insistently translates historical change into a genealogy of individual accomplishments. Alternatively, even a cursory glance at the historical record of dramas performed on English stages during the forty-year period between the opening of The Theatre in 1576 and the 1616 folio reveals a profound shift in the authorial status of plays that made it into print – a shift that not only anticipates Jonson's decision to revise and compile his plays into a collection representing the work of a single authorial presence but also may have given James I some second thoughts about available modes of royal self-representation. For The Theatre's first year of operation, Alfred Harbage lists the titles of six plays that were performed at court or offered for acting, five of which are without authorial attribution of any kind.[136] The one play that does acknowledge authorship, titled – ironically enough – *The Tide Tarrieth No Man*, is attributed to George Wapull. A year later, the number of titles jumps to thirteen, nine of which are anonymous.[137] If we skip ahead to 1615, the year in which Stansby is thought to have finalized arrangements for printing the *Workes*, only three known dramas – out of seventeen – seem to have circulated anonymously. One year later, the titles of eleven dramas appear, including three by Jonson; all of them are attributed to an author or authors. Indeed, 1616 is the first year since The Theatre opened some forty years earlier that no drama is listed without authorial attribution. Only two other years – 1631 and 1637 – can boast of the same level of named authorship, with twenty-two and twenty-one plays, respectively. If, as Saeger and Fassler observe, "the most vigorous decade for publication of plays was 1631–1640,"[138] then there would seem to be a direct correlation between concurrently high levels of publication and authorial attribution.

Given the variety of dramatic texts and performance sites recorded in the *Annals*, the shifts in the authorial status of dramas listed there cannot offer a complete picture of the theatrical context in which Jonson produced the 1616 folio. Nevertheless, the absence of anonymous titles in the year of Jonson's authorial triumph and the following decade-by-decade comparison of attribution levels are extremely suggestive:

	1580–89	1590–99	1600–09	1610–19	1620–29	1630–39
No. of Titles:	10	26	30	22	23	26
% Attributed:	58	54	75	74	81	89

Saeger and Fassler's recent statistical study of extant printed plays written for the London professional theatre, 1576–1642 indicates similar patterns of change in the authorship of drama – despite the fact that the number of extant plays (469 plays in 961 editions) accounts for little more than a third of the 1,200 titles listed in the *Annals*.[139] In their analysis, less than 20 percent of the extant plays printed in the 1580s were attributed to an author, while roughly 65 percent were attributed to a theatre company.[140] Over the next two decades, author attribution rises to 35 and 60 percent, respectively, and company attribution drops slightly to 60 percent. In the next decade, the one in which Jonson's folio appears, both author and company attribution rise to 71 and 67 percent, respectively. For the next ten-year period, during which Shakespeare's folio is published, author attribution increases no more than a few percentage points, while company attribution plunges to 45 percent. Clearly the time was right for two members of Shakespeare's company to present their dramatist's plays to the world under his name. By the last full decade before the closing of the theatres, author attribution has risen to 89 percent, and company attribution has recovered somewhat to 58 percent. Plays printed with no attribution whatsoever account for about 20 percent of the extant drama for the first thirty years of the professional theatre, then fall to ten percent in the decade of the Jonson folio, and they stay at that level for the remainder of the period.[141] Moreover, Saeger and Fassler's survey suggests a strong correlation between increases in author attribution and increases in the volume of plays printed during the same period.[142] During the first two decades, author attribution makes its steepest jump from 20 to 60 percent, while the average number of plays printed per year rises 700 percent from two to fourteen. By the time the author attribution rate is nearly 90 percent (1631–1640), an average of more than twenty-five different plays a year are being printed in one or more editions.

The consistency in this last set of figures between rising levels of print publication and increases in named authorship suggests that the transition from manuscript to print circulation had a profound effect on the authorial status of plays. In this superficial sense, Wall's claim that print "produces new authorizations and authors"[143] is at least half true. Of even greater interest, however, is the significant correlation between levels of author attribution for printed drama and the age of the London professional theatre. More than anything else, this link suggests that the "cultural circumstance" for Jonson's effort to consolidate and enhance his authorial status in print, for his effort to become, in Martin Elsky's phrase, "a serious professional author,"[144] is the increasing professionalization of the London stage. Such a close tie between the professional theatre and authorship is implied by Bentley, who, noting that medieval dramas were largely produced by men "earning their living as glovers, shipwrights, bakers, cordwainers, bowyers, fletchers, mercers, and butchers," concludes that, "[t]he plays they performed are nearly all anonymous, but there is no evidence whatever that they were written by men supporting themselves by dramatic writing, and there is much evidence to the contrary."[145] Comparably high levels of anonymity and amateurism in the first decade or so after the opening of The Theatre would indicate that the transition from lingering medievalisms to the early modern author figure, exemplified most famously by dramatic authors such as Shakespeare, Jonson, and subsequently Dryden, was facilitated by the merger of professional theatre and print publication.

Jonson and his contemporaries inevitably found themselves in the midst of this merger; but to locate the 1616 folio there, that is, to put Jonson's *Workes* – with its indelible record of printing house collaborators – back on "the loathed stage" paradoxically renders it nearly invisible within a scholarly discourse of the theatre that has nurtured itself on the notion of "the loathed page." In short, to restore the folio to the theatrical context from which it emerged is to situate it at a theoretical divide which, because it replicates what McKenzie terms the "professional *dis*junction of play-wrights and printers,"[146] is rarely crossed by scholars of early modern theatre and textual scholars. Here at this critical border, this place which is no place at all, we are, I think, finally afforded a revealing glimpse of the link between the two folios of 1616. Like the monarch in early modern England, Jonson's folio was the product of a culture to which it never really belonged.

4   "What strange Production is at last displaid": dramatic authorship and the dilemma of collaboration

> Jailer: They are famed to be a pair of absolute men.
> Daughter: By my troth, I think Fame but stammers 'em; they stand a grise above the reach of report.
>
> Fletcher & Shakespeare, *The Two Noble Kinsmen*

> The collaborative process – meeting in taverns to agree on plots, writing separate scenes apart and then coming together to edit, handing material to one playwright to finish and copy out – is a hermeneutical nightmare.
>
> Gordon McMullan, *The Politics of Unease*

The subject of this chapter is "a hermeneutical nightmare." I would like to begin, appropriately enough, with two hallucinatory seventeenth-century visions of playwrights at work. The first will be very familiar:

> [H]e was a happie imitator of Nature, was a most gentle expresser of it. His mind and hand went together. And what he thought he vttered with that easinesse, that wee haue scarse receiued from him a blot in his papers.

The second will be uncannily familiar:

> [H]is friends affirme he never writ any one thing twice: it seemes he had that rare felicity to prepare and perfect all first in his owne braine; to shape and attire his *Notions*, to adde or loppe off, before he committed one word to writing, and never touched pen till all was to stand as firme and immutable as if ingraven in Brasse or Marble.

The first account is collaboratively written by two actors, and appears near the end of an address "To the Great Variety of Readers" included in a folio that contains "Comedies, Histories, & Tragedies. Published according to the True Originall Copies." The second account is written by a single publisher, and appears near the end of an address from "The Stationer to the Reader" included in a folio that contains "Comedies and Tragedies. Never printed before, And now published by the Authours Originall Copies."

Although both accounts belong, according to Margreta de Grazia, "to a long history extending back to the pre-print era of classical rhetoric,"[1] it is also true that the first volume was published twenty-four years before the second, and, therefore, probably served as a model for the later one. Since the first account acknowledges the central role of imitation in authorship, it would be inappropriate to fault the writer of the second account for imitating the earlier account as he sets out to depict the writing process that culminated in a similar collection of plays. And both accounts, regardless of what they actually report about their respective authors, are written primarily to legitimate and authenticate the volumes which they preface. In this specific sense, Jeffrey Masten is quite right when, seeking to revise the title of Foucault's influential article on authorship, he offers an alternative question, "*Where* is an Author?" and answers, "[i]n the bookshop."[2] Masten is referring to Edward Archer's 1656 "CATALOGUE of all Plaies that were ever printed; together, with all the Authors names,"[3] and observes that this early list of dramatic titles, "reminds us, first, that dramatic authorship emerges from the publishing house and only indirectly from the theatre and, second, that authorship in its emergence is as much about marketing as about true attribution."[4]

On one level, Masten's observation pertains well to these two accounts of authorship, since both authors being described are dead by the time they are written; and both accounts, as I have suggested, are important elements within larger strategies to market two expensive and somewhat risky publishing ventures. But Masten's observation is particularly relevant to the second account. The dramatic authorship that emerges from the publishing house responsible for the second volume is indeed tenuously linked to the theatre because it was written nearly five years after the theatres were closed in 1642. Furthermore, the first volume was uncharacteristically successful in combining "marketing" and "true attribution," and therefore continues to play an extraordinary role in shaping its author's canon. The second volume rather more characteristically failed, and the attribution it promoted has rarely been taken seriously by scholars. What had worked so well for the first collection of plays did not work at all for the second, largely because in the earlier venture, two publishers named Blount and Jaggard were attempting to market a collection of plays that listed a single author on its title page. In the subsequent venture, however, a single publisher named Humphrey Moseley was attempting to market a collection of plays that listed two authors on its title page. Whereas the first volume employed the ambiguous early modern "s" to indicate that it brought together "Mr. William Shakespeares Comedies, Histories, & Tragedies" (Fig. 12), the second volume was forced to rely on a set of extra-linguistic signifiers "{ }" to indicate that its "Comedies and Tragedies" were "Written by {Francis Beavmont / And / John Fletcher}," and that both authors were "Gentlemen" (Fig. 13).

Figure 12 Title page: *Mr. William Shakespeares Comedies, Histories, & Tragedies*, 1623

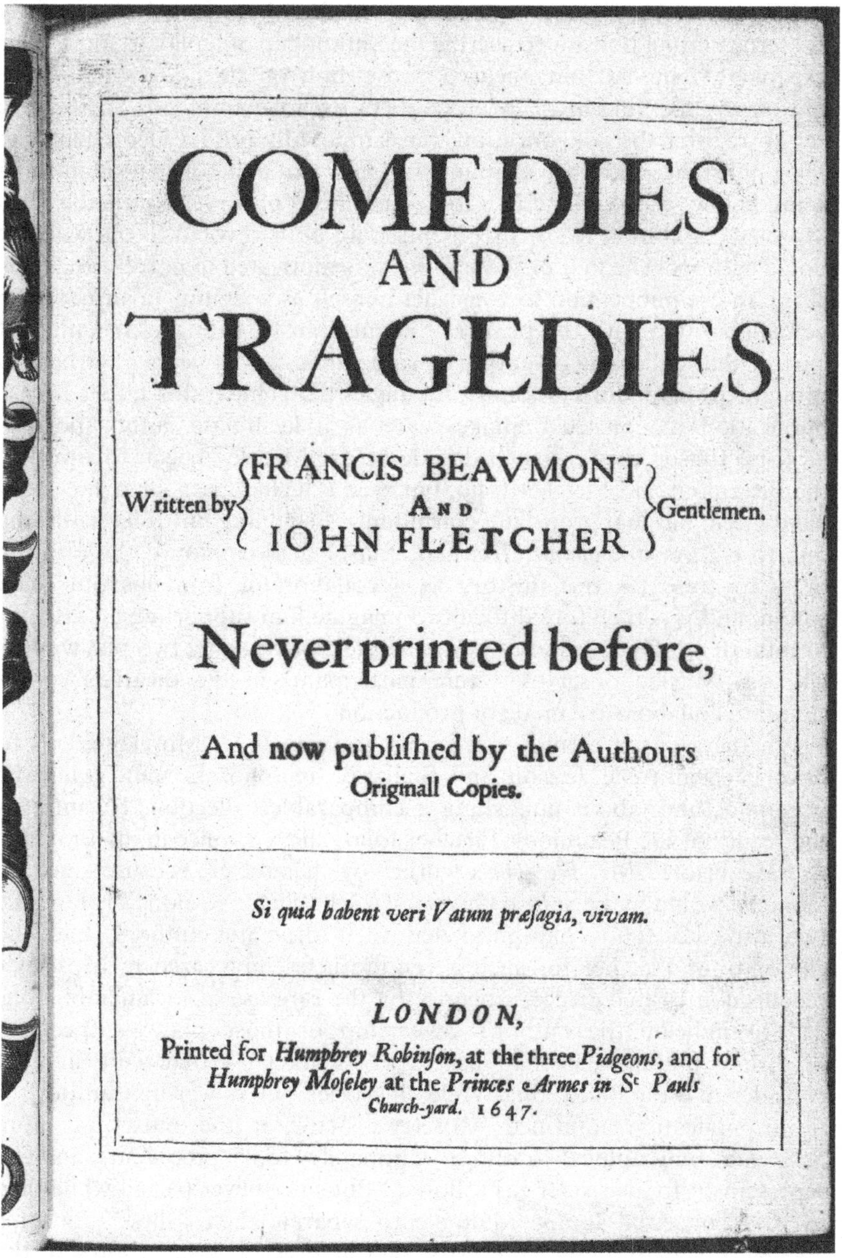

COMEDIES
AND
TRAGEDIES

Written by { **FRANCIS BEAVMONT**
AND
IOHN FLETCHER } Gentlemen.

Never printed before,

And **now** publiſhed by the Authours
Originall Copies.

Si quid habent veri Vatum præſagia, vivam.

LONDON,
Printed for *Humphrey Robinſon*, at the three *Pidgeons*, and for
Humphrey Moſeley at the *Princes Armes* in S.t *Pauls
Church-yard.* 1647.

Figure 13 Title page: *Comedies and Tragedies*, 1647

The use of "{ }" – or "dilemmas," as they were called in the early modern printing house – to ascribe the authorship of a play to more than one playwright had long been a convention on title pages of quarto editions by the time Moseley chose them over the ambiguous possessive "s" to register the collaboration that supposedly produced the plays he was publishing, and I will examine the history of that convention in some detail below. But the only two folio collections of printed dramatic texts Moseley could look to for precedents were both devoted to the work of single authors. The first of these folios was motivated in part by Jonson's desire to use publication to construct himself as a legitimate author, and he collaborated with the printer William Stansby to make a significant part of that collection as authorial as possible. Seven years later he was brought in to endorse Blount and Jaggard's comparable effort to use publication to construct Shakespeare as a legitimate author posthumously. Jonson died nearly a decade before Moseley began to work on the Beaumont and Fletcher folio, but even if he had been alive, he would have been an inappropriate consultant. Beginning in 1605 with the quarto edition of *Sejanus, His Fall*, Jonson had employed the printing press to erase his own history as a collaborator from his published canon, and it is therefore difficult to imagine him supporting an attempt to publish a folio collection of dramatic texts written by two playwrights who, as Masten observes, "were participants in the theatre's earlier standard collaborative mode of production."⁵

Whether Jonson turned over in his grave in 1647, Moseley seems to have had both the Jonson and Shakespeare folios in mind when he began to think about publishing a comparable collection. He informs the reader of the Beaumont–Fletcher folio, "[i]t was once in my thoughts to have Printed Mr. *Fletcher's* workes by themselves, because single & alone he would make a *Just Volume*" (A3r). "Single & alone" is how the two previous folios had marketed their dramatic authors, and the eligibility of Fletcher for such a venture gets emphasized in Moseley's recollection of this project's history by the rare use of an unambiguous "s" to indicate the author's ownership of those plays – specified, according to the Jonsonian usage, as "workes" – that were initially considered for publication. While this brief but powerful tradition of folio publication informed Moseley's plans at the outset, a more personal, biographical tradition ultimately took precedent, and he represents it to his readers as follows: "But since never parted while they lived, I conceived it not equitable to separate their ashes." Jonson's allegiance was to literary posterity, and he used his folio to present the volume's nine plays not as they were performed or initially written, but as he wanted them to be remembered. Blount and Jaggard's *declared* allegiance, expressed for them by Heminge and Condell, was to authenticity, and they used their folio to present Shakespeare's plays "as he conceived thē." Dedicated to honoring Beaumont and Fletcher's relationship when they were alive, Moseley claims to use his folio to preserve that relationship posthumously by mixing their literary remains into one published collection.

Ostensibly, the authorship that emerges from Moseley's publication has little to do with either marketing or true attribution, but rather with a sentimental attempt to monumentalize a relationship between two playwrights that death had done its best to break up. "Mr. *Beavmont*," Moseley reports, "dyed young . . . he left the world when hee was not full thirty yeares old. Mr. *Fletcher* survived, and lived till almost fifty; whereof the VVorld now enjoyes the benefit." It never occurs to Moseley that his commitment to keeping "their ashes" together is incompatible with the fact that Fletcher continued to write for the stage nearly two decades after his collaborator's death. Recent scholars have been much less committed to honoring the dead. Of the fifty-two extant plays that Fletcher had a hand in writing, Gordon McMullan observes that, "only fifteen can be attributed to Fletcher working alone. He wrote something like ten plays in the company of Beaumont, three with Shakespeare, six with Field, one with Rowley, and maybe nineteen with Massinger."[6] According to Cyrus Hoy, "modern scholarship is agreed that less than twelve of the vast corpus of plays which are currently designated by Beaumont and Fletcher's names are indeed products of their joint authorship."[7] Similarly, G. E. Bentley asserts, with reference to the Beaumont and Fletcher folios of 1647 and 1679, "[t]he evidence is overwhelming that Beaumont had nothing to do with most of the plays in these two collections."[8] If Moseley's folio had been motivated by more modern notions of authorship, his 1647 title page might have indicated that its "Comedies and Tragedies" were "Written by {Philip Massinger / And / John Fletcher}," or perhaps even "Written by {Philip Massinger, / Francis Beavmont / And / John Fletcher}."

Eleven years after the Beaumont–Fletcher folio appeared, Sir Aston Cokain tried to set the record straight. Cokain had contributed a commendatory poem to Moseley's collection, "On the / Deceased Author, Mr. John Fletcher, his Plays; and especially, *The Mad Lover*" (A3v), which failed to mention anything about a collaborator named Beaumont. In his 1658 poem, "*An Epitaph on Mr*. John Fletcher, *and Mr*. Philip Massinger, *who lie buried both in one Grave in St*. Mary Overie's Church *in* Southwark," he indirectly suggests that Moseley textually embalmed the wrong man:

> In the same Grave Fletcher was buried here
> Lies the Stage-Poet Philip Massinger.
> Playes they did write together, were great friends,
> And now one Grave includes them at their ends.
> So whom on earth nothing did part, beneath
> Here (in their Fames) they lie, in spight of death.[9]

Like Moseley, Cokain links the relationship between Massinger and Fletcher to the plays they wrote together, and also suggests that this collaboration has been maintained in the grave. But where Moseley's effort to preserve the collaborative authorship of Beaumont and Fletcher has not withstood scholarly scrutiny, Cokain's account can be verified by a church registry that has Massinger and Fletcher buried in the same parish graveyard.[10]

If Moseley was little bothered about whether the plays he collected were correctly attributed, his attempt to publish them is haunted at every step by other types of collaboration that require more careful attribution. First there is the matter of acquiring the manuscripts:

> 'T were vaine to mention the *Chargeablenesse* of this VVork; for those who own'd the *Manuscripts*, too well knew their value to make a cheap estimate of these Pieces, and though another joyn'd with me in the *Purchase* and Printing, yet the *Care & Pains* was wholly mine, which I found to be more then you'l easily imagine, unlesse you knew into how many hands the Originalls were dispersed (A3r).

Typographically, the italics tell a confused story of collaboration and singularity not unlike the one Moseley subsequently relates about the authorship of the volume itself. Just as the 1647 folio was initially conceived as a collection of Fletcher's plays "single & alone," but became a collection of Beaumont and Fletcher plays, the "*Care & Pains*" of the publishing project was "wholly" Moseley's, but the project's "*Chargeablenesse*" forces him to take on a co-investor to help with the "*Purchase*" of the "*Manuscripts*." Moreover, this confusion is reproduced in the information about the volume's publication. As R. C. Bald observes, "[t]he title-page bears the names of Humphrey Robinson and Humphrey Moseley as joint publishers, but *The Stationer to the Reader* is signed by Moseley alone."[11] Thus, the 1647 folio fails on both the level of authorship and publication to consistently represent the collaborative arrangements it purports to materialize.

Then there is the matter of acquiring a picture of Beaumont. Masten has noted "the apparent contradiction" in the volume's juxtaposition of a single engraved portrait of Fletcher with a title page that advertises a collection of plays "Written by {Francis Beavmont / And / John Fletcher},"[12] but what interests me about this juxtaposition is that a failed collaboration prevents Moseley from fully illustrating the collaborative authorship his folio attempts to embody and promote. Moseley informs the reader that he "was very ambitious to have got Mr. *Beaumonts* picture," and "spared no enquirie in those *Noble Families* whence he was descended, as also among those Gentlemen that were his acquaintance when he was of the *Inner Temple*," but no picture was ever made available to him. Although the two playwrights "never parted while they lived," their portraits could not be brought together after death, so Moseley assures the reader that "the best Pictures and those most like him you'l finde in this *Volume*." In other words, "Mr. *Beaumonts* picture," a genitive relation marked ambiguously by "s," is best exemplified by the texts in a collection initially planned for "Mr. Fletcher's workes," a genitive relation marked unambiguously by "'s." Appropriately, the presence or absence of a graphic, unvoiced signifier in a volume of plays "Never printed before" silently undermines Moseley's effort to textually reproduce the products of an allegedly collaborative authorship. Even Moseley's attempt to justify the missing portrait is borrowed from the most singular of authorial constructions, for as Masten observes, "the lack of Beaumont's portrait in Moseley's collection resonates with the concluding lines of the poem accompanying the engraved portrait in the Shakespeare volume: 'Reader, looke / Not on his Picture, but his Booke.'"[13] At least one extant copy of the 1647 folio (Huntington Shelf no. 112111) seems to have ignored that poem's advice by gathering and ultimately binding together two copies of Fletcher's portrait on the rectos of two successive pages (Fig. 14). Though this "mistake" is no doubt merely a rather ironic accident not uncommon to the printing houses of the period, it is, nevertheless, tempting to speculate that someone purposefully mediated between the printing and gathering phases of the book's production in order to right what they perceived to be a wrong. Seeing two names on the title page, but only one portrait within, this hypothetical good Samaritan perhaps thought that he could resolve this paradox by including a second portrait of an author in the volume. But, of course, the two portraits are identical representations of the same author, and so this particular copy which, like all other early modern printed books, is unlike any other, uniquely and singularly bears witness to the 1647 folio's desire to represent collaborative authorship as well as its inevitable failure to do so.

Contrasting Fletcher with Jonson, who "fought for authorial privilege and prerogative, and worked to deny the possibility of collaboration," McMullan notes that, "Fletcher remained doggedly a collaborator first and foremost. He quite clearly *preferred* to collaborate."[14] Given that Moseley's basic textual model was Jonson's folio, a playwright like

Figure 14 Fletcher portrait: *Comedies and Tragedies*, 1647

Fletcher, devoted to the collaborative writing environment of the theatre, was essentially incompatible with a strategy of authorial self-construction devised partly to suppress such an environment. Regardless of his stated commitment to the memory of Beaumont and Fletcher's friendship, it was no doubt the incompatibility of Fletcher's playwriting career with the Jonsonian model that influenced Moseley's decision to settle for a compromise formation. Vexed by the utter theatricality of Fletcher's authorship, Moseley stretched the format as far as he could to include Beaumont. The resulting volume's extraordinary preliminaries, consisting of thirty-five folio pages of reader addresses and commendatory poems, however, suggest the depth of Moseley's fears that such a hybrid form might fail in the bookshop.

When Moseley finally reappears between the preliminaries and the play-texts they strive to endorse, he tries one last time to assuage his own fears about the venture's success by promoting the volume as a necessary supplement to an age in which plays are no longer performed. Situating himself between texts written and signed by individuals for the printing house and texts collaboratively written for the playhouse, Moseley begins with an analogy to the theatre only to recall for his readers the fact that the theatre no longer exists:

> As after th' *Epilogue* there comes some one
> To tell *Spectators* what shall next be shown;
> So here, am I; but though I've toyld and vext,
> Cannot devise what to present ye next;
> For, since ye saw no *Playes* this Cloudy weather
> Here we have brought Ye our whole Stock together
> 'Tis new and all these *Gentlemen* attest
> Under their hands 'tis Right; and of the Best;
> *Thirty foure* Witnesses (without my taske)
> Y'have just so many *Playes* (besides a *Maske*)
> All good (I'me told) as have been *Read* or *Playd*,
> If this Booke faile, tis time to quit the Trade. (G2r)

Like an actor who steps forward to address the audience at the conclusion of a play, the stationer tries his hand at verse in the form of a textual intermezzo. The performance it follows is a kind of printing-house dumb show stitched together from scenes written by "*Thirty foure* Witnesses." The performance it precedes consists of thirty-four play-texts that were largely stitched together from scenes written by several authors, only two of whom can be more or less accommodated by the conventions of printed drama folios within which Moseley feels compelled to work. Moreover, the theatres have been darkened by the "Cloudy weather" of civil war, but by enacting within print a now prohibited bit of theatrical ritual, Moseley briefly reminds his readers of that which has been taken away from them, and simultaneously implies he can provide the next best thing. Inevitably, perhaps, he also has another closure in mind, and therefore frets at the conclusion of the speech that the sun may not shine on a certain bookshop located, according to the folio's title page, "at the Princes Armes in St. Pauls Church-yard."

James Shirley had been recruited to voice the volume's political inclinations at the beginning of the preliminaries in a commendatory verse entitled, "Upon the Printing of Mr. John Fletchers workes." Little bothered that two authors' names appear on the title page his verse follows, Shirley writes of the resurrection of a single playwright made possible through the power of print, and concludes,

> But let him live and let me prophesie,
> As I goe Swan-like out, Our Peace is nigh;
> A Balme unto the wounded Age I sing
> And nothing now wanting but the King. (A2v)

Unabashedly royalist, Shirley mourns the loss of two key early modern institutions of individualization, the author and the monarch.

When Moseley returns at the end of the preliminaries, he alludes briefly to the "cloudy weather" that has denied England both its king and its stage. Promising in a pseudo-theatrical genre to provide readers with the only theatrical experience that is available to them in 1647, Moseley can't let them have their pleasure – already frustrated for thirty-five pages of textual apparatus – without pausing to worry about the authorship of his volume one last time. Thus, what ultimately mediates between the folio's preliminary texts individually written for the printing house and the texts collaboratively written for the playhouse, is a brief "Postscript" that struggles to account for two sets of collaborations – one in the printing house, the other in the playhouse:

We forgot to tell the Reader, that some *Prologues* and *Epilogues* (here inserted) were not written by the *Authors* of this *Volume;* but made by others on the *Revivall* of severall *Playes*. After the *Comedies* and *Tragedies* were wrought off, we were forced (for expedition) to send these *Gentlemens* Verses to severall Printers, which has the occasion of their different Character; but the *Worke* it Selfe is one Continued Letter, which (though very legible) is none of the biggest, because (as much as possible) we would lessen the Bulke of the Volume. (G2r)

In the pseudo-theatrical speech that precedes this passage, Moseley had been insistent about his individuality, comparing himself to "one" who tells "*Spectators* what shall next be shown," and assuring his readers, "So here, am I; but though I've toyld and vext, / Cannot devise what to present ye next." When, however, he begins his final statement of the book and of the book's authorship and production, he slips from "I" to "We."

What follows this collaborative pronoun is a dense restaging of the 1647 folio's complex authorial predicament. In much the same way that the theatrical reality of Fletcher's playwriting career imposed collaborative authorship on a publication that was initially conceived as a single-author volume, the work of other authors, required to revive these plays in the theatre, has been added. Noting that brief and self-contained theatrical texts such as prologues and epilogues were "made by others," Moseley is either unwilling or unable to acknowledge that "severall *Playes*" themselves may not have been "written by the *Authors* of this *Volume*." Moreover, the folio's commendatory verses, each of which has been ascribed to an individual author, have been collaboratively produced by "severall Printers" – a collaboration that is betrayed by "their different Character." In other words, the extensive textual apparatus required to endorse and support the difficult task of translating the typically collaborative authorship of the theatre into a typically single-author textual format, has itself been collaboratively printed. Having alluded to the individualizing potential of the printing house when he equates the "severall Printers" with "their different Character," Moseley concludes by assuring his readers that "the *Worke* it Selfe," that is, the texts of collaboratively written plays, has been printed in "one Continued Letter." After thirty-five pages of preliminaries, Moseley has finally found a way to comfort himself and his readers that he has relocated the "Bulke of the Volume" from the collaborative writing environment of the theatre to the self-individualizing environment of the printing house. And yet, even here collaboration haunts Moseley's effort to translate the theatre into the book. Referring to Moseley's "Postscript," Bald observes,

[t]hat the preliminaries are the work of a succession of different printers is clear, but the implication that the body of the book is the work of one printing-house is . . . not to be relied upon. The plays were divided into eight rather uneven sections, and each was handed to a different printer, who signed his section with a separate alphabet.[15]

As was the case with the "severall Printers" of "these *Gentlemens* Verses," differences in "Character" – indeed, different alphabetic *signatures* – betray the collaborative nature of the folio's publication. But if, as Bald asserts, "[t]he preliminaries were, for the most part, the work of the printers who had been responsible for the body of the book,"[16] then Moseley's deliberate acknowledgment and silence, respectively, of the equally shared printing of the folio's textual apparatus and play-texts is extremely suggestive of his desire to transform collaboration into singularity. Moseley readily admits that the volume's individually authored commendatory verses have been pieced together from several printing houses. Alternatively, when Moseley turns to the collaboratively authored play-texts that constitute the main body of the folio, he tries to deceive his readers into thinking that they have come from one printer "in one Continued Letter."

The 1647 Beaumont and Fletcher folio was published some thirty years after Jonson's *Workes*, though Jonson's Oxford editors confirm a close link between the two collections that I have already intimated above.[17] Appearing well into a period in which the printing house was increasingly relied upon to assert dramatic authorship, and the "presence of an author" was no longer an anomalous aspect of a printed dramatic text, the 1647 folio nevertheless represents a very complex phase in this process. The folio collection was essentially the domain of the individual author, but the plays Moseley intended to publish were nearly all the products of multiple authorship. Inadvertently, the folio collection was also constitutively anti-theatrical, but the theatres had already been closed for four years when Moseley undertook to publish his volume. Indeed, the notorious New Bibliographic narratives of piracy are no longer even vaguely tenable, for as Bald observes,

> In 1646 the actors were no longer in the position they had been in even as late as 1641. There was no immediate likelihood that the clouds of civil strife would lift . . . the entry of thirty Beaumont and Fletcher plays in the Stationers' Register on 4 September 1646 represents the conclusion about this time of successful negotiations with the King's Men, [and] one can readily suppose that the impoverished actors had eventually approached Moseley and asked him to undertake the publication of their plays, and that, having found a partner to help him in financing the venture, he was at last prepared to do what he had for some time been anxious to undertake.[18]

In other words, the closing of the theatres had facilitated a rather earnest collaboration between playhouse and printing house to produce the first and only folio collection of collaboratively authored plays.

Attempting to adapt an essentially single-author format to collaborative authorship at a moment when the theatre had ceased to exist as an oppositional source of self-definition, Moseley's resulting folio couldn't be anything less than a record of a complexly transitional period in the history of the author's emergence. The phrase "collaborative authorship" did not exist in 1647, but the Beaumont–Fletcher folio, despite its title page attribution, suggests that it would have already been an oxymoron. I will have more to say about how the 1647 folio copes, or rather fails to cope, with the hermeneutical nightmare of collaboration below; for now, however, I want to turn to a more generalized examination of collaborative authorship in the period and some of the problems collaboration has presented to scholars of early modern dramatic texts.

If the phrase "collaborative authorship" would have been conceptually problematic in 1647, it is largely because the "moment of individualization" Foucault speaks of had already been implicated in the authorial self-construction of Jonson and the commodification of Shakespeare – both of which had been accomplished in the printing house. Thus, while author and collaborator would eventually refer respectively to functions which, at least in theory, are mutually exclusive, dramatic authorship and collaborative authorship must, in theory, represent irreconcilable modes of literary production. Consistent with this conceptual difficulty, "collaboration," as McMullan observes, "is still thought of by Shakespearean and other editors as a 'problem,'"[19] and much of this century's critical treatment of early modern drama, according to Masten, has "worked to construct an authorial univocality"[20] for extant dramatic texts, despite the fact that, as he notes elsewhere, "early modern English playwriting . . . largely resists categories of singular authorship, inalienable intellectual property, and the individual central to later Anglo-American cultural, literary, and legal history."[21]

The presence of paradox generally exhibits the force of an underlying desire, and for editors and scholars of Renaissance drama the desire is to reduce the multiple and dispersed intentions that shaped play-texts in the playhouse and the printing house into idealized, single-author works. The prototype of this editorial idealization was Jonson's involvement in the publication of his plays and masques in the 1616 *Workes* folio; and an early statement of this idealization appeared seven years later in the First Folio of Shakespeare. Lamenting that the market for published plays has been flooded "with diverse / stolne, and surreptitious copies, maimed, and deformed by the frauds / and stealthes of iniurious impostors, that expos'd them," Heminge and Condell claim to offer Shakespeare's literary remains "cur'd, and perfect of their limbes; and all / the rest, absolute in their numbers, as he conceived thẽ" (26–27). Transforming the mutilated body into a pristine corpus necessitates the production of an idealized narrative of authorship, and in the same paradoxical moment, the texts of Shakespeare's plays and the constitutive desire of Shakespearean textual scholarship are presented to the world. In short, the same single-author format that simultaneously inspired and haunted Moseley's attempt to publish a folio collection of Fletcher's plays, continues to inspire and haunt scholars and editors of printed drama.

The title page of *Love's Labour's Lost* (1598) preserves in print the lie of Heminge and Condell's depiction of Shakespearean authorship by indicating that the play had been "Newly corrected and augmented / *By W. Shakespeare*" (A1r). Apparently, the "happie imitator of Nature" decided his imitation required a second draft. The title pages of *Two Noble Kinsmen* (1634) and *The Birth of Merlin* (1662) complicate the situation enormously, because each is attributed to Shakespeare and a collaborator, John Fletcher and William Rowley, respectively. Twice within fifty years of his death, Shakespeare's publishers were willing to suggest that the playwright's mind and hand engaged with another's. Whether the material reality of Shakespeare's texts jibe with Heminge and Condell's narrative, the fantasy of a pure, unmediated authorship that underwrites their edition has proven to be as durable as the texts themselves.

There is little room in this scenario for the various webs of engagement that permit literary works to be written, printed, circulated, and read because such webs are precisely what Heminge and Condell claim to have saved Shakespeare's plays from in the first place. A comparable rescue operation subsequently became the principal goal of the New Bibliography. Writing in 1933, W. W. Greg asserted that "textual scholarship" should be defined as "the attempt to discover and expound an author's meaning in what he wrote."[22] Moreover, as was the case with Heminge and Condell, Greg contended that "the true original text" of an author could be established only after the "history of its transmission" had first been presented.[23] Where once Heminge and Condell boasted on the title page of their collection that they had published Shakespeare's plays "according to the True Originall Copies" (A1r), Greg and subsequent New Bibliographers would posit as the object of their efforts the "ideal copy" of a given work.[24]

To follow this line of interpretation from the First Folio through the New Bibliography to the work of more recent textual scholars is to notice a reversal of sorts whereby what once was viewed as deforming the text is now seen as formative; what once left the text maimed and disabled, now enables it. Where once it was deemed necessary to keep the individualized dramatic author figure immune from the taint of collaboration, recent critics such as McMullan now argue that "it has begun to be clear that collaboration – in its insistent 'impurity' – is a much more appropriate model for textual production in general than is ostensibly 'solo' writing."[25] McMullan's observation, which echoes Masten's view that "collaboration was the Renaissance English theatre's dominant mode of textual production,"[26] conflates and overturns the fundamental preoccupations that Heminge and Condell bequeathed to scholars of early modern drama. The "cur'd, and perfect" texts of a singular sovereign intelligence have given way to the "insistent 'impurity'" of collaboration as the dominant paradigm of authorship in the period, suggesting perhaps, something of a fall from innocence that bifurcates textual scholarship into pre-lapsarian and post-lapsarian modes of interpretation. Indeed, a British Library promptbook copy of *Sir Thomas More*, thought to be the collaborative effort of Anthony Munday, Henry Chettle, Thomas Dekker, Shakespeare, and possibly Thomas Heywood, intimates that the displacement of textual scholarship from the Garden of Eden was long overdue. If three pages of the play, as Scott McMillin sardonically puts it, "bear the marks of the Bard,"[27] then one of the extant "True Originall Copies" of an early modern dramatic text that exists only in manuscript preserves our most idealized and individualized author in a rather compromised authorial position. Print was much more supportive of Shakespeare's authorial singularity than manuscript.

But if writing dramatic texts for the London stage was never an autonomous authorial achievement, then it is worth asking – at the risk of arguing in a circle – how dramatists such as Shakespeare and Jonson came to be the privileged exemplars of authorial autonomy. In previous chapters, I attempted to locate the particular moment in which the process of individualizing these two dramatists was initiated. For both playwrights, I argued that what we might recognize from our post-Enlightenment perspective as an author figure emerged partly as a residual function of translating plays from the stage to the printed page. In this chapter, my subject has shifted from the pure to the impure, from individual authors and the idealizing processes by which they were dislocated from the less than ideal environment of writing for the London stage to those aspects of early modern playwriting that significantly complicate what Lisa Ede and Andrea Lunsford describe as "the pervasive commonsense assumption that writing is inherently and necessarily a solitary, individual act."[28] Given the semantic valences of the terms "collaborator" and "author" noted earlier, the most obviously complex aspect of early modern playwriting is the fact that so much of it was collaborative. Superficially, at least, the role of collaboration in the production of dramatic texts, seems to have been a prominent one. *Gorboduc* (1562), generally regarded as the earliest genuinely English tragedy, was jointly attributed to Norton and Sackville.[29] Furthermore, according to Bentley, of the 900 or so known plays that were produced by professional dramatists in the period, the evidence suggests that as many as half of these plays "incorporated the writing at some date of more than one man."[30] I will examine this evidence more carefully below, but for now, I think it is sufficient to note that, strictly speaking, the terms "collaborator" and "author" represent equally prominent modes of early modern playwriting. As such, the belief – traditionally held by editors of drama – that collaboration is an anomalous problem or a source of contamination disparages and obscures the process by which a significant number of plays were written.

It is tempting to place the blame for this obfuscation on the shoulders of New Bibliographers who bequeathed to twentieth-century editors their preoccupation with what an individual author wrote. But, in fact, the ideology of authorship that privileges the individual seems to have emerged from the very collaborative conditions that enabled the production of early modern dramatic texts. Such conditions began to exert a considerable force on how playwriting was perceived approximately halfway into the sixty-six-year life-span of the professional theatre in London. Masten has concisely depicted this force as the attempt by the producers of the 1647 Beaumont–Fletcher folio – some thirty years after Beaumont and Fletcher's working relationship had ended – "to understand their writing practice within a discursive universe where dramatic writing was increasingly imagined more as singular fatherhood than as collaborative."[31] For Masten, who views this attempt as indicative of "a shift in the printed and performative apparatus of drama away from homo-erotic collaboration and toward singular authorship on a patriarchal-absolutist model,"[32] the primary evidence for such a shift can be gleaned from the folio's introductory texts and commentary poems in which writers such as Joh. Earle, Jos. Howe, T. Palmer, Jo. Pettus, John Web, Jasper Maine, Roger L'Estrange, and Berkenhead emphasize and celebrate how two men wrote as one.

Masten's reliance on these men's verses puts him in a position that is oddly similar to Moseley's, inasmuch as both depend on the writings of individual named authors to further their projects to promote collaborative authorship. In Moseley's case, these preliminaries, as I have suggested, endorse and support his effort to translate collaborative authorship into the single-author format established by previous folio collections. In Masten's case, these preliminaries endorse and support his effort to sexualize the relationship between Beaumont and Fletcher. Masten's work is a valuable contribution to the field, especially its attempt to move beyond criticism that has traditionally viewed "collaboration as a subset or aberrant kind of authorship."[33] Nevertheless, I also think that his effort to locate "the production of texts within the discourses of a sex gender system"[34] necessarily obscures other bodies of evidence pertaining to the material, institutional, and theatrical practices that sustained playwriting in the period. Indeed, like Heminge and Condell, who offer a portrait of the author at work to validate the texts they are submitting to the literary marketplace, or Nicholas Rowe and

Thomas Betterton, who begin the first critical edition of Shakespeare's plays with the first biography of the playwright, Masten inevitably neutralizes the contaminating potential of collaboration through constant reference to individual authors and to the personal lives of collaborators. In much the same way that Gary Taylor defends his decision to substitute Falstaff with Oldcastle in the Oxford *Complete Works* edition of *1 Henry IV* by arguing that Shakespeare must have been Catholic, Masten resurrects the author – this time, paradoxically enough, in the context of collaboration – by attempting to re-embody Beaumont and Fletcher's relationship and, consequently, their authorship. In some sense, this project was already set into motion by a characteristically idiosyncratic bit of early modern English orthography in the 4 September 1646 Stationers' Register entry for the 1647 folio. Entered to "(H.) Robinson and (H.) Mosely," the collection's "several tragedies and comedies" are attributed to two authors named "Beamont and Flesher."[35]

Alternatively, I would argue that there is substantial printed evidence that the ideology of authorship that frustrated Moseley's effort to translate collaborative authorship into the single-author format of the folio collection was operating well before he began to gather manuscripts for the 1647 Beaumont–Fletcher folio. Moreover, I would assert that this ideology was already being enforced typographically in the less typical single-author format of quarto editions through the conventional use of brackets ({ }) to represent and contain collaboration on title pages of printed texts of plays. Significantly, the first title page of a play to display brackets uses them to represent brotherhood, rather than collaborative authorship. The title page of the 1607 quarto of *The Travailes of The three English Brothers* (Fig. 15), an anonymous play attributed to "J. Day" in writing, employs one bracket to link three first names, "Sir Thomas," "Sir Anthony," and "Mr. Robert," to a single patronymic, "Shirley."[36] Prior to *Travailes*, and after the opening of the first professional playhouses, the following plays were published without using brackets to represent collaboration: *A Looking Glasse for London and England* (1594), "Made by Thomas Lodge Gentleman, and / Robert Greene / In Artibus Magister"; *Dido* (1594), "Written by Christopher Marlowe and / Thomas Nash, Gent."; and *Eastward Hoe* (1605), "Made by / Geo. Chapman. Ben: Ionson. Ioh: Marston." In the same year that *Travailes* appeared, quarto editions of the following four play-texts were attributed to multiple authors, but not one of them used brackets to indicate collaboration: *Northward Hoe*, "by Thomas Decker, and / Iohn Webster"; *Westward Hoe*, "Written by Tho: Decker, and / Iohn Webster"; *Jests to Make you Merie*, "Written by T. D, and George

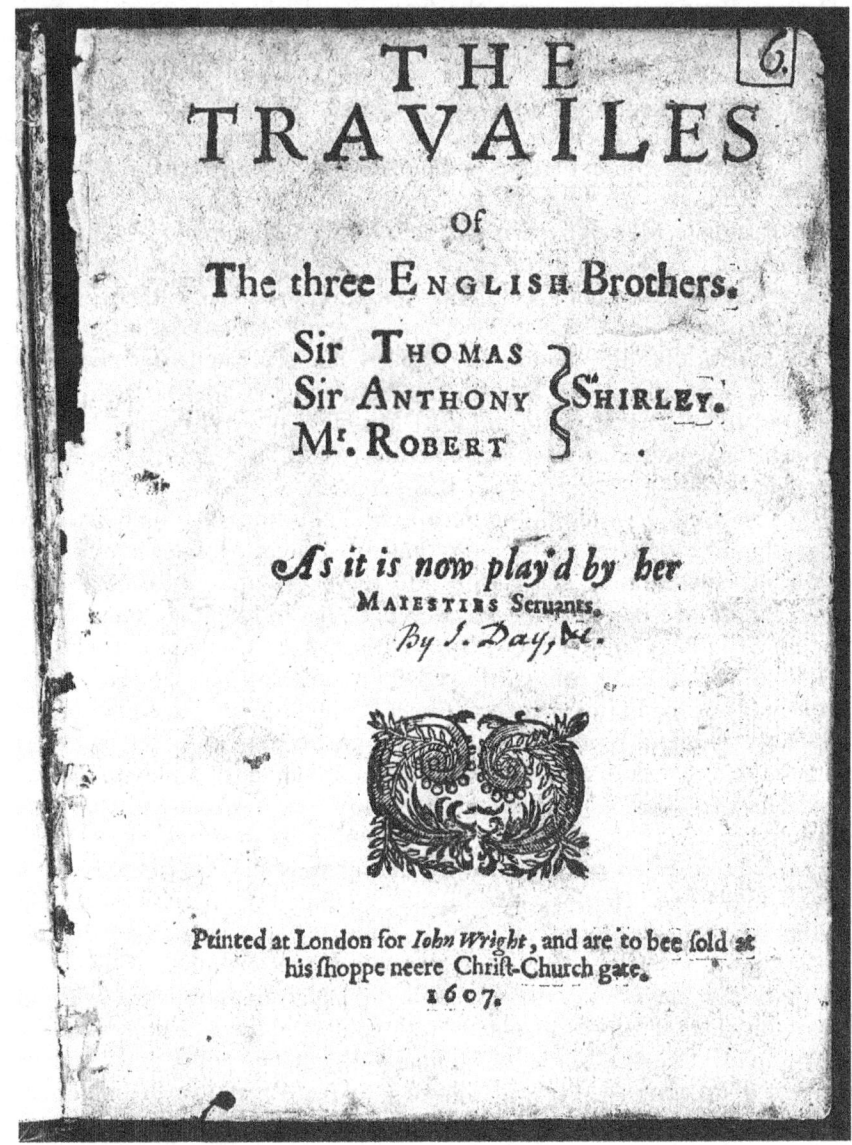

Figure 15 Title page: *The Travailes of The three English Brothers*, 1607

Wilkins"; and *The Famous History of Sir Thomas Wyat*, "Written by Thomas Dickers, / And Iohn Webster." The title page of *The Roaring Girl* (1611) indicates that the play was "Written by T. Middleton and T. Dekker," and in 1615, the title page of *The Scornful Ladie* offered the following attribution: "Written by Fra. Beaumong and Io. Fletcher, Gent." The next title page to attribute a play to multiple authors, the 1617 quarto edition of *A Faire Quarrell*, is also the first extant title page to make use of brackets to represent collaborative authorship: "Written / {by Thomas Midleton / and William Rowley.} Gentl." (Fig. 16).

Thus, one year after Jonson put the authorship of printed drama on the map by publishing the first single-author folio collection of contemporary plays, the printer of a quarto title page adapted a printing-house convention – often employed previously in printed grammar and rhetoric books to link parts of speech or verb conjugations – to the title page of a play that was written by more than one author. As if responding to the emergent paradox of collaborative authorship, the printer chose a semantically vacant, linguistically silent, typographic convention to silence the disturbance of collaborative authorship by linking the names of two authors, by representing two playwrights as if they were one. Masten might be tempted to interpret this typographic trajectory from grammar book to play-text title page as a progression from conjugation to conjugal relations between male playwrights, but what interests me about the initial effort to represent collaborative authorship typographically is that it appears on the title page of a play titled, appropriately, *A Faire Quarrell*. Furthermore, the accompanying woodcut of two men, swords drawn and crossed as if in preparation for the quarrel the title promises, embodies and reproduces the authorial struggle that had to be overcome so that two playwrights, two minds, and two pens could produce one play.

The subsequent typographic convention of putting some reference to the activity of authorship to the left of the brackets joining authors' names, and some indication of social status to the right, does not seem to have been completely established yet in 1617. Three years later, the form would come into its own on the quarto title page of "A Courtly Masque" called *The World Tost at Tennis* (1620), which featured the following attribution: "Invented and set / downe, By {Tho: Middleton / & / William Rowley} Gent." A second collaboratively authored play published in the same year featured brackets, but did not mention social status: *Phylaster*, "Written by {Francis Baymont / John Flecher}." By the time the Beaumont–Fletcher folio was published, it featured this typographic strategy of representing collaboration in its most perfected form – "Written by {Francis Beaumont / And / John Fletcher}

Figure 16 Title page: *A Faire Quarrell*, 1617

Gentlemen" – on a page that ironically faces a single portrait of John Fletcher. Prior to the 1647 folio, however, the following quartos relied on brackets to indicate multiple authorship: *The Virgin Martir* (1622), "Written by {Phillip Messenger / and / Thomas Deker"; *Herod and Antipater* (1622), "Written by {Gervase Markham / and / William Sampson} Gentlemen"; *The Two Noble Kinsmen* (1634), "Written by the Memorable Worthies / of their time {Mr. John Fletcher, and / Mr. William Shakespeare.} Gent."; *Knight of the Burning Pestle* (1635),[37] "Written by {Francius Beaumont and John Fletcher} Gent."; *Chabot Admiral of France* (1639), "Written by {George Chapman / and / James Shirley}"; *Wit Without Money* (1639), "Written by {Francis Beaumount / and / John Flecher} Gent."; and *The Ball* (1639), "Written by {George Chapman / and / James Shirley." A variant title page of *The Virgin Martir* printed in the same year (1622) has the following unbracketed attribution: "Written by Phillip Messenger and / Thomas Decker." (Fig. 17), the other includes brackets (Fig. 18). By the 1631 edition, the play's publishers settled on the use of brackets. Prior to the 1647 folio, nine first edition play quartos – published over thirty years – relied on brackets to represent multiple authorship.

After the appearance of the Beaumont–Fletcher folio, the following seven title pages of play quartos – published over fourteen years – made use of brackets to indicate multiple authorship: *The Widow* (1652), "Written by {Ben: Johnson. / John Fletcher. / Tho: Middleton.} Gent."; *The Wild-Goose Chase* (1652), "Being the Noble, Last, and Onely Remaines / of those Incomparable Drammatists / {Francis Beaumont, / and / John Fletcher,} Gent.";[38] *The Changeling* (1653), "Written by {Thomas Middleton, / and / William Rowley.} Gent."; *Fortune by Land and Sea* (1655), "Written by {Tho. Haywood / William Rowley"; *The Sun's Darling* (1656), "Written by {John Foard / and / Tho. Decker} Gent."; *The Old Law* (1656), "By {Phil. Massinger. / Tho. Middleton. / William Rowley"; and *The Spanish Gipsie* (1661), "Written by {Thomas Midleton, / and / William Rowley.} Gent." A comparison of these two sets of quarto title pages suggests that the Beaumont–Fletcher folio not only encouraged the subsequent publication of collaboratively authored plays but also helped to standardize the use of brackets to symbolize collaboration.

As Masten makes clear in his examination of the commendatory poems that preface Beaumont and Fletcher's plays, the central preoccupation of the writers enlisted to praise the collaborators is to depict the seamless univocality of their authorship. John Web, for example, writes of the "rich Conceptions of your twin-like brains" (C2v). Jasper Maine assures readers that Beaumont and Fletcher's collaborative writing

THE VIRGIN MARTIR.
A TRAGEDIE.

AS IT HATH BIN DIVERS
times publickely Acted with great
Applause,

By the seruants of his Maiesties Reuels.

Written by *Phillip Messenger* and
Thomas Decker.

LONDON,
Printed by *Bernard Alsop* for *Thomas
Iones.* 1622.

Figure 17 Title page: *The Virgin Martir*, 1622

Figure 18 Title page: *The Virgin Martir*, 1622

practices did not detract from the quality of their literary output. His standard for judging the worth of their collaboration is what either author might have written individually: "... what thus joyned you wrote, might have come forth / As good from each, and stored with the same worth" (D1v). In his commendatory poem, "On the happy Collection of Master *FLETCHER'S* Works, never before PRINTED," Berkenhead subverts the title of his own verse by asserting that "Each Piece is wholly Two, yet never splits" (E1v). Subsequently, Berkenhead legitimizes this assertion by pitting the playwriting duo against the paragon of singular authorship: "Brave Shakespeare flow'd, yet had his Ebbings too" (E2). The individualization of Beaumont and Fletcher's collaborations, already accomplished materially by binding the printed folio pages of their plays into one volume, is rehearsed a second time in the concluding lines of Berkenhead's poem:

> What strange Production is at last displaid,
> (Got by Two Fathers, without Female aide)
> Behold, two *Masculins* espous'd each other,
>   *Wit* and the World were born without a *Mother*.   (E2v, original italics)

For Masten, what is most significant about "this final burst of overdetermination" is that it "clearly employs a patriarchal model of textual reproduction; the text is begotten by, and born of, its fathers."[39] Subsequently he asserts that Berkenhead's depiction of collaboration "has radically marginalizing effects on representations of women."[40] Both of these points correspond, respectively, to the two versions of the thesis Masten offers as to the ideological transformation of collaborative authorship. On the one hand, dramatic writing is increasingly imagined "as singular fatherhood"; on the other, dramatic writing is increasingly imagined as "singular authorship on a patriarchal-absolutist model."[41]

Masten is certainly right to note the procreative metaphors in commendatory verses by Berkenhead and several other writers that Moseley enlisted to prop up his risky publishing venture. Nevertheless, to single out these metaphors as exemplary of the process by which the radicalism of Beaumont and Fletcher's collaborative authorship was domesticated "in the course of the seventeenth century"[42] is to place sixteenth-century conceptions of literary production under erasure. Observing that "[i]n the sixteenth and seventeenth centuries, many writers associate the creative imagination with the female body,"[43] Katherine Eisaman Maus concludes that "[t]he Renaissance male appropriation of the womb as a figure for the imagination, then, is perfectly consistent with an ideology that strictly limits female sexual freedom, and excludes actual women from literary endeavors."[44] Recalling Eisenstein's contention that the invention of the printing press inaugurated "the modern game of books and authors," it is significant that the link between emergent modern notions of authorship and representations of male procreation – along with their concomitant displacement of maternity – is initially figured as the link between fatherhood and print.

Inspired and enabled, perhaps, by the advent of the digital age, a number of scholars have recently shown considerable interest in the metaphorics of early modern print culture. Noting the link between the printing press and earlier technologies that made impressions, Margreta de Grazia observes:

> The astonishing thing about this machine was the degree to which it materialized the metaphorics of the signet and wax. It was made and made to function as a generational or reproductive system: made up of sexualized parts, it performed virtual copulative acts. It is not just that textual reproduction shared with sexual reproduction a vocabulary of generating issue, propagating copy, like begetting like. It materialized and mechanized that vocabulary.[45]

Prior to the advent of print, the medieval book had been the locus of considerable genealogical anxiety – kin and ink bound tightly together between the covers of a manuscript devoted to paternal uneasiness.[46] Once the printed page appeared, however, "the method of its production, the actual process of copying or printing," according to Ann and John O. Thompson, was quickly appropriated for the "patriarchal aspect of the metaphorical field" of early modern parenting.[47] "Women," observe the Thompsons, "become merely devices by which men make copies of themselves . . . their role should be as neutral as possible; the important thing is to produce a child which is an exact copy of the father."[48] Similarly, Gordon Williams notes the appearance in the period of what he calls "the book–woman equation" and "the parallel between sex and reading."[49]

Nor, for that matter, did it take long for paternity's reliance on metaphors of mechanical reproduction to be assimilated into early modern representations of authorship. In the letter that prefaces the *Countess of Pembroke's Arcadia*, Sidney tells his sister "I could well find in my heart to cast out in some desert of forgetfulness this child which I am loth to father."[50] Arguably, however, the cultural project of linking fatherhood, print, and authorship was pursued most vigorously on the London stage. Marjorie Garber, for example, observes that, "[t]he undecidability of paternity, articulated again and again in the plays by putative fathers like Lear, Leontes, Leonato, and Prospero, is analogous to, and evocative of, the undecidability of authorship."[51] Similarly, Richard Wilson observes that, "the romance, by disclaiming actuality, recounts what the history obscures: patriarchy's inability to impose mastery on the female body."[52] For Wilson, Shakespeare turns to "the proprietorial rights and productive relations of his own industry"[53] for the language of procreation while writing later romances like *The Winter's Tale*.

There are, perhaps, hundreds of examples that could be cited to demonstrate the extent to which authorship was conceptualized in terms of fatherhood well before the 1647 publication of the Beaumont–Fletcher folio. There was nothing particularly new, radical, or seventeenth-century, then, about Berkenhead's contention that the plays collected in the folio were "Got by Two Fathers, without Female aide." Rather, there was almost no other way to express authorship in the period because the printing press, which simultaneously gave birth to and served as the midwife for the modern author, had been appropriated for paternal/authorial goals just as soon as it was invented. What is significant about Berkenhead's formulation – and the sequence of the commendatory poem's final lines makes this very clear – is the "strange Production" that results from Beaumont and Fletcher's collaboration. Early modern male authors routinely fathered their works, but what is genuinely "strange" about the shared labor preserved in the 1647 folio is that it gave birth to the same child. In other words, what is truly problematic about Beaumont and Fletcher is not that they father their texts, but that they father the same text.

Both the production and the product that characterize Beaumont and Fletcher's writing arrangements – as depicted by Berkenhead – violate several norms. On the most basic level, their collaborative authorship seems to have exorcized the kind of "mimetic rivalry" which, according to René Girard, is "a persistent phenomenon" in human relations.[54] Furthermore, in the specific context of early modern drama, Berkenhead's rendering of Beaumont and Fletcher's joint fatherhood denies the working conditions of the theatre where, according to James Shapiro,

the writing of plays remained a commercial and therefore inescapably competitive enterprise, and the competitive nature of imitation meant that imitation was meant to displace and self-promote, to seal off the other, to contain its popularity, and to advance one's own.[55]

Perhaps the most famous example of this self-advancement is Jonson's use of the publication process as a strategy for individualizing the 1605 quarto text of *Sejanus*. Alternatively, in the Beaumont–Fletcher folio, as nearly all of the commendatory verses make amply clear, the "Booke" has merely captured and preserved the perfection of their collaboration – what is theirs. In short, the mediation of publication has left no trace of its mediation, except that it has elided potential for rivalry that enabled the promotion of an authorial self. Nothing has been either lost or gained in the translation from the stage to the page, except the possibility of authorship itself. The simultaneously collaborative/competitive environment of writing for the theatre is pristinely – if impossibly – embodied as a seamless collaboration. As Berkenhead puts it, "Each Piece is wholly Two, yet never splits." A strange production, indeed. And the production gets even stranger when we consider how few plays Beaumont contributed to the folio, though the fantasy of an indivisible collaboration is more interesting than the reality of who wrote what.

Arguably, the emergence of the early modern author figure, famously exemplified by the construction of Shakespeare's authorship, did represent a privileged moment of individualization. But if the starting gun for the game of books and authors was fired by the printing press, then the appearance of the Beaumont–Fletcher folio in 1647 must be seen as a rather noisy, if temporary, disruption of the game – a crack in what Foucault calls "the solid and fundamental unit of the author and the work."[56] Indeed, the situation is even more complicated. "No institutional embodiment of the author-work relation," according to Mark Rose, "is more fundamental than copyright, which not only makes possible the profitable manufacture and distribution of books, films, and other commodities but also, by endowing it with legal reality, helps to produce and affirm the very identity of the author as author."[57] And yet, copyright, as Rose subsequently notes, "is a specifically modern institution, the creature of the printing press, the individualization of authorship in the late Middle Ages and early Renaissance."[58] In other words, copyright produces and affirms the author, the author produces and affirms copyright. Locked into an irreducible symbiosis, authorship and copyright have a common origin in the invention of the printing press and share a preoccupation with individualization. Before authors benefited from such individualization, printers did.[59]

However we might approach it, what is truly disturbing about the Beaumont–Fletcher folio's preliminaries and their efforts to represent collaborative authorship is neither the conventional reliance on the patriarchal trope of fathering texts nor the conventional marginalization of women. Rather, the most unsettling aspect of collaboration, the one that the commendatory verses return to again and again is merely the math. How can two become one? How can two authors write one text? Under the recently inaugurated reign of the author, where all subjects became singular and the constitutive relation became one in which the proper name of an individual and a text were increasingly linked, there was simply no place for collaboration. Some five years after England closed down the theatres in which the culture's anxieties were routinely rehearsed, and two years before the competing institution of individuation – the monarchy – was summarily, if temporarily, dismantled, the preliminaries of the Beaumont–Fletcher folio attempt to stage and assuage an anxiety that threatens the sovereignty of the author.

Masten is certainly right to note that in the particular case of Berkenhead, the drama presented is one of same sex marriage.[60] Whereas authorship had fundamentally been the exclusive domain of the single parent, usually the father who appropriated the womb as the organ of imagination, marriage allows Berkenhead to normalize collaboration by aligning it with the one normative institution in which two commonly become one – parentage. But to privilege this version, as Masten does, is to sacrifice content for the sake of form, because the crucial mathematical conundrum of collaboration receives a number of different stagings in the folio and beyond. Web writes that "one Soule informed" "two wits," and refers to "twin-like brains" (C2v); Maine offers "the Presse" which "Sends us one Poet in a pair of Friends" (D1v); and for George Lisle, the folio is where "Two potent Wits co-operate," and their "fancies are so woven and knit" (B1). This last example unwittingly conflates collaborative authorship with the material history of books, inasmuch as the word "text," as McKenzie notes, derives "from the Latin *texere*, 'to weave,' and therefore refers, not to any specific material as such, but to its woven state, the web or texture of the materials."[61]

Within this repertory of strategic representations of collaboration, which range from anatomical to metaphysical, from social to textile, same sex marriage figures as only one among many. The most efficient of these strategies, the typographic convention of joining multiple authors' names with brackets, appropriately called "dilemmas," is the first to appear in the volume. Having been used initially to link multiple names to one family, brackets would subsequently come to represent the link between multiple authors and one text. Furthermore, their pattern of usage, briefly traced above, suggests that the commendatory verses of the Beaumont–Fletcher folio not only verbalized what had previously only been symbolized typographically, but also helped to establish brackets as a standard symbol of collaboration. In much the same way that Jonson's 1616 folio "raise[d] the contemporary existence of the generally belittled form of plays,"[62] and materially established the model for promoting dramatic authorship, the 1647 folio did what it could to assimilate the ontological anomaly of collaboration into the regime of the author,[63] even as it repeatedly articulated the inherent difficulties of such an assimilation. That this project was ultimately doomed to failure is attested by the title page of the 1679 Beaumont and Fletcher folio (Fig. 19). Appearing more than sixty years after the publication of the

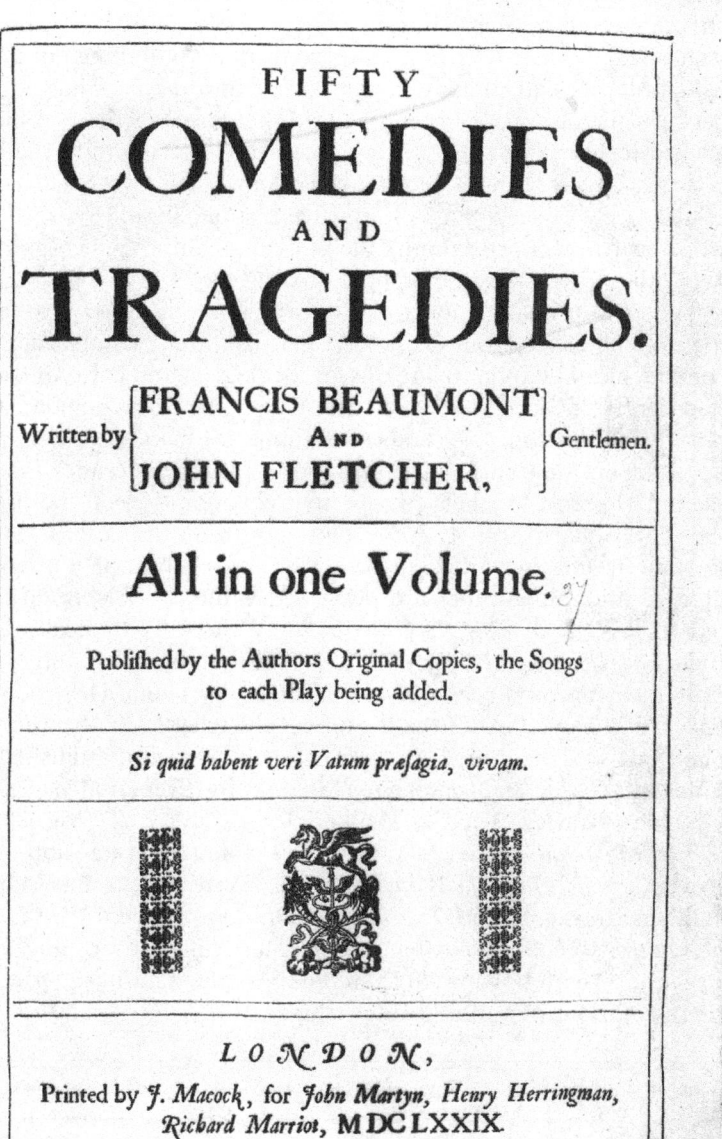

Figure 19 Title page: *Fifty Comedies and Tragedies*, 1679

first folio collection of printed drama, and thirty years before the first critical edition of Shakespeare's plays and the Statute of Anne, the title page suggests that the typographic convention of linking authors' names with brackets had already begun to fall into decay. There on the left, between the phrase "Written by" and the names of the two playwrights alleged to have done the writing, one can clearly see that the bracket is broken and has been set backward. Perhaps, these two brackets, pointing as they now do in a single, unified direction, should be read as silent, wordless banners proclaiming the individual author's ideological victory over other forms of authorship.

The extraordinary impact of Foucault's work has bequeathed to us a monolithic conception of power that is rarely compatible with the contingent and haphazard reality of ideological and cultural transformations.[64] In the specific case of the struggle between singular and collaborative authorship, one finds something less than an orderly pattern of development or transformation. During the three decades that separate the initial use of brackets to represent collaboration on the title page of the 1617 quarto of *A Faire Quarrell* from the appearance of the Beaumont–Fletcher folio, the following three extant play quartos attributed to multiple authors are published without brackets on their titles pages: *A King and No King* (1619),[65] "Written by F. Beaumont and J. Fletcher"; *The Fatall Dowry (1632)*, "Written by P. M. and N. F."; *The Late Lancashire Witches* (1634), "Written / By Thom. Heywood, / AND / Richard Broome." After the Beaumont–Fletcher folio, the following four play quartos attributed to multiple authors are published without brackets: *The Witch of Edmonton* (1658), "By divers well-esteemed Poets; / William Rowley, Thomas Dekker, John Ford, &c." (Fig. 20); *A Cure for a Cuckhold* (1661), "Written by John Webster and / William Rowley"; *The Thracian Wonder* (1661), "Written by John Webster and / William Rowley."; and *The Birth of Merlin: or The Childe Hath Found his Father* (1662), "Written by William Shakespear, and / William Rowley." The following table summarizes the data on quarto title-page representations of multiple authorship:

Publication Date	Unbracketed	Bracketed
1590–1616	10 Plays	None
1617–1647	3 Plays	9 Plays
1648–1661	4 Plays	7 Plays

Beyond indicating the progressive standardization of brackets as a symbol of collaboration after the publication of the Beaumont–Fletcher

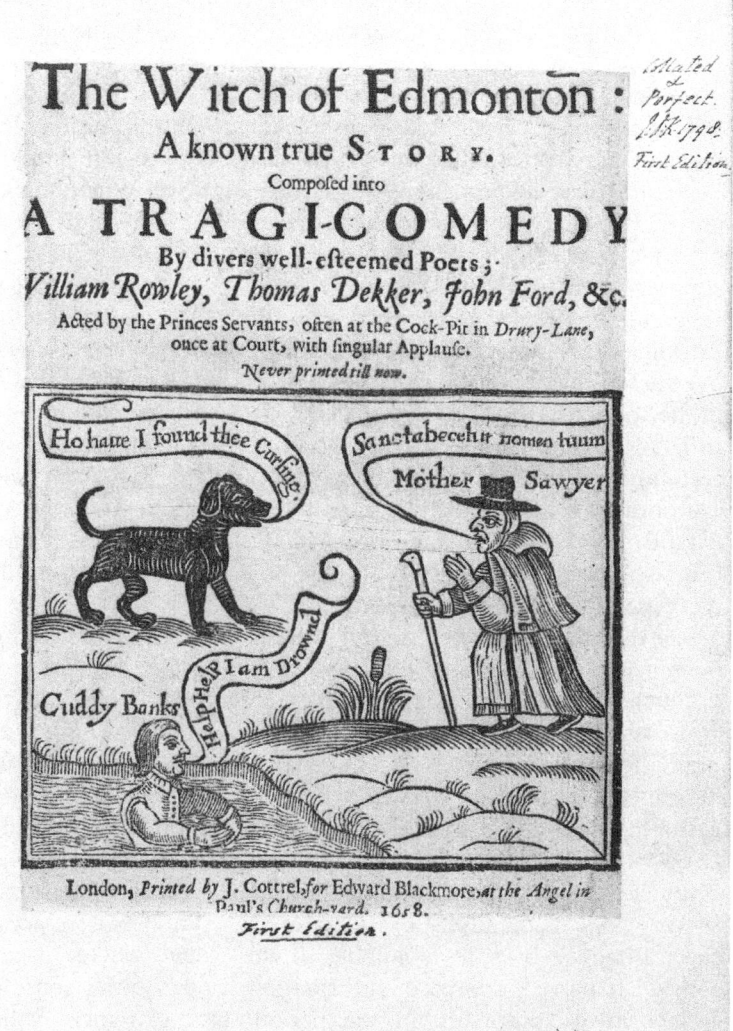

Figure 20 Title page: *The Witch of Edmonton*, 1658

folio, juxtaposing the two sets of quarto title pages attributed to multiple authors makes another important point. All of the title pages – including the 1647 folio – that place brackets on both sides of the authors' names they link also feature some full or abbreviated form of the word "Gentleman" next to the bracket on the right. However, only two of the quarto title pages attributed to unbracketed multiple authors include any form of the word. This contrast is particularly striking in the case of William Rowley, Thomas Dekker, and John Ford. When bracketed, they are gentlemen; when unbracketed, they are not. Although the number of extant title pages attributed to multiple authors is not large enough to support statistically significant claims, the available evidence does suggest that the social standing of authors is indicated only when the "strange Production" of collaborative authorship is typographically over-determined, and thus domesticated by the use of brackets. As such, in the specific case of typographically representing collaboration, authorship emerged not from the bookshop but from the printing house. It was certainly common for printers to examine, borrow from, and imitate each other's work; but if this most literal of intertextualities complicates what can be said about the published status of collaborative authorship, other sources of information about collaboration in the period generally correspond with the typographic data.

For the life span of the London professional theatre, extending from the opening of James Burbage's playhouse, The Theatre, in 1576 to the closing of the theatres in 1642, the *Annals of English Drama*[66] identifies the titles of approximately 1,200 plays.[67] Relying on the *Annals* for information about dramatic authorship can be somewhat treacherous for a number of reasons, not the least of which is the eclecticism of its approach to gathering data about the works it includes.[68] Furthermore, of the some 1,200 titles listed there, only forty percent – 469 complete plays in 961 complete editions – are extant, and nearly ten percent of these extant plays survive only in manuscript.[69] Despite these important reservations, the sheer quantity of titles available in the *Annals* makes it a useful, if somewhat flawed, source of information for an initial consideration of collaborative authorship in the period. (An extremely valuable new resource is the "Finding List" included in the Revised Edition of *An Index of Characters in Early Modern English Drama Printed Plays, 1500–1660*.)[70] One need only look at the 167 attributions appearing in "an Alphebeticall Catologue of all such plays / that ever were Printed," published in 1656 by Richard Rogers and William Levy as an appendix to the quarto edition of *The Careles Shepherdess*, to get a sense of how difficult it is to find reliable evidence of early modern dramatic authorship.[71]

The most legible pattern that emerges from even a cursory study of the

Dramatic authorship 173

data provided in the *Annals* is the change in the authorial status of play-texts from anonymous to named.[72] For The Theatre's first year of operation (1576), Harbage lists the titles of six plays that were performed at court or offered for acting, five of which are without authorial attribution of any kind. None of them are attributed to multiple authors. A year later, the number of titles jumps to thirteen, nine of which are anonymous. Of the four attributed plays, none of them was got by more than one father. For 1578, fourteen play titles are given. Nine are anonymous, and two entertainments are attributed to a writing team consisting of Churchyard, B. Garter, and H. Goldingment. For the following year, the number of titles increases to seventeen, although the number of attributed titles remains constant at five. None of the titles is attributed to more than one author. While the first four years of the professional theatre witnessed a dramatic increase in the number of works produced, anonymity remained the norm, and collaboration, barely acknowledged.

Skipping ahead to 1616, the year Jonson published the first folio collection of dramatic texts, we find the titles of eleven dramas, all of which are attributed to single authors. The concurrence of one-hundred percent attribution with the publication of Jonson's folio suggests that the proprietorial element of authorship had come into its own forty years into the professional theatre's sixty-six-year existence. Nevertheless, the newfound prominence of the dramatic author does not seem to have encouraged the attribution of collaborative authorship. Indeed, for the 1616 folio edition of *Sejanus, His Fall,* Jonson does not even feel obligated to reprint the 1605 quarto's acknowledgment that "a second Pen had good share" in the play's composition.

The following figures drawn from the *Annals* provide a year-by-year breakdown of author attribution for the six full decades that the professional theatre was in operation.

Year	Single Author	Multiple Authors	Unattributed
1580	6	0	9
1581	6	0	5
1582	5	0	7
1583	4	0	5
1584	6	0	2
1585	2	0	4
1586	3	2	5
1587	5	0	1
1588	10	3	2
1589	6	0	2

Averaging this period's total titles results in a yearly rate of 10 dramatic texts, 58% of which are attributed to an author or authors. Only 5% of these attributions indicate collaboration. One can already glimpse a developing preference for named authorship by the middle of the period. Figures for the next decade, during which the production of dramatic texts more than doubled, show a slight drop in attribution levels:

Year	Single Author	Multiple Authors	Unattributed
1590	10	2	7
1591	7	0	8
1592	13	1	11
1593	5	1	2
1594	7	1	19
1595	8	1	22
1596	7	0	15
1597	8	0	16
1598	18	19	10
1599	23	13	9

Averaging this period's total titles results in a yearly rate of twenty-six dramatic texts, 54% of which are attributed to an author or authors. Multiple-author attribution increases to 15%. Initially, it would seem, named authorship was a tenuous aspect of increased dramatic activity in Elizabethan England. Figures for the following decade, on the other hand, show a significant increase in authorial attribution.

Year	Single Author	Multiple Authors	Unattributed
1600	14	8	9
1601	17	14	4
1602	28	12	15
1603	18	5	5
1604	19	3	15
1605	13	3	6
1606	21	1	7
1607	17	1	4
1608	14	3	9
1609	7	3	2

Averaging this period's total titles results in a yearly rate of thirty dramatic texts, 75% of which are attributed to an author or authors. Collaboration reaches its peak of acknowledgment during this period, accounting for 18% of dramatic texts produced. Figures for the next decade show a similarly high level of attribution, though the number of titles drops by nearly a third:

Year	Single Author	Multiple Authors	Unattributed
1610	9	2	1
1611	20	1	4
1612	13	0	10
1613	33	3	9
1614	11	0	4
1615	14	1	2
1616	11	0	0
1617	13	3	5
1618	12	2	11
1619	16	3	15

Averaging this period's total titles results in a yearly rate of twenty-two dramatic texts, 74% of which are attributed to an author or authors. While the general attribution rate remains more or less constant with that of the previous decade, attribution to multiple authors falls significantly to 6%. Figures for the next decade show an increase in attribution, though the number of titles performed remains nearly the same:

Year	Single Author	Multiple Authors	Unattributed
1620	10	7	4
1621	21	1	5
1622	7	5	7
1623	31	4	8
1624	24	4	8
1625	12	1	4
1626	19	0	3
1627	13	0	2
1628	12	0	2
1629	16	0	1

Averaging this period's total titles results in a yearly rate of twenty-three dramatic texts, 81% of which are attributed to an author or authors. Consistent with the increased level of attribution, acknowledgment of collaborative authorship rises to 9%. Although figures for the last full decade of the professional theatre indicate a slight increase in the number of texts produced, attribution increases significantly. Multiple-author attribution, however, practically disappears.

Year	Single Author	Multiple Authors	Unattributed
1631	21	0	1
1632	18	0	2
1633	23	1	1
1634	20	3	3
1635	33	0	4
1636	15	0	5
1637	21	0	0
1638	32	0	6
1639	18	0	5
1640	23	1	3

Averaging the period's total titles results in a yearly rate of twenty-six dramatic texts, 89% of which are attributed to an author or authors. Given the high level of named authorship, it is remarkable that collaboration accounts for only 2% of 260 attributed titles.

Beyond the complex issue of periodization raised by any study that breaks up a given historical phenomenon into arbitrary units such as decades, the variety of dramatic texts and performance sites covered by the figures provided above makes the *Annals* a less than satisfactory source for determining shifts in the status of dramatic authorship, especially in the specific context of the professional theatre. Still, the following decade-by-decade comparison of attribution levels is extremely suggestive:

	1580–1589	1590–1599	1600–1609	1610–1619	1620–1629	1631–1640
No. of Titles	10	26	30	22	23	26
% Attributed	58	54	75	74	81	89
% Multiple	5	15	18	6	9	2

During the six full decades of the professional theatre, the data on known titles indicates that the production of dramatic texts more than doubled, and in the first ten years of the seventeenth century, tripled. Roughly half of the dramatic texts produced in the last two decades of the sixteenth century were anonymous, but by the end of the period nearly 90% of titles are attributed to an author or authors. In general then, increased attribution correlates with increased production. This correlation is particularly striking for the final decade of the professional theatre, especially if we limit the data to published drama. Singling out this period as the "most vigorous decade for publication of plays," Saeger and Fassler observe that "more than 25 plays were printed on

Dramatic authorship 177

average in any given year of this decade and more than 10 of them were new plays."[73] Juxtaposing Saeger and Fassler's average (twenty-five per year), based on extant title pages of published plays, with the average derived from titles listed in the *Annals* (twenty-five per year) not only lends some credence to the latter as a source of information about the London stage but also indicates – as Jonson no doubt sensed early on – that print publication could be extraordinarily kind to authorship.

Clearly, the longer playhouses, printing houses, and individual playwrights played the game of books and authors, the better they got at it. On the other hand, print seems to have been devastating to collaborative authorship. In general, multiple-author attribution remained out of step with single-author attribution for the entire period under consideration here, but it is during the final decade that the term "collaborative authorship" becomes the most starkly paradoxical. Whereas publication and single-author attribution reach their highest level during this period, multiple-author attribution falls to its lowest level, accounting for an average production of only two plays per year. If, as Eisenstein observes, the emergence of the modern author figure is fueled by "the wish to see one's work in print (fixed forever with one's name in card files and anthologies),"[74] then in the specific case of published dramatic authorship, that wish is greatly frustrated when more than one author is involved. Thus, while the 1616 Jonson folio accurately preserves the complex relation between the emergent individual author and print, the 1647 Beaumont–Fletcher folio concisely captures the status of collaboration in the age of mechanical reproduction. On its title page, directly under the bracketed names of the collaborators, the phrase "Never printed before" appears in bold type.

During the other period that sees a high level of publication, the first decade of the seventeenth century, an average of thirteen plays a year were published, with eight of them being new plays.[75] For the same period, multiple-author attribution reached its highest level, accounting for nearly 20% of all plays written. Here, however, the enormous disparity between the yearly average of titles derived from the *Annals* (thirty titles) and the yearly average of extant printed dramas examined by Saeger and Fassler (thirteen plays) suggests that an average of seventeen plays per year – a decade total of 170 plays – were lost. The most obvious conclusion to be drawn is that at the beginning of the seventeenth century the power of the printing press to embalm and preserve a given text was so limited that it could only guarantee the survival of 43% of known titles. Indeed, even this survival rate is high, because a comparison between the number of extant printed dramas and the number of titles recorded in the *Annals* indicates that 61% of known dramatic texts have been lost. If we assume that the survival rate of printed dramatic texts remained more or less constant at about 40% during the period, then the obvious question is why does evidence of multiple-author attribution peak during the second and third decades of the professional theatre, and all but disappear in the last?

A year-by-year comparison between play titles and author attributions listed in the *Annals* and playwright payment entries in *Henslowe's Diary* suggests that the answer lies in a source of information about authorship that would not have been available to book buyers in the early modern marketplace. The majority of titles and authors listed in the *Annals* for the two decades when multiple authorship attribution was unusually high are taken from the records Philip Henslowe kept during eighteen years (1592–1609) of his involvement with the professional theatre. Only when we consult *Henslowe's Diary*, which Bentley calls "far and away the most detailed record of authorship that has come down to us,"[76] do rates of multiple-author attribution begin to cohere with Bentley's estimate that "between $\frac{1}{5}$ and $\frac{1}{6}$ [of known titles] contained the work of more than one man."[77] Thus, the average rate of multiple-author attribution (16.5%) for the twenty-year period 1590–1610 represents a distortion created by Henslowe's extensive documentation of his activities with the Rose Theatre for eighteen of those years. Nevertheless, as Neil Carson notes in his study of *Henslowe's Diary*, "[t]he performance records maintained from 1592–7 list titles, but are silent on the question of authorship."[78] For the first eight years of the decade encompassing this silence, 165 known titles are produced. Sixty-five, or 39%, of those titles are attributed to single authors. Only six titles, or 4% of known titles from the period, are attributed to multiple authors. In 1598, however, the first year *Henslowe's Diary* begins to speak about authorship, forty-seven known titles are produced, eighteen (38%) of which are attributed to single authors. The presence or absence of Henslowe's documentation creates only a 1% difference in the rate of single-author attribution, suggesting, perhaps, that emic and etic knowledge of individual authorship in the period was more or less consistent.

In other words, a customer browsing the bookstalls at Paul's Churchyard was almost as likely as Henslowe to know that a Shakespeare or a Jonson or a Dekker wrote a given play. If, however, we look at multiple authorship in 1598, something remarkable happens. Of that year's forty-seven known titles, nineteen or 40% of those titles are attributed to multiple authors. In the case of multiple authorship, the presence of Henslowe's documentation creates a 36% increase in acknowledgment of collaboration. Thus, in 1600, a customer searching through the bookstalls at Paul's Churchyard for the newly published quarto edition of

1 Sir John Oldcastle was much less likely than Henslowe to know that it was written by "m^r monday m^r drayton & m^r wilsson & haythway."[79] Significantly, the play's title page gives no indication of its authorship whatsoever. Juxtaposing the effect of this kind of unpublished insider information about playwriting on the attribution of singular authorship with the effect such information has on the attribution of multiple authorship provides a reliable indication of just how extensively print publication favored dramatic texts attributed to individual authors. In 1598, the first year Shakespeare's name appeared on the title page of an extant play quarto, the game of books and authors being played in the space between the playhouse and the printing house was largely restricted to individuals. It seems likely that some fifty years later Moseley enlisted thirty-four writers to bend the rules of this game of solitaire so that Beaumont and Fletcher might be allowed on the field.

It would be a mistake to generalize about the relationship between authorship and print from available information about how plays were written in one year and for one theatre. Relying on statistics compiled by Carson from Henslowe's records of the Rose Theatre's six playing seasons for the years 1598–1600,[80] we find the seasonal average of multiple-authored plays to be 39%, considerably higher than the 18% peak figure that was derived from analyzing available data on authorship for the first decade of the seventeenth century. Even the lowest rate of multiple authorship, 25% of plays written in the 1597–1598 Fall–Winter playing season is higher than the 18% rate drawn from the *Annals*. Moreover, Carlson's statistics suggest that a play that was begun during the same period was more likely to be completed if it were collaboratively authored. Of the fifty-two finished plays written for six playing seasons, thirty plays (58%) were attributed to multiple authors. While a year-by-year comparison of author payments recorded by Henslowe with author attributions listed in the *Annals* would certainly be helpful, for now I think it is sufficient to correlate some general figures from both sources with what can be gleaned from the extant drama.

Bentley finds 282 different plays documented by Henslowe, forty of which are still extant.[81] For 170 of these plays, Henslowe's records are our only source of information. Based on these figures, Bentley concludes "that between 1590 and 1642 there probably were written as many as 500 plays of which we know not even the titles."[82] Of the dramatic texts we do know about from extant plays and titles listed in the *Annals*, what seems remarkable about Henslowe's records is the low survival rate of the plays he mentions. If we recall that the survival rate of known titles for the entire sixty-six-year span of the professional theatre is 40%, then the plays documented by Henslowe appear to have been considerably more fragile. Of the 282 plays Henslowe mentions, two-thirds of which, according to Bentley, "are the work of more than one man,"[83] only 14% are still extant. It is tempting to speculate, therefore, that a play attributed to a single author was more likely to survive. An examination of the title pages for all of the extant printed dramatic texts – as transcribed in the first two volumes of Greg's *Bibliography of Printed English Drama* – lends some support to this speculation. Of the extant printed dramas, 333 title pages (74%) are attributed either in full or abbreviated form to a single author. Only thirty-four title pages (8%), on the other hand, are attributed to multiple-authors. This figure is only slightly higher than the level of multiple author attribution (5.5%) that can be derived from averaging the number of collaboratively authored titles listed in the *Annals* for the four decades not covered by *Henslowe's Diary*. Moreover, if we examine the extant drama from the two decades documented by Henslowe, the correlation between single authorship and survival becomes even more pronounced. For the years 1590–1610, 125 dramatic texts – 29% of the total extant printed drama – indicate authorship. Of that total, 118 plays – 94% of authored texts – are attributed to single authors. The remaining seven plays – 6% of authored texts – are attributed to more than one author. This figure is significantly lower than the level of multiple-author attribution (16.5%) derived from the *Annals* for the same twenty-year period. In other words, what the publication process reports about the authorship of drama during a given period differs substantially from what the unpublished records of an eyewitness to the profession of playwriting reports during the same period.

Although this analysis could be greatly refined if the available evidence was broken down into categories that distinguished between different forms of multiple authorship such as collaboration, augmentation, and revision, I think the patterns examined suggest a great deal about an important context in which the 1647 Beaumont and Fletcher folio was published. This is not to deny the importance or relevance of other contexts. Surely Moseley and the thirty-four writers who contributed the volume's preliminaries were working in a moment of particularly intense religious, political, cultural, and ideological conflict. As I have already suggested, the 1647 folio was in part a royalist project. One need only read, for example, Sir Robert Filmer's *Patriarcha, or the Natural Power of Kings* (1642), to see the ideological links between royalist politics and Masten's claim that emergent authorship "was articulated in terms of a patriarchal-absolutist model of authority." Indeed, as Susan Dwyer Amussen observes, "[p]atriarchal political theory had a long history, and as it developed in the seventeenth century into a justification of divine-right absolutism, its assumptions about the family fitted well with the prescriptions of the writers of household manuals."[84] The establishment and enforcement of heterosexual marriage as an ideal was a major concern of such manuals. But articulating authorship is not quite the same thing as constructing or shaping it through publication, and although Masten is correct that "a notion of authorship emerged tentatively in theatrical texts of the early seventeenth century," my analysis of available evidence from the period suggests that neither patriarchalism nor absolutism had much to do with that emergence. In fact, I would argue – as I did in the case of the 1616 folio – that the emergent notion of the individual author, principally generated in the printing house and ultimately ratified in the bookshop, may have taught fathers and kings about the value of individualization.

Writing for the London stage, as *Henslowe's Diary* indicates, was predominantly a collaborative activity. Printing, as the publication history of the 1647 folio indicates, was necessarily collaborative. If Foucault is right that the author function is primarily "a principle of thrift," then certainly both the playhouse and the printing house had their respective author functions. In the early modern theatre, it might be the name of the playing company, of a well-known clown, or sometimes even a popular playwright. In the printing house, it was almost always the name of a printer, usually the owner of the house, and/or the publisher who financed the printing that appeared on the title page of a given publication. The proper name, Moseley, was the closest thing to a legitimate author function that the 1647 folio could claim, and it has appeared much more frequently in this chapter than the names of the authors listed on that volume's title page. Whereas some printed quarto editions of plays included a list of actors, no title page I know of ever listed the names of the inkers or the compositors who worked on it. Thus, in the particular case of compositor studies, the author function is often reduced, appropriately enough, to an alphabetical letter. When, however, drama began to be translated from the stage to the page, some compromise over author function had to be worked out between the two houses, though long-cherished New Bibliographic narratives about piracy precluded such an arrangement from receiving serious attention until recently.

Prior to the emergence of playing companies, printers and publishers seem to have worked from a classical or high literary notion of the author function when they set about reproducing the occasional drama manuscript that found its way into the printing house. Accordingly, the 1565 title page of *Gorboduc* chiefly strives for accuracy and fairness in its attribution: "whereof three Actes were wrytten by / *Thomas Nortone*, and the two laste by / *Thomas Sackuyle*." Seven years after the Stationers'

Company had been incorporated, the person responsible for entering this publication into the Register designated the name of the octavo's printer as the primary "principle of thrift," then did his best to dutifully transcribe the author attribution that appeared on the title page: "Receved of Wylliam greffeth for his lycense for pryntinge of a Trag[e]die of GORBODUC where[of] iij actes were Wretten by Thomas norton and the laste by Thomas Sackvyle."[85] An examination of all play entries in the Stationers' Register indicates that stationers faithfully transcribed author attributions from the title pages of printed drama for another four years, then became more or less indifferent to registering dramatic authorship until the 1620s, the first decade in which more than 80% of known titles were attributed to an author or authors.

When professional playing companies began to form in the last two decades of the sixteenth century, the name of the company that owned the manuscript to be published was frequently designated to fulfill the author function. Increasingly aware of their own proprietorial interests, printers and publishers had little difficulty attributing a printed play to the company that owned it. Moreover, because plays during this period were frequently composed by playwriting teams that generally consisted of between three to five writers, the single name of the playing company that employed and paid that team was literally a "principle of thrift," not "in the proliferation of meaning," as Foucault would have it, but merely in the proliferation of names that might have contributed an act, a scene, an augmentation, a revision, or even a prologue to a single play. No extant drama title page from that period represented this kind of company-centered authorship, except as the name of the company itself, and nearly all such title pages were published anonymously. As the following table indicates, only three extant title pages even attempted to approximate the complexly collaborative authorial environment of the professional company, and none of these attributions was reproduced in the Stationers' Register entries for the three plays.

Year	Title	Title-Page Attribution	Stationers' Register Attribution
1604	The Malcontent	Augmented by Marston, With the Additions . . . Written by Ihon Webster	
1605	Eastward Hoe	Ben. Ionson, George Chapman, John Marston	
1658	The Witch of Edmonton	By diverse well-esteemed Poets; / William Rowley, Thomas Dekker, John Ford, &c	

Dramatic authorship

During the first decade of the seventeenth century, playwrights like Jonson began to view publication as a viable and desirable alternative to performance. As they became more involved with printers and publishers, the author function on drama title pages more frequently included authors. Company attribution generally remained constant, as did printer/publisher attribution, but title pages increasingly added the names of authors – often set between the other two names. Consistent with the "principle of thrift," however, it was almost always the name of a single author that appeared. When printed drama graduated from the cheap quarto edition to the expensive folio format, it was the name of the single author that came to dominate the author function on the title page, an author function that was embodied by a portrait of the author himself. Folio publication, then, lends some credence to Foucault's observation that "the name seems always to be present, marking off the edges of the text,"[86] though on the title page of the first of these folio collections, Jonson's *Workes* (Fig. 21), an elaborate woodcut of a monument had been deployed to mark off the edges of the name.

In the decade immediately preceding Moseley's effort to publish a folio, author attribution of known titles climbed to nearly 90% and multiple-author attribution fell to its lowest point (2%) since the opening of the first professional theatre in 1576. The two folio collections of printed drama that preceded and thus legitimized Moseley's effort were both celebrations of single authors. And while a relatively small number of extant quarto editions attributed to more than one author were published, the following table suggests that, in the particular case of Beaumont and Fletcher, their collaborative presence on quarto title pages of extant first editions entered in to the Stationers' Register did not constitute a very powerful precedent for a folio title page.

Year	Title	Title-Page Attribution	Stationers' Register Attribution
1615	The Scorneful Lady	Beaumont & Fletcher	Beaumont & Fletcher
1619	A King and no King	Beaumont & Fletcher	
1620	Philaster	Beaumont & Fletcher	

Only once, a year before Jonson's folio appeared and author attribution of known titles reached 100%, did a stationer bother to enter the names of the playwriting duo "never parted while they lived" in his register. In this context, Moseley's decision to honor Fletcher's long history of collaboration by figuratively adding Beaumont's name, if not many of

Figure 21 Title page: *The Workes of Beniamin Jonson*, 1616

Dramatic authorship

his plays, to the venture was a risky one. He can hardly be faulted for not cluttering the title page of the 1647 folio with the names of Shakespeare, Field, Rowley, and Massinger, even if he did know the precise history of Fletcher's "writing arrangements." And although a single-author publication was less risky, the following table indicates that Fletcher's pre-folio history as an author function on the title page of first edition quartos entered into the Stationers' Register was less than impressive, compared to that of either Jonson or Shakespeare.

Year	Title	Title-Page Attribution	Stationers' Register Attribution
1610	The Faithful Shepheardesse	John Fletcher	
1615	Cupid's Revenge	John Fletcher	
1637	The Elder Brother	John Fletcher	John Fletcher
1639	Monsieur Thomas	John Fletcher	John Fletcher
1640	The Coronation	John Fletcher	

The "patriarchal-absolutist model" of authorship may have cohered better with the royalist politics of a volume that declared early on there was "nothing now wanting but the King," but it probably made better business sense to publish a single-author folio.[87] Whether Moseley abandoned his initial plan to publish a collection of "Fletcher's workes" to acknowledge a long collaborative writing career in the theatre, or out of homage to a close relationship, is largely a matter of speculation. What seems more certain, however, is that for a number of reasons I have elaborated, the time was not right for a folio that celebrated collaborative authorship. If the closing of the theatres five years earlier had also closed down the space of collaboration, Moseley's folio could honor such collaboration in name only, despite an emergent author function that was increasingly linked to single authors. Thus, in much the same way that the 1616 folio preserves its author's inability to extricate himself completely from the venues for which he wrote, the 1647 folio preserves its publisher's failure to translate the highly collaborative writing environment of the London stage into the single-author format of the printed drama collection. And although attribution studies have exhaustively documented what got lost in the translation, the most obvious evidence of Moseley's failure paradoxically comes from the commendatory verses he himself commissioned to underwrite the project. Of the thirty-four poems included in the preliminaries, only the following titles indicate that the folio was collaboratively authored:

(1) "Upon the Works of Beaumont / and Fletcher"
(2) "On the Edition of Mr. *Francis Beaumonts*, and Mr. *John Fletchers* Plays never printed before"
(3) "To the *Names* of the celebrated Poets and Fellow-writers, / *Francis Beaumont* and *John Fletcher*, upon the / Printing of their excellent Dramatick Poems"
(4) "On the Workes of *Beaumont* and / *Fletcher* now at length printed"
(5) "Upon the unparalelled Playes written / by those Renowned Twinnes of Poetry / Beaumont & Fletcher"

In keeping with Moseley's initial plan for the volume, the following titles refer only to Fletcher:

(1) "Upon the Printing of Mr. John Fletchers workes"
(2) "In Memory of Mr. John Fletcher"
(3) "On Mr. Fletcher, and his / Workes, never before published"
(4) "On Mr. Fletchers Works"
(5) "To the memory of the deceased but ever-living Author in these his poems, Mr. John Fletcher"
(6) "On the / Deceased Author, Mr. John Fletcher, his Plays"
(7) "On the Works of the most excellent / Dramatick Poet, Mr. John Fletcher, / Never before Printed"
(8) "On Mr. John Fletcher's Workes"
(9) "Upon Mr. Fletcher's Playes"
(10) "To Fletcher Reviv'd"
(11) "On Master John Fletchers Dramaticall Poems"
(12) "Vpon Master Fletchers Dramaticall Workes"
(13) "Upon Mr. Fletchers Incomparable Playes"
(14) "On the Dramatick Poems of Mr. John Fletcher"
(15) "Upon the report of the printing of the Dra / maticall Poems of Master John Fletcher, collected / before, and now set forth in one Volume"
(16) "Upon Master Fletchers / Incomparable Playes"
(17) "On the happy Collection of Master / Fletcher's Works, never before Printed"
(18) "To the memorie of Master / FLETCHER"
(19) "Vpon the ever to be admi– / red Mr. John Fletcher / and His Playes"
(20) "In Honour of Mr. / John Fletcher"
(21) "Master John Fletcher his dramaticall / Workes now at last printed"
(22) "On Mr. John Fletcher's Workes"
(23) "On Mr. John Fletcher's Workes"

Whereas all but one of these titles link proper name to some reference to dramatic text – and some even rely on the modern form of unambiguous possession to reinforce that link – only the following titles name Beaumont, and not one of them mentions his authorship or indicates that his plays are part of the publication the verses have been written to endorse:

(1) "To the memory of my most honoured / kinsman, Mr. Francis Beaumont"
(2) "On Mr. Beaumont"
(3) "On Mr. Francis Beaumont (then newly dead)"
(4) "To Mr. Francis Beaumont (then Living)"

Concerned primarily with his death, the titles fail to remember what Beaumont did when he was alive. And finally, the remaining two poems refer neutrally to the volume itself or a single, unnamed author: "On the Edition"; " To the desert of the Author in his most Ingenious Pieces."

Noting that, "[t]he Volume's seeming vacillation between singular authorship and dual collaboration is by no means stabilized by the extensive preliminary materials that lie between the title page and the plays themselves," Masten rightly observes that "a number of the commendatory poems are addressed to one man but speak at length of the writers' collaboration."[88] I would go further and argue that juxtaposing these poems' titles with the volume that houses them concisely illustrates the challenge that Moseley faced when he decided to put two names on the title page. In this context, the last line of his last signed address, "If this Booke faile, tis time to quit the Trade," reads more like a self-fulfilling prophecy than a confident sales pitch.

Perhaps, however, the clearest indication that the 1647 folio could not deliver what its title page promised comes in the form of one of the "*Prologues* and *Epilogues*" that Moseley – disguised as "We" – "forgot to tell the Reader" about, one of those generically theatrical pieces that, appropriately enough, was "not written by the *Authors* of this *Volume*." Here, in a poem written for the revival of a play called *The Loyal Subject*, and subsequently published in a folio collection that promises to revive the theatre for its readers and begins with a loyal subject longing for his king to return, appears a portrait of the author in all of its individualized glory:

> We need not noble Gentlemen to invite
> Attention, preinstruct you who did write
> This worthy Story, being confident
> The mirth joyn'd with grave matter, & intent.
> To yield the bearers profit, with delight

> Will speake the maker; and to do him right,
> Would aske a Genius like to his; the age
> Mourning his losse, and our now widdowed stage
> In vaine. Lamenting. I could adde, so far
> Behind him the most moderne writers are
> That when they would commend him, their best praise
> Ruins the buildings which they strive to raise,
> To his best memory, so much a friend
> Presumes to write, secure twill not offend
> The living that are modest, with the rest
> That my repine he cares not to contest.
> This debt to FLETCHER paid; it is profest
> By us the Actors, we shall do our best. (3G1r)

In 1647, Moseley also did his best, like John Daye nearly a century earlier, to pay his own debts by publishing the first collection of dramatic texts dedicated to more than one author. Unfortunately, at this late stage in the game of books and authors, the second meaning of the word subject," the thinking or cognizing agent; the self or ego," had begun to come into currency at precisely the moment in which the first meaning, "one who is under the dominion of a monarch or reigning prince," was about to become meaningless. Three years earlier, Descartes had neglected to add the phrase, "We think, therefore we are," to his solitary epiphany.

5 "So wronged in beeing publisht": Thomas Heywood and the discourse of perilous publication

> Thou hast writ much and art admir'd by those,
> Who love the easie ambling of the prose;
> But yet thy pleasingst flight, was somewhat high
> When thou did'st touch the angels Hyerarchie:
> Fly that way still it will become thy age,
> And better please then groveling on the stage.
>
> *Wits Recreations*

> Anon was created by the audience. He was writing their language for them, reflecting their idiom, giving them plots which they gathered to see. Scott McMillin, *The Elizabethan Theatre and The Booke of Sir Thomas More*

The journey from playhouse to printing house was not without hazards, though some playwrights navigated it better than others. Thomas Heywood lost his way. Perhaps the most prolific writer of his generation, he claims to have individually or collaboratively written more than two hundred plays, and he penned scores of other works in a number of genres. He began writing plays just as the professional theatres were coming into their own, and he died shortly before they were closed by an Act of Parliament. Like Shakespeare, he had a long relationship with one playing company, but like Dekker and others, he was also financially compelled at times in his life to freelance for other companies. Like Jonson, he seems to have been keenly aware of the importance of publication, but he did not share Jonson's anti-theatricalism, and he never lived to see a collection of his plays published. His authorial canon remains for the most part dispersed and unauthoritative. No playwright in the period wrote more about the vicissitudes of dramatic authorship than Heywood, and the perils of publication he documented have been frequently quoted by New Bibliographers and New Textualists to compensate for Shakespeare's frustrating silence. Having failed to play and be played by "the game of books and authors," Heywood sat noisily on the sidelines for much of his authorial career. From this marginal position, he filed a valuable, if sometimes unreliable, report on the drama of authorship in early modern England.

Searching for a discourse that exposes the "coincidental nature of state power itself as imagined by Elizabethan terminologies,"[1] Claire McEachern turns to the "social practice of the Elizabethan theatre" and observes: "[t]he survival of theatre companies had no doubt more to do with private enterprise than with royal protection and depended less on a queen's appetite than on a commodified taste for entertainment."[2] The dominant concepts here are private enterprise and commodification. Although McEachern moves directly from this general formulation to a discussion of Elizabethan anti-theatrical discourse, the career of Thomas Heywood would have served her argument well. As Kathleen E. McLuskie observes about both Heywood and Thomas Dekker:

They engaged . . . with all the opportunities available for professional dramatists in the new commercial theatre world of early modern London. As such, their work can provide an insight into the cultural movement in which literary arts began to be transformed into the commodities of a consumer economy which at the same time enacted and articulated the beliefs and aspirations of the society which produced and consumed them.[3]

Generally regarded, according to Michael Wentworth, "as a secondary figure in Renaissance literature,"[4] Heywood nevertheless began his long professional life as a dramatist somewhat ahead of the pack. As early as 14 October 1596, Philip Henslowe had paid out some thirty shillings for "hawodes bocke."[5] A second diary entry, written a year-and-a-half later, goes further and intimates that Heywood had signed on with Henslowe – in Arthur Melville Clark's apt phrase – as "a jobbing dramatist."[6]

m^r that this 25 of Marche 1598 Thomas hawoode came & hiered hime sealfe wth me as a covenante searvante for ij yeares by the Recevenge of ij syngell pence acordinge to the statute of winshester & to begine at the daye above written & not to playe any wher publicke a bowt london not while ij yeares be expired but in my howsse yf he do then he dothe forfett vnto me by the Receuinge of thes ij^d fortie powndes . . .[7]

A record of payment to Heywood and Kempe on behalf of the Earl of Worcester's players for court performances during the Christmas season of 1601/2 suggests that he was already a sharer in Worcester's company within a year of completing his term of servitude to Henslowe.[8] However, the next recorded reference to Heywood appears in Francis Meres's *Palladis Tamia* (1598), where he is praised for being one of "the best for Comedy."[9] Fourteen years letter, in a note "To the Reader" included in the 1612 quarto edition of *The White Devil*, John Webster places Heywood in a rather important group of playwrights:

For my owne part I have ever truly cherisht my good opinion of other mens worthy Labours, especially of that full and haightned stile of Maister *Chapman*. The labor'd and vnderstanding workes of Maister *Johnson*: The no lesse worthy composures of the both worthily excellent Maister *Beamont* and Maister *Fletcher*: And lastly (without wrong last to be named) the right happy and copious industry of M. *Shake-speare*, M. *Dekker*, and M. *Heywood*, wishing what I write may be read by their light.[10]

As I argued in Chapter 1, Webster's list is structured according to his desire to distance his authorship from popular theatre audiences and to promote his plays in an emergent literary market for printed drama. In this context, Heywood's position in the list is particularly suspect, though it is not altogether clear that he lacked a literary reputation. A number of his contemporaries praised him for the extent of his learning, especially his knowledge of languages.[11] It is also likely that he and the "Thomas Heywood" who entered Emmanuel College, Cambridge as a pensioner in 1591 are the same person, though a subsequent tradition, begun by William Cartwright in his 1658 edition of *An Apology for Actors* – retitled *The Actors' Vindication* – indicates that "the gentleman was a Fellow of Peter-house in Cambridge."[12] Despite this academic pedigree, Heywood was the most enthusiastic apologist for the theatre in Webster's group, and not coincidentally, the most vocal about the perils of print publication. Additionally, according to his note "To the Reader" of *The English Traveller* (1633), he was also by far the most prolific. Some eight years before his death, Heywood claims that "This *Tragi-Comedy* [is] one reserued amongst two hundred and twenty, in which I haue had either an entire hand, or at the least a maine finger."[13] This is a remarkable claim, and we will examine the preface in its entirety later. For now, it will suffice to look at what immediately precedes and follows Heywood's assertion. Writing two decades after *The White Devil*, Heywood begins the preface by granting a certain legitimacy to the play's theatre audience, presuming that some readers may have seen the play in performance: "If Reader thous hast of this Play beene an auditour? there is lesse apology to be vsed by intreating thy patience."[14] No such presumption appears in any of the preliminaries written by Webster or the first four playwrights he mentions. Instead, their primary concern is to distinguish between theatre audiences who are unable to appreciate the literary value of plays, and readers of printed texts who constitute a much more suitable audience. For playwrights like Jonson and Webster, publication is deliberate and purposeful. Heywood, on the other hand, informs his readers that the publication of *The English Traveller* was anything but purposeful. Claiming to have written more than two hundred plays, Heywood asserts that this particular play came "accidentally to the Presse," and that he attempted to make it legitimate after the fact: "I having Intelligence thereof, thought it not fit that it should passe as *filius populi*, a Bastard without a Father to acknowledge it."[15]

The paternal trope Heywood relies on here was, as Katherine Eisaman Maus has shown, commonplace in early modern writers' accounts of authorship,[16] a practice rooted in what Jeff Masten identifies as "a patriarchal model of textual reproduction."[17] And yet, Heywood's use of this trope is significant, because he proceeds to account for the illegitimacy of his offspring in astonishingly precise terms:

> True it is, that my Playes are not exposed vnto the world in Volumes, to beare the title of *Workes*, (as others) one reason is, That many of them by shifting and change of Companies, haue beene negligently lost, Others of them are still retained in the hands of some Actors, who thinke it against their peculiar profit to haue them come in Print, and a third, That it neuer was any great ambition in me, to bee in this kind Voluminously read.[18]

Although Heywood offers here three distinct ways in which his authorship has been cuckolded, they are closely inter-related. The opening dig at Jonson for publishing his plays in folio as *The Workes of Benjamin Jonson* would be succinctly explored in Epigram 269 of *Wits Recreations*:

> *To Mr. Ben Johnson demanding the reason*
> *Why he call'd his playes works.*
> Pray tell me Ben, where doth the mystery lurke,
> What others call a play you call a worke.[19]

In a note "To the Reader" included three years earlier in a quarto edition of *The Fair Maid of the West* (1631), Heywood had taken an even more bibliographically precise swipe at Jonson and folio publication:

> Cvrteous Reader, my Plaies have not beene exposed to the publike view of the world in numerous sheets, and a large volume; but singly (as thou seest) with great modesty and, small noise (A3r).[20]

By the time the later address is published, another playwright had been "exposed vnto the world in Volumes," and Heywood is possibly referring also to the publication of John Marston's *Workes* in the same year as *The English Traveller*. In his "Epistle dedicatorie" to Lady Elizabeth Cary, the publisher of Marston's volume, William Sheares, notes the use of "workes" with reference to printed drama as he attempts to protect these texts from the "approbies and aspersions" that have been "cast upon plays." Asking rhetorically if such published texts are belittled merely "because they are Playes," he answers:

> The name it seems somewhat offends them, where as if they were styled *Workes*, they might have their approbation also? I hope that I have now somewhat pacified that precise Sect, by reducing all our Authors Severall Playes into one Volume, and so stiled them the Works of Mr. John Marston (A3–A3v).

Having weighed his two options, acknowledging the downside of each – dramatic texts labeled "playes" are belittled, while those labeled "workes," as Jonson was to learn, are punished for their authors' grandiosity – he decides on the latter. No such choice may have been available or desirable to the writer of *The English Traveller*. In the same year as Sheares's epistle, Heywood observes that his plays don't "beare the title of *Workes*," and he blames this predicament on three factors. Although Heywood wrote at least half of his plays for the Earl of Worcester/Queen Anne's Men, he indicates that "many of them" were "negligently lost" due to "shifting and change of Companies." Those plays that were not lost, are being hoarded by "some Actors, who thinke it against their peculiar profit to haue them come in Print." Actors have conspired to keep Heywood from attaining the literary reputation of a Jonson or a Marston. Finally, Heywood concludes by assuring his readers that he never wanted his plays to be published in volumes anyway: "it neuer was any great ambition in me, to bee in this kind Voluminously read." His reluctance to be a "man in print" would be honored.

Over the course of a writing career that spanned nearly half a century, only the following extant plays written for the public stage were published with Heywood's name on the title page prior to his death in 1641: *A Woman Kilde with Kindnesse* (1607); *The Rape of Lucrece* (1608); *The Golden Age* (1611); *The Brazen Age* (1613); *The Silver Age* (1613); *The Foure Prentises of London* (1615); *The Iron Age* (1630); *2 The Fair Maid of the West* (1631); *The English Traveller* (1633); *A Mayden-Head Well Lost* (1634); *The Royall King and the Loyall Subject* (1637); *The Wise-Woman of Hogsdon* (1638).[21] Another play, *The Late Lancashire witches* (1634), was attributed to Heywood and Richard Brome, and *Fortune by Land and Sea* (1655), written in collaboration with William Rowley, appeared after his death. The following plays, published anonymously, have been subsequently attributed to Heywood: *The First and Second Partes of King Edward the Fourth* (1599); *A Warning for Fair Women* (1599); *The Trial of Chivalry* (1601); *How a Man may Choose a Good Wife from a Bad* (1602); *1 The Fair Maid of the West* (1604); *If You Know Not Me, You Know No Bodie* (1605); *The Second Part of, If You Know Not Me, You Know No Bodie* (1605); *The Fayre Mayde of the Exchange* (1607). A dozen or so additional masques, entertainments, or inaugural spectacles attributed to Heywood are also extant.

Less than two dozen plays reliably linked to Heywood's "entire hand" or even a "maine finger" have survived, a dismal rate that underscores the peculiarly material vulnerability of Heywood's texts, but probably has more to do with the norms of early modern dramatic publication – especially the publication of plays that were written (as most of Heywood's were) for acting companies. Although nearly forty percent of known plays produced between 1575 and 1642 were published, no more than ten percent of the plays written for companies, according to David Scott Kastan, ever made it to the press.[22] Even that rate may be high in Heywood's case. While half of his plays were probably written for the Worcester/Queen Anne's Men, after that troupe disbanded, Heywood cannot, as Bentley notes, "be shown to have been a regular dramatist for any company."[23] If, however, someone had decided to publish a folio collection of Heywood's plays after his death, we could – based on the evidence of either the first Shakespeare Folio of 1623 or the first Beaumont and Fletcher folio of 1647 – logically assume that another twenty or thirty plays would be included in his authorial canon. This would still leave more than 150 plays unaccounted for. Since no such folio collection was undertaken, the only comparable assessment of Heywood's career as a dramatist appears in Francis Kirkman's *A True, Perfect, and Exact Catalogue* (1661).[24]

Claiming to "have then been collecting plays for twenty years, and to have drawn on the experience of others whose activities covered half a century,"[25] Kirkman was an early archivist of printed drama. He ascribes twenty-five plays to Heywood, only thirteen more than those plays published under the author's name during his lifetime. Only four plays – *English Traveller*, *Golden Age*, *Love's Mistresse*, and *Mayden-Head Well Lost* – had been attributed to Heywood five years earlier in "an Alphebeticall Catalogue of all such Plays that ever were Printed" appended to the 1656 quarto edition of *The Careles Shepherdess*. Furthermore, whereas Heminge and Condell informed readers that Shakespeare was "a most gentle expresser of it. His mind / and hand, went together : And what he thought, he vttered with that / easinesse, that wee haue scarse receiued from him a blot in his papers" (A3r: 27–30), Kirkman provides the following depiction of Heywood's writing process:

I have been informed he [Heywood] was very laborious; for he not only Acted almost every day, but also obliged himself to write a sheet every day, for several years together; but many of his Playes being composed and written loosely in Taverns, occasions them to be so mean (B3r).

Like Shakespeare's literary executors, who were quite frank about their efforts to transform the playwright's corpus into a marketable commodity, Kirkman stood to gain much from promoting Heywood and the other playwrights he mentions. The 1661 *Catalogue* kept a promise Kirkman made to book buyers a few months earlier in a note from "The Stationer to the Reader" published in his quarto edition of *The Thracian Wonder* (1661). Apparently new to the art of writing preliminaries, he begins, "It is now the second time of my appearing in Print in this nature,

I should not have troubled you, but that I believe you will be as well pleased as my self" (A2r). Then, having made his humble apologies for intruding into the space between the title page and the reader's pleasure, he launches into the task at hand:

> I am sure that when I applied my self to buying and reading of Books, I was very well satisfied when I could purchase a new Play. I have promised you three this Tearm, *A cure for a Cuckold* was the first, this the second, and the third, viz. *Gamer Gurtons Needle* is ready for you. I have several others that I intend for you suddenly: I shall not (as some others of my profession have done) promise more then I will perform in a year or two, or it may never; but I will assure you that I shall never leave printing, so long as you shall continue buying. I have several *Manuscripts* of this nature, written by worthy Authors, and I account it much pity they should now lye dormant, and buried in oblivion, since ingenuity is so likely to be encouraged, by reason of the happy Restauration of our Liberties (A2r).[26]

Not only has the monarchy been restored, but the Liberties are back in the theatre business. Therefore, Kirkman logically intimates, acting companies will require printed texts of the plays he has in manuscript. Hoping to establish an archive of play books for the newly re-opened theatres, Kirkman returns to this brash marketing scheme twelve years later in the preface to *The Wits, or, Sport upon Sport* (1673). First he laments "that very few Dramatick Poems, Vulgarly called Plays, have been published,"[27] then concludes by offering some advice about how a new playing company might break into the business:

> Besides those who read these sort of Books for their pleasure, there are some who do so for profit, such as are young Players, Fidlers, &c. As for those Players who intend to wander and go a stroleing, this very Book, and a few ordinary properties is enough to set them up, and get money in any Town in England. And fidlers purchacing this Book have a sufficient stock for all Feasts and Entertainments.[28]

Clearly, Kirkman had his eye on two different markets: buyers/readers of printed drama, to whom he will return at the end of the 1661 note; and upscale theatre-goers, who he appeals to in the next line:

> We have had the private Stage for some years clouded, and under a tyrannical command, though the publick Stage of England has produc'd many monstrous villains, some of which have deservedly made their exit (A2r).

This division between the private and public stage can be traced back to elitist attitudes promulgated during the reconfiguration of the theatre companies in the first years of James I's reign and a concomitant preference for roofed city playhouses.[29] In the end, however, potential book buyers are what really matter to Kirkman, and he concludes with this rather astonishing sales pitch:

Gentlemen, I will not further trouble you at this time, onely I shall tell you, that if you please to repair to my Shop, I shall furnish you with all the *Plays* ever yet printed. I have 700 several *Plays*, and most of them several times over, and I intend to increase my Store as I sell; And I hope you will by your frequent buying, encourage (A2r).

So much for not "promise[ing] more then [he] will perform in a year or two." If we accept Heywood's perhaps exaggerated authorial claim, then nearly a third of these "700 several *Plays*" are his. But if we follow Kirkman's ascription of twenty-five plays, much "printing" and "buying" was still at stake in the sale of the Heywood corpus. Consequently, it was in Kirkman's best financial interest to take Heminge and Condell's approach to marketing a dead playwright. If the first half of his account tends to support Heywood's own claims about his extraordinary productivity, the second half conjures up less than idealized images of the author at work. Either way, Kirkman's concluding judgment that many of Heywood's plays were mediocre seems to have been made on the basis of a relatively small, poorly preserved, and, in the case of half a dozen or so ascriptions, inaccurate sample.

At the very moment that print publication was transforming a bricklayer's son into "self-creating Ben Jonson,"[30] or a committed company playwright like Shakespeare into, in Jonson's words, the "Starre of Poets" (B1v), Heywood found the journey from stage to page either formidable or unappealing. Few in the London book trade were willing to show him the way. Of the seven Heywood plays that were published prior to *The White Devil*, only *The Golden Age* (1611) was typographically dressed up for a literary readership. Appearing in print more than two decades before *The English Traveller*, *The Golden Age* includes a note "TO THE READER" from Heywood that rehearses – albeit in reverse order – the two major themes emphasized in the *Traveller*'s reader address. Whereas the later text privileges the play's theatre audience, then treats the vicissitudes of Heywood's relationship to the press, the earlier address begins with the play's publication history:

This Play comming accidentally to the Presse, and at length hauing notice thereof, I was loath (finding it my owne) to see it thrust naked into the world, to abide fury of all weathers, without either Title for acknowledgement, or the formality of an Epistle for ornament (A2r).[31]

As is the case in the subsequent address, the master trope for "accidental" publication is anxious paternal concern for an abandoned child, a concern that compels Heywood to acknowledge his "child" after the typographic fact and to dress it in swaddling clothes of his own making. Accordingly, he alludes to the play's happier prenatal experience in the theatre, then refers to its siblings:

Therefore rather to keepe custome, then any necessity, I haue fixt these few lines in the front of my Booke: neither to approue it, as tastfull to euery palat, nor to disgrace it, as able to relish none, onely to commit it freely to the generall scensure of Readers, as it hath already past the approbation of Auditors. This is the Golden Age, the eldest brother of three Ages, that have aduentured the Stage, but the onely yet, that hath been iudged to the Presse (A2r).

Two of these younger brothers, *The Silver Age* and *The Brazen Age*, were subsequently "iudged to the Presse" by Nicholas Okes in 1613, the latter printed continuously. And while both texts include addresses to the reader written by Heywood, neither address, as Bentley notes, "indicates that they had come to the press without the knowledge of the playwright."[32] Nevertheless, Heywood can't allow *The Brazen Age* out of his sight without a disavowal of sorts. Thus, he offers a prior tale of piracy in which

a Pedant about this Towne, who when all trades fail'd turn'd *Pedagogue*, & once insinuating with me, borrowed frō me certaine Translations of *Ovid*, as his three books De Arte Amandi, & two *De Remedio Amoris*, which since, his most brazen face hath most impudently challenged as his own, wherefore, I must needs proclaime it as far as *Ham*, where he now keeps schoole, *Hos ego verisculos feci tulit alter honores*, they were things which out of my iuniority and want of iudgement, I committed to view of some private friends, but with no purpose of publishing, or further cōmunicating thē (A2r).[33]

The absence of paternal anxiety over these two plays may stem from Heywood's long relationship with Okes – who also printed *The Golden Age* and *The Rape of Lucrece* (1608) – and his partner, John Norton.[34] The latter, subsequently printed quarto editions of Heywood's *How a Man May Choose A Good Wife from a Bad* in 1630 and 1634, and, according to Clark, "acted as a kind of literary agent for them in the sixteen-thirties."[35] Okes was new to the printing trade when he began to work with Heywood, but his commitment to printing drama deepened quickly, as the table of his dramatic publications for the years 1608–1611 suggests (see p. 198).

With three of the four *Ages* in print by 1613, and the fourth – *The Iron Age*, Parts 1&2 (1632) – published by Okes a year before *The English Traveller*, Heywood had both the ideal set up for a collection, and the printer to do it. The timing couldn't have been better. In the twenty-two years separating the publication of *The Golden Age* and *The English Traveller*, the following nine single-author collections of dramatic texts appeared:[36]

(1) Jonson, *The Workes of Beniamin Jonson* (1616) folio.
(2) Middleton, *Honorable Entertainments* (1621) octavo.
(3) Shakespeare, *Mr. William Shakespeares Comedies Histories & Tragedies* (1623) folio.

198   From Playhouse to Printing House

STC	Year	Author/Title/Format/Publisher
13360	1608	Thomas Heywood, The rape of Lucrece. A true Roman tragedie. 4. Printing shared with E. Alde, for J. Busby, solde by N. Butter. ent. to J. Busby and N. Butter.
17398	1608	Gervase Markham and Lewis Machin, The dumbe knight. A historical comedy. 4. for J. Bache. ent.
17888	1608	Thomas Middleton, A mad world my masters. As it hath bin lately in action. 4. Printing shared with H. Ballard, for W. Burre. ent. to Burre and E. Edgar.
22292	1608	William Shakespeare, M. William Shak-speare: his true chronicle historie of the life and death of king Lear and his three daughters. 4. for N. Butter. ent. to Butter and J. Busby 1607.
14757	1609	Benjamin Jonson, Ben: Jonson: his case is altered. 4. for B. Sutton. ent. to H. Walley and R. Bonion.
14778	1609	Benjamin Jonson, The masque of Queenes celebratted from the house of fame. 4. for R. Bonian and H. Wally. ent.
17359	1609	Gervase Markham, The famous whore, or noble curtizan; conteining the lamentable complaint of Paulina. 4. for J. Budge.
12362	1609	Fulke Greville, The tragedy of Mustapha. [anon]. 4. Printing shared with J. Windet, for N. Butter. ent 1608.
13325	1611	Thomas Heywood, The golden age. Or the lives of Jupiter and Saturne, with the deivying of the heathen gods. 4. for W. Barrrenger. ent.
17908	1611	Thomas Middleton and Thomas Dekker, The roaring girle. Or Moll Cut-purse. 4. for T. Archer

(4) Newman (Translator), *The Two First Comedies of Terence* (1627) octavo.
(5) Jonson, *The Works. Second Volume* (1631) folio.
(6) Shakespeare, *Mr. William Shakespeares Comedies Histories & Tragedies* (1632) folio.
(7) Lyly, *Sixe Covrt Comedies* (1632) twelvemo.
(8) Marston, *The Workes of Mr. John Marston* (1633) octavo.
(9) Greville, *Certaine Learned and Elegant Workes* (1633) folio.[37]

If a plan to make Heywood "Voluminously read" was in the works (as it were), the note to "To the Reader" prefacing the quarto edition of *The Iron Age* (Part 1) is curiously silent on the subject. Indeed, the address says nothing at all about publication except a parenthetical comment that the play was "(never till now Published)."[38] Instead, Heywood recounts the four *Age* plays' theatrical popularity in considerable detail:

Lastly, I desire thee to take notice, that these were the playes often (and not with the least applause.) Publickely Acted by two companies, vppon one stage at once, and have at sundry times thronged three severall Theaters, with numerous and mighty Auditories, if the grace they had then in the Actings, take not away the expected luster, hoped for in the Reading, I shall then hold thee well pleased, and therein, my selfe fully satisfied; Ever remaining thine as studious

Prodesse vt Delectare:
Thomas Heywood[39]

Rather than professing the oppositional relation between stage and page, Heywood refers to it as a kind of gap over which readers will pass easily so that they can be "well pleased," and he can be "fully satisfied." Even the phrase, "Ever remaining thine as studious," seems to locate the playwright on the side of the printed book. No other extant Heywood address is so eager to recall a play's success in the theatre. Therefore, according to the logic that underwrites the publication of those "vtterly reiected" plays by Webster and the first four playwrights he praises in 1612, the five *Age* plays would be the last ones Heywood could be expected to publish "Voluminously." The very next address "To the Reader," included in the 1632 quarto edition of *The Iron Age* (Part 2), quickly and efficiently dismantles that logic.

Whereas the year's previous address stressed the *Age* plays' popularity "with numerous and mighty Auditories" and marginalized their publication history, the later address barely mentions the theatre. Rather, for the first time since his first reader address appeared twenty-four years earlier, Heywood unambiguously promotes his plays as texts to be read:

Reade freely, and censure favourably. These Ages have beene long since Writ, and suited with the Time then: I know not how they may bee receiued in this Age, where nothing but *Satirica Dicteria*, and *Comica Scommata* are now in request: For mine owne part, I never affected either, when they stretched to the abuse of any person publicke, or private (A4r).[40]

Having previously urged his readers to make a leap of faith from the stage to the page, Heywood now emerges as a proponent of the latter. To do so necessitates the construction of an authorial identity in which the playwright offers his plays as anachronisms within the context of current theatrical fashions. In other words, for one brief Jonsonian moment, Heywood disparages the theatre in order to advance himself as a dramatist in print. The next order of business is to promote a forthcoming collection of his plays:

If the three former Ages (now out of Print,) bee added to these (as I am promised) to make vp an handsome Volumne; I purpose (Deo Assistente,) to illustrate the whole Worke, with an Explanation of all [t]he difficulties, and an Historicall Comment of every hard name, which may appeare obscure or intricate to such as are not frequent in Poetry: Which (as the rest) I shall freely devote to thy fauorable perusall, in this as all the rest industrious to thy pleasure and profit:

Thomas Heywood[41]

Now that his most theatrically popular plays are out of style and out of print, Heywood recreates himself here as Jonson, though he can't quite shake himself free of auditors who "are not frequent in Poetry." He exalts the piece as "an entire History, from *Iupiter* and *Saturne*, to the vtter subuersion of *Troy*," refers to the forthcoming publication of the collected *Age* plays as a "Volumne" and a "Worke," and even pledges to annotate his texts as Jonson did beginning with the published version of *B. Jon: HIS PART OF King James his Royal and Magnificent Entertainement through his Honorable Cittie of London* (1604).

There can be little doubt that this sudden change of heart toward the printing house was directly linked to the project of publishing a collection of the *Age* plays. Additional evidence for this view is suggested by the reader address included in the quarto edition of *The Foure Prentises of London* that also appeared in 1632. In a more typically un-Jonsonian mood, Heywood informs his "Honest and High-spirited Prentises, the Readers":

None but to you (as whom this Play most especially concernes) I thought good to Dedicate this Labour, which though written many years since, in my Infancy of Iudgment in this kind of Poetry, and my first practise: Yet vnderstanding by what meanes I know not, it was in these more exquisite and refined times to come to the Presse, in such a forwardnesse ere it came to my knowledge, that it was past preuention, and then knowing withall, that it comes short of that accuratnesse both in Plot and Stile, that these more Censorious dayes with greater curiosity acquire, I must thus excuse. That as Playes were then some fifteene or sixteene yeares agoe it was in the fashion (A2r–v).[42]

Jonson had used publication as an opportunity to radically revise the collaboratively written play book of *Sejanus*, and subsequently took advantage of the planned 1616 folio to rework earlier plays like *Every Man in his Humor* and to erase his early plays from his authorial canon. Heywood, however, alleges that accidental publication has forced him to apologize for a play which, first performed on the London stage in 1594, now embarrasses him thirty-eight years later. But if theatrical tastes and dramatic fashions have passed the play by, Heywood intimates that military history is just now catching up with it:

Nor could it have found a more seasonable and fit publication then at this Time, when to the glory of our Nation, the security of the Kingdome, and the Honor of this Renowned Citty, they have begunne againe the commendable practice of long forgotten Armes (A2v).

Taken together, the three reader addresses of 1632 indicate that Heywood was in two minds about publication late in his playwriting career. The age of the *The Foure Prentises* motivates the account of its accidental arrival at the press. Paradoxically, Heywood introduces his very purposeful effort to annotate and publish "an handsome Volumne" by notifying his readers that, "These Ages have beene long since Writ, and suited with the Time then: I know not how they may bee receiued in this Age." Perhaps, the only significant difference between these two publishing ventures is one which, ironically enough, situates the playwright between stage and page. In the case of the proposed collection, Heywood's long-standing relationship with Nicholas Okes may have given him a new sense of control over the material fate of his plays – a sense of control that manifested itself principally as a promise. In a recent astute analysis of Heywood's publishing career, Benedict Robinson points out that by 1630, Okes had actually transferred his title to print the *Age* plays to his son John Okes, who subsequently took over his father's printing business. Despite this transfer, Robinson concludes that, "it seems clear that if a collection of the *Age* plays had been published, the Okes shop would have been involved."[43]

Whether God actually intervened on Heywood's behalf to complete this project is unclear, but it seems certain that Heywood did all that was humanly possible. The excessive praise of the *Age* plays' theatrical popularity in the first *Iron Age* address constitutes the first part of a well-planned two-part marketing strategy. Part two, reserved for the second *Iron Age* address, promises its readers the forthcoming publication of those much-applauded plays in "an handsome Volumne" – a promise that was never kept. While it is impossible to know what prevented the "Volumne" from being printed, Robinson suggests that publishing rights for *The Brazen Age* may have been the problem. Initially printed by Okes for Samuel Rand in 1613, Robinson observes that "it may be that Rand or the managers of his estate were unwilling to sell the rights to that play."[44] Whatever the reason, no printed collection of the *Ages* appeared, nor was a collection of Heywood's plays undertaken during the dramatist's lifetime. The closest any of Heywood's plays came to having the bibliographical prestige bestowed on Jonson's dramatic output was the text of *The English Traveller*, his only attributed play to be printed continuously and to include a Latin epigraph on its title page.

Obviously, Heywood's 1633 declaration – in the *Traveller*'s address – that "it neuer was any great ambition in me, to bee in this kind Voluminously read" must be considered in light of the previous year's publication failure. In 1632, Heywood had indicated that he was only too aware of the publication trend sparked by Jonson's 1616 folio. By 1633, he was defining himself oppositionally against it, though it is impossible to know exactly what in the end kept his "handsome Volumne" out of readers' hands. Such a stand in relation to a specific material practice rapidly becoming integral to authorship – with its concomitants of canonization, idealization, and, eventually, authorization – would prove to be self-destructive. In an anonymous poem published in *Choice Drollery* (1656), Heywood is disparaged as "the apologetic Atlas of the Stage."[45] Two decades later, Edward Phillips, in his *Theatrum Poetarum* (1675), would remember Heywood as "a great Benefactor no doubt to the Red Bull, and other common Theaters."[46] Without a folio collection to distance his plays from the "loathed stage," Heywood's authorial ghost was compelled to haunt the "common Theaters," and his corpus was condemned to remain, like Doctor Faustus, unmonumentalized, dismembered, and dispersed.

As with most self-destructive behaviors, Heywood's reluctance to be "Voluminously read" is constitutively structured by a certain ambivalence, attested to by the longevity of his preoccupation – identically articulated in the preliminaries of quarto texts published twenty-two years apart – with accidental publication. If this preoccupation is consistent, both historically (in its repetition) and rhetorically (in its reliance on a metaphorical economy of paternal anxiety), it is not primary in the extant corpus of Heywood's efforts to publicly sort out the proprietary status of his plays. The reluctance to publish first appears eight years before the publication of Jonson's folio as a note "To the Reader" prefacing *The Rape of Lucrece*. Appearing in 1608, *Lucrece* was only the second play printed by Okes; Nathaniel Butter sold it. Had Heywood chanced upon a copy of Okes's only previous dramatic publication, the 1608 quarto edition of *King Lear*, his misgivings about being a "man in print" would have been difficult to refute. Although Peter Blayney contends that Okes's *Lear* is not "one of the worst books ever printed," he does acknowledge that "when the printing process is examined, and to an even greater extent when the findings are applied to the text [of *Lear*] itself, some of the effects of cheap-minded expediency become all too evident."[47] Such expediency was, of course, woven into the very fabric of early modern printing. As Frederick Kiefer observes, "[e]very printed page represented an investment in materials (paper and ink) and in manpower; consequently printers, who were first of all businessmen, were loath to destroy sheets containing errors . . . defective pages were routinely folded and arranged into quires that might otherwise be correct."[48] In the preface to *The Rape of Lucrece* Heywood alludes to this material liability of mechanical reproduction, but he begins his first attributed (and signed) discourse on the perils of play publication with another rationale for avoiding print:

It hath beene no custome in mee of all other men (curteous Readers) to commit my plaies to the presse: the reason, though some may attribute to my own insufficiencie, I had rather subscribe in that to their seueare censure, then by seeking to auoide the imputation of weakenes, to incurre a greater suspition of honestie: for though some haue vsed a double sale of their labours, first to the Stage, and after to the presse, For my owne part I heere proclaime my selfe euer faithful in the first, and neuer guiltie of the last (A2r).[49]

No collections of dramatic texts are available yet, so in place of claiming a lack of "any great ambition in me, to bee in this kind Voluminously read," Heywood justifies his meager credentials as a "man in print" by attributing them to a lack "of custom in me." Habit comes first, to be replaced thirty-five years later by desire, though the actual trajectory of his career as a published playwright would suggest the inverse. (Three years later in *The Golden Age* Heywood claims that he has "fixt these few lines in the front of my Booke" in order "to keepe custome.") Moreover, in 1608 it is unlikely that even Jonson had begun to think about publishing his plays in a folio collection, so Heywood merely refrains from committing his "plaies to the presse." But because Heywood is unable to define himself in opposition to writers who are "exposed vnto the world in Volumes," he is ultimately compelled to come up with an alternative term for characterizing his authorial singularity – "honestie." Whereas other playwrights duplicitously sell their wares twice, first to acting companies, then to printing houses, Heywood singles himself out as one who does not. Inevitably, however, this strategy necessitates the production of an oppositional relation between the stage and the page.

As early as 1590, Richard Jones, the printer of a quarto edition of Marlowe's two *Tamburlaine the Great* plays, had introduced a similarly oppositional structure in his note, "To the Gentlemen Readers: and others that take pleasure in reading Histories" – though, as can be expected, his loyalties were with the press. Hoping that his printed edition of the plays "wil be now no lesse acceptable vnto you to read after your serious affaires and studies, then they haue bene (lately) delightful for many of you to see, when the same were shewed in London vpon stages," Jones proceeds to describe how publication has enabled him to try his hand at authorship:

I haue (purposely) omitted and left out some fond and friuolous Iestures, digressing (and in my poore opinion) far vnmeet for the matter, which I thought, might seeme more tedious vnto the wise, than any way els to be regarded, though (happly) they haue bene of some vaine co[n]ceited fondlings greatly gaped at, what times they were shewed vpon the stage in their graced deformities.[50]

Fifteen years later, Jonson substantially reinforced the distinction between the playhouse and the printing house in the preface to *Sejanus* by differentiating between "this Booke" and the play "which was acted on the publike Stage." Quite aware, like Jones, of the transformative power of publication, Jonson does not disguise his preference for print.

Webster and other playwrights mentioned in the preface to *The White Devil* would subsequently follow Jonson's lead. Heywood, on the other hand, predictably sides with the stage, though he does so, oddly enough, in the address "to the reader" of a printed dramatic text that was first sold in manuscript to the Queen Anne's Men in 1606 or 1607, and was still a part of that company's regular repertory in 1612.[51] Heywood's next move constitutes a kind of manifesto for the New Bibliography:

> yet since some of my plaies haue (vnknown to me, and without any of my direction) accidentally come into the Printers handes, and therfore so corrupt and mangled, (coppied onely by the eare) that I haue bene as vnable to know them, as ashamde to chalenge them (A2r).

Arguing recently that a "fear of textual contamination or fragmentation"[52] has greatly shaped editorial approaches to early modern plays in general, and to Shakespeare's plays in particular, Leah Marcus asserts that such texts must

> be kept free of any taint of commercialism, because that taint is reserved for the contaminators – to some extent the printers, who sold [Shakespeare's] precious creations in cheap popular editions, but more especially those pirates the memorial reconstructors, who perverted his language out of greed and ignorance.[53]

Arguably, the most obvious manifestation of this "fear of textual contamination or fragmentation" was the institutionalization by A. W. Pollard, W. W. Greg, Leo Kirschbaum, Harry R. Hoppe, and Fredson Bowers of the terms "good" and "bad" quartos to designate the extent to which a given play-text had been exposed to the "taint of commercialism" – despite, or perhaps, because of what Randall McLeod identifies as these terms' "prejudicial connotations."[54] Recent textual scholars such as McLeod and Laurie E. Maguire have sought to move beyond this rhetoric of moral judgment in a variety of ways. Whereas McLeod has radically called for the end of editing altogether, Maguire has opted to supplant the term "bad quarto" with "the form 'suspect text' – that is, a text for which memorial reconstruction of all or part has been suspected by critics."[55] Although aware that the substitute term is not ideal, Maguire nevertheless takes some comfort in the knowledge that, as she puts it, "suspects do at least have the possibility of being acquitted."[56]

Such approaches to early modern dramatic texts, informed materially by recent advances in textual analysis and theoretically by a kind of post-structuralist or deconstructive relativism, have raised troubling questions about the ideologies, assumptions, and practices that underwrite scholarly editions of the plays we read and teach. Nevertheless, Heywood's preface to *The Rape of Lucrece* does in fact appeal to the rhetoric of contamination *and* fragmentation to describe the fate of his plays that have "accidentally come into the Printers handes" – regardless of that rhetoric's "prejudicial connotations." Indeed, he writes that these texts are "so corrupt [contaminated] and mangled [fragmented]" that he is "vnable to know them" and too "ashamde to chalenge them." As for the identity of the villains that have perpetrated these crimes against his authorship, the term "memorial reconstructors" has to wait some three centuries for its initial articulation. Instead, Heywood gives the most sophisticated bibliographic description he can, alleging that these "stolne and surreptitious" texts have been "coppied onely by the eare."[57] Subsequently, he makes this charge of aural reproduction with even greater technical precision. In short, the published plays Heywood laments here are not, to use Maguire's coinage, "suspect texts," because as far as he is concerned they do not "have the possibility of being acquitted." And while the terms "good" and "bad" quartos are not a part of the playwright's bibliographical lexicon, he acknowledges the explicit material characteristics these terms have come to represent. Referring to the text the reader is currently holding, he distinguishes it from those plays that have "accidentally come into the Printers handes":

This therefore I was the willinger to furnish out in his natiue habit: first beeing by consent, next because the rest haue beene so wronged in beeing publisht in such sauadge and ragged ornaments: accept it Curteous Gentlemen, and prooue as fauourable Readers as wee haue found you gratious Auditors. | Yours, T. H. (A2r).

Printed "by consent," *The Rape of Lucrece* is "furnish[ed] out in his native habit," whereas "the rest" have been "publisht in such sauadge and ragged ornaments." Correspondingly, the address also stages a transition from the earlier plays' auditors who copied them "onely by the eare" to the more recent play's "gratious Auditors." In other words, although publication "hath beene no custome in" Heywood, printed dramatic texts may ultimately achieve a kind of redemption because "bad" and "good" quartos are merely two points on a continuum, with accidental publication on one end, and authorial involvement on the other. This is as close as Heywood would get to endorsing the Jonsonian project of using print to transform plays into works, though even this reluctant gesture is undermined by his concluding hope that the published text will be as well received by its "Readers" as it was by its "gratious Auditors." Whereas Jonson, Webster, and Burre could only hope that the press would provide them with an alternative to the "ignorant asses" who "vtterly reiected" their plays in the theatre, Heywood imagines something like a migration from the playhouse to the bookshop.

But if Heywood was the most articulate spokesman in the campaign against the perils of print publication, he was not the first. In the specific case of printed drama, that honor would have to be bestowed on John Daye, the printer of the 1570 quarto of *Ferrex and Porrex*. Seeking to distinguish his edition from a quarto published five years earlier, we recall that Daye first asserts that the play was "never intended by the authors thereof to be published," then proceeds to narrate the tale of its accidental publication in which "one W.G. [William Griffith] getting a copie therof at some yongmans hand put it forth exceedingly corrupted (A2r).[58] Indeed, according to Daye, the previous edition was so "exceedingly corrupted" that he likens Griffith's printing practices to having "entised into his house a faire maide and done her villanie, and after all to-bescratched her face, torne her apparel, berayed and disfigured her, and then thrust her out of doors dishonested" (A2r). While Daye's rhetoric anticipates Heywood's subsequent lament that his plays are "beeing publisht in such sauadge and ragged ornaments," the oppositional relation between playhouse and printing house that structures the later preface is marginalized in Daye's account because the struggle for the text is not between the stage and the page, but rather between one printed page and another. For Daye a "bad" quarto is merely an earlier play-text published by someone else. Subsequently, quite a number of printers and writers explicitly concerned themselves with the fate of printed dramatic texts.

An early example of this concern is a note from "The Printer to the Reader" prefacing the 1576 quarto edition of *The Princelye pleasures, at the Court at Kenelwoorth*. Written by Richard Jones, the same printer who would subsequently translate Marlowe's *Tamburlaine* plays from stage to page, the address begins by acknowledging a demand:

All which have been sundrie tymes demaunded for, aswell at my handes, as also of other Printers, for that in deede, all studious and well disposed yong Gentlemen and others, were desyrous to be partakers of those pleasures by a profitable publication.[59]

Hoping to oblige these needy readers, Jones next proffers a supply:

I thought meete to trye by all meanes possible if I might recover the true Copies of the same, to gratifye all suche as had requyred them at my handes, or might hereafter bee styrred with the lyke desire. And in fine I have with much trauayle and paine obtained the very true and perfect Copies, of all that were presented & executed ... And these (being thus collected,) I have (for thy cõmoditie gentle Reader) now published.[60]

Then, as if this isn't enough to lure all those "studious and well disposed yong Gentlemen" to his bookstall, Jones refers one more time to his publication's inordinate appeal by dismissing an earlier published text of the court entertainment:

the rather because of a Report therof lately imprinted by the name of the Pastime of the Progresse which (in deede) doth nothing touche the particularitie of everye commendable action, but generally rehearseth hir Maiesties cheereful entertainement in all places where she passed.[61]

Accordingly, he concludes that the inadequacy of this "Report made verye many the more desirous to have this perfect Copy."[62]

The early modern "bad"/"good" quarto binary was essentially nothing more than the rather "prejudicial" distinction between a text previously printed by someone else, and a new text published by the person or persons writing the address to the reader. Some fifty years before Heminge and Condell would distinguish between earlier Shakespeare plays "maimed, and deformed by the frauds and stealthes of iniurious impostors" and folio texts "cur'd and perfect of their limbes" (A3r: 24–25), Jones not only assumes that his customers want an authentic and uncorrupt text, but twice promises to provide them with a "perfect Copy."[63] Three years later, Jones is still working under the same assumption, and therefore feels compelled to apologize in a note from "The printer to the Reader" prefacing *Promos and Cassandra* (1578) for not being able to furnish such a copy:

Gentle Reader, this labour of Maister *Whetstons*, came into my handes, in his first coppy, whose leasure was so lyttle (being then readie to depart his country) that he had no time to worke it a new, nor to geve apt instructions, to prynte so difficulte a worke, beyng full of variety, both matter, speache, and verse . . . so that, if I commit an error, without blaming the Auctor, amend my amisse.[64]

A decade or so later Jones might have taken it upon himself to revise and fix Whetstone's "first coppy," as he claims he has done in the preface to his Marlowe edition. For now, however, he must settle for publishing a text that he knows is defective. Similarly, I. Charlewood, the printer of a quarto edition of John Lyly's *Endimion, the Man in the Moone* (1591), also acknowledges that he is printing an imperfect text, but promises to do better next time:

Since the Plaies in Paules were dissolved, there are certaine Commedies come to my handes by chaunce, which were presented before her Maiestie at seuerall times by the children of Paules. This is the first, and if in any place it shall dysplease, I will take more paines to perfect the next. I referre it to thy indifferent iudgement to peruse, whom I woulde willinglie please. And if this may passe with thy good lyking, I will then goe forwarde to publish the rest.[65]

The "good"/"bad" quarto binary is somewhat collapsed here because the same printer is potentially capable of printing both, though the temporal aspect of the configuration noted in the other prefaces remains constant: this early text is "bad"; "the rest" will be "good." Moreover, Charlewood alludes to an instance of accidental publication from a printer's perspective: "there are certaine Commedies come to my handes by chaunce."

Taken together, these early addresses "To the Reader" substantiate many of Heywood's subsequent concerns about the publication of his plays, often relying on strikingly similar rhetoric. They suggest that printers and readers, if not writers, did value authentic and uncorrupt texts. That all of these early addresses preoccupied with textual matters were written by printers to readers seems only logical. And yet, the fact that playwrights like Heywood eventually took over the self-consciously important textual space of the reader address indicates that the space could be appropriated.[66] This appropriation points to a significant transition in the history of the relation between the early modern playhouse and printing house.

The first playwright to invade the space of the address might well have been Ben Jonson, but the note "To the Reader" included almost as an afterthought to the 1602 quarto edition of *Poetaster or The Arraignment* seems to be so aware of its own liminality that it is impossible to know for sure who wrote it:

Here (Reader) in place of the Epilogue, was meant to thee an Apology from the Author, with his reasons for the publishing of this booke: but (since he is no lesse restrain'd, then thou depriv'd of it, by Authoritie) hee praies thee to thinke charitably of what thou hast read, till thou maist heare him speake what hee hath written (N1v).[67]

Is this the printer who, in speaking for an "Author" allegedly silenced by "Authoritie," has decided to make his appearance in the last quire of the text – where one might expect to find the play's epilogue; or is this the "Author" who, in attempting to sidestep the "Authoritie" that restrains him, has decided to speak for himself – almost schizophrenically – in the third person within a discursive textual space previously reserved for the printer. Either way, the address captures and enframes a threshold moment in Jonson's career: it constitutes simultaneously the first time his authorship will be linked to the purposeful publication of a play and the last time an "Apology" will be mentioned in the context of such publication.

Three years later, Jonson will unambiguously assert the relationship between his authorship and the press in the note "To the Readers" that appears – according to tradition – immediately after the title page of *Sejanus, His Fall*. In the interim, however, *The Malcontent* (1604) had been published with a note "To the Reader" from the play's author in the initial quire of the book. Thus, the honor of being the first playwright – at least within the extant canon of printed drama – to colonize the space of the printer's address must go to John Marston. Appropriately,

Marston begins this auspicious authorial debut in a self-consciously grammatological vein: "I am an ill Oratour; and in truth, vse to indite more honestly than eloquently for t'is my custome to speake as I think, and write as I speake" (A3v).[68] With this personalized account of the relation between speech and writing in place, Marston proceeds to anticipate and foreclose on his potential critics:

In plainenesse therfore vndersand that in some thing I have willingly erred, as in supposing a Duke of Genoa, and in taking names different from that Citties families: for which some may wittily accuse me, but my defence shall bee as honest, as many reproofes vnto mee have been most malicious (A3v).[69]

Similarly, when Marston turns his attention to the subject of the play's translation into print, he once again offers up a grammatological subtext, this time to assure his readers that the text was deliberately printed. In the case of publication, however, he is forced to concede that the material reality of the early modern printing house, unlike the naming of characters and places, is beyond his control:

I would faine leave the paper; onely one thing afflicts mee, to thinke that Scenes invented, merely to be spoken, should be inforcively published to be read, & that the least hurt I can receive, is to do my selfe the wrong. But since others otherwise would doe me more, the least inconvenience is to be accepted. I have my selfe therefore set forth this Comedy; but so, that my inforced absence must much relye vpon the Printers discretion: but I shall intreat, slight errors in orthography may bee as slightly or'epassed; and that the vnhandsome shape which this trifle in reading presents, may bee pardoned, for the pleasure once afforded you, when it was presented withthe soule of lively action (A4r).[70]

In the inaugural extant address "To the Reader" from a playwright, authorship is a matter of agency, of having "willingly erred." Publication, on the other hand, engenders a masochistic narrative of grammatological/typographical affliction and injury in which the pain of being "inforcively published" can only be endured if self-inflicted. Even then, because the publication process entails the author's "inforced absence" (presumably from the printing house), "slight errors in orthography" and the play-text's "vnhandsome shape" — both of which, Marston implies, originate in "the Printers discretion" — must "bee pardoned." In a final reconfiguration of the opposition between stage and page, the ordeal that was suffered by the text in the printing house and then passed on to the reader is contrasted with the "pleasure once afforded" by the play when it was performed in the theatre.

Such denigrations of what Marston refers to as "the Printers discretion" became commonplace once playwrights settled into the textual space of the reader address. And although *The Malcontent* was the third play of Marston's to "be inforcively published," it remains unclear whether he is speaking in this, his first extant address, from experience garnered in prior encounters with the printing house. Indeed, it is also possible that he is simply borrowing stock phrases from a contemporary rhetoric that Wendy Wall characterizes as a "language of justification and disavowal" first devised as early modern "writers, printers, and compilers rethought manuscript authority and printed literary wares through a wealth of tropes, forms, and textual apparatuses."[71] Asserting that printers and booksellers "were manufactures of credit,"[72] Adrian Johns similarly observes that, "[w]hen early modern readers determined a book not to be worthy of credit, they could do so on a number of grounds. It was in the attribution of 'piracy,' however, that the issues of credibility and print particularly converged."[73] And while Johns notes that such "allegations of impropriety in general, and of piracy in particular, emerged from the practices of the printing house and bookshop,"[74] he also argues that such allegations were often contestable, partly because the assumed "veracity" of print, was in fact "extrinsic to the press itself, and has had to be grafted onto it."[75]

One of those doing the grafting was Joseph Moxon, who, when he set out to write a detailed treatment of the printer's trade nearly eighty years after Marston's address, pointed the finger in the opposite direction. Asserting that "a compositer is strictly to follow his copy, viz. to observe and do just so much and no more than his copy will bear him out for; so that his Copy is to be his rule and authority,"[76] Moxon thereupon laments that such strict adherence to copy-text is not always feasible:

But the carelessness of some good authors, and the ignorance of other authors, has forc'd printers to introduce a custom, which among them is looked upon as a task and duty incumbent on the compositer, viz to discern and amend the bad spelling and pointing of his copy, if it be English.[77]

For Moxon, "the Printers discretion" is largely a compensatory function necessitated by authorial "carelessness" and "ignorance," a task that must be undertaken for the sake of the author:

A good compositer is ambitious as well to make the meaning of his author intelligent to the reader, as to make his work shew graceful to the Eye, and pleasant in reading: Therefore if his copy be written in a language he understands, he reads his copy with consideration that so he may get himself into the meaning of the author, and consequently considers how to order his work the better both in the title page, and in the matter of the Book.[78]

No doubt, Moxon is reacting to, or over-compensating for, a 200-year-old authorial discourse of "justification and disavowal" in which printers were routinely villainized. And yet, it is also true that Marston's attitude toward publication improves the longer he is involved with it. In a subsequent address, appended to the 1606 quarto edition of *The*

Wonder of Women as an endnote, Marston commandeers the textual space commonly dedicated in early modern books to an errata page, for the purpose of holding forth again on the fate of plays in print. In the two years separating the appearance of these two quartos however, the perilous gap between playhouse and printing house narrowed considerably. Whereas the previous address views publication as a hurtful imposition only rendered tolerable if self-inflicted, the later untitled note impudently asks readers not "to taxe [Marston], for the fashion of the Entrances and Musique of this Tragedy, for know it is printed onely as it was presented by youths & after the fashion of the private stage."[79] Now that the "vnhandsome shape" of the text is attributed to the age of the actors who presented it and the venue in which it was performed, rather than to the press, Marston is also much less concerned with whatever typographic injuries his play may have sustained in the course of publication. He merely instructs his readers not to allow "some easily amended errors in the Printing afflict thee since thy owne discourse will easily setvprightany such vneuennes."[80] Indeed, the burden placed upon the reader to insert blank spaces in the typographically collapsed phrase "setvprightany" to make it intelligible seems to be a remarkably proto-Joycean attempt to literalize and reinforce this instructional point. In this context, Marston no longer feels compelled to inform the reader that he has chosen "to do my selfe the wrong" as the lesser of two evils. However, when the play is reprinted twenty-seven years later in Sheares's octavo collection, *The Workes of Mr. John Marston* (1633), the endnote is deleted, but the earlier play's assertion of authorial agency with regard to publication is reinstated, this time in a reader address fronting the penultimate play (*Parasitaster, or, The Fawne*) in the volume:

If any shall wonder why I print a Comedy, whose life rests much in the Actors voice. Let such know, that it cannot avoyd publishing: let it therefore stand with good excuse, that I have beene my owne setter out (R6r).[81]

As was the case in *The Malcontent*'s reader address, a grammatological struggle between typography and *logos* is staged so that Marston can make the double claim that the London book trade in printed drama is responsible for this unnatural conflation of mediums, and that he has made the best of a bad situation by seizing the day. Initially included in the 1606 quarto edition of the play, this address reappears, oddly enough, after Marston's death in a less than prestigious bibliographical format for which he was not his "owne setter out."

At about the same time Marston began publicly to make his peace with the printing house in *The Wonder of Women*'s reader address, an anonymous author used the address of *The Familie of Love* quarto to go on record about his experiences with accidental publication:

> Too soone and too late, this work is published: Too soone, in that it was in the Presse, before I had notice of it, by which meanes some faults may escape in the Printing. Too late, for that it was was not published when the general voice of the people had seald it for good, and the newnesse of it made it much more desired, then at this time.[82]

For this author, who is not at all bothered by the grammatological implications of translating the "Actors voice" into print, the principal difficulty with publication – as it is in many addresses written by printers and playwrights trying to differentiate between "good" and "bad" quartos – is one of temporality. Appearing in print prior to his perusal, "some faults" in the play itself, he seems to imply, "may escape." This concern is offset, however, by his worry that the play has been printed too long after it was popular, and is therefore not likely to do as well in the bookshop as it did in the theatre. In this case, it is the "general voice" of the play's theatre audience that has faltered during the journey from playhouse to printing house. The author has no problem with publication except that, in the specific case of this play, it was not undertaken in a more timely fashion. In the same year, Heywood appropriated the textual space of the address for the first time in order to define himself oppositionally with reference to playwrights who "haue vsed a double sale of their labours, first to the Stage, and after to the presse." The author of the above address may have been one of the playwrights Heywood had in mind.

Having inherited the self-appointed role of commentator on the perils of play publication first from printers, then from a few ambivalent playwrights, Heywood developed over the next thirty years into the role's most consistent and ardent performer. More than anything else, what characterizes the body of resulting reader addresses is Heywood's singular commitment to the theatre. With the exception of the two 1632 addresses that promote Parts 1 and 2 of *The Iron Age* as plays to be read and attempt to prepare the book-buying public for the forthcoming publication of an annotated collection of the *Age* plays, Heywood never wavered in his opinion that print was not the proper medium for plays and never admitted to purposefully publishing his plays. Indeed, even the second of the 1632 addresses situates this anomalous moment in Heywood's career within the larger context of a phase in the life of the London stage in which the theatre has grown improper because "nothing but *Satirica Dicteria* and *Comica Scommata* are now in request." In other words, only when he begins to suspect that his plays might be "vtterly reiected" by audiences whose tastes in drama have changed does Heywood consider publication as a viable alternative to performance.

It had taken Heywood nearly forty years to reach the point in his relationship to theatre and print that Webster and the first four authors he mentions in *The White Devil*'s reader address had reached within the first decade of their careers as playwrights. In this context, it is extremely significant that Heywood's most profound published statement of his commitment to the theatre, *An Apology for Actors*, appeared in print the same year as Webster's play.[83] Whereas Webster's text begins with an address "To the Readers" that prioritizes publication and holds the theatre and its audiences responsible for the failure of his play,[84] Heywood's initially proffers an "Epistle Dedicatory" (A2r–v) to the Earl of Worcester, the patron of the playing company he wrote for, and proceeds to an address "To my good Friends and Fellowes, / the City – Actors" (A3r) in which he introduces the subject of his treatise: "Ovt of my busiest houres, I have spared my selfe so much time as to touch some particulars concerning vs, to approu our Antiquity, ancient Dignity, and the true vse our quality" (A3r). Inasmuch as the next address is "To the Iudiciall Reader," the structure of the book materially stages a progression from stage to page that promotes the theatre over print. Here, in the reader address, Heywood raises the issue of publication in order to express his antipathy to it:

My pen hath seldome appeared in Presse till now, I have beene ever too iealous of mine owne weakenesse, willingly to thrust into the Presse: nor had I at this time, but that a kinde of necessity enioyned me to so sudden a businesse (A4r).

Having defined himself in the 1608 *Rape of Lucrece* address in opposition to playwrights who "haue vsed a double sale of their labours," now he offers an alternative explanation of his reluctance to publish that rests more on literary modesty or insecurity. While his previous texts have been less than "willingly . . . thrust into the Presse," this time "a kinde of necessity enioyned" Heywood to publish his treatise on actors. Ironically, it is in this utterly pro-theatre context that he admits for the first time he has purposefully gone to the press – though, of course, this is only true in the specific case of his career as a playwright. (In 1608 he had prepared for the press a translation of Sallust's *The Two most Worthy and Notable Histories which Remain Unmained in Posterity*: (viz.) *The Conspiracy of Catiline, Undertaken Against the Government of the Senate of Rome, and The war Which Fugarth for Many Years Maintained Against the Same State*.[85]) It will take Heywood another twenty years to entertain the idea of deliberately publishing a text linked to the theatre; but here, the actors he intends to vindicate – to borrow a word from Cartwright's 1658 edition, *The Actors' Vindication* – are so urgently in need of defense that he overcomes his fear of print for their sake. And yet, even this rare, idealized narrative moment in the troubled history of Heywood's relationship with printers may well have a grittier sub-plot. Richard H. Perkinson, who edited a facsimile edition of the text, alternatively interprets the phrase "a kinde of necessity" to mean that "Heywood had made the *Apology* available in manuscript, and that some rumor of piracy came to his attention and prompted its immediate publication."[86] Perkinson's reading is possible, but it is hard to imagine that Heywood wouldn't have delighted in recounting this tale of accidental publication in the reader address of a text devoted to extolling the virtues of the "Actors voice."

Either way, what is truly remarkable about Heywood's first purposeful publication – undertaken to validate historically the profession of playing – is the inclusion of a third address written "To my approved good Friend, / M[r.] Nicholas Okes." As was noted earlier, the first reader addresses included in printed dramatic texts were written by printers and were placed in the front of the book. Here, a rare address to a printer appears at the end of the book, a textual space traditionally dedicated to an errata page. As if responding to this textual tradition, Heywood opens the address to Okes with a rather precise horror story of prior printing errors:

The infinite faults escaped in my booke of *Britaines Troy*, by the negligence of the Printer, as the misquotations, mistaking of sillables, misplacing halfe lines, coining of strãge and never heard of words (G4r).

Buffeted on one side by a confession of reluctance to appear "in Presse," and on the other side by a remembrance of a previously botched printing, Heywood's purposefully published treatise on acting is, in some sense, textually stranded within a larger frame narrative of perilous publication. Even the dedicatory address to a printer who is an "approved good Friend" starts by recounting the brutality of another printer, in this case, William Jaggard, who would subsequently be entrusted with the task of enabling another playwright to be "Voluminously read." And just in case readers might think he is merely over-determining what Marston referred to as a "Printers discretion," Heywood then introduces the next shocking twist in the plot:

These [errors] being without number, when I would have taken a particular account of the *Errata*, the Printer answered me, hee would not publish his owne disworke-manship, but rather let his owne fault lye vpon the necke of the Author (G4r).

This is the same printer who, a decade later, would blindly oversee the project of printing Shakespeare's plays "cur'd, and perfect of their limbes; and all / the rest, absolute in their numbers, as he conceived thē."

Presumably, because *An Apology* was so well printed by Okes, the space of the errata page has been freed up to permit Heywood to recall an earlier errata page that should have been, but never was. If Moxon would have been appalled by Jaggard's unwillingness "to make the meaning of his author intelligent to the reader," he would have been heartened by what follows:

> And being fearefull that others of [Jaggard's] quality, had beene of the same nature, and condition, and finding you on the contrary, so carefull, and industrious, so serious and laborious to doe the Author all the rights of the presse, I could not choose but gratulate your honest indeauors with this short remembrance (G4r).

Working under the impression that the best way to remember Okes is to recall crimes committed by another printer, Heywood cuts short this brief moment of affirmation in order to return to Jaggard's negation:

> Here likewise, I must necessarily insert a manifest iniury done me in that worke [*Britaines Troy*], by taking the two Epistles of *Paris* to *Helen*, and *Helen* to *Paris*, and printing them in a lesse volume, vnder the name of another, which may put the world in opinion I might steale them from him; and hee to doe himselfe right, hath since published them in his owne name (G4r).

Admitting indirectly to being "Voluminously read," Heywood recounts a paranoid tale of publication in which "the name," to borrow from Foucault, that "seems always to be present, marking off the edges of the text, revealing or at least characterizing, its mode of being," is not in fact the right name. The stolen epistles, two Ovidian poems from the first published edition of *Troia Britanica* (1609), were included by Jaggard, along with seven other Heywood poems from the same text, in an augmented edition of *Passionate Pilgrim* (1612) that was based largely on his previous unauthorized edition of 1599.[87] As for the name compelled by Jaggard to reveal or characterize Heywood's "mode of being": at this particular moment in early modern publishing history it belonged to a discourse "endowed with the 'author function'" known as Shakespeare. Nevertheless, this is an address devoted to printers, not authors, so Heywood lets Shakespeare off the hook long enough to recruit him for his campaign of remembering Jaggard's abuses:

> but as I must acknowledge my lines not worthy [Shakespeare's] patronage, vnder whom [Jaggard] hath publisht them, so the Author I know much offended with *M. Jaggard* (that altogether vnknowne to him] presumed to make so bold with his name (G4r–v).[88]

Deciding in the end that the cost of printing the volume was more important than Heywood's or Shakespeare's authorship, Jaggard inexpensively resolved the dispute by printing a new title page for *Passionate Pilgrim* that omitted Shakespeare's name.[89] Apparently, no "author-function" was deemed preferable to a contested one, though Heywood did what he could within the textual and thematic context of the printing house to fetishize the conflict.

Heywood concludes his account of the dispute by exonerating Okes and longing for an authorial future in which his "pen" will have voluntarily "appeared in Presse":

> These, and the like dishonesties I know you to bee cleere of; and I could wish but to bee the happy Author of so worthy a worke, as I could willingly commit to your care and workmanship (G4v).[90]

Such a "worke," of course, was finally committed to Okes twenty years later in the shape of the promised forthcoming collection of Heywood's *Age* plays, though the materiality of its "care and workmanship" was never actualized.

If it seems somewhat odd that a text dedicated to a theatre company and written to validate the acting profession in a period of intense anti-theatricalism should conclude with the fantasy of a "happy Author" willingly committing his "worke" to a printing house, it is also the case that the trajectory of Heywood's career as a published playwright was profoundly linked to the company of which, as Andrew Gurr puts it, he "was always a loyal client."[91] Of the eleven plays individually attributed to him in print, five of them – *A Woman Kilde with Kindnesse* (1607), *The Rape of Lucrece* (1608), *The Golden Age* (1611), *The Brazen Age* (1613), *The Silver Age* (1613), and *The Foure Prentises of London* (1615) – were published during a period of relative stability for the Queen Anne's Men, the company in which he had been one of ten sharers since 1603.[92] Although that stability was shaken by the death of the Queen Anne's Men's celebrated clown, Thomas Greene, in 1612, and the subsequent transition to the management of Christopher Beeston a year later, it was after the company was fined for playing during Lent in 1616 that its future grew bleaker.[93] Exactly one year later, 4 March 1617, a Shrovetide riot severely damaged the company's recently constructed indoor theatre, the Cockpit.[94] Another attempt to pull down the Cockpit was nearly carried out on Shrove Tuesday in 1618, but, as Gurr notes, "the Privy Council got word of this second attack and prevented it."[95] Worse yet, by 2 March 1619, the company's patron, Queen Anne, was dead, and in November of that year, Beeston, the company's manager, found himself so deeply embroiled in a lawsuit brought by John Smith – to whom he owed £46 5s. 8d. – that Heywood and the other sharers parted company with him.[96]

Beeston quickly recruited Prince Charles's Men for the Cockpit, but the Queen Anne's Men, now called the Revels company, were forced to return to the Red Bull.[97] There what was left of Queen Anne's limped on for another few years until May of 1623, when, as Clark observes, "the company succumbed under ever-increasing difficulties and broke."[98] A year later, Heywood, now in his early fifties, began writing plays for the Lady Elizabeth's Men, who had recently replaced Prince Charles's Men at the Cockpit.[99] Although Lady Elizabeth's quickly became the second most important company in London, the company's future was promptly foreclosed by the death of James I in March of 1625. By the summer of 1625, a new company, Queen Henrietta's, was assembled largely from the remnants of Lady Elizabeth's, and Heywood remained with them as a company playwright until his retirement from the stage in 1630.[100] No extant printed play published under Heywood's name survives from this fifteen-year period during which the Queen Anne's Men declined and disbanded, and he was forced to sell his plays to a succession of unstable and short-lived playing companies. This conspicuous gap in the publication history of Heywood's career as a playwright gives credence to his anti-Jonsonian claim in the reader address of *The English Traveller* that his "Playes are not exposed vnto the world in Volumes, to beare the title of *Workes*" because "many of them by shifting and change of Companies, haue beene negligently lost."

During the eleven years that passed between his retirement from the stage and his death, Heywood transformed himself from playwright to, as Clark puts it, "hack-writer in good earnest and, it would appear, with some financial success."[101] Whether retirement from an extraordinarily productive thirty-five-year career led him to reconsider his stance on publication, and even to fantasize about seeing a collection of his plays in print, is uncertain. Nevertheless, despite his 1633 contention, "That it neuer was any great ambition in me, to bee in this kind Voluminously read," the last decade of his life provided readers with six plays – *The Iron Age* (1630), *The Fair Maid of the West* (1631), *The English Traveller* (1633), *A Pleasant Comedy, Called A Mayden-Head Well Lost* (1634), *The Royall King and the Loyall Subject* (1637), and *The Wise-Woman of Hogsdon* (1638) – printed under his name, as well as a host of other nondramatic publications.[102]

Near the end of this prolific period, an octavo collection of 160 leaves written "By Tho. Heywood" appeared in print. To a fan of drama collections walking quickly past the bookstalls at Paul's Churchyard, the large capital letters at the top of the unbound book's title page might have caused him or her to slow down, for it advertised that the volume contained "**PLEASANT / DIALOGVES / AND / DRAMMA'S**" (Fig. 22).

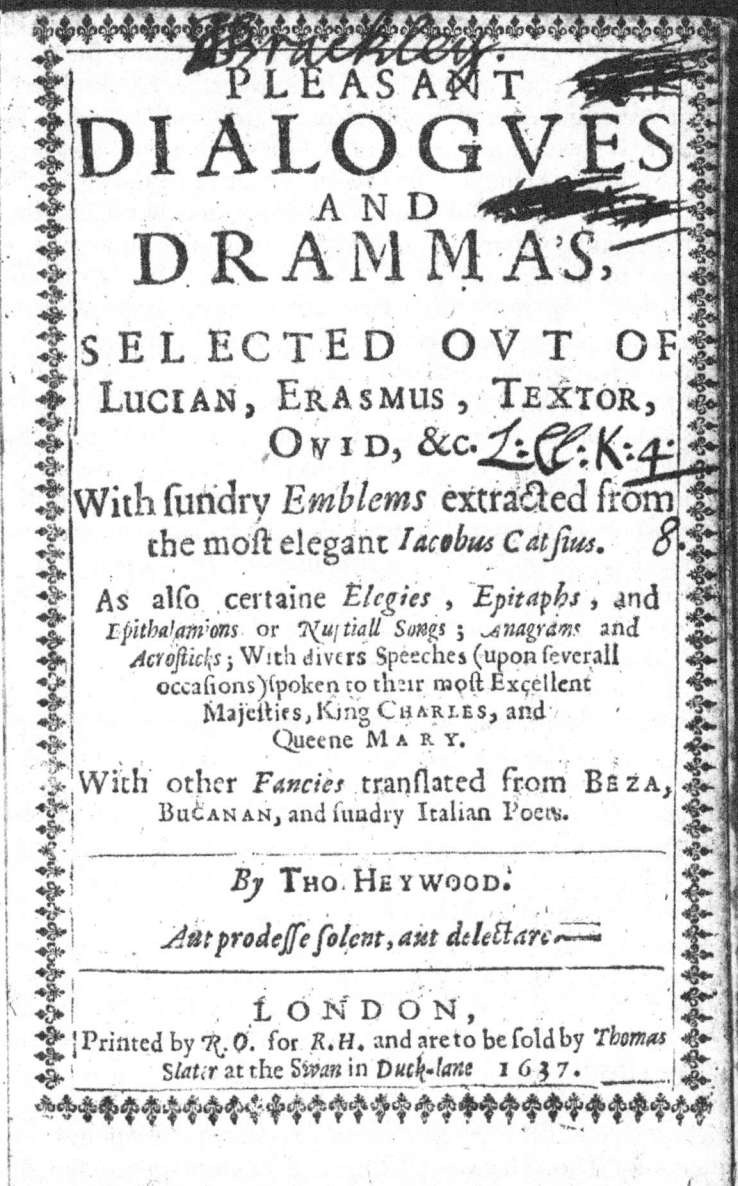

Figure 22 Title page: *Pleasant Dialogves and Dramma's*, 1637

Depending on the range of this hypothetical book-buyer's interests, however, he or she might have been quickly disappointed, because smaller capital letters in the middle of the title page indicate that these texts had been "SELECTED OVT OF / LUCIAN, ERASMUS, TEXTOR, / OVID, &c." Additionally, the title page announces in even smaller letters that it contains "sundry *Emblems* extracted from / the most elegant *Iacobus Catsius*" and "also certaine *Elegies, Epitaphs*, and / *Epithalamions* or *Nuptiall Songs*; *Anagrams* and / *Acrosticks*; With divers Speeches (upon severall / occasions) spoken to their most Excellent / Majesties, King CHARLES, and / Queene MARY. / With other Fancies translated from BEZA, / BUCANAN, and sundry Italian Poets." If this book-buyer had never encountered Heywood's published plays before, he or she would have no indication that he had been involved in the writing of more than 200 plays or had even been a playwright. On the other hand, a devotee of Heywood's published plays, especially of the five plays that had recently appeared in print prior to this 1637 collection, might have enthusiastically flipped past the dedicatory epistle, written for "the Right Honourable Sir / Henry Lord Cary" (A3r), to the address to, "the Generous Reader," in order to find out when the promised *Age* plays collection might be available, or what the latest plot twist in the saga of accidental publication was. Here again, the book-buyer might have been disappointed to learn that Heywood is oddly silent on the subject of the press, except to inform the reader that,

For such as delight in Stage-Poetry, here are divers *Dramma's*, never before published: Which though some may condemne for their shortnesse, others againe will commend for their sweetnesse (A4r).[103]

Recalling from the title page that such "divers *Dramma's*" consist merely of translations of short classical dialogues and plays,[104] our hypothetical book-buyer, eager to find some new sample of Heywood's dramatic artistry in print, might have skipped ahead to the pages of the book devoted, according to the second page of "The Table," to "Divers Speeches spoken before their too sacred Majesties, and before sundry other Noble persons upon severall occasions" (A6v). Several pages into this section, perhaps just as our book-buyer was preparing to get on with the business of the day, she or he at last would have found some satisfaction. There, within the only published collection with the word "Dramma's" on the title page attributed to the proper name of Thomas Heywood, is the most bibliographically precise lament about the perils of publication that the author would ever pen – not in the form of a note "To the Reader," but rather as the first printed edition of:

A Prologue to the Play of Queene Elizabeth as it was last revived at the Cock-pit, in which the Author taxeth the most corrupted copy now imprinted, which was published without his consent.

> Playes have a fate in their conception lent,
> Some so short liv'd, no sooner shew'd, than spent;
> But borne to day, to morrow buried, and
> Though taught to speake, neither to goe nor stand.
> This: (by what fate I know not) sure no merit,
> That it disclaimes, may for the age inherit.
> Writing 'bove one and twenty; but ill nurst,
> And yet receiv'd, as well perform'd at first,
> Grac't and frequened, for the cradle age,
> Did throng the Seates, the Boxes, and the Stage
> So much; that some by Stenography drew
> The plot: put it in print: (scarce one word trew:)
> And in that lamenesse it hath limp't so long,
> The Author now to vindicate that wrong
> Hath tooke the paines, upright upon its feete
> To teach it walke, so please you sit, and see't. (R4v)

Here author and authority finally converge – not in a fantasized meeting between a queen and a playwright, not in the coincidental publication of two folios by a playwright and his king, not in a prefatorial lament for the darkened stage and a vacant throne, but in a speech, spoken by an actor at a certain remove from the printing house, from textual production and the language of patriarchal absolutism, before the revival of a play that bears the proper name of a queen. Although no folio collection would come to serve as a sepulcher for his plays "cur'd, and perfect of their limbes," here in a meager octavo volume dedicated to anthologizing the "Stage-Poetry" of several other authors, Heywood boasts that at least one of his plays, thanks to the intervention of the playhouse not the printing house, can finally be taught to walk "upright upon its feete."

Epilogue: "Why not Malevole in folio with vs": the after-birth of the author

> It is from his new position, as an author, that he will fashion – from all he might have said, from all he says daily, at any time – the still shaky profile of his oeuvre.
> Michel Foucault, *The Discourse on Language*

> And from the point of view of posterity at least, we know to what extent this trick has succeeded: we are far from having gotten over it.
> Philippe Lacoue-Labarthe, *Typography*

In "Proofs of Holy Writ" (1934), the final short story of an incredibly prolific writing career, Rudyard Kipling offers a drama of authorship involving two of the early modern playwrights who have concerned us in this study. The one, named Ben, brags that, "I build up my own works throughout ... I build upon my own foundations; devising and perfecting my own plots; adorning 'em justly as fits time, place, and action."[1] The other, named Will, reminds his colleague that playgoers "pay their penny for pleasure – not learning" (252), then offers a strikingly different account of his authorial canon: "My *Love's Labour* (how I came to write it, I know not) is nearest to lawful issue. My *Tempest* (how I came to write *that*, I know) is, in some part, my own stuff. Of the rest, I stand guilty. Bastards all!" (253). Both sets of remarks are, of course, fictional, but the first dramatist's repeated use of the word "build" to describe his authorship recalls the architectural grandeur of the title page that fronts Jonson's 1616 folio *Workes*; while the latter's singular affirmation of *Love's Labour* as "lawful issue" recalls another title page's assertion that it has been "Newly corrected and augmented / By W. Shakespeare." As such, this effort to imaginatively reconstruct two authorial self-assessments may well be derived in part from a certain publishing practice which, A. F. Johnson asserts, was "almost unknown before the advent of the printed book" and consisted of "no more than a protective leaf" that "could then be used for the kind of identificatory and commercial material necessary for selling a book."[2] In some sense then, Kipling's tale of how these two authors work seems to takes its cues from a bit of labor that was usually undertaken after the work of authorship had been completed – produced, as Howard Marchitello observes, "narrationally out of the material objects ascribed to a particular individual."³ The birth of the author comes after his death. This somewhat awkward formulation obviously holds true for the 1623 Shakespeare Folio and the 1647 Beaumont and Fletcher folio; but it is no less true for an earlier collection of dramatic texts inasmuch as the preliminaries of Jonson's 1616 *Workes* folio were printed last and show no sign of authorial involvement whatsoever. In other words, to make explicit the diachronic narrative latent in our story's title, an integral phase of publication – "Proofs" – precedes the production of "Holy Writ." To return to Kipling's tale is to find some support for these speculations.

Ben and Will's discussion of their respective authorial canons is suddenly cut short by a "liveried serving-man" whose arrival wordlessly jogs Will's memory about a mysterious package. Here is the scene, written in the heyday of the New Bibliography:

Ben reached unsteadily for the packet of papers and read the superscription: "to William Shakespeare, Gentleman, at his house of New Place in the town of Stratford, these – with diligence from M. S." "Why does the fellow withold his name? Or is it one of your women? I'll look."

Muzzy as he was, he opened and unfolded a mass of printed papers expertly enough.

"From the most learned divine, Miles Smith of Brazen Nose college." Will explained. "You know this business as well as I. The King has set all the scholars of England to make one Bible, which the Church shall be bound to, out of all the bibles that men use."

"*I* knew," Ben could not lift his eyes from the printed page (254).

The playwright – known as "The Authour: B. I." on a number of title pages – asks why the packet's sender withholds his name, opens and unfolds "a mass of printed papers expertly enough," and seems mesmerized by "the printed page." The playwright who would spend nearly all of his professional career as a sharer in the same playing company, and claims here to have co-authored one of the few plays he deems legitimate, provides the details of a grand collaboration in which "all the scholars of England" will come together to produce a single book. Compelled to speak from beyond the grave more than three centuries after his death by an author shortly before his own death, Will could very well be describing the production of another sacred text that would subsequently command the attention of most – if not all – English scholars. Indeed, if we follow the conventional wisdom of a certain royal subjectivity/succession narrative, wherein "it is written" that James I's *Workes* begot Jonson's *Workes* which, in turn, begot the 1623 Folio, or the less conventional – and perhaps less wise – narrative I pieced together in Chapter 2, then even the point of origin of these two bestsellers is the same: the king. Royal subject and loyal subject, Cartesian agent and late medieval subordinate meet once again. According to a recent version of the narrative proffered by Jeffrey Masten about the book that will emerge from this "mass of printed papers," such a meeting had to occur because "[James] is a figure situated at the intersection of contemporaneous meanings of *author*: authority, father, instigator, ruler, writer."[4] No small wonder that Ben, whose historical counterpart was allegedly endowed with a "bibliographic ego," is unable to "lift his eyes from the printed page."

Of course, Will – not Ben – has been invited to join Miles Smith "and a half-score others" who "are cast to furbish up the Prophets – Isaiah to Malachi" (255), and Ben is left to lament that "'[t]hey never called on *me*'" as he "caresse[s] lovingly the hand-pressed proofs on their lavish linen paper" (256). The word "cast" succinctly conflates playhouse and printing house, and it is tempting to speculate here that our two playwrights' respective attitudes toward authorship determine the contours of Kipling's fantastical account. Referring casually to five lines of a soliloquy from *Macbeth* "'or something in that sort'" that initially caught Smith's attention, Will informs his rival that, "'Condell writes 'em out fair for [Smith]'" (255). Alternatively, Ben insistently speaks of "'my own foundations . . . my own plots'" and manifests something of a sexualized, fetishistic relation to the products of mechanical reproduction. While the former attitude may not bode well for a project involving "Holy Writ," the latter accords rather poorly with a collaborative effort that will include "a half-score others." Moreover, even the "privileged moment of *individualization*" underwritten by the king's mandate may not be working in Ben's favor. In fact the idea for this project came not from James I, but emerged "seemingly out of the blue" – as David Norton puts it – from a conference held at Hampton Court in January 1604 at the suggestion of a Puritan leader named John Reynolds.[5]

But Kipling, whose authorial career began at the height of Britain's imperial expansion and power and was now coming to an end just as rumors of that empire's imminent collapse were beginning to circulate, links Shakespeare to the king. As such, "Proofs of Holy Writ" takes its place in a long line of pre-natal accounts of early modern dramatic authorship spawned, perhaps, by the concurrent publication of Jonson's and James I's *Workes*. James Shirley celebrates Fletcher in this "wounded Age . . . nothing now wanting but the King"; Nicholas Rowe brings Elizabeth and Shakespeare together to decide the fate of Falstaff in the turbulent decades after the Revolution of 1688; and the editors of the *Oxford Shakespeare* exhume the author at a moment when for the first time in US history, the role of the President is being played by an actor. In the specific case of this final narrative, it is at least possible that a certain etymological kinship between "actor," "auctor," and "auctoritas" governs the editors' much-touted emphasis on stage directions and the theatre as Shakespeare's "most valuable collaborator."

What interests me most about Kipling's story, however, is the way in which the king indirectly mediates between two seemingly different sets of collaborations, the one resulting in those texts that have come down to us as Shakespeare's, the other leading to a new version of the Bible that will inevitably also bear only one proper name. In order to explore the correspondences between these two dramas of authorship a little further, I want to turn briefly to another fantastical, though no less rich, prenatal account of the same book's generation.

Inspired by Kipling's tale, and working partly from evidence of how translation committees worked on the Revised Version in the second half of the nineteenth century, David Norton has recently offered a wonderfully imaginative reconstruction of what it must have been like to work on the project to which Will has been asked to contribute.[6] The story takes place in Westminster, late in 1605, the focus of the work for the day is 1 Corinthians 4.9. Here's the scene:

Four men are seated round a large table. Ralph Hutchinson, for fifteen years president of St John's College, Oxford, is in his early fifties, but looks older. A cough shakes him now and then, and he sits closest to the fire. Death is close, but he defies it. Next to him sits John Spencer, in his mid-forties, his face still bright from a half-hour's walk from Newgate, where he is vicar at St Sepulchre's. Across from him is the youngest of the group, Roger Fenton, Rector of St Benet's Sherehog. He is already fashioning a reputation for his 'Treatise on Usury,' though it is five years and more before it will be lent to the world at large. Chairman of the group is William Barlow, Dean of Chester. He too is in his very early forties, and is known for his royalist and anti-puritan views.[7]

Four men "seated round a large table" have joined forces to piece together a book at the King's request. One of them, apparently an upstart, is "already fashioning a reputation" as an author. The other three, older and more experienced, are well-established in their respective positions. Two writers short of the six hands that have been identified in the theatrical manuscript of *Sir Thomas More*, the group nevertheless calls to mind numerically the authorship of *1 Sir John Oldcastle* or any number of other entries from *Henslowe's Diary* in which teams of four playwrights have been paid "in earneste of a boocke." No extant title page of a play from this period would adequately acknowledge such collaborations, nor would the title page of the book to which the four men in Westminster contributed. Here, according to Norton, is how their work proceeded:

In front of Barlow are sheets from the Bishops' Bible on which he is entering the results of their deliberations. To his left is Stephens' Greek Testament, to his right his notes from his own work on the chapter. The others also have Stephens and sheets from the Bishops' Bible which they have worked over. Also on the table are an assortment of other Bibles, as well as a Vulgate and a Polyglot. On shelves there are other translations, including Luther's, and a range of theological works. The other translators have been assigned to keep a special eye on particular versions. Hutchinson has Rheims and the Vulgate, Spencer has Geneva and the Great Bible, while Fenton keeps an eye on Tyndale, Coverdale and Matthew.[8]

As Linda Woodbridge observes, Roger Ascham used to counsel his teachers to "set side-by-side before students several classical authors' treatments of the same theme, myth, or story, to facilitate stylistic comparisons."[9] Such a comparative approach to learning, made possible largely by the increased availability of printed texts, characterized the humanist education received by many who went on to write plays. According to Woodbridge, "[Shakespeare] was a child of the age that broke borrowed reading into tiny reusable units in commonplace books, and that created and developed the technology of movable type – quilting, applied to books."[10] Here, of course, members of the committee "set side-by-side" different versions of the same book in preparation for producing a new version; but one only need think of the extensive annotations in some of Jonson's plays and masques, or the five volumes of Geoffrey Bullough's monumental *Narrative and Dramatic Sources of Shakespeare* to begin to see the extent to which both the Westminster committee and London playwrights – working in teams or alone – produced texts of "shreds and patches." Ben himself makes the connection in Kipling's story as he tries to imagine what it would be like to be involved in the king's new project:

The learning of Oxford and Cambridge – "most noble and most equal," as I have said – and Westminster, to sit upon a clutch of Bibles. Those 'ud be Geneva (my mother read to me out of it at her knee), Douai, Rheims, Coverdale, Matthew's, the Bishops', the Great, and so forth.
   They are all set down on the page there – text against text. And you call me a botcher of old clothes. (254–255)

Having referred earlier to "[m]y own learning which I have heaped up, lifelong" (252), Ben recalls the originary moment of that education – his mother reading the Geneva Bible to him – then directly links the committee's method of setting "text against text" with his authorial reputation as a "botcher of old clothes." As for Will, whose historical counterpart has come to signify originality and authorial genius, his approach to authorship makes him an ideal candidate for a project in which the main task is both to preserve and to re-"furbish" the textual past. As he tells his playwriting rival, "Give me the bones of any stuff, I'll cover 'em as quickly as any . . . to hatch new plots is to waste God's unreturning time" (253).

In Norton's imaginary reconstruction, the bone in question is the following verse from the Bishops' Bible: "For me thinketh that God hath set forth us which are the last Apostles, as it were men appointed to death. For we are made a gazing stock unto the world, and to angels, and to men." Taking umbrage with the word, "appointed," a member of the committee offers "approved" in its place, while another observes:

> "'Approve': 'tis strong, 'tis the language of the lawyers, yet 'tis good too: our Lord is a man approved of God, Apelles is approved in Christ. 'Approved to death,' tried, esteemed, worthy, like our Lord."
>
> There is a prolonged debate. At last Barlow, muttering, "'appointed,' 'approved,' 'tis a small change," writes it into his copy.[11]

Just one of a number of blemishes on the complexion of any collaborative effort has been temporarily covered up, and we need only look at one or two of the many extant manuscripts of early modern dramas to see comparable efforts (successful and not) to smooth things over. From here Norton moves on to a later phase of collaboration, this one at "Stationers' Hall in early autumn, 1610."[12] There, a different group of men reviews the work of the earlier committee and comes upon 1 Corinthians 4.9, whereupon they notice that, "'Approved to death' has not found agreement among the other companies, and is marked 'to be resolved' on Fenton's manuscript."[13] A member of the new committee proceeds to write "'stet' against 'approved to death,' and sets down his pen."[14]

All is set then. Nearly five years of work involving the collaborative efforts of nearly a dozen men has, in the specific case of one verse, "approved" the substitution of one word for another. This is, after all, "Holy Writ" which, at least in the case of one version of the beginning, begins with the Word. But, in fact, one important collaboration remains to be reconstructed, and it gets a brief final paragraph in Norton's tale:

> There is one last scene, some six years later in the printing house of Robert Barker, the King's Printer. A compositor is setting this same verse of 1 Corinthians. In the copy he works from, 'approved' is struck through, and 'appointed' written in the margin. He follows his copy. The one word unique to the AV has vanished.

It is impossible to know for sure whether the work of the translation committees was negated during the printing-house phase of the book's production, though a certain logocentricity – wholly appropriate for a book that opens with God's voice – makes it a fitting conclusion to a larger narrative that begins, ostensibly, with the king's voice and ends in the appearance of a book. Indeed, as Norton himself makes clear at the outset, "[w]e know too little about why the AV translators kept what they kept, and changed what they changed, to offer anything other than an imaginative – a *fictional* – reconstruction of how they worked."[15]

Like so many of the stories that have been told this century about early modern dramatic texts, Norton works back from a given book's printed, material reality to the immaterial unreality of its beginnings in the minds of those who shaped its pre-publication existence. And in both sets of stories, a printing house – like the grave – makes such backward labor difficult, if not impossible. Unlike so many of the stories that have been told this century about early modern dramatic texts, however, Norton's tale will not found a pseudo-science or a field of study, nor will it bolster one author's literary and cultural standing at the expense of others' or underwrite the "radical" re-editing of that author's works. After all, Norton's story, like the others, is nothing more than "an imaginative – a *fictional* – reconstruction."

A certain subject-ive recalcitrance, a petty act of defiance, I suppose, has prevented me from mentioning the title of the book to which our greatest author had been invited to contribute. For Miles Smith and nearly all of his contemporaries, it had no author, or at least no human author, though a few individuals may have played a fundamental role in its transcription once upon a time. Nevertheless, Smith could have referred to it as the Authorized Version, and he would have known that the prime directive for the project was that the resulting book be "as little altered as the truth of the original will permit."[16] The "original," in this case, was not some writer's hypothetical "foul papers," but the Bishops' Bible – a printed book which, like the first edition of *Gorboduc* published three years earlier, had not benefited from the emergent author's "privileged moment of *individualization*." Furthermore, despite the many collaborations that preceded the text's delivery to the printing house, and the "attendant sexualities [of such collaborations] in early modern England"[17] – or even the allegedly attendant sexuality of the name that was destined to mark off its edges – the texts that emerged from the printing house in 1611 were inadvertently hetero-sexualized. Utterly consistent with the material realities of early modern publication, the earliest copies of the first edition came to be known as *The Great He Bible* because the last six words of Ruth 3.15 read "and he went into the citie."[18] Other copies, printed in the same year, came to be known as *The Great She Bible* because the last six words of the same verse read "and she went into the citie." A single textual/sexual variant had given birth to two divergent texts which, in their gendered divergence, succinctly belied print's powers to fix and standardize even "Holy Writ." And, as would be the case with another sacred text published twelve years later, no author could be called upon to definitively declare his or her intentions. And yet, because the "privileged moment of *individualization*" was bound to have its untimely way with the book, this version would indeed come to be *author-ized* – though one sense of the word would inevitably come after the other.

Notes

PREFACE

1 D. F. McKenzie, *"What's Past is Prologue": The Bibliographic Society and History of the Book*, The Bibliographical Society Centenary Lecture, 14 July 1992 (London: Hearthstone Publications, 1993), p. 8.

PROLOGUE: "THOU GREWST TO GOVERN THE WHOLE STAGE ALONE"

1 Richard Dutton, "The Birth of an Author," in *Texts and Cultural Change in Early Modern England*, eds. Cedric C. Brown and Arthur F. Marotti (New York: St. Martin's Press, Inc., 1997), pp. 153–178; p. 175.
2 Jeffrey Masten, *Textual Intercourse: Collaboration, Authorship, and Sexualities in Renaissance Drama* (Cambridge University Press, 1997), p. 10.
3 Michael D. Bristol, "Shakespeare: The Myth," in *A Companion to Shakespeare*, ed. David Scott Kastan (Oxford: Blackwell Publishers Inc., 1999), pp. 489–502; p. 490.
4 I am grateful to Stephen Orgel for this insight. Although the *OED* credits the first use of the word to M. Clifford in 1687, referring to "this damn'd trade of a Play-wright" (p. 2204), the term had been used – with equal contempt – previously by Jonson in Epigrams 49 and 100 and some of his contemporaries. I am grateful to an anonymous reader for pointing out these earlier uses of the word to me.
5 Roland Barthes, "The Death of the Author," in *Theories of Authorship*, ed. John Caughie (London: Routledge & Kegan Paul, 1981), pp. 208–213; p. 209 (original italics).
6 Michel Foucault, "What is an Author?" trans., Catherine Porter in *The Foucault Reader*, ed. Paul Rabinow (New York: Pantheon Books, 1984), pp. 101–120; p. 101 (original italics).
7 *Ibid.*, p. 113.
8 See for example Frank Lentricchia's essay, "Foucault's Legacy: A New Historicism?" in *The New Historicism*, ed. H. Aram Veeser (New York: Routledge, 1989), pp. 231–243; Lynn Hunt, "History as Gesture, or, The Scandal of History," in *Consequences of Theory*, eds. Jonathan Arac and Barbara Johnson (Baltimore: Johns Hopkins University Press, 1991), pp. 91–107.
9 Stephen Greenblatt, "Towards the Poetics of Culture," in *The New Historicism*, ed. H. Aram Veeser (New York: Routledge, 1989), pp. 1–12; p. 12.

10 See for example, Jonathan Dollimore's discussion of the subversion/containment debate in his introductory essay, "Shakespeare, Cultural Materialism, and the New Historicism," in *Political Shakespeare: Essays in Cultural Materialism*, second edition, eds. Jonathan Dollimore and Alan Sinfield (Ithaca: Cornell University Press, 1994), pp. 2–17; pp. 11–15.
11 Masten, *Textual*, p. 10.
12 This category obviously excludes attribution studies which, in their effort to link proper names to texts, constitutively sustain a notion of the author that both Barthes and Foucault attempted to dismantle. Some other conspicuous exceptions are Jacqueline T. Miller, *Poetic License: Authority and Authorship in Medieval and Renaissance Contexts* (Oxford University Press, 1986); Martin Elsky, *Authorizing Words: Speech, Writing, and Print in the English Renaissance* (Ithaca: Cornell University Press, 1989); Barry Taylor, *Vagrant Writing: Social and Semiotic Disorders in the English Renaissance* (New York and London: Harvester Wheatsheaf, 1991).
13 These studies include Greenblatt, *Renaissance Self-Fashioning: From More to Shakespeare* (University of Chicago Press, 1980); Greenblatt, *Shakespearean Negotiations: The Circulation of Social Energy in Renaissance England* (Berkeley: University of California Press, 1988); Richard Helgerson, *Self-Crowned Laureates: Spenser, Jonson, Milton, and the Literary System* (Berkeley: University of California Press, 1983); Richard Wilson, *Will Power: Essays on Shakespearean Authority* (Detroit: Wayne State University Press, 1993); Jonathan Crewe, *Trials of Authorship: Anterior Forms and Poetic Reconstruction from Wyatt to Shakespeare* (Berkeley: University of California Press, 1990); Kevin Dunn, *Pretexts of Authority: The Rhetoric of Authorship in the Renaissance Preface* (Stanford University Press, 1994); Leah Marcus, *Puzzling Shakespeare: Local Reading and its Discontents* (Berkeley: University of California Press, 1988); Gary Taylor, *Reinventing Shakespeare: A Cultural History from the Restoration to the Present* (Oxford University Press, 1989); Michael Dobson, *The Making of the National Poet: Shakespeare, Adaptation and Authorship, 1660–1769* (Oxford: Clarendon Press, 1992); Margreta de Grazia, *Shakespeare Verbatim: The Reproduction of Authenticity and the 1790 Apparatus* (Oxford: Clarendon Press, 1991); Jean L. Marsden, *The Re-Imagined Text: Shakespeare, Adaptation, & Eighteenth-Century Literary Theory* (Lexington: University Press of Kentucky, 1995).
14 Marcus, *Puzzling*, p. 25. A pre-Foucauldian version of Marcus's position was proffered by E. K. Chambers in his 1926 British Academy Lecture, "The Disintegration of Shakespeare," subsequently published in *Shakespearean Gleanings* (Oxford University Press, 1944).
15 Bristol, *Big-Time Shakespeare* (London and New York: Routledge, 1996), p. 52. Some scholars unconvinced by the death of the author, continue to produce studies that persist in viewing Shakespeare as something more than an author function. See for example, Eric Sams, *The Real Shakespeare: Retrieving the Early Years, 1564–1594* (New Haven: Yale University Press, 1995); E. A. J. Honigmann, *Shakespeare: The "Lost Years"* (Manchester University Press, 1985); Stanley Wells, *Shakespeare: A Life in Drama* (New York: W. W. Norton & Company, 1995).
16 Ian Donaldson, "'Not of an Age': Jonson, Shakespeare, and the Verdicts of

Notes to pages 5–6

Posterity," in *New Perspectives on Ben Jonson*, ed. James Hirsh (Cranbury, NJ: Associated University Presses, 1997), pp. 197–216; p. 197.

17 David L. Gants, "A Descriptive Bibliography of the 'Workes of Beniamin Jonson' London: William Stansby, 1616" (Dissertation, University of Virginia, 1997), p. 2.

18 The term, New Textualism, was coined by Margreta de Grazia and Peter Stallybrass in their important essay, "The Materiality of the Shakespearean Text," *Shakespeare Quarterly* 44 (1993): 255–284.

19 Stephen Orgel, "What is a Text?" *Research Opportunities in Renaissance Drama* 26 (1981): 3–6. See also his essays, "The Authentic Shakespeare," *Representations* 21 (1988): 1–25; "The Poetics of Incomprehensibility," *Shakespeare Quarterly* 42 (1991): 431–437; and "What is an Editor?" *Shakespeare Studies* 24 (1996): 23–39.

20 Orgel, "What is a Text?" p. 6.

21 Orgel, "Acting Scripts, Performing Texts," in *Crisis of Editing: Texts of the English Renaissance*, ed. Randall McLeod (New York: AMS Press, Inc., 1993), pp. 251–294; p. 272.

22 Marcus, *Unediting the Renaissance: Shakespeare, Marlowe, Milton* (New York: Routledge, 1996), p. 3.

23 Randall McLeod, "FIAT *f*LUX" in *Crisis of Editing*, ed. McLeod, pp. 61–172; p. 150. See also his essay, "UnEditing Shakespeare," *Sub-Stance* 33/34 (1982): 26–55.

24 Paul Werstine, "Shakespeare," in *Scholarly Editing: A Guide to Research*, ed., D. C. Greetham (New York: Modern Language Association, 1995), pp. 253–281; p. 272.

25 See James Shapiro, "Recent Studies in Tudor and Stuart Drama," *Studies in English Literature* 37 (1996): 482–525; 482–483.

26 See for example, David Scott Kastan, "Shakespeare after Theory," *Textus* 9 (1996): 357–74; W. Speed Hill, "Where We Are and How We Got Here: Editing after Post-Structuralism," *Shakespeare Studies* 24 (1996): 38–46.

27 See for example, Howard Marchitello, "(Dis)embodied Letters and *The Merchant of Venice*: Writing, Editing, History," *English Literary History* 62 (1995): 237–265. See also Gary Taylor, "The Rhetorics of Reaction," in *Crisis of Editing*, ed. McLeod, pp. 19–60.

28 Werstine, "Narratives About Printed Shakespeare Texts: 'Foul Papers' and 'Bad' Quartos," *Shakespeare Quarterly* 41 (1990): 65–86; 65.

29 A. W. Pollard, *Shakespeare Folios and Quartos: A Study in the Bibliography of Shakespeare's Plays 1594–1685* (London: Methuen, 1909), pp. 64–80.

30 Martin Heidegger, *Being and Time*, trans. John Macquarrie and Edward Robinson (New York: Harper & Row Publishers, 1962).

31 Peter W. M. Blayney, "The Publication of Playbooks," in *New History of Early English Drama*, eds. John D. Cox and David Scott Kastan (New York: Columbia University Press, 1997), pp. 383–422; p. 383.

32 For a concise account of these developments, see Werstine, "Narratives," pp. 66–75. See also Werstine, "Plays in Manuscript," in *New History*, eds. Cox and Kastan, pp. 481–498. For an elegant account of the New Bibliography's beginnings, see Laurie E. Maguire, *Shakespearean Suspect Texts: The "Bad" Quartos and their Contexts* (Cambridge University Press, 1996), pp. 21–72.

33 For an extremely lucid account and critique of New Bibliographic narratives about "bad" quartos, especially those based on the notion of memorial reconstruction, see Maguire, *Suspect*, pp. 73–94 and pp. 323–338. See also Blayney, "Publication," pp. 384–389.
34 Blayney, "Publication," pp. 383–384.
35 See Maguire, *Suspect*, p. 26.
36 W. W. Greg, *The Editorial Problem in Shakespeare: A Survey of the Foundations of the Text*, third edition (Oxford: Clarendon Press, 1954), pp. 22–23. For a recent and extremely informative survey of extant manuscripts of plays, see William B. Long, "'Precious Few': English Manuscript Playbooks," in *A Companion to Shakespeare*, ed. David Scott Kastan (Oxford: Blackwell Publishers Inc., 1999), pp. 414–433.
37 Greg, "The Rationale of Copy-Text," in *Collected Papers*, ed. J. C. Maxwell (Oxford: Clarendon Press, 1966), pp. 374–391; p. 375.
38 *Ibid.*, p. 391.
39 Honigmann, *The Stability of Shakespeare's Text* (Lincoln, NB: University of Nebraska Press, 1965), p. 1.
40 Fredson Bowers, "Greg's 'Rationale of Copy-Text' Revisited," *Studies in Bibliography* 31 (1978): 90–162; 91.
41 Werstine, "Editing after the End of Editing," *Shakespeare Studies* 24 (1996): 47–54; 50.
42 *Ibid.*, p. 50.
43 For a concise overview of Shakespeare's plays for evidence of authorial revision see Honigmann, "Shakespeare as Reviser," in *Textual Criticism and Literary Interpretation*, ed. Jerome J. McGann (University of Chicago Press, 1985), pp. 1–22. Interestingly, Honigmann revised his own earlier authorial position on the revised status of *Lear* by the time he wrote this piece. Early on he credits "a brilliant short article by Michael J. Warren" for advancing "our understanding of the revision of *King Lear*," p. 4.
44 Honigmann, *Stability*, p. 1.
45 *Ibid.*, p. 51. For a more recent comprehensive study of Shakespeare and revision, see Grace Iappolo, *Revising Shakespeare* (Cambridge, MA: Harvard University Press, 1991). Iappolo attempts to provide a much wider context for demonstrating that Shakespeare revised his plays by examining instances of revision in extant manuscripts written by other contemporary playwrights. See especially, pp. 45–77.
46 De Grazia and Stallybrass, "Materiality," p. 255. The writers also include Michael Warren's *The Complete King Lear 1608–1623* in this progression.
47 For a concise account of the various theatrical interventions that complicated the individualization of dramatic authors in general, and Shakespeare in particular, see Scott McMillin, "Professional Playwriting," in *A Companion to Shakespeare*, ed. David Scott Kastan (Oxford: Blackwell Publishers Inc., 1999), pp. 226–238, especially pp. 229–232.
48 Quoted in Gary Taylor, *Reinventing*, p. 311.
49 *Ibid.*, pp. 311–312.
50 *Ibid.*, p. 313.
51 Masten, *Textual*, p. 10.
52 de Grazia and Stallybrass, "Materiality," 279.

53 Jonathan Goldberg, "Textual Properties," in *Shakespeare Quarterly* 37 (1986): 213–217; 214.
54 Werstine, "Editing," p. 51.
55 Dutton, "Birth," p. 172.
56 Barthes, *Sade Fourier Loyola*, trans. Richard Miller (London: Cape, 1977), p. 9.
57 Peter Thomson, *Shakespeare's Professional Career* (Cambridge University Press, 1992), p. xiii.
58 *Samuel Johnson on Shakespeare*, ed. H. R. Woudhuysen (London: Penguin Books, 1989), p. 114.
59 Dutton, "Birth," pp. 153–163.
60 Orgel, "What is a Text?" p. 6.
61 Dutton, "Birth," p. 161.
62 McMillin, "Professional," p. 237.
63 Mark Rose, *Authors and Owners: The Invention of Copyright* (Cambridge, MA: Harvard University Press, 1993), p. 27.
64 *The Workes of Beniamin Jonson, Epigrammes* 131. 1–2 (3Y5r).
65 On the relation between publishers and printers in the period, see Maguire's clear discussion of these terms in her excellent essay, "The Craft of Printing (1600)," in *A Companion to Shakespeare*, ed. David Scott Kastan (Oxford: Blackwell Publishers Inc., 1999), pp. 434–449, especially pp. 435–436.
66 James P. Saeger and Christopher J. Fassler, "The London Professional Theater, 1576–1642: A Catalogue and Analysis of the Extant Printed Plays," *Research Opportunities in Renaissance Drama* 34 (1995): 63–109; 68.
67 *Ibid.*, pp. 68–69.
68 All quotations of the First Folio here and throughout are taken from *The Norton Facsimile: The First Folio of Shakespeare*, second edition, prepared by Charlton Hinman (New York and London: W. W. Norton & Company, 1996).
69 For an astute reading of Heminge and Condell's address in the context of early modern literacy see Heidi Brayman Hackel's essay, "The 'Great Variety' of Readers and Early Modern Reading Practices," in *A Companion to Shakespeare*, ed. David Scott Kastan (Oxford: Blackwell Publishers Inc., 1999), pp. 139–157, especially pp. 139–145.
70 As Hackel notes, Heminge and Condell's equation of judgment and money recalls the rhetoric of the Scrivener's "Articles of Agreement" in the Induction to Jonson's *Bartholomew Fair* ("Great," pp. 144–145).
71 The fullest treatment of this somewhat paranoid scenario appeared in Pollard's *Shakespeare's Fight with the Pirates and the Problems of the Transmission of his Text*, second edition (Cambridge University Press, 1920).
72 Werstine, "Narratives," p. 68.
73 Marcus, *Puzzling*, p. 24.
74 Bristol, *Big-Time*, p. 36.
75 Douglas Bruster, *Drama and the Market in the Age of Shakespeare* (Cambridge University Press, 1992), p. 3.
76 These prices are based on the first two extant records of the book's purchase on the fly-leaf of *Folger 71* and in the account book of Sir Edward Dering, respectively. For an excellent survey of the Folio's sales history, see Anthony

James West, "Sales and Prices of Shakespeare First Folios: A History, 1623 to the Present (Part One)," *The Papers of the Bibliographical Society of America* 92:4 (1998): 465–528.
77 John Feather, *A History of British Publishing* (London and New York: Routledge, 1988), p. 25.

1 "A TOY BROUGHT TO THE PRESSE"

1 Louis A. Montrose, "Spenser's Domestic Domain: Poetry, Property, and the Early Modern Subject," in *Subject and Object in Renaissance Culture*, eds. Margreta de Grazia, Maureen Quilligan, and Peter Stallybrass (Cambridge University Press, 1996), pp. 83–132; p. 83.
2 See Blayney, *The First Folio of Shakespeare* (Washington: Folger Library Publications, 1991), pp. 2, 17, 21.
3 *Ibid.*, p. 2.
4 There were two eighteen-month periods (Dec. 1593–May 1595 and May 1600–Oct. 1601) during which enormous surges in the number of plays (54) registered for publication coincided with the reopening of the theatres. Blayney argues that players may have been prompted "to flood the market with scripts" in order to advertise that the theatres were back in business."Publication," pp. 383–422; p. 386.
5 Blayney, *First*, p. 2.
6 Montrose, "Spenser's," p. 83.
7 On Chaucer's early career in print, see Pask, *Emergence*, pp. 14–18.
8 Andrew Gurr, *The Shakespearean Stage 1574–1642*, second edition (Cambridge University Press, 1980), pp. 4–6.
9 McKenzie, "Typography and Meaning," in *Buch und Buchhandel in Europa im Achtzehnten Jahrhundert*, eds. Giles Barber and Bernhard Fabian (Hamburg: Dr. Ernst Hauswedell & Co., 1981), p. 82.
10 *Ibid.* p. 83.
11 Foucault, "What," p. 103.
12 Bristol, *Big-Time*, pp. 40–41.
13 Orgel, "What is a Text?" p. 3.
14 Roger Stoddard, "Morphology and the Book from an American Perspective," *Printing History* 17 (1987): 2–14; 2.
15 Feather, *History*, p. 26.
16 Greg Walker, *The Politics of Performance in Early Renaissance Drama* (Cambridge University Press, 1998), p. 225. Walker's brief, but careful survey of early attempts to regulate drama begins a few years earlier than the one I offer with Henry VIII's "Act for the Advancement of True Religion and the Abolishment of the Contrary" of 1543, pp. 225–231.
17 Quoted in Dutton, *Mastering the Revels: The Regulation and Censorship of English Renaissance Drama* (Iowa City: University of Iowa Press, 1991), p. 19.
18 *Ibid.*
19 *Ibid.*
20 See Walker, *Politics*, pp. 6–51 for a careful analysis of the printing of drama in the first half of the sixteenth century. Near the end of this analysis, Walker

concludes that, "In terms of many of the most vital and powerful traditions of early English drama, then, the printing of playbooks was, in the short term at least, only a marginal phenomenon" (p. 47).
21 Proclamation 390. "Offering Freedom of Conscience; Prohibiting Religious Controversy, Unlicensed Plays, and Printing." *Tudor Royal Proclamations Vol. II. The Later Tudors (1553–1587)*, eds. Paul L. Hughes and James F. Larkin (New Haven: Yale University Press, 1969), p. 5.
22 *Ibid.*, p. 5.
23 *Ibid.*, p. 6.
24 *Ibid.*, pp. 6–7.
25 Jürgen Habermas, "The Public Sphere," in *Jürgen Habermas on Society and Politics: A Reader*, ed. Steven Seidman (Boston: Beacon Press, 1989), p. 231.
26 Thomas Nashe's prefatory epistle to Robert Greene's *Menaphon*, in *Documents of the Rose Playhouse*, ed. Carol Chillington Rutter (Manchester University Press, 1984), p. 46.
27 Proclamation 422: Hughes and Larkin, *Tudor*, p. 57.
28 Included as Appendix D ("Documents of Control") in E. K. Chambers, *The Elizabethan Stage* vol. IV (Oxford: Clarendon Press, 1923), p. 286.
29 *Ibid.*, pp. 330–331.
30 Janet Clare, *"Art Made Tongue-Tied by Authority": Elizabethan and Jacobean Dramatic Censorship* (Manchester University Press, 1990), p. 215.
31 See Dutton, *Mastering*, pp. 97–116.
32 Feather, *History*, p. 30.
33 See Dutton, *Mastering*, pp. 107–109. The author does not really emerge as a consequence of this transgression because as Dutton notes, "dramatists and actors had been held jointly accountable for offenses," p. 164.
34 *Ibid.*, p. 164 (original italics).
35 *Ibid.*, p. 165.
36 Some three years later, a dramatic author does directly "benefit" from the individualizing potential of transgression, but it is a fleeting and elusive moment. In a letter written on 8 April 1608 by the French Ambassador in London in response to George Chapman's two-part play, *The Conspiracy and Tragedy of Charles, Duke of Byron, Marshall of France*, the Ambassador asserts that, "I caused certain players to be forbid from acting the History of the Duke of Byron ... At my suit three of them [i.e., the players] were arrested, but the principal person, the author, escaped." Quoted in G. E. Bentley, *The Profession of Dramatist in Shakespeare's Time, 1590–1642* (Princeton University Press, 1971), p. 175.
37 Cyprian Blagden, *The Stationers' Company: A History, 1403–1959* (Stanford University Press, 1960), p. 38.
38 *Ibid.*, p. 47.
39 According to the *Annals of English Drama*, the only other tragedies to be performed in English before the 1558 translation of Seneca's *Thebais* were two anti-Catholic tragedies adapted from biblical stories by James Wedderburn in 1540 when Henry's self-serving efforts to stir up anti-Catholic fervor were at their height. On the status of biblical tragedy prior to *Gorboduc*, see Howard B. Norland, *Drama in Early Tudor Britain 1485–1558* (Lincoln, NB: University of Nebraska Press, 1995), pp. 295–334. Norland notes that

approximately sixty Latin plays and nearly as many vernacular plays were derived from biblical stories between 1536 and 1556, p. 296.
40 *Troas*, trans. Jasper Heywood (1559); *Thyestes*, trans. Jasper Heywood (1560); *Hercules Furens*, trans. Jasper Heywood (1561); and *Oedipus*, trans. Alexander Neville (1563).
41 E. M. Spearing observes that, "[t]he great Greek tragedians were little studied by the Elizabethans. Greek was still unfamiliar to a large number of students; and it may be doubted whether in any case Aeschylus or Sophocles would have been appropriated by the Elizabethan public." *The Elizabethan Translations of Seneca's Tragedies* (Cambridge: W. Heffer & Sons Ltd, 1912), p. 1. The classic study of Elizabethan Senecanism is J. W. Cunliffe, *The Influence of Seneca on Elizabethan Tragedy* (New York: Macmillan, 1893). G. K. Hunter's essay, "Seneca and the Elizabethans: A Case-Study in 'Influence,'" *Shakespeare Survey* 20 (1967), 17–26, minimizes Seneca's importance to early modern England. The most recent major study is Gordon Braden, *Renaissance Tragedy and the Senecan Tradition: Anger's Privilege* (New Haven: Yale University Press, 1985).
42 Walker, *Politics*, p. 201. For E. F. J. Tucker, the play is "the earliest genuinely English Tragedy, dealing with British rather than classical or biblical history." *Intruder into Eden: Representations of the Common Lawyer in English Literature 1350–1750* (Columbia, SC: Camden House, 1984), p. 21. Noting Seneca's importance to England's efforts to produce its own tragic tradition, John Gassner observes: "Early Tudor tragedy followed classical models, and the dramatic work of Seneca was the one international model recognized wherever the influence of the Renaissance was felt in Europe. In *Gorboduc*, the five-act dramatic form, the choruses, and the reports of offstage action by a Nuntius, or Messenger, as well as the general theme of revenge, are Senecan features. To these were added allegorical pantomimes or "dumb shows" derived from Italian pageants known as *intermedi*; and a general influence from Italian Renaissance tragedy, itself patterned after Seneca's works, is to be found in the play." *Medieval and Tudor Drama* (New York: Applause Theatre Book Publishers, 1987), p. 403. Similarly, Irby B. Cauthen, Jr., remarks, "*Gorboduc* is a landmark in English drama. It is the first real English tragedy; although it adheres to the Senecan tradition, it modifies that tradition in order to express certain concepts of Tudor political theory." *Gorboduc or Ferrex and Porrex* (Lincoln, NB: University of Nebraska Press, 1970), p. xiii.
43 Philip Sidney singled out *Gorboduc* for praise and blame, mentioning Seneca along the way: "*Gorboduc* . . . is full of stately speeches and well sounding phrases, climbing to the height of Seneca his style, and as full of notable morality, which it doth most delightfully teach, and so obtain the very end of poesy; yet in truth it is very defectious in the circumstances, which grieveth me, because it might not remain as an exact model of all tragedies," *An Apology for Poetry*, ed. Forrest G. Robinson (New York: Macmillan, 1970) 74–75.
44 Quoted in Norman Jones and Paul Whitfield White, "*Gorboduc* and Royal Marriage Politics: An Elizabethan Playgoer's Report of the Premiere Performance," *English Literary Renaissance* 26 (1996): 3.

45 *Ibid.*, p. 6. Cauthen observes that, "Queen Elizabeth was not present at the first performance, but there is no doubt that she soon heard of the play. It spoke of matters so close to her subjects' hearts – the danger of an unsettled succession to the throne – that it violated her edict (19 May 1559) forbidding plays which touched on religion or politics, these 'being no meet matters to be written or treated upon but by men of authority, learning, and wisdom, not to be handled before any audience but of grave and discreet persons,'" (*Gorboduc*, p. xii).
46 Walker, *Politics*, p. 196.
47 STC 18684.
48 Beginning with Thomas Warton's *History of English Poetry* (1774–1781), there have been critics and editors who do not accept the title page's ascription. See Cauthen, *Gorboduc*, p. xi, n. 2.
49 STC 18685.
50 Fifteen years later this gesture would be literalized when, according to Michael A. R. Graves, the study in Norton's Guildhall home was searched and "[a]ll the 'bookes, papers and matters of state' found there were carried away and committed, by royal command, to the custody of Thomas Wilkes, who was clerk of the privy council." *Thomas Norton: The Parliament Man* (Oxford: Blackwell Publishers Inc., 1994), p. 147.
51 On the meaning of this phrase, see Greg, *Some Aspects and Problems of London Publishing: Between 1550 and 1650* (Oxford: Clarendon Press, 1956), pp. 41–62. For an astute and thorough analysis of what it meant to license a text in the second half of the sixteenth century, see Cyndia Susan Clegg, *Press Censorship in Elizabethan England* (Cambridge University Press, 1997), pp. 3–29.
52 *A Transcript of the Registers of the Company of Stationers of London 1554–1640 A.D.*, vol. I, ed. Edward Arber (London, 1875; reprinted Gloucester: Peter Smith 1967), p. 454.
53 As Clegg notes, the patent issued by Elizabeth to Daye in 1559, "specified not only a lifetime privilege to print William Cunningham's *The Cosmographicall Glasse*, but a privilege for seven years to print other books compiled at Daye's expense" (*Elizabethan*, p. 11).
54 Blayney, *The Bookshops in Paul's Cross Churchyard* (London: The Bibliographical Society, 1990), p. 61, n. 3.
55 I am grateful to Benedict Robinson for sharing his database of the publications of John Daye, 1546–1584, with me.
56 Drawing a distinction between the book trade and theatrical companies, Feather notes that, "[s]o far as the book trade was concerned, piracy could take place only if the established and proven rights of a Stationers' Company member were infringed." "From Rights in Copies to Copyright: The Recognition of Authors' Rights in English Law and Practice in the Sixteenth and Seventeenth Centuries," in *The Construction of Authorship: Textual Appropriation in Law and Literature*, eds., Martha Woodmansee and Peter Jaszi (Durham, NC: Duke University Press, 1994), pp. 191–210; p. 205.
57 Wendy Wall, *The Imprint of Gender: Authorship and Publication in the English Renaissance* (Ithaca: Cornell University Press, 1993), p. 21.
58 *Ibid.*, p. 184.

59 *Ibid.*, p. 182.
60 *Ibid.*, pp. 182–184.
61 Maguire, "Craft," pp. 434–449; p. 435.
62 Arber, *Transcript*, pp. 259–273, pp. 293–315.
63 *Ibid.*, p. 316.
64 *Ibid.*, p. 296. Additionally, even if Griffith's edition had not been entered into the Stationers' Register – as a number of texts printed in the period were not – the fact that he was willing to identify and give the location of his printing house on the play's title page indicates that the work was printed legally. See Clegg, *Elizabethan*, p. 18.
65 Arber, *Transcript*, p. 296.
66 Cauthen, *Gorboduc*, p. xxix. See also Cauthen, "Gorboduc, Ferrex and Porrex: The First Two Quartos," *Studies in Bibliography*, 15 (1962): 231–233.
67 Wall, *Imprint*, p. 283.
68 Edmund Spenser, *The Faerie Queene*, ed. Thomas P. Roche (New York: Penguin, 1987) 1. 13. 7–8.
69 Quoted in Dorothy Stephens, "'Newes of devils': Feminine Sprights in Masculine Minds in *The Faerie Queene*," *English Literary Renaissance* 23 (1993): 363–381; p. 381.
70 Ed. Lucy B. Campbell (New York: Barnes & Noble, Inc., 1960), p. 68.
71 Cauthen, *Gorboduc*, 5. 2. 96–97.
72 Helen King, "Once Upon a Text: Hysteria from Hippocrates," in *Hysteria Beyond Freud*, ed. Sander L. Gilman *et al.* (Berkeley: University of California Press, 1993), p. 29.
73 "Timaeus," in *Collected Dialogues of Plato*, eds. Edith Hamilton and Huntington Cairns (Princeton University Press, 1961), p. 1210, lines 91c–d (italics added).
74 Cauthen, *Gorboduc*, p. xii.
75 Wall, *Imprint*, pp. 1–23.
76 Referring to Pollard's version of this narrative, Blayney writes, "Like a folk tale, it continues to surface in whole or in part in most introductory accounts of the relations between the early theatre and the book trade . . . the old, unfounded myths persist: that acting companies usually considered publication to be against their best interests; that some publishers were so desperate to satisfy their eager customers that they would acquire plays by any dishonest means . . ." "Publication," p. 384.
77 Marcus, *Unediting the Renaissance: Shakespeare, Marlowe, Milton* (New York: Routledge, 1996), p. 78.
78 I will examine a similar anomaly in Jonson's 1616 folio in Chapter 3.
79 Greg, *A Bibliography of the English Printed Drama to the Restoration*, vol. III (London: The Bibliographical Society, 1957), p. 1196.
80 Francis Meres, *Palladis Tamia* (New York: Scholars' Facsimiles & Reprints, 1938).
81 Greg, *Bibliography*, vol. III, p. 1213.
82 Barbara A. Mowat, "The Theater and Literary Culture," in *New History*, eds. Cox and Kastan, pp. 213–230; p. 214.
83 *Ibid.*, p. 217.
84 Hackel, "'Great Variety,'" pp. 139–157; p. 145.

85 *Ben Jonson*: vol. IX eds. C. H. Herford, Percy Simpson, and Evelyn Simpson (Oxford: Clarendon Press, 1952), p. 14.
86 Zachary Lesser, "Walter Burre's Knight of the Burning Pestle," forthcoming in *English Literary Renaissance*. Lesser's argument, which elaborates a division that was theorized by Michael Neill in the context of Caroline drama ("'Wits Most Accomplished Senate': The Audience of Caroline Private Theaters," *Studies in English Literature* 18 (1978): 341–360), significantly locates the emergence of a division between popular and "select" audiences some two decades earlier than Neill does, and credits publishers like Burre for helping to generate it.
87 Greg, *Bibliography*, vol. I, p. xviii.
88 *Ibid.*, p. xviii.
89 Lesser, "Walter," p. 12.
90 *Ibid.*, p. 12.
91 *Ibid.*, pp. 11–12.
92 *Ibid.*, p. 13. Consistent with Lesser's effort to link typography to a specific readership is the fact, noted by Blayney, that after 1593 printers/publishers rarely used black letter, a typeface often associated with low levels of education and literacy, for playbooks ("Publication" pp. 414–415).
93 Ben Jonson, *Sejanus, His Fall*, ed. Philip J. Ayres (Manchester University Press, 1990), p. 49.
94 Greg, *Bibliography*, vol. III, p. 1213.
95 *Ibid.*, pp. 1206–1207.
96 *Ibid.*, p. 1213.
97 *Ibid.*, p. 1213.
98 Mowat, "Constructing the Author," in *Elizabethan Theater: Essays in Honor of S. Schoenbaum*, eds. R. B. Parker and S. P. Zitner (Newark: University of Delaware Press, 1996), pp. 93–110; p. 97.
99 The entry reads "Received of Bengemenes Johnsones Share as ffoloweth," Greg, *Henslowe's*, p. 47.
100 For an overview of Jonson's involvement with publication, see Bentley, *Profession*, pp. 289–292.
101 As Lesser observes, "of all playwrights Jonson uses the technique most consistently and prominently, for continuous printing marks the very difference between play and "legitimate Poëme" that he is so eager to mark ("Walter," p. 12).
102 Bentley, *Profession*, p. 55.
103 For an overview of Fletcher's involvement with publication, see Bentley, *Profession*, pp. 275–279.
104 Greg, *Bibliography*, vol. III, p. 1214.
105 Lesser, "Walter," p. 2.
106 Greg, *Bibliography*, vol. III, p. 1209.
107 *Ibid.*
108 Dutton, "Birth," pp. 153–178; p. 166.
109 Jacques-Alain Miller, "Microcopia: An Introduction to the Reading of *Television*," in Jacques Lacan's *Television*, trans. Denis Hollier, Rosalind Krauss, and Annette Michelson (New York: W. W. Norton, 1990), p. xxi.

110 Kathleen McLuskie, *Dekker and Heywood: Professional Dramatists* (New York: St. Martin's Press, 1994), p. 1.
111 Andrew Gurr, *The Shakespearean Playing Companies* (Oxford: Clarendon Press, 1996), p. 120.
112 For an excellent survey of Shakespeare's career in print see, Thomas L. Berger and Jesse M. Lander's essay, "Shakespeare in Print, 1593–1640," in *A Companion to Shakespeare*, David Scott Kastan, ed. (Oxford: Blackwell Publishers Inc., 1999), pp. 395–413.
113 Bentley, *Profession*, p. 280. See also Berger and Lander for a useful discussion of the poems' publication history, "Shakespeare," pp. 396–398.
114 Bentley, *Profession*, p. 280.
115 Michael J. B. Allen and Kenneth Muir, eds., *Shakespeare's Plays in Quarto: A Facsimile Edition of Copies Primarily from the Henry E. Huntington Library* (University of California Press, 1981), p. xii.
116 Bentley, *Profession*, p. 279.
117 Dutton, "Birth," pp. 153–178. An early version of Dutton's argument was rehearsed by Bentley, who examines the differences between the publication practices of professional playwrights who were attached to a particular playing company, and those professional writers who had no contractual relations with the playing companies for which they wrote (*Profession*, pp. 279–281).
118 Dutton, "Birth," p. 158.
119 *Ibid.*, p. 158.
120 Robert Clare, "'Who is it that can tell me who I am?': The Theory of Authorial Revision between the Quarto and Folio Texts of *King Lear*," *The Library* 17 (1995): 35–59; 39.
121 Dutton, "Birth," p. 174.
122 Shapiro, *Rival Playwrights: Marlowe, Jonson, Shakespeare* (New York: Columbia University Press, 1991), p. 160. See also Sara van den Berg, "'The Paths I Meant unto Thy Praise': Jonson's Poem for Shakespeare," *Shakespeare Studies* 11 (1978): 207–218.
123 David Riggs, *Ben Jonson, A Life* (Cambridge, MA: Harvard University Press, 1989), p. 276.
124 *Ibid.*, p. 276.
125 *William Shakespeare: Complete Poems*, ed. Christopher More (New York: Gramercy Books, 1993), p. 7.
126 See Dutton, "Birth," p. 154.
127 *Ibid.*, p. 155.
128 *Ibid.*
129 G. W. Wheeler, ed., *Letters of Sir Thomas Bodley to Thomas James, Keeper of the Bodleian Library* (Oxford University Press, 1926) p. 220.
130 These figures are based on my analysis of the titles of Okes's extant publications recorded in the STC. For an invaluable survey of generalized publishing trends some eight years before *Lear* appeared, see Mark Bland's essay, "The London Book-Trade in 1600," in *A Companion to Shakespeare*, ed. David Scott Kastan (Oxford: Blackwell Publishers Inc., 1999), pp. 450–463.
131 Greg, *Bibliography*, vol. III, pp. 1208–1209.

132 *Ibid.*, p. 1209.
133 *Ibid.*, p. 1209.
134 See Blayney, *First*, pp. 17–18.
135 Greg, *Bibliography*, vol. III, p. 1218.
136 McLuskie, *Dekker*, p. 5.
137 Greg, *Henslowe's*, p. 38.
138 Gurr, *Shakespearean*, p. 247.
139 *Ibid.*
140 Quoted in Gurr, *Shakespearean*, p. 247.
141 Greg, *Bibliography*, vol. III, p. 1212.
142 *Ibid.*, p. 1204.
143 Quoted in McLuskie, *Dekker*, p. 4.
144 For a useful discussion of this embodiment, see Bruster, *Drama*, pp. 1–11.
145 Paul Yachnin, *Stage-Wrights: Shakespeare, Jonson, Middleton, and the Making of Theatrical Value* (Philadelphia: University of Pennsylvania Press, 1997), p. 53.
146 According to the *OED*, from the end of the fifteenth century the word commonly meant "[o]ne who acts for another; an agent, deputy, or representative"; and "[o]ne who buys and sells for another person; a mercantile agent; a commercial merchant."
147 Wheeler, *Letters*, p. 219.
148 This praise gets distilled by Gerard Langbaine in *An Account of the English Dramatic Poets* (1691) where he writes of Heywood, "he was a general Scholar, and an indifferent linguist . . . Nay, further, in several of his Plays he has borrow'd many ornaments from the Ancients." Quoted in Michael Wentworth, *Thomas Heywood: A Reference Guide* (Boston: G. K. Hall and Co, 1986), p. xiii.
149 Quoted in Arthur Melville Clark, *Thomas Heywood: Playwright and Miscellanist* (Oxford: Basil Blackwell, 1931), p. 7.
150 For an overview of Heywood's involvement with publication, see Bentley, *Profession*, pp. 281–285.
151 Greg, *Bibliography*, vol. III, p. 1221.
152 *Ibid.*, pp. 1221–1222.
153 Elizabeth Eisenstein, *The Printing Press as an Agent of Change: Communications and Cultural Transformations in Early-Modern Europe*, vol. I and II (Cambridge University Press, 1979), p. 121.

2 "SO DISFIGURED WITH SCRAPINGS & BLOTTING OUT"

1 The principal contributions to this debate are Gary Taylor, "The Fortunes of Oldcastle," *Shakespeare Survey* 38 (1985): 85–100; Taylor, "William Shakespeare, Richard James and the House of Cobham," *The Review of English Studies*, n.s. 38 (1987): 334–354; Honigmann, "Sir John Oldcastle: Shakespeare's Martyr," in *"Fanned and Winnowed Opinions": Shakespearean Essays Presented to Harold Jenkins*, eds. John W. Mahon and Thomas A. Pendleton (London: Methuen, 1987), pp. 118–132; Pendleton, "'This is not the man': on calling Falstaff Falstaff," *Analytical & Enumerative Bibliography*, n.s. 4 (1990): 56–71; Jonathan Goldberg, "The Commodity of

Names: 'Falstaff' and 'Oldcastle' in *1 Henry IV*," in *Reconfiguring the Renaissance: Essays in Critical Materialism*, ed. Jonathan Crewe (Cranbury, NJ: Associated University Presses, 1992), pp. 76–88; Eric Sams, "Oldcastle and the Oxford Shakespeare," *Notes and Queries*, n.s. 40 (1993): 180–185; and David Scott Kastan, "'Killed with Hard Opinions': Oldcastle, Falstaff, and the Reformed Text of *1 Henry IV*," in *Textual Formations and Reformations*, eds. Thomas L. Berger and Laurie E. Maguire (Newark: University of Delaware Press, 1999), pp. 211–231. See also Kristen Poole, "Saints Alive! Falstaff, Martin Marprelate, and the Staging of Puritanism," *Shakespeare Quarterly* 46 (1995): 47–75; *The Oldcastle Controversy*, eds. Peter Corbin and Douglas Sedge (Manchester University Press, 1994), pp. 1–34; Robert J. Fehrenbach, "When Lord Cobham and Edmund Tilney 'were att odds': Oldcastle, Falstaff, and the Date of *1 Henry IV*," in *Shakespeare Studies* 18, ed. J. Leeds Barroll (New York: Burt Franklin & Co., Inc., 1986), pp. 87–101; Rudolph Fiehler, "How Oldcastle Became Falstaff," *Modern Language Quarterly* 16 (1955): 16–28; and George Walton Williams, "Second Thoughts on Falstaff's Name," *Shakespeare Quarterly* 30 (1979): 82–84.
2 For a concise analysis of the Pavier quartos, see Berger and Lander's essay, "Shakespeare," pp. 395–413, especially pp. 403–405.
3 See Blayney, "Publication," pp. 383–422; pp. 384–389.
4 Blayney, *First Folio*, p. 4.
5 Feather, "From," pp. 191–210; p. 200.
6 Although no English statute defined the author as the creator and owner of literary property before the Copyright Act of 1814 (Feather, "From," p. 191), the proto-form of copyright law was inaugurated by the Statute of Anne in 1709 and subsequently ratified by the case of *Donaldson v. Becket* decided before the House of Lords on 22 February 1774. See Mark Rose, "The Author as Proprietor: Donaldson v. Becket and the Genealogy of Modern Authorship," *Representations* 23 (1988): 51–85; 51.
7 Quoted in Feather, "From," p. 205.
8 George Walton Williams, *The Craft of Printing and the Publication of Shakespeare's Works* (Cranbury, NJ: Associated University Presses, 1985), p. 83. See also, Werstine, "Shakespeare," pp. 253–281; 265.
9 Since Pollard, the "bad quarto" has been generally coterminous with the hypothetical pirated text. See Werstine, "Narratives," pp. 65–86.
10 *The Complete Works of Shakespeare*, third edition, ed. David Bevington (New York: HarperCollins Publishers, 1980), p. 1380. See also Blayney, *First*, p. 17. In their recent edition of the play in the New Cambridge series, Doreen DelVecchio and Anthony Hammond assert that they "do not regard the stylistic differences in the play (which have often been exaggerated) as in any way conclusive evidence of collaboration," *Pericles, Prince of Tyre, The New Cambridge Shakespeare* (Cambridge University Press, 1998), p. 11.
11 Jonathan Rittenhouse, *A Critical Edition of 1 Sir John Oldcastle* (New York: Garland Publishing, Inc., 1984), pp. 1.
12 I am relying here and throughout on a Huntington Library photostat edition of the play. Critical editions cited will be identified in accompanying notes.

13 For a detailed study of Simmes's work on the printing of early modern dramatic texts see Craig W. Ferguson, *Valentine Simmes. Printer to Drayton, Shakespeare, Chapman, Greene, Dekker, Middleton, Daniel, Jonson, Marlowe, Marston, Heywood, and Other Elizabethans* (Columbia, SC: University of South Carolina Press, 1968).
14 McMillin, "Professional," pp. 226–238; p. 236.
15 *Henslowe's Diary: Part I*, ed. Walter W. Greg (Folcraft Press, Inc., 1904), p. 113.
16 *Ibid.*, p. 113.
17 Samuel Schoenbaum's observation that "[i]n 1599 a quartet of dramatists from the rival Admiral's Men pooled their inconsiderable talents to produce *The First Part of the True and Honourable History of the Life of Sir John Oldcastle, the Good Lord Cobham*," is representative of the play's critical reception. *Shakespeare's Lives: New Edition* (Oxford: Clarendon Press, 1991), pp. 49–50. Emphasis added.
18 Quoted in Rittenhouse, *Critical*, p. 1.
19 Corbin and Sedge, *Oldcastle*, pp. 1–34; p. 32.
20 A comparable desire for authorial individuality underwrites recent critical references to *Oldcastle* as "Henslowe's play."
21 Corbin and Sedge, *Oldcastle*, p. 33.
22 Referring to how publishers/printers acquired copy, Blayney observes that, "Modern notions of literary property simply would not apply: what is being sold is a manuscript, not what we would call a copyright (an eighteenth-century word for an eighteenth-century innovation), "Publication," p. 394.
23 All quarto title pages examined are from Allen and Muir, *Shakespeare's Plays in Quarto*.
24 Blayney, *The Texts of King Lear and their Origins, Volume I: Nicholas Okes and the First Quarto* (Cambridge University Press, 1982), p. 83.
25 See Stallybrass, "Shakespeare, the Individual, and the Text," in *Cultural Studies*, eds. Lawrence Grossberg, Cary Nelson, and Paula Treichler (New York: Routledge, 1992), pp. 593–610.
26 Greenblatt, *Renaissance*, p. 1.
27 In fact, the type for the head-title was re-imposed from the top of the title page (Blayney, *Texts*, p. 97, Fig. 6, p. 148).
28 *Ibid.*, p. 82.
29 *Ibid.*
30 Foucault, "What," pp. 101–120; p. 108. It is also true that by the time *1 Henry IV* was published, Shakespeare had become popular and/or reputable enough as a playwright that the use of his name on a title page may have made good business sense to a publisher.
31 In identifying William Brooke as the seventh Baron Cobham, most scholars follow the *Dictionary of National Biography*. However, David McKeen includes a genealogy of the Cobham Lordship indicating that Brooke was the tenth holder of the title. *A Memory of Honor: The Life of William Brooke, Lord Cobham* (Universität Salzburg, 1986), vol. I: 2 and vol. II, Appendix 2, pp. 700–702.
32 Gary Taylor and Stanley Wells's Oxford Shakespeare edition of *1 Henry IV* is at the center of the restoration controversy, yet in many ways their editorial

Notes to pages 74–76

self-confidence is a development that follows from the work of Alice-Lyle Scoufos. Scoufos takes the notion that Shakespeare purposefully chose Oldcastle as the name for his fat knight further than any other commentator before her. She argues in her book-length study that the dramatist not only deliberately made use of "a conflation technique in which past elements of history are blended skillfully with recent and contemporary events" to satirize the Cobhams because they were rivals of the Essex–Southampton group, but also attempted to use the Falstaff–Cobham satire "to predict the future." *Shakespeare's Typological Satire: A Study of the Falstaff-Oldcastle Problem* (Chicago: Ohio University Press, 1979), p. 19. Honigmann observes, "[t]he enmity of Essex and the Cobhams cannot be ignored by students of the Oldcastle plays, even if it may also be overemphasized ... Whatever Shakespeare's original purpose, his Sir John Oldcastle was later seen as a significant factor in the complicated power-struggle that finally destroyed Essex and very nearly led to the execution of Southampton." "Martyr," pp. 120, 124. McKeen makes much of the brevity of Brooke's Lord Chamberlainship, and suggests that Shakespeare merely dragged "out of the obscurity of the roistering *Famous Victories of Henry the Fifth* onto the queen's own stage a scandalous character explicitly identified with another lord Cobham" (*Memory*, II, pp. 648–649). Another influential critical position, first put forth by Dover Wilson, maintains that Shakespeare was deliberately using Oldcastle to get back at the Cobham family for their purported opposition to the players. "The Origins and Development of Shakespeare's *Henry IV*," *The Library* 4:26 (1945): 2–16. However, Janet Clare finds "no concrete evidence that Cobham was personally antagonistic towards the theatre," *Art*, p. 77. Similarly, McKeen asserts that "it is hard to imagine [Brooke] as the wrathful inhibitor of genius, Puritan, obsessed by both hatred of the stage and/or aristocratic pride in his ancestry, that conjectural reconstructions of the circumstances in which Shakespeare laboured under his rule have made him" (*Memory*, II, p. 649).

33 McKenzie, *Bibliography and the Sociology of Texts* (London: The British Library, 1985), p. 26. McKenzie holds "Saussure's insistence upon the primacy of speech" (26) primarily responsible for the subordinate epistemological status of typographic conventions.
34 Here I am following the chronology of Shakespeare's work on the histories proposed by Giorgio Melchiori, *Shakespeare's Garter Plays: Edward III to Merry Wives of Windsor* (Newark: University of Delaware Press, 1994) pp. 98–101. *The Famous Victories of Henry V* was not published in quarto until 1598. Presumably, Shakespeare was working from a circulating manuscript copy of a prompt book.
35 Corbin and Sedge, *Oldcastle*, p. 146.
36 Gary Taylor, "James," p. 347.
37 Fehrenbach, "When," p. 96.
38 A. R. Humphreys, ed. *2 Henry IV* (London: Penguin Books, 1966), p. 186
39 Clare, *Art*, p. 77.
40 I am grateful to an anonymous reader for pointing out these two uses of "author" to me.
41 See for example, Gurr, *Shakespearean*, p. 19.

42 *Oldcastle*'s literary fortunes have soared of late. Two important critical editions of the play have appeared since 1984. One is Rittenhouse's edition, the other is the edition that Corbin and Sedge include in their collection of related texts, *The Oldcastle Controversy*.
43 "Great Britain, Historical Manuscripts Commission Report, de L' Isle Manuscripts," 2: 445–446. Quoted in Scoufos, *Shakespeare's*, p. 36.
44 Greg, *Henslowe's*, p. 181.
45 Sams, "Oldcastle," pp. 181–182.
46 Scoufos, *Shakespeare's,* p. 37; Kastan, "Killed," p. 214; Gary Taylor, "Fortunes," p. 90.
47 Nathan Fields, *Amends for Ladies* (London: Mathew Walbancke, 1618), G1r. Quoted in Scoufos, *Shakespeare's*, pp. 37–38.
48 Jane Owen, *An Antidote Against Purgatory* (English College, St. Omer, 1634). Quoted in R. W. F. Martin in "A Catholic Oldcastle," *Notes and Queries*, n.s. 40 (1993): 185–186; 185 (original italics). Martin concludes that "[e]vidently Owen knew Sir John as Oldcastle, perhaps from past stage performances" ("Catholic," p. 185). That a Catholic writer, as Martin notes, was citing Oldcastle with approval, will be considered later in this chapter.
49 See Scoufos, *Shakespeare's*, pp. 37–40.
50 Demonstrating the ways in which the early modern stage frequently ignored the containment imposed upon it by Greenblatt, Shapiro portrays *The Spanish Tragedy*'s Hieronimo as another character – like the Falstaffian Oldcastle – whose cultural after-life strays beyond the theatre. "'Tragedies naturally performed': Kyd's Representation of Violence," in *Staging the Renaissance: Reinterpretations of Elizabethan and Jacobean Drama*, eds. David Scott Kastan and Peter Stallybrass (New York: Routledge, 1991), pp. 99–110, especially pp. 108–110.
51 The dedicatory epistle is Bodleian Library, MS James 34 or British Library, Add. MS 33785. I am following the account of the James epistle provided by Gary Taylor ("William," p. 335).
52 I am using Taylor's transcription here ("William," pp. 334–335).
53 Taylor, "Fortunes," pp. 85; p. 100.
54 The gap between performance text and printed edition offers a complex of problems, but this gap remains untheorized in Taylor's account.
55 John Dennis, *The Comical Gallant: or The Amours of Sir John Falstaffe* (London: A. Baldwin, 1702), A2.
56 It is worth noting that by the time Falstaff gets revived for *Merry Wives*, he, like his author, has come to be closely associated with printing. Indeed, as was the case with Shakespeare's indifference to publication, Falstaff "cares not what he puts in press" (*MWW* 2. 1. 78). See de Grazia, "Imprints: Shakespeare, Gutenberg and Descartes," in *Alternative Shakespeares*, vol. II, ed. Terence Hawkes (New York: Routledge, 1996), pp. 63–94, esp. pp. 76–77.
57 *The Works of Mr. William Shakespeare*, 7 vols (London: E. Curl and E. Sanger, 1709–1710), I: viii. Quoted in Scoufos, *Shakespeare's*, p. 23.
58 Rose, "Author," p. 52. While it is true that the Copyright Act limited protection to a set time period, it is also true that the law focused on author-held copyright, as opposed to publisher-held copyright. Despite the cruel legal

realities of the period, on paper at least, authors stood to gain more under the new law than did booksellers.
59 A thorough reading of the events that shaped Shakespeare's career in 1709 is provided by Gary Taylor, *Reinventing*, pp. 52–99.
60 Shakespeare's authorship has been linked with Elizabeth recently by Leah Marcus. Taking seriously Heminge and Condell's claim in the reader's preface to the First Folio that "what [Shakespeare] thought, he vttered with that easinesse, that wee haue scarse receiued from a blot in his papers" (A3r), Marcus suggests that the playwright may "have composed orally," and asserts that "Queen Elizabeth I apparently had the same skill." *Unediting*, p. 162, p. 163.
61 See Masten, *Textual*, p. 151.
62 Rose, "Author," p. 52.
63 On these convergences see J. S. Peters, "The Bank, the Press, and the 'Return of Nature': On Currency, Credit, and Literary Property in the 1690s," in *Early Modern Conceptions of Property*, eds. John Brewer and Susan Staves (London: Routledge, 1995), pp. 365–388; esp. pp. 367–372.
64 Sharon Achinstein examines the relation between king and printer as it was reconfigured during the pamphlet wars of the English Revolution in her study, *Milton and the Revolutionary Reader* (Princeton University Press, 1994), especially pp. 78–101. Also of considerable value is Harold Love's analysis of the link between state authority and material practices of linguistic reproduction in his study, *Scribal Publication in Seventeenth-Century England* (Oxford: Clarendon Press, 1993), pp. 157–176. Love locates this link in the relationship between "the relative status accorded to voice, script and print within the political structure" and the prominent social fiction that "located the origin of all secular power in the king's person" (p. 161). For Love, the regicide of 1649 precluded royalty in the future from placing "any excessive trust in the power promised by legitimating fictions" (p. 176). Kevin Sharpe also examines the relation between Tudor–Stuart royal authorship and print culture, "The King's Writ: Royal Authors and Royal Authority in Early Modern England," in *Culture and Politics in Early Stuart England,* eds. Kevin Sharpe and Peter Lake (Stanford University Press, 1993), pp. 117–138. The relation between power and representation is given a useful general treatment by Michael Taussig, "Maleficium: State Fetishism," in *The Nervous System* (New York: Routledge, 1992), pp. 111–141.
65 Gary Taylor, "William," p. 335.
66 *Ibid.*, p. 341.
67 Alexander Pope echoes the young Gentle Ladie's observation in his 1723 edition of Shakespeare, but by then he has come upon a simple solution to the conundrum of the fat knight's double life: "*Falstaffe* is here introduc'd again [in *Henry VI*], who was dead in *Henry V*; the Occasion whereof is, that this Play was written before *Henry IV* or *Henry V*." Quoted in George Walton Williams, "Fastolf or Falstaff," *English Literary Renaissance* 5 (1975): 309. Ten years later, Lewis Theobald dismisses Pope's solution as "but an idle piece of Criticism" and offers the following explanation in its place: "It is the Historical Sir *John Fastolfe*, (for so he is call'd by both our Chroniclers) that is here mention'd; . . . and not the *Comic* Character afterwards introduced by

Notes to pages 82–84

our Author; and which was a Creature merely of his own Brain." *Works of Shakespeare* (1733), IV, 114–115. Quoted in Williams "Fastolf," p. 309.
68 Scoufos, *Shakespeare's*, p. 48
69 This is the account provided by John Capgrave, *The Chronicle of England* (London: Longman, Brown, Green, Longmans, and Roberts, 1858), pp. 303–304. In a subsequent chronicle Capgrave returns to the session between Cobham and Henry, but abbreviates it considerably: "This same Oldcastle, having been led before the king, and an accusation laid against him on account of certain erroneous bills to which he gave his support, they first attempted to soften him by kindnesse, that he should desist from the course he had taken; then he was terrified by threats, but not even thus could he be moved from his purpose." *The Book of Illusstrious Henries*, trans. Francis Charles Hingeston (London: Longman, Brown, Green, Longmans, and Roberts, 1858), pp. 126–127.
70 In addition to Capgrave, substantive chronicle accounts of Oldcastle are provided by Thomas Walsingham, Thomas Netter, Thomas Otterbourne, Thomas Eltham, and Hocclleve.
71 Capgrave, *Chronicle*, p. 303. As Fiehler notes, Oldcastle "was not openly characterized as a martyr until the time of the reformation" ("How," p. 20). See also Scoufos, *Shakespeare's*, p. 56.
72 G. R. Elton, *Policy and Police: The Enforcement of the Reformation in the Age of Thomas Cromwell* (Cambridge University Press, 1972), p. 34.
73 *The English Works of Sir Thomas More*, eds. W. E. Campbell and A. W. Reed, 2 vols. (London: Eyre and Spottiswoode, 1927) p. 2: 274.
74 John Bale, *A Brefe Chronycle Concerning the Examination and Death of the Blessed Martyr of Christ, Sir John Oldcastle, the Lord Cobham* (1544; STC 1276), 45r. Bale's account proved to be enormously popular and went through three printings in four years.
75 By 1559, however, when it began to be clear that matters of state would dominate matters of doctrine in Elizabeth's church policy, Sir Anthony Cooke and other eager reformers schooled in continental Protestant theology would no doubt have argued that the top half of the edifice remained to be built. As William Fuller puts it in his "Booke to the queene," "but halflie by your Majesty hath God bene honoured, his Church reformed and established, his people taught and comforted, his enemies rejected and subdued." Quoted in Patrick Collinson, *The Elizabethan Puritan Movement* (Berkeley: University of California Press, 1967), p. 29.
76 On the play's propagandistic qualities, see Kastan, "'Holy Wurdes' and 'Slypper Wit': John Bale's King Johan and the Poetics of Propaganda," in *Rethinking the Henrician Era: Essays on Early Tudor Texts and Contexts*, ed. Peter C. Herman (Champaign, IL: University of Illinois Press, 1994), pp. 267–282.
77 Annabel Patterson quotes these lines as a rebuttal of Archbishop Arundel's position that Oldcastle suffered from a "lack of learning." *Reading Holinshed's Chronicle* (University of Chicago Press, 1994), p. 137.
78 Kastan, "Killed," p. 215.
79 P.T., "Observations on Shakespeare's Falstaff," *Gentleman's Magazine*, 22 (October, 1752): 459–461. Quoted in Fiehler, "How," p. 18.

80 John Foxe, *Acts and Monuments*, 1571 (STC 11222).
81 Foxe's book, which went through six English editions during Elizabeth's reign and 14 more editions by the middle of the seventeenth century (Corbin and Sedge, *Oldcastle*, p. 7), was a rather unstable printed text in an era that had allegedly come to depend on the fixity of the printing press for securing presence and permanence. Oldcastle's martyrdom, however, seems to have been one of the book's constants since the 1563 edition, even meriting a woodcut of the knight's "horrible and cruell martirdome" (1563; 277). For an astute analysis of how Foxe's book changes over successive editions see Jesse Lander, "Foxe's *Book of Martyrs*: Printing and Popularizing the *Acts and Monuments*," in *Religion and Culture in Renaissance England*, eds. Claire McEachern and Debora Shuger (Cambridge University Press, 1997), pp. 69–92.
82 Collinson, *Elizabethan*, p. 25.
83 Kastan, "Killed," p. 216.
84 *Acts and Monuments, Newly Revised*, 2 vols. (STC 11225). Published by Richard Day, this is the last authorial edition of the work.
85 The prominence of the typographic element in Foxe's attempt to aggrandize Oldcastle's status as a proto-Protestant martyr is entirely consistent with the role of the printing press in the Reformation, a role that has received critical attention from Kastan, "'The noyse of the new Bible': Reform and Reaction in Henrician England," in *Religion and Culture in Renaissance England*, eds. Claire McEachern and Debora Shuger (Cambridge University Press, 1997), pp. 46–68; John N. Wall, "The Reformation in England and the Typographical Revolution: 'By this printing ... the doctrine of the Gospel soundeth to all nations,'" in *Print and Culture in the Renaissance*, eds. Gerald P. Tyson and Sylvia S. Wagonheim (Newark: University of Delaware Press, 1986), pp. 208–221; Jane O. Newman, "The Word Made Print: Luther's 1522 New Testament in an Age of Mechanical Reproduction," *Representations* 11 (1985): 95–133; Greenblatt, "The Word of God in the Age of Mechanical Reproduction," in *Renaissance*, pp. 75–114; Benedict Anderson, *Imagined Communities: Reflections on the Origin and Spread of Nationalism* (London: Verso, 1983), pp. 37–47; Eisenstein, *Printing*, pp. 302–440; Lucien Febvre and Henry-Jean Martin, *The Coming of the Book: The Impact of Printing 1450–1800*, trans. David Gerard (London: NLB, 1976), pp. 287–318.
86 Foucault, "Two lectures: Lecture One: 7 January 1976," in *Power/Knowledge: Selected Interviews and Other Writings 1972–77*, ed. Colin Gordon (Brighton: Harvester Press, 1980), p. 81.
87 Quoted in Eisenstein, *Printing*, p. 378.
88 Raphael Holinshed, *The Firste volume of the Chronicles of England, Scotlande, and Irelande* (STC 13568) (London: John Harrison, 1577), p. 1189.
89 In fact, Holinshed seems to be quoting Edward Hall's 1548 account nearly verbatim. Hall writes, "The Lorde Cobham not onely thanked the kyng of his most favourable clemencye, but also declared firste hym by mouthe and afterwarde by writyng the foundacion of his faith, the ground of his belefe and the bottome of his stomacke ..." *The Union of the Two Noble & Illustre Famelies of Lancastre & Yorke*, ed. Henry Ellis (1548; repr. London, 1809; New York, 1965), p. 48. Quoted in Patterson, *Reading*, p. 143. Nevertheless,

as Patterson notes, Foxe argued in the 1570 edition of *Acts* that Hall's source was Bale's *Brefe Chronycle* (p. 144).
90 On the significance of this title to the Elizabethan settlement, see Elton, *England Under the Tudors*, third edition (New York: Routledge, 1991) pp. 269–276.
91 Holinshed's source for this passage, as Patterson notes, was Thomas Walsingham's *Historia Anglicana* (Patterson, *Reading*, p. 151).
92 Holinshed, the anonymous author of *Famous Victories*, and Shakespeare all treat Oldcastle as a satellite figure to the king.
93 Hunter, "Religious Nationalism in Later History Plays," in *Literature and Nationalism*, eds. Vincent Newey and Ann Thompson (Savage: Barnes & Noble Books, 1991), p. 92. Similarly, Gary Taylor observes that, "[t]he team of playwrights who in 1599 produced Henslowe's derivative potboiler ... specifically contrasted their play, which presents 'faire truth,' with the 'forg'de invention' of Shakespeare's – just as Foxe had contrasted his pietistic interpretation with that of earlier chroniclers" ("Fortunes," p. 97).
94 Hunter, "Religious," p. 92.
95 *Ibid.*, p. 95.
96 *Ibid.*, p. 95.
97 *Ibid.*, p. 95
98 In *The Mirror of Martyrs or The life and death of that thrice valiant Captain and most godly Martyr Sir John Oldcastle Knight, Lord Cobham* (1601), John Weever condenses the link between author and martyr into a single couplet referring to the second meeting with Henry: "I come to Court and written with me bring / My swan's last funeral dirge to the King" (996–997). Included as Appendix D in Corbin and Sedge, *Oldcastle*, pp. 223–253.
99 For a recent study of representations of reading and writing on the early modern stage, see Eve Rachele Sanders, *Gender and Literacy on Stage in Early Modern England* (Cambridge University Press, 1998). Although Sanders examines a number of staged representations of men writing, for example in *Richard III* (pp. 156–162), she does not include *Oldcastle*'s scene of writing in her analysis.
100 Honigmann points out that Weever "asserted that his was the 'first true Oldcastle', having been 'made fit for the press' two years before its publication in 1601" ("Martyr," p. 124).
101 According to Corbin and Sedge, the lost sequel was ready for performance by March of 1600 (*Oldcastle*, p. 9).
102 Even the knight's last line of the play – spoken to Lord Powis, his betrayer – echoes Christ's final words on his own betrayal: "Tis true my Lord, and God forgive him for it" (K4v).
103 *The Mirror for Magistrates*, ed. Lily B. Campbell (New York: Barnes & Noble, Inc., 1938), pp. 8–20.
104 Honigmann, *Lost*, p. 51.
105 *Ibid.*, p. 57.
106 Honigmann offers the following lines from the poem as an example: "I dare here speak it, and my speech maintain, / That Sir John Falstaff was not any way / More Gross in body, than you are in brain ... (*Ibid.*).
107 In fact, subsequent references to the knight in Thomas Fuller's *Church*

History of Britain (1655) and Peter Heylyn's *Examen Historicum: Animadversions on the Church History of Britain* (1659) suggest that Oldcastle's fortunes as the ur-figure of the Protestant state plummeted tremendously during the half-century that followed Shakespeare's play.

108 Michael Dobson, *The Making of the National Poet: Shakespeare, Adaptation and Authorship, 1660–1769* (Oxford: Clarendon Press, 1992), p. 187.
109 *Ibid.*, p. 185.
110 Honigmann, who sees close similarities between Falstaff's role in *Merry Wives* and Lord Cobham's ill-fated effort to woo Lady Montague after the death of Lord Cobham's second wife in 1592, takes Elizabeth's anecdotal role in the play's conception seriously because "Lord Cobham's deceased wife had been a favourite attendant of Queen Elizabeth; his wooing of a third wife was evidently no secret, and an oblique allusion to his discomfiture would probably have appealed to the queen's earthy humour" ("Martyr," pp. 130–131).
111 Quoted in Scoufos, *Shakespeare's*, p. 23.
112 Dobson, *Making*, p. 184.
113 Gary Taylor, *Reinventing*, p. 65.
114 *The Merchant of Venice*: 5. 1. 94–95.
115 Feather, "From," p. 192.
116 Slavoj Zizek, *For they Know not What they Do: Enjoyment as a Political Factor* (London: Verso, 1991), p. 269.
117 Nicholas Rowe, *Works* I: viii.
118 Rowe, *The Tragedy of Jane Shore*, ed. Harry William Pedicord (Lincoln, NB: University of Nebraska Press, 1975) p. 9. Quoted in Dobson, *Making*, p. 91.
119 Dobson, *Making*, p. 1.
120 Colonel Joseph Hart, *The Romance of Yachting* (New York, 1848), pp. 210–212. Quoted in Dobson, *Making*, p. 1.
121 For a useful overview of the critical assault on authorship see Sean Burke, *The Death and Return of the Author: Criticism and Subjectivity in Barthes, Foucault and Derrida* (Edinburgh University Press, 1992), pp. 8–19.
122 Kastan, "Killed," p. 219.
123 It is worth noting that although *The Norton Shakespeare* advertises itself as being "Based on the Oxford Edition," the Norton edition of *1 Henry IV* returns Oldcastle to textual exile. Referring to the Oxford text, Greenblatt, the general editor of the Norton edition, writes, "[b]ut this decision [to restore Oldcastle] is a problem for several reasons. It draws perhaps too sharp a distinction between those things that Shakespeare did under social pressure and those he did of his own accord. More seriously, it pulls against the principle of a text that represents the latest performance version of a play during Shakespeare's lifetime: after all, even the earliest title page advertises "the humorous conceits of Sir John Falstaff" (New York: W. W. Norton and Company, 1997, p. 75).
124 Taylor, "Fortunes," p. 95. Similarly, Stanley Wells writes of Oldcastle/Falstaff, "Awareness of the character's origins adds to the play's historical resonances." *Shakespeare: A Life in Drama* (New York: W. W. Norton & Company, 1995), p. 140.

125 Gary Taylor, "Fortunes," p. 99.
126 Werstine has persuasively argued a similar point in the context of the editorial tradition that underwrites Taylor and Michael Warren's work on the texts of *King Lear*. See his essay, "Editing," pp. 47–54; p. 50.
127 Taylor, "Fortunes," p. 100.
128 *Ibid.*, p. 100.
129 See Goldberg's essay, "Commodity," pp. 76–88.
130 Quoted in Kastan, "Killed," p. 216.
131 See Martin, "Catholic," p. 185.
132 Taylor, "Fortunes," p. 99.
133 Sams, *Real*, p. 11.
134 Sams, *Real*, p. 32. If the document Sams is referring to is legitimate, then Shakespeare's father would have remained Catholic all his life. Schoenbaum, however, offers some grounds for skepticism, noting that the first part of the document is not authentic, the document's signature could have been forged, and there were other John Shakespeares living in Warwickshire (*Shakespeare's*, p. 538). Then there is the fact, noted by Schoenbaum and Sams, that the father's Testament comes down to us, via Malone, in the form of a 1784 copy of the lost original.
135 Honigmann, *Lost*, p. 125.
136 Taylor, "Fortunes," p. 100, n. 61.
137 Honigmann, *Lost*, pp. 119, 122.
138 Sams, *Real*, pp. 34–35.
139 On this point, see Kastan, "Killed," pp. 218–219.
140 Taylor, "Fortunes," p. 99.
141 *Ibid.*, p. 99.
142 Taylor himself compares Wells to Rowe in his discussion of the Oxford Shakespeare's publication. Noting that Wells "is a theatre historian as well as an editor, both a governor of the Royal Shakespeare Theatre and a Fellow of Balliol College," Taylor observes that, "[l]ike Rowe, but in contrast to the subsequent editorial tradition initiated by Pope, Wells edits Shakespeare in the light of theatrical practice." (*Reinventing*, p. 311).

3 "IF HE BE AT HIS BOOK, DISTURB HIM NOT"

1 Eisenstein, *Printing*, p. 33.
2 Saeger and Fassler, "London," pp. 63–109; p. 67.
3 STC 17471.
4 Bentley, *Profession*, pp. 55–56.
5 Joseph Loewenstein, "The Script in the Marketplace," *Representations* 12 (1985): 101–114; 101.
6 Richard C. Newton, "Jonson and the (Re-)Invention of the Book," in *Classic and Cavalier: Essays on Jonson and the Sons of Ben,* eds. Claude J. Summers and Ted-Larry Pebworth (University of Pittsburgh Press, 1982), pp. 31–58; p. 34.
7 Love, *Scribal*, p. 146.
8 Elizabeth Hanson, *Discovering the Subject in Renaissance England* (Cambridge University Press, 1998), p. 120.

9 Barthes, "Death," pp. 208–213; pp. 210–211.
10 In fact, Gants's analysis of the 1616 folio suggests that Jonson did not regularly visit William Stansby's shop at all because Stansby had enough type to print six full formes and printed by quires, "thus allowing early pulls to be examined and corrected off-premises at Jonson's residence . . ." "The Printing, Proofing and Press-Correction of Ben Jonson's Folio Workes," in *Re-presenting Jonson: Text, Performance, History* (New York: Macmillan, 1999), pp. 39–58; p. 55.
11 Kevin J. Donovan, "Jonson's Texts in the First Folio," in *Ben Jonson's 1616 Folio*, eds. Jennifer Brady and W. H. Herendeen (Newark: University of Delaware Press, 1991), pp. 23–37; p. 23.
12 This prejudice, which has often been attributed to Jonson himself, becomes a major theme, for example, in Richard Helgerson's influential analysis of what he calls "Jonson's laureate self-presentation," *Self-Crowned*, pp. 144–165.
13 See, for example, Loewenstein's discussion of Jonson's reliance on Martial, "Printing and 'The Multitudinous Presse': The Contentious Texts of Jonson's Masque," in *Ben Jonson's*, eds. Brady and Herendeen, pp. 168–191; pp. 173–175. See also Stella P. Revard, "Classicism and Neo-Classicism in Jonson's *Epigrammes* and *The Forrest*," in *Ben Jonson's*, eds. Brady and Herendeen, pp. 138–167.
14 Johan Gerritsen, "Stansby and Jonson Produce a Folio: A Preliminary Account," *English Studies* 40 (1959): 52–65; 52.
15 Donovan, "Jonson's," p. 23.
16 Gants, "Descriptive." The sections of Gants's dissertation that are of particular interest to me in this chapter (pp. 92–285, and pp. 302–356) have formed the basis of two recent articles that I will be relying on here.
17 See for example Bland's article, "Jonson, Biathanatos, and the Interpretation of Manuscript Evidence," *Studies in Bibliography* 51 (1998): 154–182.
18 See for example Bland's article, "William Stansby and the Production of *The Workes of Beniamin Jonson*, 1615–1616," *The Library* 20 (1998): 1–34.
19 *Ben Jonson*, vol. IX (Oxford: Clarendon Press, 1952), p. 72.
20 Herford and Simpson, *Jonson*, vol. VII, p. 420.
21 *Ibid.*, p. 420.
22 Goldberg, *James I and the Politics of Literature: Jonson, Shakespeare, Donne, and Their Contemporaries* (Baltimore: Johns Hopkins University Press, 1983), p. 136.
23 James A. Riddell, "The Concluding Pages of the Jonson folio of 1616," *Studies in Bibliography* 47 (1994): 147–154.
24 Gants, "Printing," p. 40.
25 *Ibid.*, p. 41.
26 *Ibid.*, p. 42. See Table 3.1 (p. 43) for a complete distribution of textual variants made by Jonson, and those made by Stansby or his corrector.
27 *Ibid.*, p. 45.
28 Donovan, "Jonson's," p. 26. For a recent discussion of copy-text see G. Thomas Tanselle, "Editing without a Copy-Text," *Studies in Bibliography* 47 (1994): 1–22.
29 D. C. Greetham, *Textual Scholarship: An Introduction* (New York: Garland Publishing, Inc., 1994), p. 333.

Notes to pages 109–111

30 For a useful recent discussion of this decision see Donaldson, "A New Edition of Ben Jonson?" in *Ben Jonson Journal* 2 (1995): 223–228. Consistent with this authorial fantasy, Gants notes that the Oxford editors chose a large-paper setting of the twice-set first gathering of *Epicoene* over the regular-paper setting because they "assumed Jonson would have insisted his large-paper presentation copies contain as few flaws as possible." "Printing," p. 46.

31 T. H. Howard Hill, "Towards a Jonson Concordance," *Research Opportunities in Renaissance Drama* 15–16 (1972–1973): 17–32; 23.

32 Greg's main concern was the evolving notion of the term "copy-text" in McKerrow's editorial practice. What had begun in McKerrow's edition of Nashe's *The Unfortunate Traveller* as a general term for an early text of a work, subsequently developed into a restrictive (tyrannical) concept which, by his *Prolegomena for the Oxford Shakespeare* excluded, for example, a later edition of a Shakespeare play even if its corrections could be shown to have come from the author ("Rationale," pp. 374–381).

33 This was especially the case for *Richard III* and *King Lear*.

34 Evelyn Tribble, *Margins and Marginality: The Printed Page in Early Modern England* (Charlottesville: University of Virginia Press, 1993), pp. 130–157.

35 *Ibid.*, p. 161.

36 Eisenstein, *Print Culture and Enlightenment Thought: The Sixth Hanes Lecture Presented by the Hanes Foundation for the Study of the Origin and Development of the Book* (Chapel Hill: Hanes Foundation, 1986), p. 6. The most recent critique of Eisenstein's notion of the fixity of print is offered in Adrian Johns's recent study, *The Nature of the Book: Print and Knowledge in the Making* (University of Chicago Press, 1998), especially pp. 28–40.

37 Bowers, "Greg's," 90–162; 109.

38 Questioning Herford and Simpsons' reliance on folio editions of masques where quarto editions are extant, Greg concludes, "[t]he only excuse for following the folio (whether of 1616 or 1642) is that the text shows signs of having been touched up before it was reprinted. But the changes made were sporadic and could easily have been introduced into a text based on the quarto" "Jonson's Masques – Points of Editorial Principle and Practice," *The Review of English Studies* 18 (1942): 144–66; 145.

39 Van den Berg, "Ben Jonson and the Ideology of Authorship," in *Ben Jonson's 1616 Folio*, eds. Brady and Herendeen, pp. 111–137; p. 117.

40 For a discussion of the relation between pre-performance masque printing and post-performance masque printing, see Berger, "Textual Problems in English Renaissance Masques, Pageants, and Entertainments: A Summary," *Research Opportunities in Renaissance Drama* 17 (1974): 13–16.

41 Of course Jonson himself had been down this path many times, as any number of studies of his relationship to censorship and authority have documented. For example the alterations made between the quarto and folio editions of *Every Man Out of His Humour* represent instances of authorial tampering with a play-text that most closely parallel the changes made in *The Golden Age Restored*. See H&S vol. III, pp. 602–604 and vol. IX, pp. 76–77.

42 Timothy Murray, *Theatrical Legitimation: Allegories of Genius in Seventeenth-Century England and France* (Oxford University Press, 1987), p. 68.

43 Berger, "Textual," p. 15.

44 James K. Bracken, "Books from William Stansby's Printing House, and Jonson's folio of 1616," *The Library* 10 (1988): 19–29; 28. For a discussion of such authorial involvement in the context of one play, see Dutton, "The Significance of Jonson's Revision of *Every Man in his Humor*," in *Modern Critical Views: Ben Jonson*, ed. Harold Bloom (New York: Chelsea House Publishers, 1987), pp. 129–139.
45 Greg, "Rationale," pp. 389–390.
46 *Ibid.*, p. 390. See Bowers's discussion of these two positions, "Greg's," pp. 110–11.
47 Gants, "Printing," p. 42, Table 3.1.
48 Quoted in Nigel Alexander, *Poison, Play and Duel: A Study in Hamlet* (Lincoln, NB: University of Nebraska Press, 1971), p. 177. See also Marie Axton, *The Queen's Two Bodies: Drama and the Elizabethan Succession* (London: Royal Historical Society, 1977). Axton usefully characterizes the Elizabethan version of this medieval theory as follows: "It was found necessary by 1561 to endow the Queen with two bodies: a *body natural* and a *body politic* . . . The body politic was supposed to be contained within the natural body of the Queen. When lawyers spoke of this body politic they referred to a specific quality: the essence of corporate perpetuity. The Queen's natural body was subject to infancy, error, and old age; her body politic . . . was held to be unerring and immortal" (12).
49 Loewenstein, "Script," p. 108.
50 STC 14774.
51 Loewenstein, "Script," p. 108.
52 See Riddell, "Jonson and Stansby and the Revisions of *Every Man in his Humor*," *Medieval and Renaissance Drama in England* 9 (1997): 81–91, 91. Gants's reconstruction of the folio's printing sequence based on paper evidence supports Riddell's findings. See Gants, "Patterns of Paper Use in the *Workes of Beniamin Jonson* (William Stansby, 1616),'" *Studies in Bibliography* 51 (1998): 127–153; 134–135.
53 See Riddell, "The Printing of the Plays in the Jonson folio of 1616," *Studies in Bibliography* 49 (1996): 149–168; 149, 161. Gants's analysis of the folio's gatherings indicates the *Epigrammes* were printed after *Every Man in* ("Printing," p. 43, Table 3.1.)
54 Herford and Simpson, *Jonson*, vol. VIII, p. 16.
55 *Ibid.*, p. 16.
56 Herford and Simpson give *The Forrest* a title page of their own making in their edition. (*Jonson*, vol. VIII, p. 91). They do not, however, provide a facsimile of the first page, as they do for all of the masques in vol. VII.
57 van den Berg, *The Action of Ben Jonson's Poetry* (Newark: University of Delaware Press, 1987), p. 129.
58 For a discussion of extant manuscripts see Herford and Simpson, *Jonson*, vol. VIII, pp. 7–10.
59 Focusing only on Jonson's substantive revisions of *Every Man in*, Dutton suggests that "there would be good reason for supposing that the revision might occupy some of the time that Jonson was off the public stage, after *Volpone* (1605) and before *Epicoene* (1609)," and argues that the play's revisions contribute to our understanding of how Jonson matured as a

playwright ("Significance," p. 131). Much of the interest in dating the play's revisions and interpreting them in terms of Jonson's maturation as a writer has been fueled by the play's primary position in the *Workes*. However, textual scholars have long noted that it was not in fact the first play in the folio that was printed, but rather presswork began with *Every Man Out*. And recently Riddell has convincingly demonstrated that in fact *Every Man In* was the last play printed and that many of its substantive revisions – especially the extensive cuts made in the folio version's final pages – including the excision of Lorenzo Junior's defense of poetry from the quarto version were probably motivated by print shop practices, rather than artistic considerations. Noting that exactly six quires of paper were set aside for printing the play, Riddell concludes that "the extensive cuts made in the last few pages of *Every Man In* were influenced by a compelling, if awkward, reality. Jonson and Stansby had run out of space" ("Jonson," p. 15).

60 See Gerritsen, "Stansby," p. 55.
61 Herford and Simpson, *Jonson*, vol. IX, p. 72.
62 *Ibid.*, p. 14.
63 See Gerritsen's concise critique of the Survey, "Review of H&S vol. IX–XI," *English Studies* 38 (1957): 120–126.
64 For an overview of these refutations, see Gerritsen, "Stansby," pp. 52–53.
65 *Ibid.*, p. 55.
66 Bland, "William," p. 10. Donovan's analysis of headline rules that were used on the final quires of the folio and another book Stansby was printing intermittently suggests that the presswork on the folio was completed sometime in late November or early December. "The Final Quires of the Jonson 1616 *Workes*: Headline Evidence," *Studies in Bibliography* 40 (1987): 106–119; 120–121.
67 Bland, "William," p. 14.
68 Donovan, "Jonson's," p. 25.
69 Gants, "Patterns," p. 135.
70 W. David Kay, for example, discusses the division between public and private theatre in Jonson's plays, not between theatre and court. "The Shaping of Ben Jonson's Career: A Re-examination of Facts and Problems," *Modern Philology* 67 (1976): 224–239; especially 231–233. In a recent study, Alvin Kernan examines Shakespeare's later plays in the context of James I's court: *Shakespeare, the King's Playwright: Theater in the Stuart Court* (New Haven: Yale University Press, 1995).
71 Jerome McGann, "Theory of Texts," *London Review of Books*, 10:14 (18 February 1988): 20.
72 Lowenstein, *Responsive Readings: Versions of Echo in Pastoral, Epic, and the Jonsonian Masque* (New Haven: Yale University Press, 1984), p. 95.
73 *Ibid.*
74 Miller, *Poetic*, p. 3.
75 Hanson convincingly argues for a comparable conflict within Jonson's use of print to assert his authorial individuality, only she locates it not – as I am suggesting – within the text of the 1616 folio, but rather between the folio and *Bartholomew Fair* (*Discovering*, p. 119).
76 STC 14782.

77 For a useful analysis of the Jonson canon prior to *Every Man In* see Kay, "Shaping," pp. 224–227.
78 Tribble, *Margins*, p. 131.
79 STC 14756.
80 Riggs argues sensibly enough that "the new spelling proclaimed [Jonson's] uniqueness ... the change of name set him apart from his real father and his three children, all of whom had been Johnsons" (*Ben Jonson*, p. 114). More recently, however, Bruce Thomas Boehrer concludes that "[Jonson] drops the 'h' from his name in 1605, apparently just after his imprisonment for *Eastward Ho*." "The Poet of Labor: Authorship and Property in the Work of Ben Jonson," *Philological Quarterly* 72 (1993): 290.
81 Tribble, *Margins*, p. 131.
82 Goldberg examines the differences between Elizabeth's and James's respective inaugural entertainments at great length, mostly to argue for the Roman character of the latter's reign (*James I*, pp. 28–55).
83 In the dedicatory epistle, Mulcaster refers to *The Queenes Maiesties Passage* as "the first fruites of my publik writing," *Mulcaster's Elementarie*, ed. E. T. Campagnac (London: Clarendon Press, 1925), A2.
84 Loewenstein, "Script," p. 106.
85 See Robert C. Evans's excellent discussion of these difficulties in the specific context of writing the masques. *Ben Jonson and the Poetics of Patronage* (Cranbury, NJ: Associated University Presses, 1989), pp. 222–246.
86 Loewenstein refers to other distinguishing elements linked to venue, noting that the masques "contain no cast lists, few stage directions, virtually no descriptions of scenery, no mention of Jonson's collaborators" ("'Multitudinous Presse,'" p. 181).
87 Bland, "William," p. 28.
88 Orgel, *The Illusion of Power* (Berkeley: University of California Press, 1975), p. 24.
89 The most exhaustive study of the architectural significance of the masques is A. W. Johnson's recent book, *Ben Jonson: Poetry and Architecture* (Oxford: Clarendon Press, 1994), especially pp. 115–242. Johnson's objective is to "examine the structural coherence of Jonson's early masques and the way in which scenography, music, and even choreography are related to Jonson's 'Fables' through a common symbolism of number" (p. 116). My interest here, however, is merely to point out that architecture offers Jonson another strategy for locating the authority of his text beyond his own authorship.
90 Murray, *Theatrical*, p. 57.
91 Herford and Simpson, *Jonson*. These title pages appear on the following pages of vol. VII: 161, 201, 243, 265, 321, 337, 357, 373, 387, 397, 407, 419.
92 Loewenstein, "Script," p. 108.
93 On this link, see Richard Helgerson, "Barbarous Tongues," in *The Historical Renaissance: New Essays on Tudor and Stuart Literature and Culture*, eds. Heather Dubrow and Richard Strier (University of Chicago Press, 1988), pp. 273–293; p. 289.
94 Murray, *Theatrical*, p. 56.
95 In "To Penshurst" it is the banqueting table, not the hall, that brings Jonson and James I together. And yet, the metonymic link in both cases between

Jonson's authority and food should remind of us the author's oft-remarked bulk.
96 Anthony Vidler, *The Architectural Uncanny: Essays in the Modern Unhomely* (Cambridge, MA: MIT Press, 1992), p. 70.
97 *Ibid.*, p. 71.
98 Mark Wigley, "Untitled: The Housing of Gender," in *Sexuality & Space: Princeton Papers on Architecture*, ed. Beatriz Colomina (Princeton Architectural Press, 1992), p. 357.
99 *Ibid.*, p. 369.
100 Orgel, *The Jonsonian Masque* (New York: Columbia University Press, 1981), p. 65.
101 Orgel, "What is a Text?" 3–6; 5.
102 Montrose, "The Elizabethan Subject and the Spenserian Text," in *Literary Theory/Renaissance Texts*, eds. Patricia Parker and David Quint (Baltimore: Johns Hopkins University Press, 1986), pp. 303–340; p. 306.
103 STC 1344.
104 See Don Wayne's discussion of lines 65–66, "And I not faine to sit (as some, this day, / At great mens tables) and yet dine away," *Penshurst: The Semiotics of Place and the Poetics of History* (University of Wisconsin Press, 1984), pp. 76–77.
105 See, for example, Sharpe's "King's," pp. 117–138. In the "epistle dedicatorie" to James's *Workes*, the publisher James Winton suggests to Prince Charles that royal authorship is essentially a father–son affair (A4).
106 On the formation of the English Stock, see H. S. Bennet, *English Books and Readers 1603–1640: Being a Study in the History of the Book Trade in the Reigns of James I and Charles I*, (Cambridge University Press, 1970), pp. 50–55.
107 For a concise overview of the early years of the press in England see Feather, *History*, pp. 7–18.
108 For details of Pynson's career as the king's printer see Colin Clair, *A History of Printing in Britain* (Oxford University Press, 1966), p. 39.
109 Masten, *Textual*, p. 151.
110 *Ibid.*, p. 73.
111 *Ibid.*, pp. 63–73.
112 Hanson, *Discovering*, p. 116.
113 van den Berg, "Ben," p. 113.
114 *Ibid.*, p. 113.
115 *Ibid.*, p. 113.
116 On Jonson's weight see Boehrer, "Renaissance," pp. 1071–1082. For Boehrer, gluttony is to Jonson what sex is to Foucault's effort to historicize sexuality, simultaneously "an instrument and an effect of power."
117 STC 14771.
118 See Richard Burt, *Licensed by Authority: Ben Jonson and the Discourses of Censorship* (Cornell University Press, 1993), p. 26. Burt makes much of the link between the two meanings of "corpus" in his initial examination of Jonson's relation to court and market censorship (pp. 26–78). Jennifer Brady examines the posthumously published collection of poems, *The Underwood*, for the metaphorical links between Jonson's body and his folio,

"'Noe fault, but life': Jonson's folio as Monument and Barrier" in *Ben Jonson's*, eds. Brady and Herendeen, pp. 192–216; pp. 195–200.
119 Meres, *Palladis*, p. 238.
120 van den Berg, "Ben," p. 117. This argument also ignores the more obvious fact that James had been an author in print since the 1580s.
121 Wall, *Imprint*, p. 343.
122 Meres, *Palladis*, p. 278.
123 Noting a similar conflation of king and poet in this epigram, Goldberg remarks, "[i]n the economy of Jonson's discourse, the same language celebrates the power of both roles, monarch and poet, just as a single crown marks them" (*James*, p. 17).
124 Blayney, *Texts*, p. 81.
125 Bracken, "Books," p. 23.
126 On the question of whether Jonson and/or his printers were using legal dating, i.e. the year reckoned from Lady Day on March 25, or calendar dating, reckoned according to the almanacs of the period from January 1, see Greg, "The Riddle of Jonson's Chronology," in Maxwell, ed., pp. 366–373.
127 Bland, "William," pp. 15–16.
128 Bracken, "Books," p. 21.
129 *Ibid.*, p. 23.
130 Murray, *Theatrical*, p. 57.
131 On Jonson's anti-theatricalism see Jonas Barish, *The Anti-Theatrical Prejudice* (Berkeley: University of California Press, 1981), pp. 132–155.
132 Quoted in Herford and Simpson, vol.IV, p. 13.
133 Foucault, "What," pp. 103–104. Hans-Georg Gadamer offers an important discussion of the relation between play and work in *Truth and Method*, second revised edition, translation revised by Joel Weinsheimer and Donald G. Marshall (New York: Crossroad, 1992), pp. 101–110.
134 Steven Mullaney, *The Place of the Stage: License, Play, and Power in Renaissance England* (Ann Arbor: University of Michigan Press, 1996), p. 47.
135 Jean E. Howard, *The Stage and Social Struggle in Early Modern England* (New York: Routledge, 1994), p. 24.
136 *Annals of English Drama*, Alfred Harbage, ed., third edition (London: Routledge, 1989), p. 46.
137 I am using the term "anonymous" here in the rather simplistic, literal sense of "without a name." Masten makes much of the word's history and meaning (*Textual*, p. 13), but my goal here is merely to get a sense of attribution trends for play-texts written, performed, and printed during the period of the professional London stage, 1576–1642.
138 Saeger and Fassler, "London," p. 65.
139 Although Saeger and Fassler's study is based primarily on facsimiles of the title pages and front matter of extant editions of printed professional drama, they note that, "[t]he primary authority for accepted attributions is *Annals*" ("London," p. 70).
140 Saeger and Fassler, "London," p. 106, Fig. 4.
141 *Ibid.*, p. 107, Fig. 6.

142 *Ibid.*, p. 105, Fig. 2.
143 Wall, *Imprint*, p. 347.
144 Elsky, *Authorizing*, p. 106.
145 Bentley, *Profession*, p. 3.
146 McKenzie, "Typography," p. 82.

4 "WHAT STRANGE PRODUCTION IS AT LAST DISPLAID"

1 de Grazia, *Shakespeare Verbatim*, p. 44.
2 Masten, "Playwriting," pp. 357–382; p. 371.
3 *Ibid.*, p. 370.
4 *Ibid.*, p. 371.
5 Masten, "My Two Dads: Collaboration and the Reproduction of Beaumont and Fletcher," in *Queering the Renaissance*, ed. Jonathan Goldberg (Durham, NC: Duke University Press, 1994), pp. 280–309; p. 281.
6 Gordon McMullan, *The Politics of Unease in the Plays of John Fletcher* (Amherst: University of Massachusetts Press, 1994), p. 134.
7 Cyrus Hoy, "The Shares of Fletcher and His Collaborators in the Beaumont and Fletcher Canon," *Studies in Bibliography* 8 (1956): 129–146; p. 129.
8 Bentley, *Profession*, p. 197.
9 Quoted in Masten, *Textual*, p. 1.
10 *Ibid.*
11 R. C. Bald, *Bibliographical Studies in the Beaumont & Fletcher Folio of 1647* (Oxford University Press, 1958), p. 2.
12 Masten, "Dads," p. 284.
13 *Ibid.*
14 McMullan, *Politics*, p. 133 (original italics).
15 Bald, *Bibliographical*, p. 13.
16 *Ibid.*, p. 14.
17 Herford and Simpson, eds., *Ben Jonson*: Vol. IX, p. 13. See also Masten, *Textual*, p. 126.
18 Bald, *Bibliographical*, p. 6.
19 McMullan, "Collaboration and the Problem of Editing," *Textus* 9 (1996): 437–460; 437.
20 Masten, "Beaumont and/or Fletcher: Collaboration and the Interpretation of Renaissance Drama," *English Literary History* 59 (1992): 337–356; 337.
21 Masten, "Playwriting," pp. 360–361.
22 Greg, "The Function of Bibliography in Literary Criticism Illustrated in a Study of the Text of 'King Lear,'" *Neophilogus* 17 (1933): 241–262; 241.
23 Greg, "Function," p. 241.
24 See Maguire, *Suspect*, pp. 38–41.
25 McMullan, "Collaboration," p. 438.
26 Masten, "Beaumont," p. 339.
27 McMillin, *The Elizabethan Theatre and The Booke of Sir Thomas More* (Ithaca and London: Cornell University Press, 1987), p. 136. In his remarkable analysis of hand D and the scholarly controversy it has generated (pp. 135–159), McMillin neither fully endorses nor argues against the long-cherished belief that the hand was Shakespeare's.

28 Lisa Ede and Andrea Lunsford, *Singular Texts/Plural Authors: Perspectives on Collaborative Writing* (Carbondale, IL: Southern Illinois University Press, 1990), p. 51.
29 Bentley points to *Gorboduc* as evidence that "before the appearance of the regular commercial theatres in London collaboration was a well-known phenomenon in the drama" (*Profession*, p. 198).
30 *Ibid.*, p. 199.
31 Masten, "Dads," p. 281.
32 *Ibid.*, p. 282.
33 Masten, "Playwriting," pp. 371–372.
34 Masten, *Textual*, p. 5.
35 Quoted in Greg, *Bibliography*, vol. III, p. 1013.
36 Unless otherwise noted, my discussion of title pages here will refer to first editions. My survey of subsequent editions of plays attributed to multiple authors – too long and detailed a subject to include here – suggests that the pattern of representing collaboration over the course of a given play's publication history is consistent with the pattern of representing collaboration within the larger body of extant drama.
37 The first edition of *Knight of the Burning Pestle* was published anonymously in 1613.
38 The publisher, Humphrey Moseley, and his printer are so dedicated to the notion of collaboration on this title page that they include a second pair of bracketed names directly underneath the Beaumont–Fletcher attribution: "Retriv'd for the publick delight of all the Ingenius; / And Private Benefit / Of {John Lowin, / And / Joseph Taylor,} Servants to His late Majestie."
39 Masten, "Dads," p. 292.
40 *Ibid.*, p. 293.
41 *Ibid.*, p. 282.
42 *Ibid.*, p. 282.
43 Katherine Eisaman Maus, *Inwardness and Theater in the English Renaissance* (University of Chicago Press, 1995), p. 182.
44 *Ibid.*, p. 193.
45 de Grazia, "Imprints," pp. 63–94; pp. 82–83.
46 For several examples of this anxiety, see Jan-Dirk Müller, "The Body of the Book: The Media Transition from Manuscript to Print," in *Materialities of Communication*, eds. Hans Ulrich Gumbrecht and K. Ludwig Pfeiffer, trans. William Whobrey (Stanford University Press, 1994), pp. 32–44.
47 Ann Thompson and John O. Thompson, *Shakespeare: Meaning & Metaphor* (Brighton: Harvester Press, 1987), p. 178.
48 *Ibid.*, p. 178.
49 Gordon Williams, *Shakespeare, Sex and the Print Revolution* (London: The Athlone Press Ltd, 1996), pp. 46–50.
50 Sidney, *Countess of Pembroke's Arcadia*, ed. Maurice Evans (New York: Viking Penguin, 1977), p. 57.
51 Marjorie Garber, *Shakespeare's Ghost Writers: Literature as Uncanny Causality* (New York: Methuen, 1987), p. 26.
52 Richard Wilson, *Will*, p. 171.
53 *Ibid.*, p. 165.

Notes to pages 166–178

54 René Girard, *Things Hidden Since the Foundation of the World*, trans. Stephen Bann and Michael Metteer (Stanford University Press, 1987), p. 9.
55 Shapiro, *Rival*, p. 14.
56 Foucault, "What," p. 101.
57 Rose, *Authors*, pp. 1–2.
58 *Ibid.*, p. 3.
59 See Feather, "From," pp. 191–210; especially pp. 191–201.
60 Masten, "Dads," pp. 292–293.
61 McKenzie, *Bibliography*, p. 5.
62 Bentley, *Profession*, p. 56.
63 Masten makes a similar point with reference to the 1623 folio, noting that "[p]rior to the first collection of Beaumont and Fletcher plays in the 1647 folio, forty-six editions of plays eventually associated with their names had appeared in quarto. Of these forty-six, all of the editions that were printed *without* a title-page attribution of authorship (eight in all) appeared before 1623, the date of the Shakespeare folio." *Textual*, p. 116.
64 For a useful corrective, see Pierre Bourdieu, *The Field of Cultural Production: Essays on Art and Literature*, ed. Randall Johnson (New York: Columbia University Press, 1995), especially pp. 29–73, 176–191. Asserting that "it is not possible to treat cultural order, the *épisteme*, as an autonomous and transcendent system," Bourdieu rightly accuses Foucault of having "succumbe[d] to that form of essentialism or, if one prefers, fetishism, that is manifested so clearly in other domains, notably in mathematics" (p. 179).
65 The third edition of *A King and No King*, published in 1631, does bracket the playwrights' names.
66 *Annals*, Harbage, ed.
67 For the period 1590–1642, Bentley puts the total number of known titles at 1,500, though the source for this figure is not given (*Profession*, p. 199).
68 For a useful discussion of the difficulties that such lists pose to scholarly analysis, see Bruce R. Smith, "Reading Lists of Plays, Early Modern, Modernist, Postmodern," *Shakespeare Quarterly* 42 (1991): 129–144.
69 Saeger and Fassler, "London," pp. 63–109; p. 67.
70 *An Index of Characters in Early Modern English Drama Printed Plays, 1500–1660*, Thomas L. Berger, William C. Bradford, and Sidney L. Sondergard eds., (Cambridge University Press, 1998), pp. 105–146.
71 For a useful discussion of this list, see Greg, "Authorship Attributions in the Early Play-Lists, 1656–1671" *Edinburgh Bibliographical Society Transactions*, vol. II (1938–1945): 305–329.
72 In relying on the data provided by the *Annals*, I have counted only certain attributions. Speculative single authors or collaborators – indicated parenthetically in the author column – have been counted as anonymous or singular, respectively.
73 Saeger and Fassler, "London," p. 67.
74 Eisenstein, *Printing*, p. 121.
75 Saeger and Fassler, "London," pp. 67–68.
76 Bentley, *Profession*, p. 199.
77 *Ibid.*

78 Neil Carson, *A Companion to Henslowe's Diary* (Cambridge University Press, 1988), p. 56.
79 *Henslowe's Diary: Part I*, ed. Walter W. Greg (Folcraft Press, Inc., 1904), p. 113.
80 Carlson, *Companion*, p. 58.
81 Bentley, *Profession*, p. 15.
82 *Ibid.*, p. 16.
83 *Ibid.*, p. 199.
84 Susan Dwyer Amussen, *An Ordered Society: Gender and Class in Early Modern England* (New York: Columbia University Press, 1988), p. 55.
85 Arber, *Transcript*, p. 296.
86 Foucault, "What," p. 107.
87 Although the 1679 Beaumont and Fletcher folio reproduced nearly all of the commendatory verses published in the preliminaries of the 1647 folio, Shirley's poem was not included.
88 Masten, "Dads," pp. 283–284.

5 "SO WRONGED IN BEEING PUBLISHT"

1 Claire McEachern, "*Henry V* and the Paradox of the Body Politic," *Shakespeare Quarterly* 45: 1 (1994) 33–56; p. 36.
2 *Ibid.*, p. 38.
3 McLuskie, *Dekker*, p. 2.
4 Wentworth, *Thomas*, p. xi.
5 *Henslowe's Diary: Part I*, ed. Walter W. Greg (Folcraft Press, Inc., 1904), p. 45.
6 Clark, *Thomas*, p. 8.
7 Greg, *Henslowe's*, p. 204.
8 Clark, *Heywood*, p. 20.
9 Meres, *Palladis Tamia* (New York: Scholars' Facsimiles & Reprints, 1938), p. 238.
10 Greg, *Bibliography*, vol. III, p. 1213.
11 This praise is distilled by Gerard Langbaine in *An Account of the English Dramatic Poets* (1691) where he writes of Heywood, "he was a general Scholar, and an indifferent linguist . . . Nay, further, in several of his Plays he has borrow'd many ornaments from the Ancients." Quoted in Wentworth, *Thomas*, p. xiii.
12 Quoted in Clark, *Heywood*, p. 7.
13 Greg, *Bibliography*, vol. III, p. 1221.
14 *Ibid.*
15 *Ibid.*, pp. 1221–1222.
16 Maus, "A Womb of his Own: Male Renaissance Poets in the Female Body," in *Sexuality and Gender in Early Modern Europe: Institutions, Texts, Images*, ed. James Grantham Turner (Cambridge University Press, 1993), pp. 266–288.
17 Masten, "Dads," pp. 280–309, p. 292.
18 Greg, *Bibliography*, vol. III, p. 1222.
19 Quoted in Herford and Simpson, *Ben Jonson*, vol. IV, p. 13.

20 Not reproduced in Greg, *Bibliography*, vol. III.
21 Other dramatic texts attributed to Heywood are *London's Ius Honorarium* (1631); *Londini Scaturigo* (1632); *Londini Emporia* (1633); *Londini Sinus Salutis* (1635); *Love's Mistress* (1634); *A Challenge for Beauty* (1635); *Londini Speculum* (1637); *Jupiter and Io* (1637); *Appollo and Daphne* (1637); *Amphrisa* (1637); *Porta Pietatis* (1638); and *Londini Status Pacatus* (1639). The title of one lost text, *Love's Masterpiece* (1640), was attributed to Heywood, and the title of a lost anonymous play, *Godfrey of Bouillon*, has been attributed to him.
22 Kastan, "Shakespeare," pp. 357–374; p. 367.
23 Bentley, *Profession*, p. 285.
24 For an analysis of this and the three other mid-seventeenth-century play lists see Greg's "Authorship," pp. 305–329. For an account of Kirkman's publishing activities, especially what the stationer reports about the practices and prevalence of piracy, see Johns, *Nature*, pp. 162–169.
25 Greg, "Authorship," p. 318.
26 A strikingly similar sales pitch was made in 1591 by I. Charlewood, the printer of Lyly's *Endimion, the Man in the Moone*.
27 Greg, *Bibliography*, vol. III, p. 1244.
28 *Ibid.*, p. 1246.
29 See Gurr, *Shakespearean*, pp. 104–119.
30 Helgerson, *Self-Crowned*, p. 101.
31 See Greg, *Bibliography*, vol. III, pp. 1209–1210.
32 Bentley, *Profession*, p. 284.
33 See Greg, *Bibliography*, vol. III, p. 1214.
34 A year before Okes published these two *Age* plays, Heywood had concluded the text of *An Apology for Actors* with an address to the printer that will be considered later in this chapter.
35 Clark, *Heywood*, pp. 22–23, n. 4.
36 Arguably, the number is ten if Thomas Pavier's thwarted 1619 collection of ten Shakespeare plays is counted.
37 Compiled from Greg, *Bibliography*, vol. III, pp. 1009–1139.
38 *Ibid.*, p. 1219.
39 *Ibid.*
40 *Ibid.*, p. 1220.
41 *Ibid.*
42 Not reproduced in Greg, *Bibliography*, vol. III.
43 See Benedict Robinson, "'Voluminous' Reading; or, why Thomas Heywood Wrote no Works," forthcoming in *Studies in English Literature*.
44 *Ibid.*
45 Quoted in Wentworth, *Thomas*, p. xii.
46 *Ibid.*, p. xiii.
47 Blayney, *Texts*, p. 30.
48 Frederick Kiefer, *Writing on the Renaissance Stage: Written Words, Printed Pages, Metaphoric Books* (Newark: University of Delaware Press, 1996), p. 61.
49 Greg, *Bibliography*, vol. III, p. 1208.
50 *Ibid.*, p. 1196.

51 Gurr, *Shakespearean*, p. 323.
52 Marcus, *Unediting*, p. 76.
53 *Ibid.*, p. 78.
54 McLeod, "The Marriage of Good and Bad Quartos," *Shakespeare Quarterly* 33 (1982): 421–431; 422.
55 Maguire, *Suspect*, p. 16.
56 *Ibid.*
57 Such allegations of a text being been "coppied onely by the eare" were not uncommon when Heywood made his, though, as Adele Davidson has shown, they were more commonly made with reference to sermons that were taken down by means of one of the recently available systems of shorthand and then published. "Some by Stenography: Stationers, Shorthand, and the Early Shakespearean Quartos," *The Papers of the Bibliographical Society of America* 90 (1996): 417–450.
58 Greg, *Bibliography*, vol. III, p. 1193.
59 *Ibid.*, p. 1195.
60 *Ibid.*, pp. 1195–1196.
61 *Ibid.*, p. 1196.
62 *Ibid.*
63 A more direct precursor to Heminge and Condell's address can be found in Thomas Walkley's address "To the Reader" of his 1622 quarto edition of Fletcher's *Philaster*. Referring to two previously printed texts (*Philaster* and *Arethusa*), Walkley writes that they "have laine so long a bleeding, by reason of some dangerous and gaping wounds, which they receiued in the first Impression, that it is wondered how they could goe abroad so long, or travaile so farre as they have done. Although they were hurt neither by me, nor the Printer; yet I knowing and finding by experience how many well-wishers they haue abroad, have aduentured to bind vp their wounds, & to enable them to visite vpon better tearmes, such friends of theirs, as were pleased to take knowledge of them, so mained and deformed, as they at the first were." Greg, *Bibliography*, vol. III, p. 1217.
64 *Ibid.*, p. 1195.
65 *Ibid.*, p. 1196.
66 On the "prehistory" of prefatorial addresses, see Gerard Genette, *Paratexts: Thresholds of Interpretation*, trans. Jane E. Lewin (Cambridge University Press, 1997), pp. 163–170.
67 Greg, *Bibliography*, vol. III, p. 1200.
68 *Ibid.*, p. 1201.
69 *Ibid.*
70 *Ibid.*, pp. 1201–1202.
71 Wall, *Imprint*, p. 21. On "disavowing authorial prefaces," see Genette, *Paratexts*, pp. 280–284.
72 Johns, *Nature*, p. 33.
73 *Ibid.*, p. 32.
74 *Ibid.*, p. 33.
75 *Ibid.*, p. 2.
76 Joseph Moxon, *Mechanick Exercises, or the Doctrine of Handy-Works Applied to the Art of Printing* (London: 1683–1684). Facsimile reprint, eds.

Herbert Davis and Harry Carter (New York: Dover Publications Inc., 1958), p. 191.
77 *Ibid.*, p. 192.
78 *Ibid.*, p. 212.
79 Greg, *Bibliography*, vol. III, p. 1204.
80 *Ibid.*
81 Not reproduced in Greg, *Bibliography*, vol. III.
82 Greg, *Bibliography*, vol. III, p. 1206.
83 It was also a good year for Heywood's company, for as Gurr notes, "To some extent 1612 can be seen as a high point in the Queen Anne's Company's development. That was the year when Heywood's plays triumphed on the Red Bull stage" (*Shakespearean*, p. 323). By contrast, so disaffected was Webster by *The White Devil*'s reception, that he left the company and the Red Bull that year for the King's Men's hall playhouse.
84 In his dedicatory poem to the *Apology*, Webster praises Heywood for giving actors "authority to play; / Even whilst the hottest plague of envy raignes'" (A2r) and seems to have a much higher opinion of the theatre when the success of his play isn't at stake: "What a full set of Poets, have you cited, / To iudge your cause? and to our equall veiw / Faire Monumentall Theaters recited: / Whose runnes had bene ruin'd but for you" (A2v).
85 For details of Heywood's non-theatrical publishing career, see Clark, *Heywood*, pp. 44–85.
86 Thomas Heywood, *An Apology for Actors* (1612) / *A Refutation of the Apology for Actors* (1615) ed. Richard H. Perkinson (New York: Scholars' Facsimiles & Reprints, 1941), p. xvi.
87 Perkinson, *Apology*, pp. xii–xiii. See also *The New Variorum Edition of Shakespeare: The Poems*, ed. Hyder Edward Rollins (London: J. B. Lippincott Company, 1938), pp. 533–538. Rollins observes: "That the P. P. was a piratical venture of William Jaggard's has never been seriously questioned" (p. 533). Subsequently, Rollins claims he was the first to discover that the pirated text actually included nine Heywood poems, rather than two (p. 534).
88 Shakespeare may have returned the favor. According to Rollins, "It is not unlikely also that Shakespeare, who certainly had good reason to be much offended with Master Jaggard, added his protest to that of his acquaintance, Heywood" (*Variorum*, p. 535).
89 Perkinson, *Apology*, p. xiii. See also Rollins, *Variorum*, p. 535.
90 Similarly, a descendant of Jaggard, Captain Jaggard, defended the printer, arguing that, "the manuscript brought to the printer may have been written entirely in Sh———'s hand. It is quite feasible that Sh— copied the others' poems and added them to his own for some alterior purpose, as an anthology, like 'Tottel's Miscellany,' or jotted them down for use in unborn plays." Quoted in Rollins, *Variorum*, p. 536.
91 Gurr, *Shakespearean*, p. 317.
92 *Ibid.*, p. 322.
93 Clark, *Heywood*, pp. 86–87.
94 Gurr, *Shakespearean*, p. 325. Ironically, the destruction may have been carried out by the "ignorant asses" that Webster and Jonson had denigrated a few years earlier, for as Gurr notes, "There is reason to believe that the

apprentices were registering their anger at the company's transfer from the Red Bull, where they could see the plays for a penny, to the much costlier Cockpit."
95 *Ibid.*, p. 325.
96 Clark, *Heywood*, pp. 86–7.
97 Gurr, *Shakespearean*, p. 325.
98 Clark, *Heywood*, p. 89.
99 *Ibid.*, p. 91.
100 *Ibid.*, pp. 103–104. According to the title page of *2 The Fair Maid of the West* (1631), the play was "lately acted before the King and Queen with approved liking. By the Queens Majestys Commedians" during the 1630–1631 Christmas season, and was entered in the Stationers' Register on 16 June 1631. Additionally, Heywood's retirement was temporarily interrupted by performances of *The Iron Age* (part 2) in 1632, and a revival of Marlowe's *The Jew of Malta*, which Heywood revised and presented, in 1633.
101 *Ibid.*, p. 105–141. A number of Heywood's masques and pageants were performed during the years 1631–1634.
102 *Ibid.*, pp. 143–186.
103 Not reproduced in Greg, *Bibliography*, vol. III.
104 The generic division between these two sets of translations isn't readily discernible. As Greg notes, "In this collection the distinction between dramatic and undramatic is particularly hard to draw." Greg, *Bibliography*, vol. III, p. 1070.

EPILOGUE: "WHY NOT MALEVOLE IN FOLIO WITH VS"

1 Rudyard Kipling, *Mrs. Bathurst and Other Stories*, ed. Lisa Lewis (Oxford and New York: Oxford University Press, 1991), pp. 251–263; p. 252.
2 A. F. Johnson, "Title Pages: Their Forms and Development," in *Books and Printing: A Treasury for Typophiles*, ed. Paul A. Bennett (Savannah, TN: Frederic C. Beil, 1951), pp. 52–65; p. 52.
3 Marchitello, *Narrative and Meaning in Early Modern England: Browne's Skull and Other Histories* (Cambridge University Press, 1997), pp. 128–129.
4 Masten, *Textual*, p. 66.
5 David Norton, *The King James Bible: A Textual History* (forthcoming from Cambridge University Press).
6 David Norton, "Imagining translation committees at work: the Authorised and the Revised Versions," unpublished conference paper.
7 *Ibid.*
8 *Ibid.*
9 Linda Woodbridge, "Patchwork: Piecing the Early Modern Mind in England's First Century of Print Culture, *English Literary Renaissance* 23 (1993): 5–45; 18.
10 *Ibid.*, p. 17.
11 Norton, "Imagining."
12 *Ibid.*
13 *Ibid.*
14 *Ibid.*

15 *Ibid.*
16 A. W. Pollard, *The Holy Bible. A Facsimile . . . of the Authorized Version . . .* (Oxford University Press, 1911), pp. 29–30. Quoted in Norton, "Imagining."
17 Masten, *Textual*, p. 2.
18 See Alfred Sutro, *The Great She Bible* (San Francisco: Grabhorn Press, 1938), pp. 3–4. The entire verse in these copies reads "Also hee said, Bring the vaile that thou hast / upon thee, and hold it. And when she held it, he / measured sixe measures of barley, and laid it on / her: and he went into the citie."

Bibliography

Achinstein, Sharon. *Milton and the Revolutionary Reader*. Princeton University Press, 1994.
Allen, J. B. and Kenneth Muir. *Shakespeare's Plays in Quarto: A Facsimile Edition of Copies Primarily from the Huntington Library*. Berkeley: University of California Press, 1981.
Alexander, Nigel. *Poison, Play and Duel: A Study in Hamlet*. Lincoln, NB: University of Nebraska Press, 1971.
Amussen, Susan Dwyer. *An Ordered Society: Gender and Class in Early Modern England*. New York: Columbia University Press, 1988.
Anderson, Benedict. *Imagined Communities: Reflections on the Origin and Spread of Nationalism*. London: Verso, 1983.
Arber, Edward, ed. *A Transcript of the Registers of the Company of Stationers of London 1554–1640 A.D.* Vol. I. London, 1875. Reprinted Gloucester: Peter Smith, 1967.
Axton, Marie. *The Queen's Two Bodies: Drama and the Elizabethan Succession*. London: Royal Historical Society, 1977.
Bald, R. C. *Bibliographical Studies in the Beaumont & Fletcher Folio of 1647*. Oxford University Press, 1958.
Bale, John. *A Brefe Chronycle Concerning the Examination and Death of the Blessed Martyr of Christ, Sir John Oldcastle, the Lord Cobham*. 1544. STC 1276.
Barish, Jonas. *The Anti-Theatrical Prejudice*. Berkeley: University of California Press, 1981.
Barthes, Roland. "The Death of the Author." *Theories of Authorship*. Ed. John Caughie. London: Routledge & Kegan Paul, 1981, 208–213.
Sade Fourier Loyola. Trans. Richard Miller. London: Cape, 1977.
Bennet, H. S. *English Books and Readers 1603–1640: Being a Study in the History of the Book Trade in the Reigns of James I and Charles I*. Cambridge University Press, 1970.
Bentley, Gerald Eades. *The Profession of Dramatist in Shakespeare's Time, 1590–1642*. Princeton University Press, 1971.
Berger, Thomas L., William C. Bradford, and Sidney L. Sondergard, eds. *An Index of Characters in Early Modern English Drama Printed Plays, 1500–1660*. Revised Edition. Cambridge University Press, 1998.
Berger, Thomas L. and Jesse M. Lander. "Shakespeare in Print, 1593–1640." *A*

Companion to Shakespeare. Ed. David Scott Kastan. Oxford: Blackwell Publishers Inc., 1999. 395–413.

Berger, Thomas L. "Textual Problems in English Renaissance Masques, Pageants, and Entertainments: A Summary." *Research Opportunities in Renaissance Drama* 17 (1974): 13–16.

Blagden, Cyprian. *The Stationers' Company: A History, 1403–1959*. Stanford University Press, 1960.

Bland, Mark. "The Appearance of the Text in Early Modern England." *Text* 11 (1998): 67–130.

"Jonson, Biathanatos, and the Interpretation of Manuscript Evidence." *Studies in Bibliography* 51 (1998): 154–182.

"The London Book-Trade in 1600." *A Companion to Shakespeare*. Ed. David Scott Kastan. Oxford: Blackwell Publishers Inc., 1999. 450–463.

"William Stansby and the Production of *The Workes of Beniamin Jonson*, 1615–1616." *The Library* 20 (1998): 1–34.

Blayney, Peter W. M. *The Bookshops in Paul's Cross Churchyard*. London: The Bibliographical Society, 1990.

The First Folio of Shakespeare. Washington, DC: Folger Library Publications, 1991.

"The Publication of Playbooks." *New History of Early English Drama*. Eds. John D. Cox and David Scott Kastan. New York: Columbia University Press, 1997, 383–422.

The Texts of King Lear and their Origins. Volume I: Nicholas Okes and the First Quarto. Cambridge University Press, 1982.

Bodley, Sir Thomas. *Letters of Sir Thomas Bodley to Thomas James, Keeper of the Bodleian Library*. Ed. G. W. Wheeler. Oxford University Press, 1926.

Boehrer, Bruce Thomas. "The Poet of Labor: Authorship and Property in the Work of Ben Jonson." *Philological Quarterly* 72 (1993): 289–313.

Bourdieu, Pierre. *The Field of Cultural Production: Essays on Art and Literature*. Ed. Randall Johnson. New York: Columbia University Press, 1995.

Bowers, Fredson. "Greg's 'Rationale of Copy-Text' Revisited." *Studies in Bibliography* 31 (1978): 90–162.

Bracken, James K. "Books from William Stansby's Printing House, and Jonson's Folio of 1616." *The Library* 10 (1988): 19–29.

Braden, Gordon. *Renaissance Tragedy and the Senecan Tradition: Anger's Privilege*. New Haven: Yale University Press, 1985.

Brady, Jennifer. "'Noe fault, but life': Jonson's Folio as Monument and Barrier." *Ben Jonson's 1616 Folio*. Eds. Jennifer Brady and W. H. Herendeen. Newark: University of Delaware Press, 1991. 192–216.

Bristol, Michael D. "Shakespeare: The Myth." *A Companion to Shakespeare*. Ed. David Scott Kastan. Oxford: Blackwell Publishers Inc., 1999, 489–502.

Big-Time Shakespeare. London and New York: Routledge, 1996.

Bruster, Douglas. *Drama and the Market in the Age of Shakespeare*. Cambridge University Press, 1992.

Burke, Sean. *Death and Return of the Author: Criticism and Subjectivity in Barthes, Foucault and Derrida*. Edinburgh University Press, 1992.

Burt, Richard. *Licensed by Authority: Ben Jonson and the Discourses of Censorship*. Ithaca: Cornell University Press, 1993.

Capgrave, John. *The Book of Illusstrious Henries.* Trans. Francis Charles Hingeston. London: Longman, Brown, Green, Longmans, and Roberts, 1858.
   The Chronicle of England. London: Longman, Brown, Green, Longmans, and Roberts, 1858.
Carson, Neil. *A Companion to Henslowe's Diary.* Cambridge University Press, 1988.
Cauthen Jr., Irby B. "Gorboduc, Ferrex and Porrex: The First Two Quartos." *Studies in Bibliography* 15 (1962): 231–233.
   Gorboduc or Ferrex and Porrex. Lincoln, NB: University of Nebraska Press, 1970.
Chambers, E. K. *Shakespearean Gleanings.* Oxford University Press, 1944.
   The Elizabethan Stage Vol. IV. Oxford: Clarendon Press, 1923.
Clair, Colin. *A History of Printing in Britain.* Oxford University Press, 1966.
Clare, Janet. *"Art Made Tongue-Tied by Authority": Elizabethan and Jacobean Dramatic Censorship.* Manchester University Press, 1990.
Clare, Robert. "'Who is it That Can Tell me Who I am?': The Theory of Authorial Revision between the Quarto and Folio Texts of *King Lear.*" *The Library* 17 (1995): 35–59.
Clark, Arthur Melville. *Thomas Heywood: Playwright and Miscellanist.* Oxford: Basil Blackwell, 1931.
Clegg, Cyndia Susan. *Press Censorship in Elizabethan England.* Cambridge University Press, 1997.
   "Taking Liberties, Keeping Privileges: The Stationers' Company, the Crown, the Church, and the Estate of Thomas Middleton, 1580–1627." Forthcoming in *The Oxford Companion to the Works of Thomas Middleton.* Ed. Gary Taylor.
Collinson, Patrick. *The Elizabethan Puritan Movement.* Berkeley: University of California Press, 1967.
Corbin, Peter and Douglas Sedge, eds. *The Oldcastle Controversy.* Manchester University Press, 1994.
Cox, John D. and David Scott Kastan, eds. *New History of Early English Drama.* New York: Columbia University Press, 1997.
Crewe, Jonathan. *Trials of Authorship: Anterior Forms and Poetic Reconstruction from Wyatt to Shakespeare.* Berkeley: University of California Press, 1990.
Crockett, Bryan. *The Play of Paradox: Stage and Sermon in Renaissance England.* Philadelphia: University of Pennsylvania Press, 1995.
Cunliffe, J. W. *The Influence of Seneca on Elizabethan Tragedy.* New York: Macmillan, 1893.
Davidson, Adele. "Some by Stenography: Stationers, Shorthand, and the Early Shakespearean Quartos." *The Papers of the Bibliographical Society of America* 90 (1996): 417–450.
De Grazia, Margreta. "Imprints: Shakespeare, Gutenberg and Descartes." *Alternative Shakespeares*, Vol. 2. Ed. Terence Hawkes. New York: Routledge, 1996. 63–94.
   "The Materiality of the Shakespearean Text." With Peter Stallybrass. *Shakespeare Quarterly* 44 (1993): 255–284.
   Shakespeare Verbatim: The Reproduction of Authenticity and the 1790 Apparatus. Oxford: Clarendon Press, 1991.

Dennis, John. *The Comical Gallant: or The Amours of Sir John Falstaffe*. London: A. Baldwin, 1702.
Dobson, Michael. *The Making of the National Poet: Shakespeare, Adaptation and Authorship, 1660–1769*. Oxford: Clarendon Press, 1992.
Dollimore, Jonathan. "Shakespeare, Cultural Materialism, and the New Historicism." *Political Shakespeare: Essays in Cultural Materialism*. Second edition. Eds. Jonathan Dollimore and Alan Sinfield. Ithaca: Cornell University Press, 1994. 2–17.
Dominik, Mark. *Shakespeare-Middleton Collaborations*. Beaverton: Alioth Press, 1988.
Donaldson, Ian. "A New Edition of Ben Jonson?" *Ben Jonson Journal* 2 (1995): 223–228.
— "'Not of an Age': Jonson, Shakespeare, and the Verdicts of Posterity." *New Perspectives on Ben Jonson*. Ed. James Hirsh. Cranbury, NJ: Associated University Presses, 1997), 197–216.
Donovan, Kevin J. "Jonson's Texts in the First Folio." *Ben Jonson's 1616 Folio*. Eds. Jennifer Brady and W. H. Herendeen. Newark: University of Delaware Press, 1991. 23–37.
— "The Final Quires of the Jonson 1616 *Workes*: Headline Evidence." *Studies in Bibliography* 40 (1987): 106–119
Dunn, Kevin. *Pretexts of Authority: The Rhetoric of Authorship in the Renaissance Preface*. Stanford University Press, 1994.
Dutton, Richard. *Mastering the Revels: The Regulation and Censorship of English Renaissance Drama*. Iowa City: University of Iowa Press, 1991.
— "The Significance of Jonson's Revision of *Every Man in his humor*." *Modern Critical Views: Ben Jonson*. Ed. Harold Bloom. New York: Chelsea House Publishers, 1987. 129–139.
— "The Birth of an Author." *Texts and Cultural Change in Early Modern England*. Eds. Cedric C. Brown and Arthur F. Marotti. New York: St. Martin's Press, Inc., 1997. 153–178.
Ede, Lisa and Andrea Lunsford. *Singular Texts/Plural Authors: Perspectives on Collaborative Writing*. Carbondale, IL: Southern Illinois University Press, 1990.
Eisenstein, Elizabeth. *The Printing Press as an Agent of Change: Communications and Cultural Transformations in Early-Modern Europe*, Vols. I and II. Cambridge University Press, 1979.
— *Print Culture and Enlightenment Thought: The Sixth Hanes Lecture Presented by the Hanes Foundation for the Study of the Origin and Development of the Book*. Chapel Hill: Hanes Foundation, 1986.
Elsky, Martin. *Authorizing Words: Speech, Writing, and Print in the English Renaissance*. Ithaca: Cornell University Press, 1989.
Elton, G. R. *England Under the Tudors*. Third edition. New York: Routledge, 1991.
— *Policy and Police: The Enforcement of the Reformation in the Age of Thomas Cromwell*. Cambridge University Press, 1972.
Evans, Robert C. *Ben Jonson and the Poetics of Patronage*. Cranbury, NJ: Associated University Presses, 1989.
Feather, John. "From Rights in Copies to Copyright: The Recognition of

Authors' Rights in English Law and Practice in the Sixteenth and Seventeenth Centuries." *The Construction of Authorship: Textual Appropriation in Law and Literature*. Eds. Martha Woodmansee and Peter Jaszi. Durham, NC: Duke University Press, 1994. 191–210.

A History of British Publishing. London and New York: Routledge, 1988.

Febvre, Lucien and Henry-Jean Martin. *The Coming of the Book: The Impact of Printing 1450–1800*. Trans. David Gerard. London: NLB, 1976.

Fehrenbach, Robert J. "When Lord Cobham and Edmund Tilney "were att odds': Oldcastle, Falstaff, and the Date of *1 Henry IV*." *Shakespeare Studies* 18. Ed. J. Leeds Barroll. New York: Burt Franklin & Co., Inc., 1986, 87–101.

Ferguson, Craig W. *Valentine Simmes. Printer to Drayton, Shakespeare, Chapman, Greene, Dekker, Middleton, Daniel, Jonson, Marlowe, Marston, Heywood, and Other Elizabethans*. Columbia, SC: University of South Carolina Press, 1968.

Fiehler, Rudolph. "How Oldcastle Became Falstaff." *Modern Language Quarterly* 16 (1955): 16–28.

Foucault, Michel. *Power/Knowledge: Selected Interviews and Other Writings 1972–1977*. Ed. Colin Gordon. Brighton: Harvester Press, 1980.

"What is an Author?" Trans. Catherine Porter. *The Foucault Reader*. Ed. Paul Rabinow. New York: Pantheon Books, 1984. 101–120.

Foxe, John. *Acts and Monuments, Newly Revised*. 2 vols. London: Richard Day, 1583. STC 11225.

Gadamer, Hans-Georg. *Truth and Method*, second revised edition. Translation revised by Joel Weinsheimer and Donald G. Marshall. New York: Crossroad, 1992.

Gants, David L. "A Descriptive Bibliography of the '*Workes of Beniamin Jonson*.' London: William Stansby, 1616." Ph. D. Dissertation, Charlottesville: University of Virginia, 1997.

"Patterns of Paper Use in *The Workes of Beniamin Jonson* (William Stansby, 1616)." *Studies in Bibliography* 51 (1998): 127–153.

"The Printing, Proofing and Press-Correction of Ben Jonson's Folio Workes." *Re-presenting Jonson: Text, Performance, History*. New York: Macmillan, 1999. 39–58.

Garber, Marjorie. *Shakespeare's Ghost Writers: Literature as Uncanny Causality*. New York: Methuen, 1987.

Gassner, John. *Medieval and Tudor Drama*. New York: Applause Theatre Book Publishers, 1987.

Genette, Gerard. *Paratexts: Thresholds of Interpretation*. Trans. Jane E. Lewin. Cambridge University Press, 1997.

Gerritsen, Johan. "Review of H&S vol. IX–XI." *English Studies* 38 (1957): 120–126.

"Stansby and Jonson Produce a Folio: A Preliminary Account." *English Studies* 40 (1959): 52–65.

Girard, René. *Things Hidden Since the Foundation of the World*. Trans. Stephen Bann and Michael Metteer. Stanford University Press, 1987.

Goldberg, Jonathan. "The Commodity of Names: 'Falstaff' and 'Oldcastle' in *1 Henry IV*." *Bucknell Review Reconfiguring the Renaissance: Essays in Critical*

Materialism. Ed. Jonathan Crewe. Cranbury, NJ: Associated University Presses, 1992. 76–88.

James I and the Politics of Literature: Jonson, Shakespeare, Donne, and Their Contemporaries. Baltimore: Johns Hopkins University Press, 1983.

"Textual Properties." *Shakespeare Quarterly* 37 (1986): 213–217.

Graves, Michael A. R. *Thomas Norton: The Parliament Man.* Oxford: Blackwell Publishers Inc., 1994.

Greenblatt, Stephen. *Renaissance Self-Fashioning: From More to Shakespeare.* University of Chicago Press, 1980.

Shakespearean Negotiations: The Circulation of Social Energy in Renaissance England. Berkeley: University of California Press, 1988.

"Towards the Poetics of Culture." *The New Historicism.* New York: Routledge, 1989. 1–14.

Greetham, D. C. *Textual Scholarship: An Introduction.* New York: Garland Publishing, Inc., 1994.

Greg, W. W. "Authorship Attributions in the Early Play-Lists, 1656–1671." *Edinburgh Bibliographical Society Transactions.* Vol. II (1938–1945): 305–329.

A Bibliography of the English Printed Drama to the Restoration. Vol. I–IV. London: The Bibliographical Society, 1939–1963.

The Editorial Problem in Shakespeare: A Survey of the Foundations of the Text. Third edition. Oxford: Clarendon Press, 1954.

"The Function of Bibliography in Literary Criticism Illustrated in a Study of the Text of 'King Lear.'" *Neophilogus* 17 (1933): 241–262.

"Jonson's Masques – Points of Editorial Principle and Practice." *The Review of English Studies* 18 (1942): 144–166.

"The Rationale of Copy-Text." *Collected Papers.* Ed. J. C. Maxwell. Oxford: Clarendon Press, 1966. 374–391.

Some Aspects and Problems of London Publishing: Between 1550 and 1650. Oxford: Clarendon Press, 1956.

Gurr, Andrew. *The Shakespearean Playing Companies.* Oxford: Clarendon Press, 1996.

The Shakespearean Stage 1574–1642. Second edition. Cambridge University Press, 1980.

Habermas, Jürgen. *Jürgen Habermas on Society and Politics: A Reader.* Ed. Steven Seidman. Boston: Beacon Press, 1989.

Hackel, Heidi Brayman. "'Rowme' of its Own: Printed Drama in Early Libraries." *A New History of Early English Drama.* Eds. David Scott Kastan and John D. Cox. New York: Columbia University Press, 1997. 113–132.

"The 'Great Variety' of Readers and Early Modern Reading Practices." *A Companion to Shakespeare.* Ed. David Scott Kastan. Oxford: Blackwell Publishers Inc., 1999. 139–157.

Hanson, Elizabeth. *Discovering the Subject in Renaissance England.* Cambridge University Press, 1998.

Harbage, Alfred, ed. *Annals of English Drama.* Third edition. London: Routledge, 1989.

Hart, Colonel Joseph. *The Romance of Yachting.* New York, 1848.

Heidegger, Martin. *Being and Time*. Trans. John Macquarrie and Edward Robinson. New York: Harper & Row Publishers, 1962.
Helgerson, Richard. "Barbarous Tongues." *The Historical Renaissance: New Essays on Tudor and Stuart Literature and Culture*. Eds. Heather Dubrow and Richard Strier. University of Chicago Press, 1988, 273–293.
— *Self-Crowned Laureates: Spenser, Jonson, Milton, and the Literary System*. Berkeley: University of California Press, 1983.
Henslowe, Philip. *Henslowe's Diary: Part I*. Ed. Walter W. Greg. Folcraft Press, Inc., 1904.
Heywood, Thomas. *An Apology for Actors* (1612) / *A Refutation of the Apology for Actors*. 1615. Ed. Richard H. Perkinson. New York: Scholars' Facsimiles & Reprints, 1941.
Hill, T. H. Howard. "Towards a Jonson Concordance." *Research Opportunities in Renaissance Drama* 15–16 (1972–1973): 17–32.
Hill, W. Speed. "Where We Are and How We Got Here: Editing after Poststructuralism." *Shakespeare Studies* 24 (1996): 38–46.
Holinshed, Raphael. *The Firste Volume of the Chronicles of England, Scotlande, and Irelande*. London: John Harrison, 1577. STC 13568.
Honigmann, E. A. J. "Shakespeare as Reviser." *Textual Criticism and Literary Interpretation*. Ed. Jerome J. McGann. University of Chicago Press, 1985, 1–22.
— *Shakespeare: The "Lost Years."* Manchester University Press, 1985.
— "Sir John Oldcastle: Shakespeare's Martyr." *"Fanned and Winnowed Opinions": Shakespearean Essays Presented to Harold Jenkins*. Ed. John W. Mahon and Thomas A. Pendleton. London: Methuen, 1987. 118–132.
— *The Stability of Shakespeare's Texts*. Lincoln, NB: University of Nebraska Press, 1965.
Howard, Jean E. *The Stage and Social Struggle in Early Modern England*. New York: Routledge, 1994.
Hoy, Cyrus. "The Shares of Fletcher and His Collaborators in the Beaumont and Fletcher Canon." *Studies in Bibliography* 8 (1956): 129–146.
Hughes, Paul L. and James F. Larkin, eds. *Tudor Royal Proclamations Vol. II. The Later Tudors (1553–1587)*. New Haven: Yale University Press, 1969.
Hunt, Lynn. "History as Gesture, or, The Scandal of History." *Consequences of Theory*. Eds. Jonathan Arac and Barbara Johnson. Baltimore: Johns Hopkins University Press, 1991. 9–107.
Hunter, G. K. "Religious Nationalism in Later History Plays." *Literature and Nationalism*. Eds. Vincent Newey and Ann Thompson. Savage: Barnes & Noble Books, 1991.
— "Seneca and the Elizabethans: A Case-Study in 'Influence.'" *Shakespeare Survey* 20 (1967): 17–26.
Iappolo, Grace. *Revising Shakespeare*. Cambridge, MA: Harvard University Press, 1991.
Johnson, A. F. "Title Pages: Their Forms and Development." *Books and Printing: A Treasury for Typophiles*. Ed. Paul A. Bennett. Savannah, TN: Frederic C. Beil, 1951. 52–65.
Johnson, A. W. *Ben Jonson: Poetry and Architecture*. Oxford: Clarendon Press, 1994.

Johnson, Samuel. *Samuel Johnson on Shakespeare*. Ed. H. R. Woudhuysen. London: Penguin Books, 1989.

Jones, Norman and Paul Whitfield White. "Gorboduc and Royal Marriage Politics: An Elizabethan Playgoer's Report of the Premiere Performance." *English Literary Renaissance* 26 (1996): 3–16.

Johns, Adrian. *The Nature of the Book: Print and Knowledge in the Making*. University of Chicago Press, 1998.

Jonson, Ben. *The Workes of Beniamin Jonson*. 1616.

    Ben Jonson, vols. I–XI. eds. C. H. Herford, Percy Simpson, and Evelyn Simpson. Oxford: Clarendon Press, 1952.

    Sejanus, His Fall. Ed. Philip J. Ayres. Manchester University Press, 1990.

Kantorowicz, Ernst. *The King's Two Bodies*. Princeton University Press, 1959.

Kastan, David Scott, ed. *A Companion to Shakespeare*. Oxford: Blackwell Publishers Inc., 1999.

    "'Holy Wurdes' and 'Slypper Wit': John Bale's King Johan and the Poetics of Propaganda." *Rethinking the Henrician Era: Essays on Early Tudor Texts and Contexts*. Ed. Peter C. Herman. Champaign, IL: University of Illinois Press, 1994. 267–282.

    "'Killed With Hard Opinions': Oldcastle, Falstaff, and the Reformed Text of *1 Henry IV*." *Textual Formations and Reformations*. Eds. Thomas L. Berger and Laurie E. Maguire. Newark: University of Delaware Press, 1999, 211–231.

    "'The Noyse of the New Bible': Reform and Reaction in Henrician England." *Religion and Culture in Renaissance England*. Cambridge University Press, 1997, 46–68.

    "The Mechanics of Culture: Editing Shakespeare Today." *Shakespeare Studies* 24 (1997): 23–30.

    "Shakespeare after Theory." *Textus* 9 (1996): 357–374.

Kay, W. David. "The Shaping of Ben Jonson's Career: A Re-examination of Facts and Problems." *Modern Philology* 67 (1976): 224–239.

Kernan, Alvin. *Shakespeare, the King's Playwright: Theater in the Stuart Court*. New Haven: Yale University Press, 1995.

Kiefer, Frederick. *Writing on the Renaissance Stage: Written Words, Printed Pages, Metaphoric Books*. Newark: University of Delaware Press, 1996.

King, Helen. "Once Upon a Text: Hysteria from Hippocrates." *Hysteria Beyond Freud*. Eds. Sander L. Gilman *et al*. Berkeley: University of California Press, 1993.

Kipling, Rudyard. *Mrs. Bathurst and Other Stories*. Ed. Lisa Lewis. Oxford University Press, 1991. 251–263.

Lacan, Jacques. "Microcopia: An Introduction to the Reading of Television." *Television*. Trans. Denis Hollier, Rosalind Krauss, and Annette Michelson. New York: W. W. Norton, 1990.

Lander, Jesse. "Foxe's *Book of Martyrs*: Printing and Popularizing the *Acts and Monuments*." *Religion and Culture in Renaissance England*. Eds. Claire McEachern and Debora Shuger. Cambridge University Press, 1997. 69–92.

Lentricchia, Frank. "Foucault's Legacy: A New Historicism?" *The New Historicism*. Ed. H. Aram Veeser. New York: Routledge, 1989. 231–243

Lesser, Zachary. "Walter Burre's Knight of the Burning Pestle." Forthcoming in *English Literary Renaissance*.
Loewenstein, Joseph. "Printing and 'The Multitudinous Presse': The Contentious Texts of Jonson's Masque." *Ben Jonson's 1616 Folio*. Eds. Jennifer Brady and W. H. Herendeen. Newark: University of Delaware Press, 1991. 168–191.
  Responsive Readings: Versions of Echo in Pastoral, Epic, and the Jonsonian Masque. New Haven: Yale University Press, 1984.
  "The Script in the Marketplace." *Representations* 12 (1985): 101–114.
Long, William B. "'Precious Few': English Manuscript Playbooks." *A Companion to Shakespeare*. Ed. David Scott Kastan. Oxford: Blackwell Publishers Inc., 1999, 414–433.
Love, Harold. *Scribal Publication in Seventeenth-Century England*. Oxford: Clarendon Press, 1993.
Maguire, Laurie E. "The Craft of Printing (1600)." *A Companion to Shakespeare*. Ed. David Scott Kastan. Oxford: Blackwell Publishers Inc., 1999. 434–449.
  Shakespearean Suspect Texts: The "Bad" Quartos and their Contexts. Cambridge University Press, 1996.
Marchitello, Howard. "(Dis)embodied Letters and The Merchant of Venice: Writing, Editing, History." *English Literary History* 62 (1995): 237–265.
  Narrative and Meaning in Early Modern England: Browne's Skull and Other Histories. Cambridge University Press, 1997.
Marcus, Leah. *Puzzling Shakespeare: Local Reading and its Discontents*. Berkeley: University of California Press, 1988.
  Unediting the Renaissance: Shakespeare, Marlowe, Milton. New York: Routledge, 1996.
Marotti, Arthur. *Manuscript, Print, and the English Renaissance Lyric*. Ithaca: Cornell University Press, 1995.
Marsden, Jean L. *The Re-Imagined Text: Shakespeare, Adaptation, & Eighteenth-Century Literary Theory*. Lexington, KY: The University Press of Kentucky, 1995.
Martin, R. W. F. "A Catholic Oldcastle." *Notes and Queries* n.s. 40 (1993): 185–186.
Masten, Jeffrey. "Beaumont and/or Fletcher: Collaboration and the Interpretation of Renaissance Drama." *English Literary History* 59 (1992): 337–356.
  "My Two Dads: Collaboration and the Reproduction of Beaumont and Fletcher." *Queering the Renaissance*. Ed. Jonathan Goldberg. Durham, NC: Duke University Press, 1994. 280–309.
  "Playwriting: Authorship and Collaboration." *A New History of Early English Drama*. Eds. David Scott Kastan and John D. Cox. New York: Columbia University Press, 1997. 357–382.
  Textual Intercourse: Collaboration, Authorship, and Sexualities in Renaissance Drama. Cambridge University Press, 1997.
Maus, Katherine Eisaman. *Inwardness and Theater in the English Renaissance*. University of Chicago Press, 1995.
  "A Womb of his Own: Male Renaissance Poets in the Female Body." *Sexuality and Gender in Early Modern Europe: Institutions, Texts, Images*. Ed. James Grantham Turner. Cambridge University Press, 1993. 266–288.

McEachern, Claire. "*Henry V* and the Paradox of the Body Politic." *Shakespeare Quarterly* 4 (1994): 33–56.
McGann, Jerome J., ed. *Textual Criticism and Literary Interpretation*. University of Chicago Press, 1985.
"Theory of Texts." *London Review of Books* 10:14 (18 February 1988): 20.
McKeen, David. *A Memory of Honor: The Life of William Brooke, Lord Cobham*. Universität Salzburg, 1986.
McKenzie, D. F. *Bibliography and the Sociology of Texts*. London: The British Library, 1985.
"Typography and Meaning." *Buch und Buchhandel in Europa im Achtzehnten Jahrhundert*. Eds. Giles Barber and Bernhard Fabian. Hamburg: Dr. Ernst Hauswedell & Co., 1981.
'*What's Past is Prologue*': *The Bibliographic Society and History of the Book*. The Bibliographical Society Centenary Lecture, 14 July 1992. London: Hearthstone Publications, 1993.
McLeod, Randall. "FIAT *f*LUX." *Crisis of Editing: Texts of the English Renaissance*. Ed. Randall McLeod. New York: AMS Press, Inc., 1993, 61–172.
"The Marriage of Good and Bad Quartos." *Shakespeare Quarterly* 33 (1982): 421–431.
"UnEditing Shakespeare." *Sub-Stance* 33/34 (1982): 26–55.
McLuskie, Kathleen. *Dekker and Heywood: Professional Dramatists*. New York: St. Martin's Press, 1994.
McMillin, Scott. "Professional Playwriting." *A Companion to Shakespeare*. Ed. David Scott Kastan. Oxford: Blackwell Publishers Inc., 1999. 226–238.
The Elizabethan Theatre and The Booke of Sir Thomas More. Ithaca: Cornell University Press, 1987.
McMullan, Gordon. "Collaboration and the Problem of Editing." *Textus* 9 (1996): 437–460.
The Politics of Unease in the Plays of John Fletcher. Amherst: University of Massachusetts Press, 1994.
Melchiori, Giorgio. *Shakespeare's Garter Plays: Edward III to Merry Wives of Windsor*. Newark: University of Delaware Press, 1994.
Meres, Francis. *Palladis Tamia*. 1598. New York: Scholars' Facsimiles & Reprints, 1938.
Miller, David Lee. *The Poem's Two Bodies: The Poetics of the 1590 Faerie Queene*. Princeton University Press, 1988.
Miller, Jacqueline T. *Poetic License: Authority and Authorship in Medieval and Renaissance Contexts*. Oxford University Press, 1986.
Montrose, Louis A. "The Elizabethan Subject and the Spenserian Text." *Literary Theory/Renaissance Texts*. Eds. Patricia Parker and David Quint. Baltimore: Johns Hopkins University Press, 1986. 303–340.
"Spenser's Domestic Domain: Poetry, Property, and the Early Modern Subject." *Subject and Object in Renaissance Culture*. Eds. Margreta de Grazia, Maureen Quilligan, and Peter Stallybrass. Cambridge University Press, 1996. 83–132.
More, Sir Thomas. *The English Works of Sir Thomas More*. 2 vols. Eds. W. E. Campbell and A. W. Reed. London: Eyre and Spottiswoode, 1927.

Mowat, Barbara A. "The Theater and Literary Culture." *New History of Early English Drama*. Eds. John D. Cox and David Scott Kastan. New York: Columbia University Press, 1977. 213–230.

"Constructing the Author." *Elizabethan Theater: Essays in Honor of S. Schoenbaum*. Eds. R. B. Parker and S. P. Zitner. Newark: University of Delaware Press, 1996. 93–110.

Moxon, Joseph. *Mechanick Exercises, or the Doctrine of Handy-Works Applied to the Art of Printing* (London: 1683–1684). Facsimile reprint. Eds. Herbert Davis and Harry Carter. New York: Dover Publications, Inc., 1958.

Muir, Kenneth and Michael J. B. Allen. *Shakespeare's Plays in Quarto: A Facsimile Edition of Copies Primarily from the Huntington Library*. Berkeley: University of California Press, 1981.

Mulcaster, Richard. *Mulcaster's Elementarie*. Ed. E. T. Campagnac. London: Clarendon, 1925.

Mullaney, Steven. *The Place of the Stage: License, Play, and Power in Renaissance England*. Ann Arbor: University of Michigan Press, 1996.

Müller, Jan-Dirk. "The Body of the Book: The Media Transition from Manuscript to Print." *Materialities of Communication*. Eds. Hans Ulrich Gumbrecht and K. Ludwig Pfeiffer. Trans. William Whobrey. Stanford University Press, 1994.

Murray, Timothy. *Theatrical Legitimation: Allegories of Genius in Seventeenth-Century England and France*. Oxford University Press, 1987.

Newman, Jane O. "The Word Made Print: Luther's 1522 New Testament in an Age of Mechanical Reproduction." *Representations* 11 (1985): 95–133.

Newton, Richard C. "Jonson and the (Re-)Invention of the Book." *Classic and Cavalier: Essays on Jonson and the Sons of Ben*. Eds. Claude J. Summers and Ted-Larry Pebworth. University of Pittsburgh Press, 1982. 31–58.

Niell, Michael. "'Wits most Accomplished Senate': The Audience of Caroline Private Theaters." *Studies in English Literature* 18 (1978): 341–360.

Norland, Howard B. *Drama in Early Tudor Britain 1485–1558*. Lincoln, NB: University of Nebraska Press, 1995.

Norton, David. "Imagining Translation Committees at Work: the Authorised and the Revised Versions." Unpublished conference paper.

The King James Bible: A Textual History. Cambridge University Press, forthcoming.

Orgel, Stephen. "Acting Scripts, Performing Texts." *Crisis of Editing: Texts of the English Renaissance*. Ed. Randall McLeod. New York: AMS Press, Inc., 1993. 251–294.

"The Authentic Shakespeare." *Representations* 21 (1988): 1–25.

The Illusion of Power. Berkeley: University of California Press, 1975.

The Jonsonian Masque. New York: Columbia University Press, 1981.

"The Poetics of Incomprehensibility." *Shakespeare Quarterly* 42 (1991): 431–437.

"What is an Editor?" *Shakespeare Studies* 24 (1996): 23–39.

"What is a Text?" *Research Opportunities in Renaissance Drama* 26 (1981): 3–6.

Pask, Kevin. *The Emergence of the English Author: Scripting the Life of the Poet in Early Modern England*. Cambridge University Press, 1996.

Patterson, Annabel. *Censorship and Interpretation: The Conditions of Writing and Reading in Early Modern England*. Chicago: University of Wisconsin Press, 1984.
  Reading Holinshed's Chronicle. University of Chicago Press, 1994.
Pendleton, Thomas A. "'This is not the man': on calling Falstaff Falstaff." *Analytical & Enumerative Bibliography* n.s. 4 (1990): 56–71.
Peters, Julie Stone. *Theatre of the Book: Print and Stage 1480–1880*. Forthcoming, Oxford: Clarendon Press, 2000.
  "The Bank, the Press, and the 'Return of Nature': On Currency, Credit, and Literary Property in the 1690s." *Early Modern Conceptions of Property*. Eds. John Brewer and Susan Staves. London: Routledge, 1995. 365–88.
Plato. *Collected Dialogues of Plato*. eds. Edith Hamilton and Huntington Cairns. Princeton University Press, 1961.
Pollard, A. W. *Shakespeare's Fight with the Pirates and the Problems of the Transmission of his Text*. Second edition. Cambridge University Press, 1920.
  Shakespeare Folios and Quartos: A Study in the Bibliography of Shakespeare's Plays 1594–1685. London: Methuen, 1909.
Poole, Kristen. "Saints Alive! Falstaff, Martin Marprelate, and the Staging of Puritanism." *Shakespeare Quarterly* 46 (1995): 47–75.
Revard, Stella P. "Classicism and Neo-Classicism in Jonson's *Epigrammes* and *The Forrest*." *Ben Jonson's 1616 Folio*. Eds. Jennifer Brady and W. H. Herendeen. Newark: University of Delaware Press, 1991. 138–167.
Riddell, James A. "The Concluding Pages of the Jonson Folio of 1616." *Studies in Bibliography* 47 (1994): 147–154.
  "Jonson and Stansby and the Revisions of *Every Man in his Humor*." *Medieval and Renaissance Drama in England* 9 (1997): 81–91.
  "The Printing of the Plays in the Jonson Folio of 1616." *Studies in Bibliography* 49 (1996): 149–168.
Riggs, David. *Ben Jonson: A Life*. Harvard University Press, 1989.
Rittenhouse, Jonathan. *A Critical Edition of 1 Sir John Oldcastle*. New York: Garland Publishing, Inc., 1984.
Robinson, Benedict. "'Voluminous' Reading; or, why Thomas Heywood Wrote no Works." Forthcoming in *Studies in English Literature*.
Rose, Mark. "The Author as Proprietor: Donaldson v. Becket and the Genealogy of Modern Authorship." *Representations* 23 (1988): 51–85.
  Authors and Owners: The Invention of Copyright. Harvard University Press, 1993.
Rousseau, G. S. "Once Upon a Text: Hysteria from Hippocrates." *Hysteria Beyond Freud*. Eds. Sander L. Gilman *et al*. Berkeley: University of California Press, 1993. 91–224.
Rowe, Nicholas. *The Tragedy of Jane Shore*. Ed. Harry William Pedicord. Lincoln, NB: University of Nebraska Press, 1975.
Rutter, Carol Chillington, ed. *Documents of the Rose Playhouse*. Manchester University Press, 1984.
Sackville, John and Thomas Norton. *Gorboduc or Ferrex and Porrex*. Ed. Irby B. Cauthen, Jr. Lincoln, NB: University of Nebraska Press, 1970.
Sackville, John *et al. The Mirror for Magistrates*. Ed. L. B. Campbell. New York: Barnes & Noble, Inc., 1960.

Saeger, James P. and Christopher J. Fassler. "The London Professional Theater, 1576–1642: A Catalogue and Analysis of the Extant Printed Plays." *Research Opportunities in Renaissance Drama* 34 (1995): 63–109.

Sams, Eric. "Oldcastle and the Oxford Shakespeare." *Notes and Queries* n.s. 40 (1993): 180–185.

  The Real Shakespeare: Retrieving the Early Years, 1564–1594. New Haven: Yale University Press, 1995.

Sanders, Eve Rachele. *Gender and Literacy on Stage in Early Modern England*. Cambridge University Press, 1998.

Schoenbaum, Samuel. *Shakespeare's Lives: New Edition*. Oxford: Clarendon Press, 1991.

  William Shakespeare: A Documentary Life. Oxford University Press, 1975.

Scoufos, Alice-Lyle. *Shakespeare's Typological Satire: A Study of the Falstaff-Oldcastle Problem*. Chicago: Ohio University Press, 1979.

Shakespeare, William. *The Complete Works of Shakespeare*. Third edition. Ed. David Bevington. New York: HarperCollins Publishers, 1980.

  The Complete Works of Shakespeare. Eds. Gary Taylor and Stanley Wells. Oxford University Press, 1986.

  The New Variorum Edition of Shakespeare: The Poems. Ed. Hyder Edward Rollins. Philadelphia and London: J. B. Lippincott Company, 1938.

  The Norton Facsimile: The First Folio of Shakespeare. Second edition. Prepared by Charlton Hinman. New York: W. W. Norton & Company, 1996.

  Shakespeare's Plays in Quarto. Eds. Michael J. B. Allen and Kenneth Muir. Berkeley: University of California Press, 1981.

  William Shakespeare: Complete Poems. Ed. Thomas More. New York: Gramercy Books, 1993.

  2 Henry IV. Ed. A. R. Humphreys. London: Penguin Books, 1966.

  The Works of Mr. William Shakespeare. 7 vols. Ed. Nicholas Rowe. London: E. Curl and E. Sanger, 1710.

  Pericles, Prince of Tyre, The New Cambridge Shakespeare. Eds. Doreen DelVecchio and Anthony Hammond. Cambridge University Press, 1998.

Shapiro, James. "Recent Studies in Tudor and Stuart Drama." *Studies in English Literature* 37 (1996): 482–525.

  Rival Playwrights: Marlowe, Jonson, Shakespeare. New York: Columbia University Press, 1991.

  "'Tragedies naturally performed': Kyd's Representation of Violence." *Staging the Renaissance: Reinterpretations of Elizabethan and Jacobean Drama*. Eds. David Scott Kastan and Peter Stallybrass. New York: Routledge, 1991. 99–113.

Sharpe, Kevin. "The King's Writ: Royal Authors and Royal Authority in Early Modern England." *Culture and Politics in Early Stuart England*. Eds. Kevin Sharpe and Peter Lake. Stanford University Press, 1993.

Sidney, Philip. *An Apology for Poetry*. Ed. Forrest G. Robinson. New York: Macmillan, 1970.

  Countess of Pembroke's Arcadia. Ed. Maurice Evans. New York: Viking Penguin, 1977.

Smith, Bruce R. "Reading Lists of Plays, Early Modern, Modernist, Postmodern." *Shakespeare Quarterly* 42 (1991): 129–144.

Spearing, E. M. *The Elizabethan Translations of Seneca's Tragedies.* Cambridge: W. Heffer & Sons Ltd, 1912.
Spenser, Edmund. *The Faerie Queene.* Ed. Thomas P. Roche. New York: Penguin, 1987.
The Yale Edition of the Shorter Poems of Edmund Spenser. Eds. William Oram et al. New Haven: Yale University Press, 1989.
Stallybrass, Peter. "Shakespeare, the Individual, and the Text." *Cultural Studies.* Eds. Lawrence Grossberg, Cary Nelson, and Paula Treichler. New York: Routledge, 1992. 593–610.
Stephens, Dorothy. "'Newes of devils': Feminine Sprights in Masculine Minds in *The Faerie Queene.*" *English Literary Renaissance* 23 (1993): 363–381.
Stoddard, Roger. "Morphology and the Book from an American Perspective." *Printing History* 17 (1987): 2–14.
Sturgess, Keith. "Introduction." *Three Elizabethan Domestic Tragedies.* Middlesex: Penguin, 1969.
Sutro, Alfred. *The Great She Bible.* San Francisco: Grabhorn Press, 1938.
Tanselle, G. Thomas. "Editing without a Copy-Text." *Studies in Bibliography* 47 (1994): 1–22.
Taussig, Michael. "Maleficium: State Fetishism." *The Nervous System.* New York: Routledge, 1992. 111–141.
Taylor, Barry. *Vagrant Writing: Social and Semiotic Disorders in the English Renaissance.* New York and London: Harvester Wheatsheaf, 1991.
Taylor, Gary. "The Fortunes of Oldcastle." *Shakespeare Survey* 38 (1985): 85–100.
Reinventing Shakespeare: A Cultural History from the Restoration to the Present. Oxford University Press, 1989.
"The Rhetorics of Reaction." *Crisis of Editing: Texts of the English Renaissance,* ed. Randall McLeod. New York: AMS Press, Inc., 1993. 19–60.
"William Shakespeare, Richard James and the House of Cobham." *The Review of English Studies* n.s. 38 (1987): 334–354.
Thompson, Ann and John O. *Shakespeare: Meaning & Metaphor.* Brighton: Harvester Press, 1987.
Thomson, Peter. *Shakespeare's Professional Career.* Cambridge University Press, 1992.
Tracy, James D. "Erasmus Among the Postmodernists: Dissimulatio, Bonae Literae, and Docta Pietas Revisited." *Sixteenth Century Essays & Studies 32 Erasmus' Vision of the Church.* Ed. Hilmar M. Pabe. Kirksville: Sixteenth Century Journal Publishers, Inc., 1995, 1–40
Tribble, Evelyn. "Genius on the Rack: Authorities and the Margins in Ben Jonson's Glossed Works." *Exemplaria* 4 (1992): 317–363.
Margins and Marginality: The Printed Page in Early Modern England. Charlottesville: University of Virginia Press, 1993.
Tucker, E. F. J. *Intruder into Eden: Representations of the Common Lawyer in English Literature 1350–1750.* Columbia, SC: Camden House, 1984.
Urkowitz, Steven. *Shakespeare's Revision of King Lear.* Princeton University Press, 1980.
Van den Berg, Sara. *The Action of Ben Jonson's Poetry.* Newark: University of Delaware Press, 1987.
"Ben Jonson and the Ideology of Authorship." *Ben Jonson's 1616 Folio.* Eds.

Jennifer Brady and W. H. Herendeen. Newark: University of Delaware Press, 1991. 111–137.

——"'The Paths I Meant unto Thy Praise': Jonson's Poem for Shakespeare." *Shakespeare Studies* 11 (1978): 207–218.

Vidler, Anthony. *The Architectural Uncanny: Essays in the Modern Unhomely*. Cambridge, MA: MIT Press, 1992.

Walker, Greg. *The Politics of Performance in Early Renaissance Drama*. Cambridge University Press, 1998.

Wall, John N. "The Reformation in England and the Typographical Revolution: 'By this Printing . . . the Doctrine of the Gospel Soundeth to all Nations.'" *Print and Culture in the Renaissance*. Eds. Gerald P. Tyson and Sylvia S. Wagonheim. Newark: University of Delaware Press, 1986.

Wall, Wendy. *The Imprint of Gender: Authorship and Publication in the English Renaissance*. Ithaca: Cornell University Press, 1993.

Warren, Michael and Gary Taylor. *The Division of the Kingdoms*. Oxford: Clarendon Press, 1983.

——"Quarto and Folio *King Lear* and the Interpretation of Albany and Edgar." *Shakespeare, Pattern of Excelling Nature*. Newark: University of Delaware Press, 1978. 95–107.

Watt, Tessa. *Cheap Print and Popular Piety, 1550–1640*. Cambridge University Press, 1992.

Wayne, Don. *Penshurst: The Semiotics of Place and the Poetics of History*. Chicago: University of Wisconsin Press, 1984.

Weever, John. *The Mirror of Martyrs or The Life and Death of that Thrice Valiant Captain and Most Godly Martyr Sir John Oldcastle Knight, Lord Cobham*. 1601.

Wells, Stanley. *Shakespeare: A Life in Drama*. New York: W. W. Norton & Company, 1995.

Wentworth, Michael. *Thomas Heywood: A Reference Guide*. Boston: G. K. Hall and Co., 1986.

Werstine, Paul. "Editing after the End of Editing." *Shakespeare Studies* 24 (1996): 47–54.

——"Narratives About Printed Shakespeare Texts: 'Foul Papers' and 'Bad' Quartos." *Shakespeare Quarterly* 41 (1990): 65–86.

——"Plays in Manuscript." *New History of Early English Drama*. Eds. John D. Cox and David Scott Kastan. New York: Columbia University Press, 1977. 481–498.

——"Shakespeare." *Scholarly Editing: A Guide to Research*, Ed. D. C. Greetham. New York: Modern Language Association, 1995. 253–281.

West, Anthony James. "Sales and Prices of Shakespeare First Folios: A History, 1623 to the Present (Part One). *The Papers of the Bibliographical Society of America* 92:4 (1998): 465–528.

Wheeler, G. W. Ed. *Letters of Thomas Bodley to Thomas James, Keeper of the Bodleian Library*. Oxford University Press, 1926.

Wigley, Mark. "Untitled: The Housing of Gender." *Sexuality & Space: Princeton Papers on Architecture*. Princeton Architectural Press, 1992.

Williams, George Walton. *The Craft of Printing and the Publication of Shakespeare's Works*. Cranbury, NJ: Associated University Presses, 1985.

"Second Thoughts on Falstaff's Name." *Shakespeare Quarterly* 30 (1979): 82–84.

"Fastolf or Falstaff." *English Literary Renaissance* 5 (1975): 308–312.

Williams, Gordon. *Shakespeare, Sex and the Print Revolution*. London: The Athlone Press Ltd, 1996.

Wilson, Dover. "The Origins and Development of Shakespeare's *Henry IV*." *The Library* 4:26 (1945): 2–16.

Wilson, Richard. *Will Power: Essays on Shakespearean Authority*. Detroit: Wayne State University Press, 1993.

Woodbridge, Linda. "Patchwork: Piecing the Early Modern Mind in England's First Century of Print Culture." *English Literary Renaissance* 23 (1993): 5–45.

Yachnin, Paul. *Stage-Wrights: Shakespeare, Jonson, Middleton, and the Making of Theatrical Value*. Philadelphia: University of Pennsylvania Press, 1997.

Žižek, Slavoj. *For they Know not What they Do: Enjoyment as a Political Factor*. London: Verso, 1991.

Index

Achinstein, Sharon, 246 n. 64
Acton, Sir Roger, 85
Actors' Vindication, The, 191, 214
Acts
   Beggars and Vagabonds, 17–18
   Enforcing Statute against Heresy, 20
   Freedom of Conscience, 18
   Prohibiting Religious Controversy, Unlicensed Plays, and Printing, 18–19
Acts and Monuments
   1583 edition of, 85; *see also* Foxe, Lander
Admiral's Men, 68
Alchemist, The
   reader address of, 51
   typographical distinction of, 52
Allen, Michael J. B., 55
Amends for Ladies, 77
Amussen, Susan Dwyer, 180
Anderson, Benedict, 248 n. 85
Annals of English Drama, 137, 172–3, 176–7, 179–80, 235 n. 39, 261 n. 72
Anne, Statute of, 80, 170
Antidote Against Purgatory, An, 77
Apology for Actors, An, 213–14
   1658 edition of, 64, 191
Arber, Edward
   on first edition of *Gorboduc*, 33
Archer, Edward, 141
Archer, Thomas
   publisher of *The White Devil*, 46
Arundel, Archbishop, 86, 88
Ascham, Roger, 226
   translation of *Philoctetes*, 23
author attribution
   on title pages, 10
Authorized Version, 227
Axton, Marie, 254 n. 48

Bald, R. C., 146, 151–2,
Baldwin, William
   preface to *A Mirror for Magistrates*, 34
Bale, John, 66, 247 n. 74
   on Oldcastle, 82–4, 86, 91, 97–8

Ball, The, 161
Barish, Jonas, 107, 258 n. 131
Barker, Robert, 226
Barthes, Roland, 9, 100, 110
   "The Death of the Author," 3, 106
Beaumont, Francis, 52, 147, 187
   as collaborator, 14, 15
Beaumont and Fletcher, 1, 149, 161, 166, 179, 183, 186
   1647 folio, 43, 141, 144, 151, 156–7, 159–61, 166–8, 170, 177, 180–1, 185, 187–8, 194, 222, 262 n. 87; title page of, 143
   1679 folio, 145, 168, 262 n. 87; title page of, 169
   involvement with Walter Burre, 53
   position in Webster's list, 52
   typography and literary ambition, 54
Beeston, Christopher, 216
Bennet, H. S., 257 n. 106
Bentley, G. E., 139, 145, 155, 194, 197, 239 n. 100, 239 n. 103, 240 n. 117, 241 n. 150, 260 n. 29, 261 n. 67
   on collaborative authorship, 178–9
   on Jonson's 1616 *Workes*, 52, 105
   on publication of Shakespeare's poems, 55
Berger, Thomas L., 240 n. 112, 240 n. 113, 242 n. 2, 253 n. 40
   on Jonson's *Masques*, 111
Berkenhead, John, 156, 164, 166–8
Betterton, Thomas, 99, 102, 157
Bevington, David, 68
Birth of Merlin, The, 153, 170
Bishops' Bible, 226–7
Blackfriars Boys, 55
Blagden, Cyprian, 23
Bland, Mark, 107, 240 n. 130, 252 n. 17, 252 n. 18
   on the printed page, 127
   on the printing of Jonson's *Workes*, 118, 134
Blayney, Peter W. M., 29, 202, 232 n. 33, 238 n. 76, 239 n. 93, 243 n. 22

Index

New Bibliographic melodrama, 5
unfounded myths of New Bibliography, 6, 234 n. 4
on 1623 Folio, 14–15
on customers of printed drama, 71
Blount, Edward, 14, 38, 60, 122, 126, 141, 144
Bodley, Sir Thomas, 63
on lowly status of plays, 59
Boehrer, Bruce Thomas, 256 n. 80, 256–7 n. 95, 257 n.116
Booke of Sir Thomas More, The, 155, 224
Bourchier, Henry, 78
Bourdieu, Pierre, 261 n. 64
Bowers, Fredson, 204
on "Rationale of Copy-Text," 7
on Greg, 110–11
Bracken, James K.
on Jonson and revision, 111
Braden, Gordon, 236 n. 41
Brady, Jennifer, 257–8 n. 118
Brazen Age, The, 197, 201, 216
Bristol, Michael D., 4, 13
on myth of Shakespeare, 2
on political outlook of shareholders, 16
Brome, Richard, 170, 193
Brooke, Elizabeth, 73
Brooke, William (Lord Cobham), 66, 73, 81, 89, 243 n. 31
death of, 76
Browne, Thomas
translation of *Thebais*, 23
Bruster, Douglas, 13, 241 n. 144
Bullough, Geoffrey, 225
Burbage, James, 104, 172
Burke, Sean, 250 n. 121
Burre, Walter, 44–6, 134, 205
dedication to Robert Keysar, 52
involvement in publication of Jonson plays, 53; *see also* Lesser
Burt, Richard, 257 n. 118
Butter, Nathaniel, 59, 202
publisher of *King Lear*, 59, 70–1
publisher of *Whore of Babylon*, 63

Caius, Thomas
translation of *Euripides*, 23
Camden, William, 135
Capgrave, John, 82, 91, 247 n. 69
Careles Shepherdess, The, 172, 194
Carson, Neil, 178–9
Cartwright, William, 64, 191
Cary, Lady Elizabeth, 136, 192
Case is Altered, The
typographical distinction of, 52

Catiline, his Conspiracy, 113, 132
dedication to, 51
typographical distinction of, 52
Cauthen, Irby B., 33, 35, 236 n. 41, 237 n. 45
Caxton, William, 15, 104
Certayne Masques, 134
Chabot Admiral of France, 161
Chambers, E. K., 58, 230 n. 14
Changeling, The, 161
Chapman, George, 44, 161, 235 n. 36
as collaborator with Jonson and Marston, 50
commendatory poem for *The Faithful Shepheardesse*, 54
dedication to Sir Thomas Howard, 50
literary reputation of, 49, 64
on reception of *Bussy d'Ambois*, 50
plays written by, 50
translations of Homer, 49–50
Charles I, 81
Charlewood, John, 207–8, 263 n. 26
Chaucer, Geoffrey, 15
Chettle, Henry, 155
Children of the Queen's Revels, 55
Choice Drollery, 202
Clair, Colin, 257 n. 108,
Clare, Janet, 20, 74–5, 244 n. 32
Clare, Robert, 56
Clark, Arthur Melville, 190, 197, 217, 265 n. 85
Clegg, Cyndia Susan, 237 n. 51, 237 n. 53
Cockpit, 216–17, 220
Cokain, Sir Aston, 145–6
Collinson, Patrick
on John Foxe, 84
Comical Gallant or: The Amours of Sir John Falstaffe, The, 79
continuous printing, 45, 52; *see also* Greg, Lesser
Copus, Alanus, 85
Corbin, Peter, 69–70
Coronation, The, 185
Coryate, Thomas, 135
Cotton, Sir Robert, 78
Countess of Pembroke's Arcadia, 165
Creede, Thomas
Printer of *Famous Victories*, 74
Crockett, Bryan, 19
Cunliffe, J. W., 236 n. 41
Cupid's Revenge, 185
Cure for a Cuckhold, A, 170, 195
Cynthia's Revels, 53

Davidson, Adele, 264 n. 57
Daye, John, 28–43, 48, 188, 206

286   Index

De Certeau, Michel, 110
De Grazia, Margreta, 140, 231 n. 17
  on parenting and printing, 165
  on Shakespeare as reviser, 8–9
  on the *Oxford Shakespeare*, 8
deconstruction, 5
Dekker, Thomas, 155, 159, 161, 170, 172, 189–90
  as collaborator on *Westward Hoe*, 46
  as freelancer, 61
  collaborations with Webster, 63
  criticism of playwrights, 62–3
  on Jonson, 62
  on the Queen's Men, 62
  Whole Magnificent Entertainment, The, 124
Dennis, John, 79, 81, 96–7
Descartes, Renee, 188
Dido, 157
dilemmas
  as printers' term, 144
  use of on title pages, 157, 159, 161, 168, 170, 172
Dobson, Michael, 95, 98
Dollimore, Jonathan, 230 n. 10
Donaldson, Ian, 253 n. 30
  on Shakespeare scholarship, 4
Donovan, Kevin J., 130, 255 n. 66
  on copy-text for the Oxford Jonson, 109
  on Jonson scholarship, 106–7
Downton, Thomas, 69
Dryden, John, 139
Dutton, Richard, 2, 254 n. 44, 254–5 n. 59
  on censorship, 18, 235 n. 33
  on company-held copyright, 56, 240 n. 117
  on granting of licenses, 58
  on over-length plays, 54
  on Oxford edition, 9
  on *Sejanus* and censorship, 22
  on Shakespeare's attitude toward publication, 9–10, 56

Eastward Hoe
  authorship of, 50, 157, 182
Ede, Lisa, 155
Edward VI, 17
Eisenstein, Elizabeth, 64, 104, 110, 177
Elder Brother, The, 185
Elizabeth I, 29, 34–5, 38, 79–80, 89, 97, 112, 122, 133, 220, 223
  as "Supreme Governor," 87
  collaboration with Shakespeare, 81
  confirmation of Stationers' Company Charter, 23

Elsky, Martin, 138
Elton, G. R., 249 n. 90
  on Lollardy, 82
Endimion, the Man in the Moone, 207, 263 n. 26
English Stock, The, 131
English Traveller, The, 194, 196, 197,
  reader address of, 64, 191–3, 201, 217
Epigrammes, 113
  title page of, 115
Euripides, 49
Evans, Robert, 256 n.85
Every Man in his Humor, 113, 200
  publisher of, 53

Fabian, Robert, 85
Fair Maid of the West, The, 217, 266 n. 100
  reader address of, 192
Faire Quarrell, A., 159, 170
  title page of, 160
Fatall Dowry, The, 170
Faithful Shepheardesse, The, 185
  publication of, 53
Falstaff, Sir John, 73, 78, 94–5, 133, 157, 223, 245 n. 56
  as play title, 77
Familie of Love, The, 48, 212
Famous Victories of Henry V, The, 73, 75, 98
  authorship of, 74
Faques, William, 131
Feather, John, 257 n. 107
  on "rights in copies," 67
  on literature as commodity, 13
  on piracy, 237 n. 56
  on professional authorship, 17
  on regulation of book sales, 21, 242 n. 6
Fehrenbach, Robert J.
  on Oldcastle/Falstaff switch, 74
Ferguson, Craig W., 243 n. 13
Ferrex and Porrex, 35, 38, 206
  title page of, 28
Fiehler, Rudolph, 247 n. 71
Field, Nathan, 77, 145, 185
Filmer, Sir Robert, 180
Fletcher, John, 52, 147, 151, 153–4, 161, 183, 185–6, 223
  as collaborator, 14
  dedicatory poem to *The Alchemist*, 53
  portrait of, 148
  preface to *The Faithful Shepheardesse*, 53; *see also* Beaumont and Fletcher
Florio, John, 135
Ford, John, 170, 172
Forrest, The, 113, 116, 254 n. 56
  title page of, 117; *see also* Van den Berg

Index

Fortune by Land and Sea, 161
Fortune Theatre, 62
Foster, John, 118
Foucault, Michel, 33, 87, 130, 141, 153, 215, 221
  author function, 3, 129, 181–3
  influence on New Historicism, 4
  on authorship and transgression, 16, 73, 106
  on notions of the work, 136, 167
Foure Prentises of London, The, 200, 216
Foxe, John, 66, 90–1
  Acts and Monuments, 82, 84, 97–8
  editions of, 248 n. 81
  on Oldcastle and treason, 85–6
  on other chroniclers, 85
  on the benefits of printing, 87
Freud, Sigmund, 54
Fuller, William, 247 n. 75

Galen, 34
Gadamer, Hans-Georg, 258 n. 133
Gants, David L., 107, 252 n. 10, 252 n. 16, 253 n. 30, 254 n. 52, 254 n. 53
  on Anglo-American bibliography, 4
  on substantive authorial revisions, 108–10
  on textual variants in Jonson's *Workes*, 112
  on the printing sequence of Jonson's *Workes*, 119
Garber, Marjorie, 165
Gassner, John, 236 n. 42
Genette, Gerard, 264 n. 66, 264 n. 71
Geneva Bible, 225
Gentleman Usher, The
  publication style of, 50
Gerritsen, Johan, 107, 118, 255 n. 63, 255 n. 64
Girard, René, 166
Goldberg, Jonathan, 100, 108, 256 n. 82, 258 n. 123
  on Shakespeare as reviser, 9
Golden Age Restored, The, 108, 111, 119, 253 n. 41; *see also* Herford, Riddell
Golden Age, The, 194, 197, 216
  reader address of, 196–7, 203
Gorboduc, 23–5, 32–4, 37–8, 40, 155, 181–2, 227, 236 n. 42, 236 n. 43
  first performance of, 23
  title page of, 25
Graves, Michael A. R., 237 n. 50
Greenblatt, Stephen, 4, 33, 71, 109, 248 n. 85, 250 n. 123
Greene, Robert, 37, 157
Greene, Thomas, 216

Greetham, D. C., 109, 112
Greg, W. W., 19, 154, 204, 253 n. 32, 253 n. 38, 258 n. 126, 261 n. 71, 263 n. 24, 266 n. 104
  Bibliography of Printed English Drama, 180
  on "continuous printing," 45
  on copy-text, 109–10
  on Jonson's approach to his texts, 110–11
  on the Oxford Jonson, 112
  narratives about "bad" quartos, 6
  The Editorial Problem in Shakespeare, 6
  "The Rationale of Copy-Text," 6–7, 109, 111
Grenville, George, 96
Greville, Fulke
  Certaine Learned and Elegant Workes, 198
Griffith, William, 32–6, 206, 238 n. 64
Gull's Hornbook, The, 63
Gurr, Andrew, 16, 31, 48, 61, 216, 265 n. 83, 265–6 n. 95

Habermas, Jürgen, 19
Hackel, Heidi Brayman, 233 n. 69, 233 n. 70
  on marketing playbooks, 44
Hall, Edward, 248 n. 89
Hamlet, 101
Hanson, Elizabeth, 255 n. 75
  on Jonson's authorship, 106
  on Jonson scholarship, 132
Harbage, Alfred, 137, 172–3
Harpfield, Nicholas, 85
Heidegger, Martin
  Sein und Zeit, 5
Helgerson, Richard, 252 n. 12, 256 n. 93
Heminge, John and Condell, Henry, 36–8, 40–2, 64, 76, 79, 81, 145, 154, 156, 194, 196
  "To the great variety of readers," 11–16, 57, 140–1
  on piracy of Shakespeare's texts, 207
Henry IV, part 1, 81, 100–3
  controversy over, 66, 73–4
Henry IV, part 2
  attribution of, 67
  epilogue to, 75
  title-page attribution of, 71, 133
  title page of, 72
Henry V
  epilogue to, 75
Henry V
  relations with Oldcastle, 82, 84, 87–8, 91–3, 97

288 Index

Henslowe's Diary, 17, 61, 69, 77, 178–81, 224
Henslowe, Philip, 178, 180,
  payment to Thomas Downton, 69
  payments to Thomas Heywood, 189
  payments to playwrights, 38
Herford, C. H. and Percy and Evelyn Simpson, 44, 107–8, 113, 152, 254 n. 56, 254 n. 58
  on Jonson and revision, 109, 116
  on the ending of *The Golden Age Restored*, 108
  on William Stansby, 118
Herod and Antipater, 161
Heywood, Thomas, 63–4, 155, 170, 189–94, 196–205, 212–20
  as apologist for the theatre, 64, 263 n. 34
  attitude toward publication, 64
  plays written by, 193, 263 n. 21
  Webster's praise of, 43, 265 n. 84
Hinman, Charlton, 107
Hoccleve, Thomas, 78
Holinshed, Raphael, 248 n. 89
  on Oldcastle, 87, 92
Homer
  Chapman's translation of, 49–50
Honigmann, E. A. J., 7–8, 101–2, 230 n. 15, 232 n. 43, 244 n. 32, 250 n. 110
  on Weever, 94–5, 249 n. 100, 249 n. 106
Hoppe, Harry R., 204
Horace
  as quoted by Webster, 46
  Jonson's translation of *Ars Poetica*, 68
Howard Hill, T. H., 109
Howard, Jean, 136
Howard, Sir Thomas, 50
Hoy, Cyrus, 145
Humphreys, A. R., 75
Hunt, Lynn, 229 n. 8
Hunter, G. K., 236 n. 41
  On *1 Sir John Oldcastle*, 89–90
Hymenaei, 112, 128

Iapollo, Grace, 232 n. 45
If This Be Not a Good Play
  dedication to, 62
Inner Temple, 23–4, 37, 147
Inns of Court
  views on succession, 23
Iron Age, The, part 1, 197–8, 201
  reader address of, 198–9, 212
Iron Age, The, part 2, 199, 201, 266 n. 100
  reader address of, 199–200, 212
Isle of Dogs, 21

Jaggard, Captain, 265 n. 90

Jaggard, Isaac, 14, 38, 141, 144
Jaggard, William, 30, 60, 214–5, 245
  involvement in Pavier collection, 67–8
James I, 108, 111–12, 122, 195, 217, 222–4, 258 n. 120
  his *Workes*, 122, 131–5, 222
James, Dr. Richard, 78, 81
  on shift from Oldcastle to Falstaff, 78, 88
James, Thomas, 59
Jests to Make you Merie, 157
Jew of Malta, The, 266 n. 100
Johns, Adrian, 210, 253 n. 36, 263 n. 24
Johnson, A. F., 221, 256 n. 89
Johnson, Samuel, 9, 55
Jones, Inigo, 120
Jones, Norman, 24
Jones, Richard, 206–7
  preface to *Tamburlaine*, 43, 203
Jonson, Ben, 23, 44, 147, 159, 161, 185, 189, 196, 203, 205, 208
  1616 *Workes* folio, 35, 38, 44, 67, 105–12, 118–20, 130–9, 153, 173, 177, 182, 185, 192, 194, 198, 201, 221–2; title page of, 184
  attitude toward publication, 51, 55
  career as an author, 126–7
  commendatory poem for *The Faithful Shepheardesse*, 54
  dedication to Earl of Pembroke, 51
  exclusion of early plays from 1616 *Workes*, 40, 121
  influence on 1623 Folio, 13
  on authorial predicament, 10
  on Dekker, 62
  on reception of *Catiline* in theatre, 51
  on reception of *Sejanus* in theatre, 46
  preface to *Sejanus*, 22, 121
  "To the memory of my beloved," 57
  typography and literary ambition, 51
  views on printing, 9
Jorden, Edward
  discourse on hysteria, 34
Joseph Hart, Colonel, 98, 102
Julius Caesar, 68

Kastan, David Scott, 194, 247 n. 76, 248 n. 85
  on Oldcastle, 84–5, 99
Kay, W. David, 255 n. 70, 256 n. 77
Kernan, Alvin, 255 n. 70
Keysar, Robert, 52
Kiefer, Frederick, 19, 202
King and No King, 170, 183, 261 n. 65
King Johan, 83
King Lear, 89,
  first print run of, 71

Index

folio text as copy-text, 6
head title of, 71
printing of, 59, 202
title page of, 59, 70–1
King Leir, 71
King's Entertainement, The, 122, 124, 126, 200
title pages of, 123, 125
King's Men, 14, 17, 56, 58, 67, 265 n. 83
staging of *Sejanus*, 22
King, Helen
on hysteria, 34
Kipling, Rudyard, 221–4
Kirkman, Francis, 194–6
Kirschbaum, Leo, 204
Knight of the Burning Pestle, The, 44, 161, 260 n. 37
continuous printing of, 53
reception in theatre of, 52; *see also* Burre, Lesser
Kyd, Thomas, 73

Lacoue-Labarthe, Philippe, 221
Lady Elizabeth's Men, 217
Lander, Jesse, 240 n. 112, 240 n. 113, 242 n. 2, 248 n. 81
Langbaine, Gerard, 241 n. 148, 262 n. 11
Late Lancashire Witches, The, 170
Lentricchia, Frank, 228 n. 8
Lesser, Zachary, 53, 239 n. 86, 239 n. 92, 239 n. 101
on "continuous printing," 45
on marketing plays to an upscale readership, 45
on Walter Burre, 44
Licensing Act of 1637, 80
Lisle, George, 168
Lodge, Thomas, 37, 157
Loewenstein, Joseph, 252 n. 13, 256 n. 86
on *Cynthia's Revels*, 127
on Jonson's collaborations with Inigo Jones, 120
on Jonson's *Workes*, 105
on publication of Jonson's *Masques*, 112–13
Lollardy, 82–3
Looking Glasse for London and England, A, 157
Lord Chamberlain's Men, 56
Long, William B., 232 n. 36
Love, Harold, 105–6, 246 n. 64
Love's Labour's Lost
title page of, 71, 153
Love's Mistress, 194
Loyal Subject, The, 187
Lunsford, Andrea, 155

Lyly, John, 198, 207, 263 n. 26

Maguire, Laurie E., 204–5, 231 n. 32, 232 n. 33, 233 n. 65
on distinction between publishers and printers, 32
Maine, Jasper, 161, 164, 168
Malcontent, The, 46, 182,
reader address of, 208–10
Marchitello, Howard, 222, 232 n. 26
Marcus, Leah, 4, 5, 12, 246 n. 60
on contamination, 36, 204
Markham, Gervase, 161
Marlowe, Christopher, 43, 157, 206
Marston, John, 46, 104–5, 192, 208–11
1633 *Workes*, 136, 192, 198, 211
reader address of *The Wonder of Women*, 62, 211
Martin, R. W. F., 245 n. 548
Mary I, 18
Masque of Blacknesse, The, 120, 127–9
preface to, 121
Massinger, Philip, 145–6, 161, 185
Masten, Jeffrey, 141, 144, 146–7, 153–4, 156–7, 161, 164, 168, 180–1, 187, 192, 258 n. 137, 261 n. 63
on authorship/royal authority, 80, 131–2, 223
on New Historicism, 4
on Shakespeare as reviser, 23
on Shakespeare's reputation, 2
Master of the Revels, 58
Maus, Katharine Eisaman, 164, 192
Mayden-Head Well Lost, A, 194, 217
McEachern, Claire, 190
McGann, Jerome, 120
McKeen, David, 243 n. 31, 244 n. 32
McKenzie, D. F., 7, 31, 43, 168, 244 n. 33
on dialects of written language, 74
on relations between playwrights and printers, 16, 18
McKerrow, R. B.
narratives about "bad" quartos, 6
McLeod, Randall, 204
on unediting, 5
McLuskie, Kathleen E., 54, 61, 190
McMillin, Scott, 10, 68, 155, 232 n. 47, 259 n. 27
McMullan, Gordon, 140, 145, 147, 153–4
Measure for Measure, 102
Melchiori, Giorgio, 244 n. 34
Meres, Francis, 43–4, 132–3
Palladis Tamia, 43, 190
Merry Wives of Windsor, The, 74, 96–7
title page of, 77
Middleton, Thomas, 159, 161, 197

290   Index

Miller, Jacqueline T.
  on authorship, 120, 130
Miller, Jacques-Alain, 54
Monsieur Thomas, 185
Montrose, Louis A., 14–15, 130
More, Christopher, 58–9
More, Sir Thomas
  on Oldcastle, 82
Moseley, Humphrey, 141, 144–7, 149–53,
  156–7, 164, 179–83, 185–8, 260 n. 38
Mowat, Barbara A., 44
  on Homer and early modern authorship,
  50
Moxon, Joseph, 210, 215
Muir, Kenneth, 56
Mulcaster, Richard, 122, 124, 256 n. 83
Müller, Jan-Dirk, 260 n. 46
Mullaney, Steven, 136
Munday, Anthony, 69, 155
Munday–Drayton–Hathway–Wilson, 69,
  76–7, 79, 89–94, 179
Murray, Timothy, 111, 127–8, 135

Nashe, Thomas, 157, 253 n. 32
  "To the Gentlemen Students of Both
  Universities," 19
Neill, Michael, 239 n. 86
Newman, Jane O., 248 n. 85
New Bibliography, 19, 35, 68, 105, 152, 154,
  181, 189, 204, 222
New Textualism, 5, 9, 189
Newton, Richard C., 105
Norland, Howard B., 235–6 n. 39
Northbrooke, John, 136
Northward Hoe, 46, 63, 157
Norton and Sackville, 23, 27, 31–4, 36–7,
  41–2, 155, 181–2
Norton, David, 223–7
Norton, John, 197
Norton, Thomas, 29, 38–42
  "All such treatises," 38–41; title page of,
  39

Okes, John, 201
Okes, Nicholas, 59, 63, 197–8, 201, 214–16,
  263 n. 34
  printer of *King Lear*, 59, 70–1
  printer of *Othello*, 61
  printer of *The White Devil*, 46
  printing activities of, 60, 198; *see also*
  Robinson, Benedict
Old Law, The, 161
Oldcastle, Sir John
  as author, 83
  as Shakespeare character, 73, 89
  becomes Falstaff, 74, 97–8

  martyrdom of, 66
  name change, 78; *see also* Kastan, Taylor
Oldcastle, Sir John, part 1, 70, 76, 179, 224
  publication of, 68
  prologue to, 89
Orgel, Stephen, 229 n. 4
  edition of the *Masques*, 121
  on company shareholders, 16
  on Jonson's authorship, 129–30
  on publishers of plays, 10
  on theatrical space, 127
  "What is a Text?," 5
Othello
  preface to, 61
Owen, Jane, 77
*Oxford William Shakespeare: The Complete
  Works*, 66, 102; *see also* De Grazia,
  Dutton, Stallybrass, Taylor, Wells

Parasitaster, or, The Fawne, 104, 211
Parker, Archbishop Matthew
  letter on behalf of John Daye, 29, 36, 42
Pask, Kevin, 234 n. 7
Passionate Pilgrim, 215–16
Patriarcha, or the Natural Power of Kings,
  180
Patterson, Annabel, 247 n. 77, 248–9 n. 89
Pavier, Thomas, 59, 69, 78
  attitude toward authorship, 70
  efforts to publish Shakespeare collection,
  67–8, 71, 134, 263 n. 36
  publisher of *Sir John Oldcastle*, 68, 94
"Penshurst, To," 128, 131, 256–7 n. 95
Pericles, 242 n. 10
  exclusion from 1623 Folio, 40
  status as Shakespeare play, 68
Perkinson, Richard H., 214
Peters, J. S., 246 n. 63
Phillips, Edward, 202
Phylaster, 159, 183
Plato
  on hysteria, 34
Pleasant Dialogves and Dramma's, 217, 219
  title page of, 218
Poetaster, 62, 122, 208
Pollard, A. W., 5, 19, 58, 109, 204
  on "good" and "bad" quartos, 6
  on "piracy," 12, 233 n. 71; *see also*
  Blayney, Werstine
Pope, Alexander, 246 n. 67
Prince Charles's Men, 217
Prince's Men, 61
Princelye pleasures, The, 206
Privy Council, 17, 20–3
Promos and Cassandra,
  reader address of, 207

Index

Pynson, Richard, 131

Queen Anne's Men, 193–4, 204, 216–17
Queen Henrietta's Men, 217

Raleigh, Walter, 135
Rand, Samuel, 201
Rape of Lucrece, The, 197, 216
  reader address of, 202–5, 212
Raworth, Robert, 63
Red Bull, 202, 217, 265 n. 83
Revard, Stella P., 252 n. 13
Revels Company, 217
Revenge of Bussy d'Ambois, The,
  dedicatory epistle to 50; *see also*
  Chapman
Reynolds, John, 223
Richard III, 101
  folio text as copy-text, 6
Riddell, James A., 254 n. 52, 254 n. 53,
  254–5 n. 59
  on the ending of *The Golden Age
  Restored*, 108
Riggs, David, 256 n. 80
  on "To the Great Variety of Readers,"
  57
Roaring Girl, The, 61, 159
Robinson, Benedict, 237 n. 55, 263 n. 43
  on Heywood and Okes, 201
Robinson, Humphrey, 146, 157
Rogers, Richard and William Levy
  An Alphabetical Catalogue . . ., 172, 194
Rollins, Hyder Edward, 265 n. 87, 265 n. 88
Romeo and Juliet, 75
Rose, Mark, 167, 242 n. 6
  on Jonson's authorship, 10
Rose Theatre, 178–9
Rowe, Nicholas, 99, 102, 156, 223
  on Oldcastle, 97–8
  on shift from Oldcastle to Falstaff, 79–80
Rowley, William, 145, 154, 159, 170, 172,
  185, 192, 218
Royall King and the Loyall Subject, The, 217

Saeger, James P. and Christopher J. Fassler,
  137–8, 176–7, 258 n. 139
Sams, Eric, 77, 101–2, 230 n. 15, 251 n. 134
Sanders, Eve Rachele, 249 n. 99
Satiromastix, 62
Schoenbaum, Samuel, 243 n. 17
Scornful Lady, The, 183
Scoufos, Alice-Lyle, 244 n. 32
Sedge, Douglas, 69–70
Sejanus, His Fall, 46, 62, 132, 144, 166, 173,
  200, 208
  censorship of, 22
  preface to, 51
  reader address of, 22, 121, 203
  typographical distinction of, 52; *see also*
  Jonson
Selden, John, 135
Seneca, 23–4, 36, 135, 236 n. 40, 236 n. 41,
  236 n. 42
Shakespeare, William 2, 18, 40, 59–61, 89,
  134, 170, 185, 189, 215–16, 221–3
  1623 Folio, 43, 153, 194, 198, 222; title
  page of, 142
  as author of *Sir John Oldcastle*, 68
  as corrector/augmentor, 71, 75
  as Catholic, 100–3
  attitude toward publication, 9, 55–7
  authorial image, 2, 130, 140–1, 194
  death of, 57
  final years of career, 59
  plays published anonymously, 11, 69
  position in Webster's list, 61
  status as sharer, 56
  typographic emergence of, 73–5, 90
Shakespeare, John, 101
Shapiro, James, 57, 166, 245 n. 50
Sharpe, Kevin, 246 n. 64
Sheares, William, 136, 192–3, 211
Shirley, James, 150, 161, 223, 262 n. 87
Sidney, Sir Philip, 165, 236 n. 43
Sidney, Sir Robert, 76
Silver Age, The, 197, 216
Simmes, Valentine, 68, 126
Smith, Bruce R., 261 n. 68
Smith, John Miles, 223, 227
Spanish, Gipsie, The, 161
Spanish Tragedy, The, 73
Spearing, E. M., 236 n. 41
Speed, John, 100–1
Spenser, Edmund
  as precedent for Jonson Folio, 15
  Faerie Queene, The, 34
Stallybrass, Peter, 231 n. 17
  on Shakespeare as reviser, 8–9
  on the *Oxford Shakespeare*, 8
Stansby, William, 32, 110, 112, 118–19,
  126–7, 134, 137, 144
  collaboration with Jonson, 15; *see also*
  Bland, Gants
Stationers' Company, 12, 21, 24, 131
  incorporation of, 23, 182
Stationers' Register, 20, 69, 182–3
Stoddard, Roger, 17
Sun's Darling, The, 161
Sutro, Alfred, 267 n. 18

Tamburlaine the Great, 43, 203, 206; *see also*
  Richard Jones

292   Index

Tanselle, G. Thomas, 252 n. 28
Taylor, Gary, 7, 157, 246 n. 59, 249 n. 93, 251 n. 142
  on editorial method of Oxford edition, 8
  on Oldcastle, 99
  on Oldcastle's restoration 79
  on Oldcastle/Falstaff change, 74, 157
  on Richard James, 81
  on Shakespeare as Catholic, 100–3
Taussig, Michael, 246 n. 64
Theatrum Poetarum, 202
Theobald, Lewis, 246–7 n. 67
Thomas Wyat, Sir, 63, 159
Thompson, Ann and John O., 165
Thomson, Peter, 9
Thracian Wonder, The, 170, 194
Tilney, Edward, 20
Titus Andronicus
  title page of, 24, 26
Tragedy of Jane Shore, The, 98
Travailes of the Three English Brothers, The, 157
  title page of, 158
Tribble, Evelyn, 106, 110, 121–2, 124, 126
Troia Britanica, 215
Troylus and Cresseid, The Famous Historie of
  preface to, 60
True, Perfect, and Exact Catalogue, A, 194–6
Tucker, E. F. J., 236 n. 42
Twelfth Night, 102
Two Noble Kinsmen, 140, 153, 161
  exclusion from 1623 Folio, 40
Tyndale, William, 66
  Book of Thorpe, 82

Urkowitz, Steven, 7

Van den Berg, Sara
  on authorship, 132–3
  on Jonson's *Workes*, 111–12, 122, 240 n. 122
  on *The Forrest*, 116
Vavasour, Nicholas, 63
Vidler, Anthony, 129
Virgilius, Polydorius, 85
Virgin Martir, The, 161,
  title pages of, 162–3
Vives, Juan Louis, 34
Volpone
  typographical distinction of, 52

Walden, Thomas, 85
Walker, Greg, 234 n. 16, 234–5 n. 20
  on *Gorboduc*, 24
  on impact of printing, 17

Walkley, Thomas
  preface to *Othello*, 61
  preface to *Philaster*, 264 n. 63
Wall, John N., 248 n. 85
Wall, Wendy, 210
  on Daye's preface to *Ferrex and Porrex*, 31–5
  on textual/cultural authority, 133, 138
Walley, Henry
  dealings with Blount and Jaggard, 60
  reader address of *Troylus and Cresseid*, 60
Wapull, George, 137
Warren, Michael J., 232 n. 43
  on Shakespeare as reviser, 7
Warton, Thomas, 237 n. 48
Wayne, Don, 257 n. 104
Web, John, 161, 168
Webster, John, 43, 170, 190–1, 204–5
  and Euripides, 49
  attitude toward publication, 9, 48–9, 64
  attribution of *The White Devil*, 46
  on Heywood's *Apology*, 265 n. 84
  on distinction between low and high art, 49
  on reception of *The White Devil* in theatre, 46–8, 265 n. 83
  reader address of *The White Devil*, 43–6, 54, 190–1
  typography and literary ambition, 59
Weever, John, 249 n. 98
  on Oldcastle, 94–5
Wells, Stanley, 100–2, 230 n. 15, 250 n. 124
  on editorial method of *Oxford Shakespeare*, 8
Wentworth, Michael, 190
Werstine, Paul, 231 n. 31
  on New Bibliography's origins, 5
  on "Rationale of Copy-text," 7
  on *King Lear* controversy, 9, 251 n. 126
  on Pollard's theories, 12–13
  on twentieth-century editing, 5
West, Anthony James, 233–4 n. 76
Westward Hoe, 63, 157
White Devil, The, 43, 63, 191, 196
  reader address of, 46–7, 190–1, 213
  reception of, 46; see also Webster
White, Hayden, 104
White, Paul Whitfield, 24
Whore of Babylon, The, 61
  marketing of, 83; see also Dekker
Whyte, Rowland, 76
Widow, The, 161
Wigley, Mark, 129
Wild-Goose Chase, The, 161

Wilson, John Dover, 244 n. 32
  narratives about "bad" quartos, 6
Wilson, Richard, 110, 165–6
Winter's Tale, The, 165–6
Winton, James, 135, 257 n. 105
Wise-Woman of Hogsdon, The, 217
Wit Without Money, 161
Witch of Edmonton, The, 170, 182
  title page of, 170
Wits, or, Sport upon Sport, The, 195
Wits Recreations, 136, 192
Woman Hater, The
  attribution of, 52
Woman Kilde with Kindnesse, A, 216

Wonder of a Kingdom, The
  printing of, 63
Wonder of Women or the Tragedie of Sophonisba,
  reader address of, 210–11; *see also* Marston
Woodbridge, Linda, 225
World Tost at Tennis, The, 159

Yachnin, Paul, 63
Yorkshire Tragedy, A
  authorship of, 68

Žižek, Slavoj, 97

Cambridge Studies in Renaissance Literature and Culture

General editor
STEPHEN ORGEL
Jackson Eli Reynolds Professor of Humanities, Stanford University

1. Douglas Bruster, *Drama and the market in the age of Shakespeare*
2. Virginia Cox, *The Renaissance dialogue: literary dialogue in its social and political contexts, Castiglione to Galileo*
3. Richard Rambuss, *Spenser's secret career*
4. John Gillies, *Shakespeare and the geography of difference*
5. Laura Levine, *Men in women's clothing: anti-theatricality and effeminization, 1579–1642*
6. Linda Gregerson, *The reformation of the subject: Spenser, Milton, and the English Protestant epic*
7. Mary C. Fuller, *Voyages in print: English travel to America, 1576–1624*
8. Margreta de Grazia, Maureen Quilligan, Peter Stallybrass (eds.), *Subject and object in Renaissance culture*
9. T. G. Bishop, *Shakespeare and the theatre of wonder*
10. Mark Breitenberg, *Anxious masculinity in early modern England*
11. Frank Whigham, *Seizures of the will in early modern English drama*
12. Kevin Pask, *The emergence of the English author: scripting the life of the poet in early modern England*
13. Claire McEachern, *The poetics of English nationhood, 1590–1612*
14. Jeffrey Masten, *Textual intercourse: collaboration, authorship, and sexualities in Renaissance drama*
15. Timothy J. Reiss, *Knowledge, discovery and imagination in early modern Europe: the rise of aesthetic rationalism*
16. Elizabeth Fowler and Roland Greene (eds.), *The project of prose in early modern Europe and the New World*
17. Alexandra Halasz, *The marketplace of print: pamphlets and the public sphere in early modern England*
18. Seth Lerer, *Courtly letters in the age of Henry VIII: literary culture and the arts of deceit*
19. M. Lindsay Kaplan, *The culture of slander in early modern England*
20. Howard Marchitello, *Narrative and meaning in early modern England: Browne's skull and other histories*

21. Mario DiGangi, *The homoerotics of early modern drama*

22. Heather James, *Shakespeare's Troy: drama, politics, and the translation of empire*

23. Christopher Highley, *Shakespeare, Spenser, and the crisis in Ireland*

24. Elizabeth Hanson, *Discovering the subject in Renaissance England*

25. Jonathan Gil Harris, *Foreign bodies and the body politic: discourses of social pathology in early modern England*

26. Megan Matchinske, *Writing, gender and state in early modern England: identity formation and the female subject*

27. Joan Pong Linton, *The romance of the New World: gender and the literary formations of English colonialism*

28. Eve Rachele Sanders, *Gender and literacy on stage in early modern England*

29. Dorothy Stephens, *The limits of eroticism in post-Petrarchan narrative: conditional pleasure from Spenser to Marvell*

30. Celia R. Daileader, *Eroticism on the Renaissance stage: transcendence, desire, and the limits of the visible*

31. Theodore B. Leinwand, *Theatre, finance, and society in early modern England*

32. Heather Dubrow, *Shakespeare and domestic loss: forms of deprivation, mourning and recuperation*

33. David Posner, *The performance of nobility in early modern European literature*

34. Michael C. Schoenfeldt, *Bodies and selves in early modern England: physiology and inwardness in Spenser, Shakespeare, Herbert, and Milton*

35. Lynn Enterline, *The rhetoric of the body from Ovid to Shakespeare*

36. Douglas A. Brooks, *From playhouse to printing house: drama and authorship in early modern England*

Made in the USA
Monee, IL
28 April 2026

49136481R00184